Tatiana Bazzichelli

Networking
The Net as Artwork

Preface by Derrick de Kerckhove

Digital Aesthetics Research Center
www.digital-aestetik.dk

Layout and front cover by Jonas Frankki
Cover image: "Giovanotti Mondani Meccanici" by Antonio Glessi-Andrea Zingoni, published in "Frigidaire" issue 42, May 1984, Primo Carnera Edition.

Italian editing by Simonetta Fadda
English translation of chapters 1, 2, 7, Acknowledgements, Webliography, Captions and Afterword by Maria Anna Calamia, editing by Grace Wright
English translation of chapters 3, 4, 5, 6 by Helen Pringle
First proofreading by Jonas Frankki
Last proofreading by Helen Pringle

ISBN 87-91810-08-6
EAN 9788791810084

This research is part of the Digital Urban Living research centre, partly funded by the Danish Council for Strategic Research grant number 2128-07-0011

A copy of the book can be found at www.digital-aestetik.dk
Other reference materials on the subject: www.networkingart.eu

To Musti, Sergio and Bepi
and to the infinite possibilities of being

Table of Contents

Acknowledgements

I wish to thank all those who contributed to the creation and the realization of this book: Simonetta Fadda, for her irreplaceable advice and her passionate critical sense, for having followed the draft of this book, step by step, with her precise editing and for writing the Afterword; Derrick de Kerckhove for our stimulating conversations and for having enthusiastically embraced the topics explored here, allowing himself to be involved in writing the Preface; Florian Cramer for his brilliant insights and his numerous suggestions and for having put up with me in thinking critically from afar; Federico Bucalossi, Antonio Glessi, Ferry Byte and Oedipa_m, Giacomo Verde, Claudio Parrini, Francesco Galluzzi, Tommaso Tozzi, Massimo Cittadini, Flavia Alman and Sabine Reiff because without our exchange this book would have never existed and I would have become a less enthusiastic T_Bazz; Franca Formenti for her active participation and her constant and effervescent moral support; Mariano Equizzi, Fabrizio Manizza, Vittore Baroni, Luca Lampo, Lee Felsenstein, Alessandro Ludovico for having shared the story of their own journeys, thus helping my writing; Gaia/Nina and all the Sexyshock's Betties, Francesco "Warbear" Macarone Palmieri, Roberto Paci Dalò for having given me illuminated suggestions and precious information; all those registered on the AHA mailing list for having always been active and stimulating, and Eleonora Calvelli and Loretta Borrelli for having put up with me in the moderation of difficult moments; Asbesto, Jaromil, Andrea Natella, Giancarlo "Ambrogio" Vitali, Heath Bunting, Eva and Franco Mattes for having answered my questions; Strano Network, Isole nella Rete, AvANa.net, "Neural", Candida TV, CopyDown, Decoder/Shake, Luther Blissett, The Thing Roma, all the hackers, the Hackmeetings, the Forte Prenestino and the Social Centres, for having played a fundamental role in my techno-political journey and for having been fundamental for many other people; Massimo Canevacci, Alberto

Abruzzese, Andrea Fusco, Ninì Candalino, Pier Luigi Capucci, Mariacristina Cremaschi, Luisa Valeriani for having enlightened my theoretical course; to all my friends and colleagues in Berlin for having been present, facilitating my work and to my friends in Rome for always being there; the city of Berlin, because thanks to her I was able to stop and think, and to the city of Rome, because she allowed me to be who I am; and lastly, but fundamentally important, to my family, to Marilena for her constant love, to Roberto because he is a real Steinerian anarchist and he taught me to be free, to Tamara because she believes in love and depth, to Giovanni because he believes in simple things, to Matteo because he means the future.

For the English edition of this book, I would like to thank first of all the Digital Aesthetics Research Center of Århus University in Denmark for supporting this publication and hosting it on its website; Søren Pold for his interest on the subject and help with the promotion of the book; Helen Pringle for her fundamental work as English translator, for her great willingness and availability to solve all my lexicon problems and for our very inspiring Skype-talks; Maria Anna Calamia for her initial translation; my colleagues at the Department of Information and Media Studies at Århus University, in particular Lars Bo Løfgreen and Morten S. Riis, to create a really nice work atmosphere; and finally all my love and all my greatest thanks go to my partner Jonas Frankki for his invaluable support and extraordinary love, which allowed me to bring this work to the end with serenity and passion.

Preface
by Derrick de Kerckhove

Tatiana Bazzichelli is a rising scholar and critic of digital culture. This book is a milestone in the critical theory she began developing in the 1990s while studying Sociology. Her interest in the connections between art and media matured within academic environments, to consider their social and political implications. She went on to concentrate more fully on the themes of art and hacker ethics and collaborated directly with independent Italian hacker communities and networking activists in the art industry.

This book follows the itinerary in the art field and in digital activism that she has documented over time. A quest that is not exclusively personal; but that also recounts some of the experiences of many other people in Italy who began to work experimentally in art and technology during the 1980s. This type of writing I call "global autobiography", meaning that it connects the personal to the larger connected realm of global activities. The book takes its place in the evolution of the artistic networking project *AHA: Activism-Hacking-Artivism*. An initiative started in 2001 by Bazzichelli as part of her plan to promote art on the Internet and to give greater visibility to the Italian digital culture, AHA has contributed to the creation of a vast network of relations and projects.

Italian hacktivism and net art are little known to the rest of the world. That situation ought to be remedied, since Italians, as in so many other fields, are just as innovative on line as off, in their own inimitable way. Exporting Italian thinking on media and network technology is a sort of vocation I am presently following within a few institutions in Italy: the Faculty of Sociology in the University Federico II in Naples, and the M Node research centre within the Fine Arts Academy in Milan (NABA). The McLuhan Program at the University of Toronto is a possible platform for the diffusion of Italian hacktivist and artistic paths such as are mentioned in this book.

Penetrating at the heart of current networking dynamics, of complex processes in the Internet, one may notice that instead of the usual focus on technology, there is a growing trend towards interest in people, in their way of connecting and their social-cultural friendships and relations, their direct connection to the reality in which they live. Not long ago people talked a lot about the virtual, but today it's clear that the people in flesh and blood are the destiny of the network and not just machines.

The *network of participation* and the formation of networks and relations through technology is an increasingly pervasive and global phenomenon, and the analysis of the methods with which these networks are formed is becoming a necessity for those who deal with digital culture. One must not limit oneself to solely analyzing singular contents which are present on the internet, but instead should try and understand how people who create such contents are connected between themselves in a present, extended way. One must therefore consider the social dimensions of connectivity. This book attempts to do this for the Italian communities of networkers.

Quoting the famous phrase by Marshall McLuhan "the medium is the message"[1], today one may say that *the network is the message of the medium Internet*. The networking phenomenon was anticipated by the practice of mail art long before Internet evolved, just as the *pointillism* of Seurat could be considered prophetic with respect to the subsequent development of the television image. Until recently in America the term network was used to describe the television medium, but today it regards a much larger and vaster connective dimension, which is the Internet. Network becomes "the net of social relations", it is the message transmitted by the Internet medium, which is in turn the net which technically permits transmission.

The net of relations represents the message of the technical net. If the medium conditions the message (though converging on the Internet, TV, books, radio, telephones, cell phones do transmit specific messages), on the Internet (a medium based on the creation of connection nets), the message is the social relationships that all these media generate.

11

All this leads to the role of the user. McLuhan often jested that "If the medium is the message, then the user is the content". What he implied, I think, is that media were not just support or even conditioners of messages; they were prime and foremost *environments*. The medium thus could shape both the content and the user. If the medium conditions the message, the user becomes the content of this message, and this goes for all the forms of networking. With the extension of the Internet, one's position within the flow of information changes: today the net allows us to diffuse our thoughts in a global manner; whereas before these affirmations were merely a utopia, now one may experiment with them as a concrete phenomenon. Once on line we quite literally become content for the Internet.

The structure of the medium also conditions one's perception of one's own identity: the fact that one becomes an active lever in the distribution and creation of digital contents also determines a change in the net structures and in our way of communicating and relating with the outside world. People carry an aura of communications around them.

In the case of TV, television images speak directly to the body of the viewer. Television addresses one's inner state and the electron beam paints its sensorial and emotional dimensions directly onto the viewer's nervous system; it is a form of physical action, which is conveyed through sound and moving images. But with the Internet, we share the responsibility of making sense with the technology; we are not just consumers of information, but also producers, creators, and our production becomes an active part of network dynamics. Just check this out on YouTube. The Internet is a medium, which contains in itself all the other media, even as the cellular phone recaps the history of all media by bringing the convergence of speech, writing and electricity to a single portable appliance.

With the Internet or mobile phones, intended as network platforms, a flow of connective information is generated and extended globally and our existence, with its own particular inclinations, preferences and connections, becomes a lever in the production and reception of relationships as well as information.

How does the user become Internet content? First, we need to abandon the illusion of being containers of information. The user, instead, becomes an active producer of this information in such practices as *social bookmarking*[2] or *tagging*. Social software either for personalized encyclopaedias such as *Del.icio.us* <http://del.icio.us>, or for human and professional contacts such as *Small World* <www.asmallworld.net>, or for sharing personal media such as *Flickr* <www.flickr.com> or YouTube <www.youtube.com>, are professional and amateur at the same time. Each innovation augments the strength and the capabilities of the network.

The creation of expanded communities on the basis of common interests, in which it is possible to interact with and involve diverse media, is something I explain by examining the concept of "hypertinence". This is a neologism which I created to describe the progressive precision of the rapport between offer and demand (and vice-versa) within the Internet contents and within the information contexts which are created on the Internet. An example of hypertinence is the story of the particular refinement of search engines and the access of information on the net: thus one passes from Yahoo to Google and from Google to *Del.icio.us*. Through these platforms of social networking as *Del.icio.us,* one moves on from Wikipedia, a more or less anonymous albeit genial form of collaboration on the net, to the formation of myriads of just-in-time-on-line-on-demand connective intelligence networks that involve diverse individuals sharing their own specific interests.

Here, one gives free access to a personal homepage from which various *tags* branch off, which allow for the organisation of digital elements such as photos, text, and videos, which are all under a specific index, a key word which may be shared with other people too. At the same time these indexes become accessible to anyone who connects to the platform and has the intention of exchanging information with a similar content to their own. The evolution of the net demonstrates that progressively more and more situations are being created whereby the creation and the production of knowledge is evermore pertinent and the access of information becomes common ground - a process which involves people directly, the individual user who refines him or herself periodically with the aim to create more harmony with his or her own personal preferences.

The structural characteristic of the net is packet switching, through which all these processes come about on the net. The technical principle supporting packet switching is to fragment each message in tiny information packets, before sending them on line and give each one both a specific address/identity and a code to indicate the order in which they are to be recombined on arrival. Thanks to tagging it is possible to make one's own contents accessible to a global community of individuals without creating a hierarchy between them and between the access paths. The shared information, the exchanged messages, the personal preferences indexed on the net through associated *tag* systems, give way to a more profound development of the social networking dimension and allow the addition of a level of great maturity on the net. In *Del.icio.us,* anyone may participate freely and gratuitously without restrictions. One may insert one's own material, be it photographic or text, and associate particular *tags* to it, key words which are interpreted as connections. These key words circulate within the community and on the vaster net and may attract other people with similar interests, who access the networking platform and exchange information and documents. Thus thematic interest groups are generated which are the connective evolution of blogs, which were the first form of personalization of the net and a concrete example of the network of participation, if associated with other friends' or acquaintances' blogs through related topics.

A simple example to explain how social software works on the net is *Flickr.* Suppose you have been invited to a wedding and have taken some photographs. The website allows you to publish them on line and describe them by typing in the names of the people who appear on them. Chances are you may not know or recall the name of everybody who appears. You may leave those in blank, hoping that someone else who was at that wedding, and has connected to *Flickr* either to post pictures or to see those already posted, might know the missing names. Flickr allows surfers to add the forgotten names. This is just to say that through these networking platforms one may give life to an intricate web of connections, as if one had many personalized Wikipedia regarding one's own activities.

Platforms such as Wikipedia, with strategic interconnections, use a similar mechanism, which is coherent with the idea of partaking, but opposite through the modalities of its practice. Wikipedia is an anonymous and free Internet encyclopaedia and produced by anonymous people. The *tagging* of platforms such as *Del.icio.us* or *Flickr,* on the other hand, allow for the emphasizing of the presence of the user on the net and gives the public a configuration of indexed information based on one's own interests. In this sense, there is room on line both for useful but anonymous contributions as well as personalized information.

Both projects are examples of technological systemization of connective thought which arise from the intelligence of the few who create something useful and accessible for a vaster community.

Throughout inter-connective strategies, which give people the possibility to share their own information through evermore sophisticated methods, we are presented with what I recently described as "connective intelligence", which makes auto-organisational strategies a central part of the net. In these platforms there is no limit to the contents which may be published and one may share them with the entire planet, attracting more specifically those who have similar interests to our own. *Tagging* is a form of *social networking* refinement, and gives the possibility to create a plural and extended conscience. In these forms of connectivity I see a resurrection of the aura, intended as that tactile but unperceivable halo, created by the informational connections of each and every one of us, such as our sentimental and personal bonds and our friendships, which are all organised in a whole and extended fashion - a web of relations which represents how we relate to the world and what we have shared so far.

The artist becomes a networker and creates possibilities for exchange between people who become a part of the conceived network, which means to open up the idea of aura to all possible connections, which may come about in that network. The aura of a person connected in a professional and friendly information net system represents the communicability of that person and the interconnection of all his or her bonds. For example, our computer, our mobile phone, also contain the aura of our cohabitation in this world, consisting of the messages we send and receive, the list of friends or acquaintances in our address book, files we have saved and archived, the configuration of the system we have created, etc. This web belongs to us personally, and makes us a part of a community that reunites in hyper-cognitive systems in the information-sphere. It is part of our digital persona, although much of that escapes our control entirely.

In Tatiana Bazzichelli's book, connection is seen as an artistic practice. Interaction platforms, free operative systems such as GNU/Linux, independent experimental or community projects and *hacktivist* movements are presented as works of art. The network in itself becomes a work of art. When I was member of the jury at the Ars Electronic Festival in Linz in 1994, I, along with the other four members, Joi Ichi Ito, Franz Manola, Morgan Russell and Mitsuhiro

Takemura, we were confronted with the need to formalize the criteria to judge the works submitted in the newly created category of art developed on the net. We asked ourselves how we could judge these forms of art, if the www was the medium that supported them, and so we decided that the connectivity was the message[3]. Among the criteria for evaluating the artistic validity of a web site, I proposed *webness*. With *webness* I mean the quality of connectivity of projects. These criteria led us to attribute the Golden Nica award to no less then Linus Torvalds, for having invented and spread the use of Linux the following year.

In 1979, at the first ever edition of the Ars Electronic Festival in Linz, digital culture was an avant-garde theme. Today we are no longer relating to Utopias, but rather dealing with tentatively interpreting an economic and social phase in which technological progress has become the grammar of the present. On the one hand we live in a progressive segmentation and specialization, as demonstrated by the technique of *tagging*, and on the other hand we are experimenting an extended inclusion which involves common people who have access to technology which 20 years ago was unimaginable (like video conferencing or the multi-medial or multi-sensorial use of mobile phones). People become the active content and the producers of connected information.

The Italian thoughts and activities relating to the net become central in the explanation of this mechanism of media evolution, which sees the presence of the user as being evermore active and pertinent. The experiences told in this book show a network of individuals who act as an alternative to the standardized production of culture, information and art. These are people who pour their own political, social, artistic relations and friendships directly into a creative use of the media; a net which exists before the evolution of the Internet, through the alternative use of BBSes and even before that through mail art. Through the projects and activities contained in this book, it is possible to understand how the central component of networking in Italy is the web of relations: going to a conference, participating in a festival, talking and sharing projects with others, organising a thematic meeting and at the same time, meeting in a bar or a restaurant with people who share our interests, become creative occasions to produce new activities and projects.

Tatiana Bazzichelli's work proposes that we understand our cultural present through art itself. Art can be used to explain current cultural processes, and this kind of study, which is still in progress even now - like this book - is a precious instrument whereby to understand who we are and where we are going. It is a slice of Italian culture inside the network, an important lesson for young people and for many students, academics, critics and artists who may gather their inspiration from this text and who don't really know the origins of Internet art and of Italian digital culture.

Italy is a country which is controlled by one-way communication media and particularly by television: it is quite apposite that to resist a collective medium, one must use a connective one, and, at the same time, give life to an artistic tradition of networking which involves the entire country and is still in evolution. In the creation of such an extended connectivity, the free access to the net creates an occasion to develop one's own communication from the bottom, moulding it to one's own needs - needs which become subversive artistic practice in order to create new stages for free participation and to give visibility to all. I support Tatiana Bazzichelli's effort in that direction. And so does this book.

Endnotes

[1] Even if he never spoke of anything close to the Internet, in a certain way Marshall McLuhan had anticipated it in the fifth chapter of *Understanding Media* predicting the development of electronic technologies as vehicles through which to expand not only our senses, but our consciousness itself (the book was written in 1962 and published in 1964).

[2] For a deeper knowledge of concepts such as *tagging* and *social bookmarking*, look at the description on the respective Wikipedia at: <en.wikipedia.org/wiki/Tags> and <en.wikipedia.org/wiki/Social_bookmarking>.

[3] The statement of the judge panel for the www category is online at the site of the Ars Electronic Festival, 1995 edition: <www.aec.at/en/archives/prix_archive/prixjuryStatement .asp?iProjectID=2554>.

Introduction

The concept that networking is art is loaded with meaning, since it unites two seemingly different worlds: the practices of networking with that of art. In this context, however, the two are perfectly integrated. To network means to create relationship networks, in order to share experiences and ideas in the context of a communicative exchange, and an artistic experimentation in which the sender and the receiver, the artist and the public, act on the same plane.

In Italy, over the course of twenty years of experimentation, thanks to the alternative use of the Internet, a vast national network of people who share political, cultural and artistic objectives was created. These projects, which are active among underground movements, integrate different media (computers, video, television, radio, magazines) and individuals who are involved in the technological experimentation also known as "Hacktivism", customary terminology in use in Italy, where the political component is key. The Italian network proposes a form of critical information, spread through independent and collective projects that share the common value of freedom of expression. At the same time, it reflects the new role of the artist and author who becomes a networker, an operator of collective networks, reconnecting himself with the artistic practices of the Neo-Avant-garde of the 1960s (Fluxus being the first), but also with mail art, and with Neoism and Luther Blissett.

The art of networking is shaped by weaving open relational dynamics that are coming into being, and, in many cases, difficult to define. Even those who produce this type of art (or have produced it) often do not define it as such, or rather prefer to not limit it with some agreed upon categorization.

Until recently, the term "art" has rarely been used to connote artistic activities on line. Instead an attempt was made to define these practices by creating micro categories, often sources of ambiguities (and vivid contrasts!) even among those in the know. A point of view that is perfectly rooted in the rejection of the concept of art belonging to the artistic Avant-garde; from Dadaism to Futurism and Surrealism, up until the Neo-Avant-garde of the 1960s, which, in any case, took place within the art circuits.

In general, there seems to be great confusion surrounding the various definitions, which go from net art (or net.art, with a period between net and art) to web art, hacker art, new media art, cyber art, electronic art and digital art. In many cases however the difference among these practices is real and can be documented.

Terms like net.art (with a dot between net and art) or hacker art refer to a series of practices and events that are created during specific phases of the development of a critical approach to the web, as we will see in the following pages. Sometimes however, categorical definitions run the risk of delimiting a scope of action on the basis of how it came into being, generating distinctions of belonging among those who recognize a term as more or less valid as another, on the basis of "community perception" or on one's own artistic history.

At the same time, it is no longer enough to define these practices in terms of the medium used. The art of networking is transversal to the arts that are characterized by a medium of communication and realization: it can travel through mail art, web art, video art, computer art, net.art, software art, ASCII art, media art in the broad sense. For this reason, it is possible to say, without reading too much into it, that Networking was an art and it still is. *The Net as Artwork*, therefore freeing itself from the prejudices of the past and re-appropriating itself of a term that, in its conceptual vastness, allows it to embrace different practices, without forcing them into rigid forms, leaving them free to transform themselves through the inter-weaving of links that are always new. It is art outside the box, which comprises, as we shall see, numerous spheres of action.

The term "art" can help to critically refer to a series of activities that hinge on the construction of connections, community networks and relationship networks between heterogeneous subjects. The works of networking mentioned here allow for the reconstruction of the development of realities that, from the 1980s, had proposed a shared creative use, conscious of the technology, from video to computers, contributing to the formation of an Italian hacker community. A journey that goes from mail art to BBSes (alternative computer networks widespread throughout Italy before the internet), to Hackmeetings, to Telestreet, and to the practice of networking and net.art.

The main research field of this book is Italy, since it is here that networking practices have determined the construction of a network of projects unparalleled in any other country. A scene with a strong identity and with its own artistic, technological and political feeling has been formed in Italy. The forms of artistic activism (artivism) and technological activism (hacktivism) are tightly interconnected in an extensive network diffused throughout the nation.

In Italy, the idea of cyberpunk and hacking has taken on a very particular typology, tightly connected with the history of the underground digital network and the radical political movement, something that has not happened in most other countries. In Italy we prefer to use the term hacktivism to define artistic and mass media practices, giving them an artistic and political value which is not always recognized as such, outside of Italy. In some ways, our country constitutes a laboratory of underground experimentation that can become a model for many others. At the same time however, it represents a sort of creative "island" that is not always able to export its own creations. The idea that the "Italian scene" has been virtually marginalized comes from here.

Surely this affirmation derives from the fact that in many experimental environments a linguistic gap has existed, and to a certain extent, still exists, so that artists and activists tend to only use the Italian language and to disseminate their activities via local channels. Furthermore, it has very often been the "community" dynamics of political activism that have made some processes slower. In any case, several Italian realities described here are conceptually tied to international ones, which frequently represent very important inspirational sources.

This book wants to shed light on a series of activities that starting from the 1980s, in and outside of Italy, has transformed the conception of art as object into art as a network of relationships, possibilities of personally and collectively intervening in the creation of an artistic product. The formation of art as networking laid down its theoretical and practical bases a long time ago.

The Avant-garde of the 1900s had already shifted its attention from the artistic object to daily life, further tarnishing the notion of "originality". But it is with the Neo- Avant-garde of the 1960s that the public enters directly into the process of creation of the work with the *happening* in which everyone is, at least ideally, simultaneously a producer and a consumer of information. In the *happenings* and in Fluxus, art becomes inter-action, inviting the spectator to eliminate the distance between himself and the artistic product, with the goal of making the dichotomy of artist-spectator obsolete (however, it does in part survive).

It is above all in contexts outside of the gallery and museum circuit that the possibility of experimenting with art as collective inter-action is truly materialized: moving the debate from the artistic realm to daily social reality. This dates back to the 1970s with the graffiti artists and with the punk movement and is carried through to the counterculture digital networks and the current hacker movement. This network is comprised of activists, artists, and collectives that promote and apply the self-managed use of media in their own actions, defining self-management as the self-organization and self-production of communication media and artistic practices.

In punk, a movement which constitutes the basis for many practices of future artistic and technological activism in Italy, the concept of self-management (DIY) is manifested in the willingness to undermine the opposition between the amateur and the professional, showing that it is possible to self produce one's own art (music, magazines, information material, etc.) outside of the market circuits.

Within the sphere of the practices of the graffiti artists, DIY is manifested in the act of personalizing the walls surrounding their lives with *tags*, activating a moving communication between various anonymous identities.

The concept of DIY is also a key for the development of the alternative Italian digital culture and for future forms of networking. The scene of Italian cyberpunk and the hacker movement show that, starting with a conscious use of technology and the instruments of language, it is possible to conceive of a type of art in which it is possible to personally intervene: activating an open process of creation. These dynamics have been widespread throughout Italy since the mid 1980s, especially within the circle of the *Centri Sociali Occupati* [Squatted Social Centres], developing by means of an independent use of technology through the creation of collective practices, and artistic and political objectives, forming a web of projects that was diffused throughout the country.

At the same time, the course of analysis and critical thinking about the culture of the internet had begun. It saw the height of its expression in the 1990s, giving way to the first Virtual Reality experimentations; forging the foundations for an Italian *net culture*. These processes involve different artists, such as, just to name a few: Giacomo Verde, Antonio Glessi and Andrea Zingoni from the *Giovanotti Mondani Meccanici*, Massimo Contrasto, Tommaso Tozzi, Federico Bucalossi, Claudio Parrini and the collective from *Strano Network*, Simonetta Fadda, Mario Canali and the *Correnti Magnetiche* group, Flavia Alman e Sabine Reiff of the *Pigreca* group, Helena Velena, Mariano Equizzi, together with the editors of specialized publications such as Francesco Galluzzi and the editorial staff of *La Stanza Rossa*, Alessandro Ludovico from *Neural*, the collective from *Decoder/ Shake Edizioni* and those of *Isole nella Rete, FreakNet, AvANa.net, Tactical Media Crew* and different other artists, theorists, activists and hackers who have already acted in the arena of Italian underground digital culture.

Some of the aforementioned have developed an aptitude towards the artistic experimentation with media (from video to computers) which presents a strong community character, making us talk more about the "art of the hackers" or Hacker art in general. With hacker art the meaning of the work of art should no longer be looked at in its manifestation as object, but in the network of relations and in the collective processes that have contributed to its creation. The story of hackers in Italy is closely knit to that of the digital culture and the formation of underground alternative networks.

In Italy the concept of the hacker developed at the same time as the development of a critical conscience about the use of technology. A hacker is not only someone who uses technology to test its limits, but above all someone who believes in the freedom of information (and let us add, art), within the accessibility of information and in the sharing of knowledge, who perhaps has never seen a computer in his life. For this reason, the hacker ethic is the attitude of thought that best accompanies many of the practices described here.

In this sense, the social component gains a central importance: that is why often in Italy many experiences between the 1980s and the 1990s are defined as social hacking, in which experimentation in technology and in programming code is tied to the idea of sharing resources and knowledge. Following this objective, Italian artists, activists and hackers act concretely in person and on the internet, putting protest practices like Netstrike, into play; constructing counterculture sites and independent magazines, hacker laboratories (Hacklabs) and organizing collective meetings regarding self-teaching and the exchanging of skills. (Hackmeetings).

Naturally projects of artistic networking do not exist solely in Italy. On an international scale, in the last ten years, mailing lists, festivals and on-line projects have been, and in many cases are still now, a territory for primary experimentation and development of net.art and, more in general, of the international *net culture*. These experiences have involved numerous theorists and artists for years, and are fundamental in order to develop a critical approach to the network. The networking scene in Italy has acquired a particular character, and, due to its participation and diffusion, it does not have any equals anywhere. The Italian scene links itself directly with the hacker practices, as evident in the work of the activist Jaromil and, following the Blissettian tradition of the "viral" participation on communication, the works of 0100101110101101.ORG and of [epidemiC], to name those who had major contact with international reality.

Between the 1990s and 2000, the culture of networking in Italy developed through the proliferation of collective projects that work critically in media and on the internet, which are by now available to everyone instead of only to a few experts. Many activists, hackers and artists take advantage of the diffusion of low priced technology, from computers to video cameras, to realize far-reaching projects providing a concrete turning-point for the Italian networking culture in terms of its diffusion throughout the nation.

Realities are born: such as Indymedia Italia, the Telestreet network, the collective New Global Vision, and the Autistici/Inventati free server, which experiments with computers, video and the Internet with a critical point of view. Many other local projects are tied to these national realities which share these same political and technological objectives. Among these, the collectives: Candida TV, Serpica Naro, Molleindustria and other groups who actively respond to the post neo-economy social problematics, such as ChainWorkers and in the realm of strategic marketing tactics of Guerrigliamarketing.it.

The majority of the above-mentioned projects emerged after the G8 anti-summit in Genova in 2001; a stage not only for difficult clashes, repression and violence, as the majority of the official media highlighted, but also for an important experience for anyone who constructs grassroots information, with amateur video cameras, underground internet sites or independent radio networks. The three days in Genoa not only dealt a harsh blow to Italian activist groups through violence and repression, but also contributed to rendering a more incisive critical reflection on media, technology and the forms of political activism.

Together with the projects of networking described above, there is a network of people who answer to the strategies of the opposition with a ludic-tactic frivolity, putting one's own body into play and subverting the idea of political action as "resistance": which showed its strength as well as its limits in Genoa. In this network, the body becomes a fundamental channel through which to create new openings, to initiate experimentation on the "bordering" - even sexual - territories. There are many projects that aim to form a larger network, commonly described by the term "queer" or "pink". Among these, the collective Sexyshock in Bologna, Phag-Off in Rome, and the Pornflakes in Milano stand out, whose activity is inserted in a discourse of reflection on sexuality, pornography and artistic experimentation ranging from cyberfeminism to Netporn to indie-porn on the Internet.

The description of the ties that exist in this dynamic Italian network of artistic, technological and political experimentation, intends to show how it is possible to create successful critical and creative routes that involve "alternative" channels, compared to those dominated by the economy of the market, by the politics of control and by commercial information, often presented in Western society as the only possibilities. A criticism of the *status quo* which overruns, not only the social and political plane, but also the artistic plane, as, for example happens with the episode of the Tirana Conspiracy at the beginning of the 21st century. This event which few know about, dealt a harsh blow to the Italian system, which is based on commercial dynamics. The Tirana Conspiracy illustrated the inanity of the collector-market-artist system, and showed that the current artistic challenge lies in the invention of new courses of action and new contents.

The networking projects described in this book act within these spaces, in the social and cultural fractures that are apparently on the margins of daily life, but which in reality constitute an important territory for the re-invention and rewriting of symbolic and expressive codes with which to transform and decode our present. It is not surprising, therefore, that the Internet, with which we all work today is in reality the fruit of connections, battles and relationships which see hackers playing a leading role. Just like it is not surprising that many individuals here mentioned were precursors of different artistic and cultural processes which have contributed to the shaping of the current Italian mass media and technological imagination.

This book wants to give the proper weight and worth to the many artistic, social and cultural practices which, through their network of political, artistic, technological and affective ties, have contributed to making the instruments with which we interact daily, more fascinating; from the computer to the Internet. With the hope that the experiences written here become a model for all those who would like to continue to work creatively in the spaces and fractures of the everyday, or for those who will fight to ensure that everything comes out in the open, allowing anyone to make it his or her own.

Naturally, the components of personal networking play a central role in approaching subjects like these. My analysis should therefore be thought of as one of the many possibilities, and I expect others to follow, dictated by the personal worlds that we each have built, following one's own network dynamics. I welcome a future of new connections and sharing; opening the contents of this book to future reflections and re-elaborations, with the same passion, enthusiasm and even idealism that have characterized these past twenty years in the history of Italian networking.

Networking Cultures

Networking as Art

The art of networking can be seen as a metaphor for art as a network; art that creates a network. To be able to correctly categorize the many artistic practices of media art over the last twenty years, it becomes fundamental to reconstruct the concept of networking. This concept is often used by new media publications. Yet it is rarely analyzed within its own particular characteristics, apart from a few publications which are for the most part widespread in independent circles or promoted by specialized publishing houses[1].

Instead, the art of networking is an artistic practice whose origins are rooted in the distant past. To network means to create relationship networks, to share experiences and ideas. It also means to create contexts in which people can feel free to communicate and to create artistically in a "horizontal" manner. It means creating the aforementioned in a way that the sender and the receiver, the artist and the public, are fused/confused; they lose their original meaning.

The art of networking is based on the figure of the artist as a creator of sharing platforms and of contexts for connecting and exchanging. This figure spreads through those who accept the invitation and in turn create networking occasions. For this reason, it no longer makes sense to speak of an artist, since the active subject becomes the network operator or the networker. Perhaps it is also the most difficult type of contemporary art to define, for it is not based on objects, nor solely on digital or analogical instruments, but on the relationships and processes in progress between individuals. Individuals who can in turn create other relationship contexts, or give life to creative products, which are important if considered within the larger idea of sharing.

Business logic, often connected with the traditional environments of contemporary art, allows for the "exchange" of that spontaneous gift. Perhaps it is for this reason that few publications exist on the subject, because it has always been considered more important to live out certain dynamics, rather than to write about them. Furthermore, in art show circles and in written texts, one must necessarily carry out a selection process. However, this aspect does not exist within the world of networking: everyone can participate by recommending their own materials, and total freedom exists.

Let's therefore start at the beginning. According to my reconstruction, the first forms of art as network are found in the sixteenth century, and in particular, in the Mannerism period. This period is strongly characterized by the interconnection between artists living in different countries, ranging from Northern Europe to Italy. Albrecht Dürer, a key protagonist who among his numerous works created xylographs and engravings of extraordinary interest, greatly influenced the iconography of the era. Let's think for example about the famous 1514 xylograph *Melancolia*. In the second half of the fifteenth century in Germany, the technique of producing images on paper and in a serial manner had already been widespread. For example, Gutenberg printed his *42 Line Bible* in Mainz, and had approximately 180 copies circulated. In those years a real revolution was seen in the field of creating images "in a series", a phenomenon that really can be compared to the advent of television and computers and to the digital reproduction techniques invented almost five hundred years later.

With Albrecht Dürer we find characteristics of strong modernity which allowed him to disseminate his images throughout Europe, giving life to a network of exchanges and relationships that even gave him a presence in Italy. In the first part of the sixteenth century Albrecht Dürer's activity set the foundation for the formation of a unified European culture. His engravings and xylographs were found in many countries, and as was the case of Marcantonio Raimondi in Venice, sometimes they were even counterfeited. Dürer formed a noteworthy relationship with Italy, as he was interested in coming into contact with Renaissance thinking and with the prominent individuals of the time such as Giovanni Bellini and Jacopo de' Barbari, creator of, among other works, the famous xylography of Venice[2].

Returning to networking dynamics, the interest in diffusing one's own works in a serial and reticular manner is found in other, diverse contexts, be they international or Italian. The contemporary phenomenon that best connects these practices is mail art. It is a line of transmission that leads to the types of video and artistic language experimentation present in Fluxus practices. These practices fit together like Chinese boxes and are visible in the widest vein of artistic experimentation, especially in the Avant-garde of the first decades of the twentieth century.

Moving quickly through time we see that in the 1980s networking developed a strong identity in Italy (in the European context it started to develop at the end of the 1970s). It evolved as a dimension that spanned different media, favoured by their progressive development. In those years copy machines were widespread and their use became increasingly more constant within the milieu of "dissent". Just think of the massive production of punkzines and fanzines within the Social Centres, as well as their production outside of this environment. Furthermore, within punk ideology the idea of the death of art often comes up in order to open up creative possibilities for everyone. Anyone can play, as long as there is the desire to do it. The *Do It Yourself* concept is then found in the subsequent phenomena of networking; combining with the influxes of mail art, from Neoism to Plagiarism to Luther Blissett, up until the 1990s, when the network dynamic is affirmed on a mass level through the use of computers and the internet.

In the 1990s, the idea of networking was developed further, taking on new shapes in the world of the hacker ethic. Much like an artistic *happening*, this idea of networking cannot overlook the notion that technology should be critically seen as an open medium. Within the computer domain the term *hack* literally means "ingenious find". It is associated with the concepts of exchange and social sharing; whose goal is the spreading of information and free knowledge. The intent of this approach to technology is not to destroy, but to create; to give life to open processes in which the use of the computer is an important medium, but not as a means to an end. This "aptitude" emerges at the end of the 1980s with the advance of the Bulletin Board Systems (BBSes); electronic databases through which it is possible to send and propagate information from hub to hub, connecting through a computer and a modem, thereby creating the sharing platforms which marked the future history of the internet.

The idea of networking as art is also found in many works of net.art. Italians Marco Deseriis and Giuseppe Marano define net.art as "the art of Connection". In their book Deseriis and Marano recount its birth and its advance, describing a great part of this phenomenon which developed at the international level in the 1990s.[3] In fact, most of the net.art current was propagated through collective platforms. Along with many others, mailing lists such as "Nettime" <www.nettime.org> are a concrete example of this.

The art of networking goes beyond the idea of media as containers, and it should be interpreted as a conceptual work, in which what counts is connecting; subverting the idea of art that is created by a single person. Therefore *Art is easy*, as the artist Giuseppe Chiari said in 1972, freeing the spectator from his inhibitions with respect to a "superior" art.[4]

From Ready-made to Fluxus

This journey begins at the time of the historic Avant-gardes. During this era we moved towards constructing a mass society as a direct consequence of the *metropolitan crowd* affirming itself as a social object (clearly visible in the first Universal Expositions of the second half of the nineteenth century)[5].

In the Cubist and Dadaist collages, fragments of daily life such as train tickets, newspaper articles, snapshots, common objects like bottles, hats, bicycle wheels, irons become part of the art world. In Marcel Duchamp's famous 1917 work *Fountain,* a urinal becomes a work of art, simply through the artist's "gesture" of legitimizing it as such, by signing it. The practice of "readymade" de-contextualizes an object, attributing new and different meanings to it. "Readymade" gives way to the beginning of those artistic practices that turn everyday objects into works of art; unhinging the traditional concept of the work of art itself. The work can also be a common object, which becomes art simply after the artist decides that it does.

The practice of "readymade" was advanced in the 1950s by the New Dada in the United States and by the *Nouveau Realisme* in Europe; not only giving life to compositions of daily objects, which are reconnected to the *collages* of the historic Avant-garde, but also inserting discarded objects. For example, the *Poubelles* series by Fernandez Arman reminds us of the work of the Dadaist Kurt Schwitters, who composed *assemblages* with used and degraded materials. Instead, Robert Rauschenberg associates the gestural painting of Action Painting with fragments of the everyday.

The same presence of the everyday is in the Pop art of the 1960s, in which the standardization of industrial production takes on an artistic value. The idea of reinserting life within art is also found in Piero Manzoni, who worked in the wake of the pop wave in the 1960s. In 1961 he produced a work composed of a numbered series of tin cans of the now famous "Artist's Shit". Simonetta Fadda remarks that, in any case, the figure of the artist as creator is central.

Piero Manzoni renders "Artist's Shit" because he himself has produced it. He himself legitimizes it as such. It is a paradoxical affirmation of the power that an artist has over reality, which makes life become included in art (as Marcel Duchamp had done earlier). Only after, with the artistic practices of networking on the internet, does the point of view become inverted: the goal is no longer to reinsert life into art, but to reinsert art into life. This is the real revolution of our present (Fadda, 2006, private conversation with the author).

Research on the "art-life" relationship is reconnected to the performances and to the *happenings* of the end of the 1950s. Work-events that affirmed themselves especially in the following decade, determined an ever-increasing bond between artistic practices and concrete experiences. The work of art materializes until it becomes an event, following the path initially laid by Giacomo Balla and Fortunato Depero in the *Theatre of Futuristic Objects* and with the Dada evening shows. With the *happenings,* a form of art gained ground and it continued to develop, almost completely, eliminating the objectual component. Art becomes action and the spectator is invited to personally intervene; to participate in the process. In these artistic practices the non-predictable is played upon: art wants to be discovery, experience, compartmental practice, interaction.

During the "actions" of Allan Kaprow, the creator of the *happenings* as work-events, the collaborators acted by following a script. Even though the starting point was known, the work resulted from the combined action of the artists and spectators. With the practice of the *happenings* we see the beginning of a form of *Intermedial art* that unites theatrical, musical, literary, pictorial and sculptural expressions. For example the Merce Cunningham Dance Company and musician John Cage, the inspiration for Fluxus, work in the same artistic milieu. Furthermore, Fluxus is the principal core of our discussion on networking, because it brings with it some assumptions that would be later encountered in much of the subsequent collective art, laying the foundations for the networking culture as we understand it today.

Fluxus has tried to eliminate the barriers between composer and those who listen, between the artist and those who observe, actively maintaining a constant dialogue composed of concrete, minimal, ephemeral and iconoclastic practices, in which the components of surprise and irony are key. According to Ken Friedman, it is a "philosophy thrown into reality", which completely revolutionized the concept of the artistic event. Fundamental presumptions notwithstanding, almost all Fluxus events take place on the *stage*. In its performances Fluxus still maintains, in fact, a distance from the audience members who connect more with its "being" than with its performed actions. In any case, Fluxus is fundamental for interpreting future phenomena ranging from mail art to Neoism to many subsequent video and computer experimentations.

The birth of the Fluxus movement is set in the period that dates from the end of the 1950s to the beginning of the 1960s. Fluxus gathers together heterogeneous artistic presences, which initially come into contact in New York, in Manhattan, in the SoHo district, and which see Marcel Duchamp active in this practice. Many of John Cage's students, from Allan Kaprow to Dick Higgins, Alison Knowles, Jackson McLow, Richard Maxfield, George Brecht and Al Hansen meet in 1958 in the New School for Social Research. They constitute the core nucleus of the movement which would then be diffused throughout Europe, thanks to the actions of George Maciunas, a key figure for Fluxus.

Maciunas, the real networker of the group, gave birth to the A/G gallery together with Almius Salcius, in 1961, contributing to the formation of a vast network made up of many active personalities within the literary circle, in theatre, in philosophy, in music, in dance, in performance and in contemporary art in general. These artists, including, La Monte Young, Yoko Ono, Terry Riley and Simone Forti, just to name a few, gravitate between New York and, later, San Francisco.

At the beginning of the 1960s, it is thanks to Maciunas and Higgings that Fluxus was spread within Europe, meeting personalities such as Robert Filliou, Joseph Beuys, Nam June Paik, Wolf Vostell, and musicians like the Italian Giuseppe Chiari, who are fundamental for their contributions in the field of contemporary art.

Fluxus was central in giving life to the notion of *intermedia*, which is found in the future practices of networking, as well as to the notion of the collective procedural event. The effects called *fluxus-events* or *flux-concerts* depending on the case, are based on public performances of instructions which are openly banal, simple life gestures, contained in short scripts (*fluxus-event scores*).

The idea of *intermedia*, a term which was used in more modest measure for the first time by the poet philosopher Samuel Taylor Coleridge[6], describes the practice of putting together different media and different types of artistic expression, which range from design to poetry, from painting to theatre. An almost natural concept for Fluxus considering the many and interdisciplinary elements present in the movement. In the *fluxus-events*, the traditional expressive schemes are broken down, while the often ironic and provocative intervention of the micro-objects of daily life becomes fundamental, from hats to ping-pong racquets, equipped with recurring icons that become almost "mystical". Common actions are de-contextualized and become concepts, taking on a new, often unforeseeable, meaning.

The first form of the *fluxus-events* collection is found in the *fluxus-concerts'* scores: the performers would read the action directions, or proposals, to be followed: a sort of "open composition" to carry out during the *happening*. Later, the events were organized in other ways, from the collection of postcards like *Water Yam* by George Brecht to small books like *Grapefruit* by Yoko Ono, to the pamphlets produced under the Great Bear emblem, a collection published in the 1960s by Dick Higgins for Something Else Press, the publishing house he founded in 1964.

George Maciunas is another figure who was greatly concerned about leaving visible traces of Fluxus. He ensured it by editing editions of individual and collective events and works, like the publication of *An Anthology*, or *Fluxus Yearbook*, producing the *fluxfilms* collections or creating the so-called *fluxboxes*: small boxes containing small "subversive" objects and multiple works. The

Fluxus boxes are total multimedia works, each one different from the other. They bear an authenticity that makes it ever clearer that the networker is not only a creator of collective contexts/events, but also a real net artist[7].

Fluxus Diagrams

From 1953 to 1973 George Maciunas created real hyper-textual maps, through sketches and diagrams drawn by his own hand on note pad pages according to the concept of Fluxus as an "alternative attitude in making art, culture and life"[8]. In 1961 it is Maciunas who coined the term Fluxus: art was supposed to be *amusement*, fun, simple, non-pretentious and it was to concentrate on the insignificant aspects of life, not presupposing large competencies in order to be understood and without any institutional value. Fluxus operated on the border between art and non-art and is interpreted more like a thought attitude; a life-practice more than an artistic movement. The term Fluxus derives from the Latin verb *fluere*, and the individual is seen as in a state of flux, a sort of active current in which daily life makes its entrance into art. *You don't do Fluxus, you simply are it*[9].

For Maciunas, Fluxus did not manifest itself simply in an attitude of thought, but was seen as a life practice and a "being" within art in an open way, total, and at the same time, free. In opposition to the *glamour* of Pop art, Fluxus was created as a form of "easy" art. Knowledgeable of the history of the then Soviet Union (his childhood was spent in Lithuania), Maciunas united his conviction in the democratic values of art with the idea of progressively realizing a sort of Total art, taking his cue from the Russian constructivist currents and from the anarchical movements of the early 1920s and working on concepts such as "Slavophilism" in opposition to "Westernism" (he coined the definitions). In fact, his biography tightly reconnects him to three countries, the USA, Germany and Lithuania, and this is found in his works and also in his creation of Fluxus as a real, expanded network of "hypermedial" artists. In his position, to which he held fast through the years, Maciunas is also inspired by the Left Front of the Arts (LEF), founded in 1917. LEF is an association of social artists at which he was hinting with his objective of overcoming bourgeois art - the traditional idea of music, theatre, sculpture, painting and poetry - in light of a new form of "expanded" art.

In his *Fluxcharts* (the Fluxus diagrams), Maciunas applies the concept of the expansion of space-time directly to the experimental music of John Cage in the reconstruction of macro historical periods. The first diagram *Atlas of Russian History* was started in the spring of 1950 and was followed by the *Atlas of Prehistoric Chinese Art* in 1958, and then by *Greek and Roman History of Art Chart*; themes that Maciunas explored in his university studies. Even if constructed with simple notepad paper, Maciunas' historical diagrams are decisively hypertexutal and three-dimensional. Subdivided into sections containing writings with an elegant and minute calligraphy, inserted inside the spatial-temporal axis, which in reality were to be read by opening the next "window", constructed with other pieces of paper glued close to the text in order to delve deeper, as if they were paper pop-ups.

The first diagram expressly relative to Fluxus is dated December 1961 and was publicly presented during a small, summer-time, neo-Dada demonstration organized by Maciunas in the Galerie Parnass in Wuppertal. No one knew Fluxus in Europe at the time and so it was publicized as a re-reading of the works of John Cage and an aesthetic presentation of the post-Cage art in America. The event was presented in a rigidly academic way. Maciunas himself prepared a reading of his work *Neo-Dada in Music, Theater, Poetry and Art*, translated into German and recited by actor Arthus C. Caspari. In the text, Fluxus is not expressly mentioned and the focus seems to be on something else.

In this context we see the entrance of Fluxus onto the European artistic scene. As a surprise, Nam June Paik came on stage behind Caspari, and showed one of Macianus' diagrams, drawn on a large scale on white Bristol board, provoking laughter in the audience. The diagram is a re-publication in German of *Time/time projected in 2dim.space POETRY GRAPHICS/space projected in time GRAPHIC MUSIC/Time/Time projected in space MUSIC THEATRE*; abbreviated with: *Time-Space Chart*. The scheme anticipated the concept of the subsequent *Fluxcharts* by Maciunas.

The ample ray of artistic practices in which Fluxus has operated is reconstructed in the *Fluxcharts* in a linear flow from Dada to Futurist sonorous poetry, to the *Dada collages* of Kurt Schwitters. The categories of poetry, graphics, music and theatre are subdivided into thirteen other categories inserted within an artistic dimension of space-time, called *time-art* and *space-art*. The different *Fluxartists* are placed within the thirteen categories on the basis of their fields of expression and some like Jackson Mc Low and Dick Higgins are included many times due to their heightened sense of being "intermedial".

Maciunas was a pioneer of our times, periodically creating a *Fluxnewsletter* to directly ask for advice or direction from group members, with regards to including names of the artists and diverse practices in his diagrams, tediously collecting information on each one of them, and archiving the material.

Another Fluxus diagram dated 1966, called *Fluxus (Its historical Development and Relationship to Avant-garde Movements)*, is divided into two parts. In the top half, Maciunas tries to give a definition of what art and non-art are. The bottom half is a schematization of what Fluxus is, and its relationship to all the different –*isms* distinguishing it from Modernism. The roots of Fluxus are found, according to Maciunas, in the Baroque theatre and in the "multimedia" shows of the Versailles gardens, up until Marcel Duchamp's Readymade and John Cage's music, Fluxus' immediate predecessors. Therefore, they are classified into spatial-temporal categories of the artists who belong or do not belong to Fluxus. In this scheme however, as in the *Expanded Art Diagrams*, which come later, it is interesting to note that Maciunas did not create a simple list of names, but he divided people into four major categories.

Perhaps it is here that we find the "dark side" of this fascinating operation of George Maciunas' historicization, a trait that certainly makes it less "machine-like" and more human. The Achilles' heel of the networker is often his mania of schematism and cataloguing. This is also the most delicate aspect of the Art of networking, closely connected with the personal and experiential components of whoever carries it forward.

The first category of the scheme includes the pre-Fluxists George Brecht and Ben Vautier, already active in this context before the birth of Fluxus. The core base of the group appears next on the spatial-temporal line: George Brecht and Ben Vautier, George Maciunas, Robert Watts, Philip Corner, Dick Higgins, Alison Knowles, Benjamin Patterson, Nam June Paik, Jackson Mac Low, Tomas Schmit, Emmett Williams, Henry Flynt, inserted in the "Fluxus" category.

Subsequently the "independents" appear, ranging from Joseph Beuys to Ray Johnson to La Monte Young who had only temporarily worked with Fluxus. Lastly, still following the line of temporal progression which goes from 1959 to 1966, the group of the "excluded" appear, former members of Fluxus, who according to Maciunas had decided to alienate themselves from the group. They are recognizable in the diagrams with a dotted line in the continuity of the temporal axis.

The justifications put forth by Maciunas for this list of expelled members are: anti-collective attitude; excess of individualism; desire for personal glory; "prima donna complex". Numerous internationally recognized exponents of this movement are included in this group and listed in the introduction to the diagram[10]. Secondary reasons, but not enough to warrant being "excluded", were "opportunism, transfer into rival groups following the offer of more publicity, competitive attitudes and the creation of rival practices". Nam June Paik was later "expelled from Fluxus" in Maciunas' diagrams, like other artists, and this position provoked strong internal controversy. The members of the group started to ask themselves what Fluxus really was and what its limits were, accusing Maciunas of applying the same practices of expulsion as Guy Debord in the Situationist International sphere or as André Breton with the creation of the belonging criterion of Surrealism. Despite these accusations, due, above all, to the differences in ideological positions, Maciunas continued his methodical and untiring historicization of Fluxus and of the related artistic practices.

In 1966 he gave life to the *Expanded Art Diagram*, describing the development of art up until 1966: the year in which the Fluxus experience is generally considered over. The diagram is on the reverse of the *Fluxfest Sale* flyer and approximately 2,000 copies were printed. This diagram follows the schema of the preceding ones, including however the notion of Political Culture, whose origin is pegged at 1964, inside the temporal line which goes from the iconoclastic Byzantine to the actions of the Chinese Red Guard, clearly highlighting Maciunas' point of view in perceiving art as anti-Bourgeois and popular (a position which brings him closer in the diagram to Henry Flynt). This point of view became increasingly more predominant in the last years of his work.

Nevertheless, Maciunas' complete work was the *Diagram of Historical Development of Fluxus and other 4 Dimensional, Aural, Optic, Olfactory. Epithelial and Tactile Art Forms* (1973) and it measured 1m x 3m. It included all Fluxus activities starting from 1948 until 1971, therefore adding even the posthumous activities. The Fluxus diagrams drew attention even in Italy and Maciunas set himself to work on the publication of the 1973 *Diagram of Historical Development of Fluxus* [11]. The diagram was published only in 1979, a year after Maciunas' death and on a reduced scale, by the Swedish publishing house Kalejdoskop.

The Mail Art Network

Mail art is a network of relationships constructed through the postal circuit, and in practice it is exercised by sending and receiving letters, cards or anything else one wants, from all over the world, establishing "virtual" ties with many other individuals, united simply by the interest in communicating. Mail art, especially because it remains outside of the artistic business circuits, has always been considered the Cinderella of art, but in the end, this was its fortune, because no one ever really historicized it and it has always preserved that character of originality and novelty that today makes it unique and always current.

Mail art is a form of art open to all. It does not foresee the selection of the artists and in the few organized shows on this theme the works of all the participants in the various projects have always been displayed. There is an amusing pun in Italian: "mail art = mai l'art" [mail art = never art]. This shows how several mail non-artists have wanted to deliberately keep themselves far removed from the worlds of institutional collecting and museums, such that those who compile fragments of mail art in never-ending archives do so out of pure passion.

Despite being recognized by few, or rather by those few who have directly experimented with mail art directly, this form of art is the true mother of *networking*.

It is not for nothing that the term that can best define it is *Eternal Network*, created by the French artist-sociologist Robert Filliou[12]. An eternal network that starting from the 1950s has involved hundreds of people, made up of envelopes and rubber stamps and any other self-produced object or pieces of paper turned into creative art sent by mail. It involves individuals linked by belonging to a non-formalized network, who because of who they know are included, as time goes on in the network which consists of exchanging addresses and one-to-one and one-to-many mailings.

An artistic process that unites within it public and private dimensions in a harmonious manner, mail art takes shape in a network of small works mailed to everyone who enter in the collective postal circuit and at the same time giving life to friendly bi-directional relationships, which are lived out in the intimacy of one's own mail box.

Most of the time, a work-process of mail art comes to life when the networker on duty proposes themed projects and sends a sort of "call" out to the people involved in the network. If they want to they can accept the invitation and send their mail art works to the specified address. A collective collection, which stays with the network operator, is produced from the projects sent, while the participants are compensated by the former with a small publication at the end of the project, or with other forms of independent editions of the works obtained.

For a brief historical reconstruction, the birth of mail art is usually placed at the beginning of the 1960s, but has its origins in the 1950s. Vittore Baroni, who together with Piermario Ciani[13] was pivotal in the diffusion and development of mail art in Italy, maintains that in reality there is no real starting point to mail art, considering the infinite possibilities that the postal medium can offer and the ease with which networks can be created through the use of envelopes and stamps[14].

Commonly, the origin of mail art is connected to the figure of Ray Johnson (1927-1995) and to his New York Correspondence School, created in 1962. The name NYCS recalls the many art academies of that period which bloomed along the East Coast. Ray Johnson left us many works of mail art: whole collections of postcards, stamps, invitations to events that never took place, sketches and small drawings, among which the icon of the likeable bunny with the long and sinuous nose that has become a symbol today. Johnson died in 1995. All dressed up, he dove from a New York bridge into the gelid waters, an act considered by many as his last performance. He created a fundamental activity of networking, which was naturally not highly recognized by official critics when he was alive, except for isolated events such as the *New York Correspondence School Show*, curated by Marcia Tucker at the Whitney Museum of New York in 1970.

After his death, in 1999, a huge retrospective was organized at the Whitney Museum, signalling in some way the end of the journey, which nevertheless has no beginning and no end, precisely because of its open and "eternal" way of being. Ray Johnson was, and remains, a very important icon for mail art and his notoriety among the members of the network place him among the principal proponents of the art of networking[15].

Vittore Baroni quotes Futurism, underlining the connection between mail art and other artistic movements with the creative correspondence created by Giacomo Balla and Francesco Cangiullo and Dadaism, with Marcel Duchamp's and Kurt Schwitters' collages. In the text *The Early Days of Mail Art* in the anthology *Eternal network*, the artist Ken Friedman remembers Yves Klein's famous "Blue Stamp", which circulated via mail in the mid 1950s, causing a sensation among the bureaucracy of the time. It is certain however that the area in which mail art has mostly shown its influence is Fluxus, in which the members operated in close postal contact. Dick Higgins' newsletter, famous for the dissemination of the activities of the Something Else Press publishing house and of George Maciunas, was directed toward the creation of the Fluxus diagrams. Even Ben Vautier, Robert Watts and Mieko Shiomi were supporters of interesting experiments with postage stamps, rubber stamps and artists' postcards.

In fact, the field of mail art experimentation extends not only to the sending of "creating" mail, but also to the creation of stamps, rubber stamps, stickers and other self-produced material. The principal channel for the Italian diffusion of these practices was the Mail art magazine "Arte Postale!" edited by Vittore Baroni, which involved hundreds of people from Ray Johnson to children; presenting musical projects, texts, catalogues, postcards, postage stamps, rubber stamps and postal poetry. The first issue, dated October 1979, initiated the twenty-year journey of a published periodical, later followed by the "Real Correspondence" bulletin distributed by e-mail. Every issue of "Arte Postale!" is different from the next and has a specific theme, often paired with exhibition projects.

In the summer of 2000, the Museo d'arte moderna of Bassano del Grappa featured *Sentieri Interrotti. Crisi della rappresentazione e iconoclastia nelle arti dagli anni '50 alla fine del secolo,* with a section on mail art curated by Vittore Baroni. The show presented works and materials from movements such as Cobra, Letterism, Gutaj, Viennese Actionism, Fluxus, Visual Poetry, etc. In the section dedicated to Postal art, Vittore Baroni showed a few collective projects created between the 1960s and the 1990s, as well as a few publications representative of the field, and a sample of individual works in a chronological journey from the works of Ray Johnson to mail art transmitted through the internet. A collective project named "*Il tavolo del piccolo iconoclasta*" [The Table of the Small Iconoclast] was conceived for the occasion. It was a long white table positioned in the centre of the exhibition space dedicated to mail art, with a series of rubber stamps and a few different coloured ink pads on the table and pile of sheets of paper with the target motif of concentric circles stamped on different iconic symbols (faces of politicians, religious heads, television celebrities, famous artists, works of art, multinational corporation trademarks, etc.) The visitors were encouraged to use the rubber stamps as "make-shift arms" in the iconoclastic act of annulling the image-targets as they deemed appropriate, preserving the work created as a memento of the show. This, in order to render the collaborative and inclusive character of Postal art comprehensible and verifiable in practice: open-to-everyone[16].

An important aspect that emerges from this reflection is precisely the meaning of gifting, the idea of making art to then give it away. It is the capacity of creating horizontal networks not based on profit, but based rather on the notion of creating spontaneous relationships and therefore central to mail art. Even for this reason, mail art is also alive today, for it is based on relational mechanisms part of our daily living and feeling, which go beyond the fashion of the moment[17].

In the image "Real Correspondence 6" (Vittore Baroni, 1981)[18], this process is made clear as it passes from a linear communication, inherent in the circuits of traditional art, to that of the reticular art of mail art and of the successive networking art. It is interesting to note how the figure of the network operator is inserted in the middle of the circuit and how it interacts at the same level with the public, who becomes the creator through the combined use of the different mass media.

Real Correspondence – Six

● Notwithstanding the wide range of old and new visual topics covered (e.g. rubber stamp,stamp,postcard,photocopy,audiocassette,etc.) Mail Art is not just another art trend. Mail Art affects firstly the structure of cultural work,the way art and information is produced and circulated.This is an INTRODUCTORY SCHEME to Mail Art tactics.

THE ARTWORK.

THE ARTIST.

THE AUDIENCE.

VICIOUS CIRCLE

ONE WAY

PEDESTAL.

N.B.All generalizations hide part of the truth.

ART DEALER-MUSEUM.

MAIL

BEFORE

ART

AFTER

MIXED MEDIA PRODUCTS.
AUDIO VISUAL TEXT ETC.

ALL POSSIBLE COMBINATIONS

THE NETWORK OPERATOR.

MASS MEDIA.

In a network system the audience may at all times become actively involved in a direct communication.

FLEXIBILITY OF ROLES

TWO-WAY

THE AUDIENCE.

● Scheme one devised by Vittore Baroni.Send corrections and suggestions.

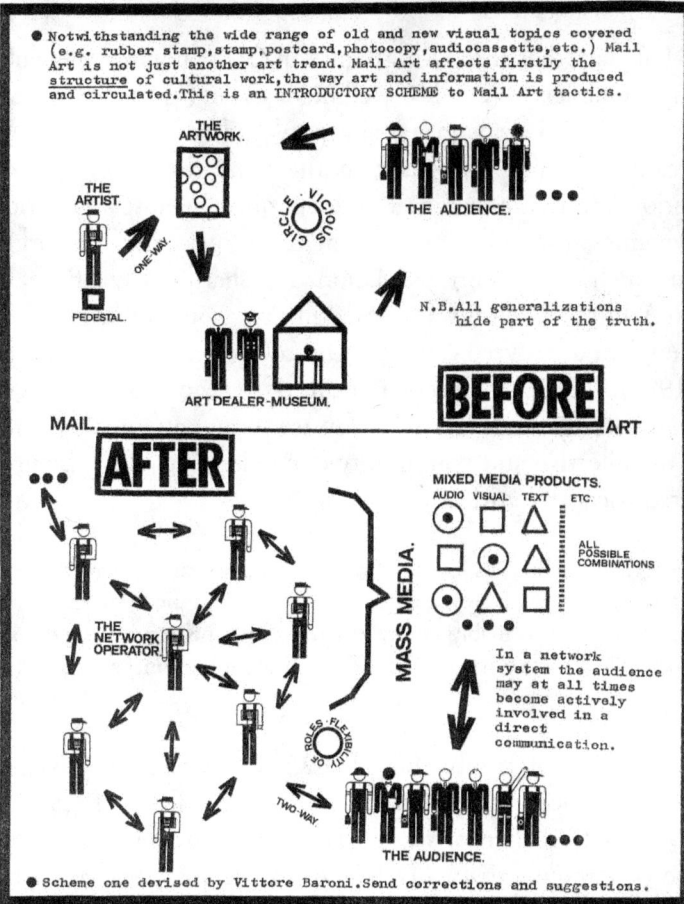

Vittore Baroni, "Real Corrispondence 6", 1981 (part of series of flyers by the same name). The diagram was then repaginated by Ragged Edge Press in 1990, in a postcard called "The Evolution of Art".

The image shows the network operator of mail art as a figure that connects well with the future figure of the art networker via computer, with the re-combining of the different media in the creation of a platform of interaction and common procedural action. It is not by accident that the idea of the *network Congress,* the first meetings in Italy dedicated to those who work on the networks, be they, postal or computer-based, as an open communication vehicle (the first took place in 1992, in the "Mu" space of Vittorio Veneto) rises out of the circuit of mail art.

Also in Italy, another interesting figure in the panorama of mail art and of networking is Guglielmo Achille Cavellini, or CAG, (1914-1990) a central figure in the history of mail art who has always played with the system mechanisms of art, creating an ambitious and, at the same time, ironic piece of auto-historicization. His figure is of interest to our quest because it is a bridge between artistic dynamics inserted in the system of business and networking art as a process, in which the network of relations and sharing play a fundamental role. Guglielmo Achille Cavellini was quoted in numerous works by Vittore Baroni, who defines him as "a very central figure to the entire adventure of mail art" (Baroni, 1997). Cavellini reinserts the cult of the ego and the individual genius into the network dynamics, usually adverse to any attempt of self-celebration in favour of collective and community dynamics. The effect is simultaneously ironic, paradoxical and critical.

Already one of the most famous Italian collectors of modern art, a friend of the major talents of his generation, he cultivates even through time, a fervid pictorial activity, but it is only in 1971 that, feeling unjustifiably ignored by the critics, he decided to go out on his own, making himself the object of art, a series of fantastical promotional strategies (Baroni, 1997, p. 194).

A fervid activity of production follows: catalogues of Cavellinian shows that never took place, stamps bearing large scale effigies of Cavellini, stickers and autobiographical diaries, self promotional postcards, self portraits paired with those of famous artists. "Delivery Exhibitions" that recall those of the Avant-garde, sent via mail to friends and acquaintances of the world of art and afterwards to all the members of the mail art circuit, which Cavellini discovers and makes it a main channel for his auto-historicization, concerning himself with answering all those who write to him.

His capacity for ironic and creative interpretation of artistic business mechanisms makes him one of the first *culture jammers* of our time. Even more interesting because his refusal of the art system does not force him to distance himself from this, but makes him play with his language and his strategies in the first person, working on the promotion of his own ego without making him anonymous, anticipating many of the creative marketing techniques and the current guerrilla media.

Multi-identity, Neoism and Luther Blissett

Founded in 1979 by Monty Cantsin, the multiple-identity located in Montreal, Canada and in Baltimore in the USA, Neoism was quickly diffused throughout all of America, Europe and Australia involving dozens of people. Until the 1980s the mail art network was used as a channel and propaganda for Neoism, which was expressed through the Neoist Apartment Festival in North America, Europe and Australia between 1980 and 1988 through different publications. Among these the magazine "Smile" should be remembered, as it started to be distributed in 1984, giving rise to a network of people who produced and circulated their own magazine in a self made way, contaminating it with that of others and following a procession-like path. According to the Neoist tENTATIVELY a cONVENIENCE, "Neoism is an international prefix more than a suffix, without anything in between. Neoism does not exist, and it is a pure invention of its enemies, of the anti-neoists."[19].

Neoism expresses itself through artistic practices and experimentation in media. It embraces a philosophy that presupposes the use of multiple identities, the collection of pseudonyms, the discussion of concepts like identity and originality and the realization of *pranks*, paradoxes, plagiarism and *fakes*, components that come up again later in collective movements such as the Luther Blissett Project (LBP) and in the actions of different net.artists , including the Italian 0100101110101101.org.

Neoism is above all known through the texts of Stewart Home, which were fundamental for diffusion, but very much related to Home's personal experience, according to other Neoists, inclined to not define and historicize the movement and to not create forms of belonging. In the definition given in Wikipedia, the free encyclopaedia, Neoism is considered an international subculture, which unites and combines within it experimental art (currents such as Dada, Surrealism, Fluxus and Conceptual art), together with punk culture, industrial music, electro-pop, religious movements and libertarian and desecrated politicians, Science Fiction and speculative science, graffiti and street-performance, mail art, gay and lesbian culture and the first Church of the Subgenius[20].

An interesting and ironic description of Neoism is found in the *Ultimate Manifest of Neoism*, on the site <www.neoism.net>. The site was a result of an experiment created with wiki technology, allowing the screens to be freely edited and to create new links and definitions according to one's liking, in line with the Neoist idea of collectivity and contamination. Despite the fact that the wiki experiment did not bring about the desired results, the site often presents new contents, giving the idea of being a truly fluctuating project, as mutating as the Monty Cantsin personality is.

Symbol-icons of Neoism are the flaming steam iron; the clothes hanger used as an antenna to create a telepathic flow between people; the improvisational haircut during the performances; the red cross; a particular type of spicy food like *chili* and *chapatti*. Monty Cantsin was not only a multiple identity, but a real way of life for many people who embraced being a Neoist in daily life; opening experimental video stores, creating performances, publishing magazines, giving life to independent projects.

The element that makes Neoism an art out of networking is evident in the description of the Apartment Festival found in the booklet *What is an uh, uh, Apartment Festival* of 1981, called "The APT Project, The Practice of a Common Cause".

The APT Festivals are usually one week events with various activities such as conferences and performances, but the main purpose of these "friendship gatherings", "drills", "habitation manoeuvres" is to create a simple and comfortable situation for personal meeting between the concerned collaborators. The APT fests are NEITHER "performance-art" NOR "installation" festivals. The APT fests are the "*fêtes mobiles*" [travelling celebrations] of the neoist-network-web.

WHAT IS A uh uh APARTMENT FESTIVAL??????

The APT Project

the practice of a common cause

The APT festivals are usually one week events with various activities such as conferences and performances,but the main purpose of these "friendship gatherings" "drills","habitation manoeuvres" is to create a simple and confortable situation for personal meetings between the concerned collaborators.

The APT fests are NEITHER "performance-art" NOR "installation" festivals.

The APT fests are the "fêtes mobiles" of the neoist-network-web.

"What is an uh, uh, Apartment Festival", image from the *Centre de Recherche Neoiste*, publication, 1981.

It is the Neoists who talked about a "Web-network" in 1981, giving life to a discourse on systemized libertarian networking based on the idea of the *Centre de Recherche Neoiste* (CRN). The Centre of Neoist Research originated in Montreal, in 1980 as a consequence of the Neoist cultural conspiracy. The idea was to "promote collaborative research between different recruits at a national and international level, with the goal of sharing and diffusing innovative ideas and developing new forms of creative communication"[21].

We are talking about "Open Situations", in which people who can catalyze their own energy, give life to a series of collaborations between the members of the network. The Centre of Neoist Research gave life to the APT Festival Project in 1979, starting a series of apartment events in Montreal, Baltimore and Toronto.

To coordinate the collective events and projects, the Neoists used Mail art as a principal channel, inventing a *spider web strategy* conceived in the world of their network-Web. Between the various examples of mail art created in the Neoist circuit we have Pete Horobin's "DATA" project[22] and naturally the activity of Vittore Baroni, who was also in contact with the Neoist network.

The Plagiaristic practices of the 1980s, of which Neoism was one of the greatest driving forces, converged during the Plagiarism Festival. The first Plagiarism Festival took place in London in 1988, organized by Stewart Home and Graham Hardwood. Stewart Home organized the Plagiarism Festival once he had distanced himself from Neoism. On one hand opening him up to a wider public of participants (from mail artists to different people active in the underground environments), on the other hand circumscribing practices that had been defined on a theoretical level. In a criticism of the Plagiarism Festival by John Berndt we read:

[the Plagiarims Festivals] were born as a product of the Neoist Apartment Festivals, events that were themselves products of a plagiarism of the Fluxusfestivals of a few years earlier. The main difference between the Plagiarism Festivals and the Neoist Apartment Festivals was the intention to have [the former] centred on the theme of plagiarism, to the detriment of the more eclectic approach of the latter. Nevertheless [the Neoist Apartment Festivals] embraced a broader field of activity and did not represent a singular theme (such as that of originality or artistic intellectual property, which was the theme of the first Festival in London in 1988)[23].

The last Festival of Plagiarism was held in Glasgow in 1989, during the week of August 4-11, organized by Stewart Home and Billy Clark, the founder of the now famous underground gallery "Transmission" of Glasgow. Other participants were Lloyd Dunn (of TapeBeatles), Matthew Fuller, Klaus Maeck and Walter Hartmann (author of the famous "Decoder Handbuch", 1984, which accompanied the German movie *Decoder* written and produced by Maeck[24]), Tom Vague, Jamie Reid, Florian Cramer and the Italians Raf Valvola and Gomma, of "Decoder/Shake Edizioni" magazine (which takes its name from the Klaus Maeck film).

The latter describe the event in the fifth issue (1990) of the magazine "Decoder":

The demonstration was organized with the radical, base theory of the concept of the "artist" and of art in general. The base hypothesis is that the artist should not be seen as a unique genius. This is the vision of romantic origin which is inadequate to witness the current reality. Against this "bourgeoisie" idea and vision of art, the official controversial proposal was to read in the plagiaristic practice, in the cloning and in the *déturnament* of the sense, the only valid alternative. In fact it was quoted as being the practice of over 100 artists from all over the world to sign their work with a single name (Karen Eliot). Adherent to this analysis the project declared at the Festival to implement and propagate an "art strike", a strike including any type of artistic practice and "objectification" in general until 1993[25].

The term plagiarism was a re-elaboration by Stewart Home of the situational concept of *détournement*. Guy Debord coined the term *détournement* (which most of the time is translated as "detournement" in English) on the pages of the *Internazionale Lettrista*, hybridizing Cahiers Lautréamont's concept of *plagiat* and Bertolt Brecht's *Verfremdungseffekt* (estrangement) (cfr. Cramer, 2006). By *détournement* we mean the act of subverting daily forms of communication – from advertising posters to film images – appropriating oneself of the linguistic sign to create a "semiotic rewriting", isolating and inserting it in another context, unveiling the fiction of communication to look at reality with different eyes.

The situational practices have their roots in Lettrism, in the Cobra Group and in the International Movement for an Imaginist Bauhaus (IMIB). Central to these is the radical criticism of theorized art of the Situationist International (1957-1972), the opposition to traditional bourgeois values, the subversion and upheaval of traditional cultural values and of the mediocre daily way of life, the transformation of architecture in anti-architecture, the revolutionary potential of free time, the creation of "situations" defined as "moments of life concretely and deliberately constructed through the organized collective of a unitary environment and of a play on events" ("Internationale Situationniste", 1, 1958). Tied to these practices is the practice of psycho-geography, with the emotional exploration of the territory through the *dérivé*[26].

The idea of psycho-geography and of the *dérivé* are naturally taken from Isidore Isou's proposal of an infinitesimal architecture, which proposed to substitute the constructive elements of space according to the sense and will of those who lived there.

Psycho-geography has the function of a spontaneous and ludic exercise of daily life with the *dérivé*, a free-walk without a fixed itinerary (of which the antecedent is the surrealist *flânerie*) realizes in a new human dimension, founded on the liberation of the desire and on the exploding of subjectivity, in opposition to the conditioning of the consumeristic need (Debord, 1958).

Situationism is always cited as the inspiring philosophy of different radical practices; even if it is necessary to say that over the years it was very mitigated, removing the dogmatic-theoretical imprinting that has characterized a part of the Situationist International's history, to make room for the diverse libertarian concepts and forms of multiple actions.

At the core of this discussion it becomes natural to associate another collective practice of "multiple singularity" Luther Blissett's *condividualità* [shared identity]. A transmission wire ties together the three multiple identities of Monty Cantsin, Karen Eliot and Luther Blissett, even if some core differences exist[27].

Monty Cantsin was created like an *open pop star* and a real and living multiple identity. The name was suggested by David Zack to Istvan Kantor and Maris Kundzins, but only Istvan Kantor adopted it concretely in his artistic and performance journey. Because it was possible to associate it with people "in the flesh", often risking being identified with Istvan Kantor, it was used as a collective identity only in the first part of Neoism. Many Neoists are in fact known by other pseudonyms such as tENTATIVELY a cONVENIENCE, Kiki Bonbon, Reinhardt U. Sevol, etc.

The name Karen Eliot was suggested by Stewart Home as a multiple and anonymous name, to be used as a collective signature for works of art or written texts, to go against the idea of a single author. It was not created so it could be associated with physical people, even if in the course of time it was always linked to Stewart Home.

Luther Blissett was born a media ghost, a mythological figure to which an even more mythical tradition attached the legendary names of Harry Kipper and Coleman Healy. A mysterious figure; an identity which is quite different from a pseudonym, not created to be shown in public, and a little like Kaiser Soze in the movie *The Usual Suspects*[28].

Luther Blissett is not anyone, and at the same time everyone can be him. He was born like an urban myth, with the goal of sabotaging the power control centres through culturally destabilizing activities, introducing himself into the media infrastructure like a worm in an apple, who corrodes everything inside, leaving only the peel intact. Luther Blissett is born through the conjoined action of active characters in different worlds, from Mail art to Neoism to the external radical practices, following in the wake of the Monty Cantsin and Karen Eliot multi-identities, but distancing himself from the artistic environment in order to potentially open himself to anyone. It does not make sense in my opinion, to write down the names of people who had the idea of launching this project since, among others, the meaning of the Luther Blissett Project (LBP) was to go beyond the mentality of individualistic belonging.

The name Luther Blissett derives from the name of the former Jamaican footballer who played centre forward for Watford and also for Milan. Among the sources of inspiration for the name was a networking project of an English mail artist who had diffused compositions and collages of football players including Luther Blissett. A happy union of sounds like *looter* and *bliss*[29].

When asked: "What does one have to do to become a *sharer*?", Luther Blissett, replies:

It is enough to renounce one's own identity, with all the advantages that this entails. Dive into the wave of emotions of anger and joy that you feel flowing around you, re-elaborate without leaving your imprint, your signature. Because those like you don't know what to do with a signed work: it is something finite, to which you yourself have decreed the end, and to which no one will be able to add anything new. The non-identity of the sharer goes hand in hand with incompleteness (Blissett, 1996, p. 19).

Formally born in 1994, the Luther Blissett Project spread from Italy to the United Kingdom, the United States, Holland, Germany, Austria, Finland, and Hungary. Like a true virus the LBP landed to give rise to deeply impacting media pranks, together with *happenings*, shows and performances in the subway, articles in publications, actions of overcoming art in favour of the everyday, becoming one of the most active projects of the period.

In Italy, the LBP reached the height of its diffusion between 1994 and 1999, giving life to diversified creative experiences and media pranks from Bologna to Rome. The libertarian component of the LBP, united in the idea of creating a web of many multi-viduals and of subverting the rigid categories (including "politics", "show", "media communication") found fertile ground in our country, in which one tends to talk through images and through the fixed identity of belonging, from work, to family, to the house, to politics, etc.

Among the various pranks is the one where Luther Blissett takes part in the television show "Chi l'ha visto?" [Who Saw Him/Her?], in which investigators and the like search for a fictitious artist named Harry Kipper. Luther Blissett says that the artist disappeared on the Italo-Jugoslav border while on a mountain bike tour of Europe, during which the artist intended to trace the word "ART" on the map of the continent. Here a paradoxical game begins in which the television crew follows the (false) traces of the missing person and only just before the show goes on the air the crew discovers that the identity of the one they are looking for is that of a ghost.

Another famous prank is the creation of the fake book to be published by Mondadori, called *net.gener@tion, manifesto delle nuove libertà* [New Freedoms Manifesto], signed by Luther Blissett and published by the Milanese publishing house in 1996. Initially it seemed fine, but going beyond the surface, the contents were discovered to be made up, with false internet addresses. Naturally the book gets taken off the market very quickly, as soon as the editor realizes the prank (after the book had been published and circulated...).

One activity that remained historic for those who were part of the scene at the time is the psycho-geographic *happening Neoist Bus*. It took place in 1995 on the

Number 30 night bus in Rome. During this *happening*, the bus was hijacked to throw a Neoist party through the streets of Rome, subverting the bored daily life of a public means of transportation. The people involved had a live feed via telephone to Radio Città Futura (Future City Radio), on which the show Radio Blissett was airing, to create a hypermedial action that would connect cars, busses, public and private telephones, radios, computers.

The bus, the "moving body of the metropolis", travelled through the streets of Rome with unusual passengers, who all had the same name: Luther Blissett. The irony of this, naturally, was not understood by the police who intervened with the readiness typical to these occasions, shooting their guns off in the sky, sheriff style, as if they were in a Western movie, and bringing in eighteen of the "bus occupants" who refused to show identification and who all claimed to be named Luther Blissett! This event became a real myth of the Italian underground, transforming into a legend sustained by varying believers who, as always, did not worry about digging too deeply. In many articles and publications on the subject we read that the episode took place on a train, culminating in March of the following year with a court case, charged with insurrection, resisting arrest, and insulting a public official, in which for all the accused in the subpoena we read: Blissett Luther born on XX.XX.19XX in XXXX, residing in XXXX Road[30].

In reality in the Wu Ming Foundation website it is highlighted that the episode took place on the night bus. As posted on the site:

It wasn't a train, it was a night bus. It happened in Rome on June 17th, 1995. A few dozen ravers occupied and "hijacked" a night bus. A rave party took place on the vehicle until the police decided to block the street and stop it. When the ravers came out of the bus, the policemen attacked them, one of them even fired three shots in the air. A journalist from an independent radio station (Radio Città Futura) was also on the bus, he was covering the event on the phone for a live chat show, thus the shots were heard by thousands of listeners. Eighteen people were arrested. Some of them said that they were "Luther Blissett", but none of them actually claimed that at the police station, later on. The media extensively covered the event, which showed how much the "Luther Blissett" name was penetrating youth subcultures. We really don't know how this turned into that four-people-on-a-train story. Years later, it keeps popping up here and there. We used to find it funny, now it's just... uncanny.[31]

The most complex prank took place in Lazio in 1997, broadcasting the news that around the area of Viterbo, black masses and Satanic rituals had taken place, documented by physical, textual and audiovisual traces left by the presumed "demon cultists". The prank lasted a year, generating a total "mass paranoia" (Wu Ming, 2006), so much so that the television show *Studio aperto* shown on the Italia1 channel, dedicated an episode to this event. As always, Luther Blissett reveals the "behind the scenes" of the case, showing how the so-called "urban legends" are born and revealing mechanisms by which sensationalist news is diffused through the information circuits[32].

The history and the documentation of the Luther Blissett Project (LBP) can be read on the <www.lutherblissett.net> internet site, which describes Luther's other activities and documents the press coverage of the most famous cases. The "veterans" of the Luther Blissett Project proclaimed the ritual suicide of the LBP in December 1999, a collective *Seppuku* which put an end to a five-year experience, giving life to other plans[33]. Among these are the most famous Wu Ming group and the duo 0100101110101101.ORG. Despite the *Seppuku*, the pseudonym Luther Blissett will continue to live on in different countries and through other experiences.

In the three years from 1996 to 1998 four LBP members from Bologna wrote the novel *Q*, signed by Luther Blissett. It was published by Einaudi in 1999 with a Copyleft licence and it was distributed in translation in many other countries. At the same time, the four writers of the novel revealed their real names during an interview with the daily paper "La Repubblica", claiming to represent less than 0.04% of the Luther Blissett Project. In January 2000, after the arrival of another person in the Blissettian writer's group, the Wu Ming experience began. Wu Ming means "anonymous" in Mandarin Chinese, as stated in their website: <www.wumingfoundation.com>.

Following the LBP tradition, the books were written by five different members whose names have been publicized (Roberto Bui, Giovanni Cattabriga, Luca di Meo, Federico Guglielmi e Riccardo Pedrini), but who prefer to be called Wu Ming 1, 2, 3, 4, 5 (the number is determined by the alphabetical order of their last names). In the Wu Ming site we read:

The name of the band is understood as a tribute to dissidence and a refusal of the role of the Author as *star*. The identity of the five Wu Ming members is not secret, but we feel that our works are more important than our single biographies or faces.

The Wu Ming have generated different novels of great breadth, and all are the result of detailed historical research. Among these, the already mentioned *Q* (1999), a work of non-fiction set in the sixteenth century, and defined as a "western theologic" whose protagonist is a spy hired by the Cardinal Carafa, *Asce di Guerra* [*Hatchets of War*](2000), *54* (2002), and other works of which there is only one Wu Ming signature[34].

The Wu Ming novels are "open source" and they can be downloaded free from their internet site. Wu Ming also periodically publishes two newsletters. *Giap* (2000) and *Nandropausa* (2001)[35], through which one can learn about new publications and read various commentaries by members on different subjects.

Another work by Wu Ming is the screenplay written together with Guido Chiesa who directed *Lavorare con lentezza* [Working slowly] (Fandango, 2004), <www.lavorareconlentezza.com>. The film, part documentary and part fiction, centres on *Radio Alice* and the 1970s movement in Bologna, going through the history, the ideals and the practices that inspired a great part of the Italian phenomenon of future political activism. It is enough to read the book *Alice è il diavolo* [Alice is the Devil] (1976, reprinted Shake 2002) that explores the story of Radio Alice of Bologna and of the activities of the A/traverso group, to understand just how many of the aesthetics and practices of movements in Italy today originated at the end of the 1970s, during a period of free radio, in which politics was lived radically, a battle paid for by many in prison. The actions are also depicted in the movie *Alice è in Paradiso* [Alice is in Paradise] (2002), produced by Fandango once again, and also directed by Guido Chiesa, who revisits the adventure of a collective of real communication hackers where, instead of the computer we find radio.

To conclude the discussion on the multiple identities and the anti-artistic movements, uniting them with those of the anarchical utopias of the 1970s, the events in Monte Capanno, in Umbria in 1970, will be described briefly here. Very few know that a group of thirty American students from San Jose State College (California) led by David Zack, formally the creator of the Monty Cantsin multiple identity, carried out a collective and self-manage learning experiment from January to June 1970. An experiment with an intense study program of seminars organized by the students themselves and coordinated by David Zack, in which they read books, wrote, developed artistic actions, and concentrated on social concepts and alternative politicians, whose documentation is posted today on <http://montecapanno1970.com/>. A first attempt to give life to a "Learning Community" called Monte Capanno, which sounds a lot like Monty Cantsin...

Endnotes

1   Among these Vittore Baroni and Piermario Ciani's AAA Edizioni publishing house, whose activity is described in the paragraph dedicated to Mail art in this chapter.

2   To read more about Albrecht Dürer's influence in Italy, consult the Triennale Europea dell'Incisione website at <http://karaartservers.ch/udine/durer/durer.i.html>.

3   Marco Deseriis, Giuseppe Marano, *Net.art, l'arte della connessione*, Milan, Shake Edizioni, 2003.

4   For a detailed biography and analysis of Giuseppe Chiari's work, we suggest the paragraph found at <www.wikiartpedia.org/index.php/Chiari_Giuseppe> on *WikiArtPedia, La Libera Enciclopedia dell'Arte e le Culture delle Reti Telematiche*, idealized by Tommaso Tozzi.

5   On the process of affirmation of the metropolitan crowd as a social subject, cf. Alberto Abruzzese, *Lo splendore della TV*, Genova, Costa & Nolan, 1995. In Abruzzese's work, the splendour of artificial images inherent in television language starting with the first demonstrations of the metropolitan civilization, according to a path which, stating from the spectacularization of the square-market, spans the non-places of the first Universal Expositions, of the metropolitan crowd, of the first trips with a steam engine train, touching the fantasmatic simulacra of the postcards, of photographs, of the world of merchandise, of the radiophonic, cinematographic universe up until the television network.

6   Samuel Taylor Coleridge (1772-1834), poet, philosopher and critic, is considered among the founders of English Romanticism. About Coleridge's use of the concept of intermedia we read, in the text written by Dick Higgins "Synesthesia and Intersenses: Intermedia" originally published in 1965 in *Something Else Newsletter 1, No. 1* (Something Else Press, 1966), and today on UBUWEB, a site specialized in Avant-garde Art. Higgins affirms that Coleridge used the term intermedia in 1812: "The vehicle I chose, the word 'intermedia', appears in the writings of Samuel Taylor Coleridge in 1812 in exactly its contemporary sense – to define works which fall conceptually between media that are already known, and I had been using the term for several years in lectures and discussions before my little essay was written" (<www.ubu.com/papers/higgins_intermedia.html>).

7   Subsequently even Ken Friedman, artist associated with Fluxus, worked on cataloguing different *fluxus-events*, inserting even posthumous performances, among which the *52 Events*. His last publication is the *FluxusPerformanceWorkBook* (2002), which follows the preceding 1990 edition; edited with Owen Smith e Lauren Sawchyn. This e-book which can be downloaded for free in PDF format, contains numerous *fluxus-events* and *fluxus-concerts* scores as well as posthumous works by other artists who were assimilated with Fluxus for their orientation. Ken Friedman's interpretation (even if personal) of the movement plays an important role and the publication contains texts which are normally difficult to access. It can be downloaded at <www.thecentreofattention.org/artists/Fluxus.pdf>. More information on Friedman's works are found on The Centre of Attention site curated by Pierre Coinde and Gary O'Dwyer, at <www.thecentreofattention.org>.

8   In 2005 in Germany a catalogue of the *Maciunas' "Learning Machines", From Art History to a Chronology of Fluxus*, show was published held at Berlin's Kunstbibliothek from October 2003 to January 2004 (Schmidt-Burkhardt A. 2005). A fundamental publication in order to see what Fluxus had been trough the diagrams created by George Maciunas.

9   Cf. Owen F. Smith, *Fluxus. The History of an Attitude*, San Diego, 1998.

10   The complete list of the "excluded" is found published in the diagram created by George Maciunas in1966, called *Fluxus (Its historical Development and Relationship to Avant-garde Movements)* and published in Astrit Schmidt-Burkhardt, *Maciunas' Learning Machines, From Art History to a Chronology of Fluxus*, The Gilbert and Lila Silverman Fluxus Collection, Vive Versa Verlag, Berlin, 2005.

11   In the show catalogue we read: *Maciunas' "Learning Machines", From Art History to a Chronology of Fluxus*, held at the Berlin Kunstbibliothek which the Milanese Multhipla publishing house managed by Gino Di Maggio, offered to organise the distribution of one thousand copies of the diagram.

12   A term that lent itself to one of the more important publications on mail art, *Eternal network, A Mail Art Anthology*, edited by Chuck Welch, University of Calgary Press, 1995.

13   Piermario Ciani, born in 1951 in Bertiolo (Udine), disappeared recently overnight on July 2, 2006. As is posted on the AAA Edizioni website, he was a "student of Luther Blissett at the Psycho-geographical Art School of London. He produced images using manual, photochemical, electrostatic and digital methods. He published and displayed his works beginning in 1976: first paintings, then photographs, xerographs, mail art, multimedia installations and collages. He prefers paper media but often his works are immaterial and are perceived along the boundaries between telepathy and data transmission," as translated from a quote from <www.aaa-edizioni.it/Ciani.htm>

14   In 1996, Vittore Barone and Piermario Ciani established the AAA Edizioni publishing house, fundamental to the reconstruction of the idea of networking in Italy. They offered fascinating publications to the Italian and international counterculture world, from mail art and Internet culture, to Fluxus, Neoism, Situationism, and on all the iconoclastic and anti-art phenomena of the last few decades. Among the various works published by AAA Edizioni, we find *Arte Postale* [Postal Art] (1997), *L'arte del timbro* [The Art of the Rubber Stamp] (1999), and *Artistamps* (2000), texts that are key to understanding the phenomenon of mail art and reconnecting it with many earlier practices. The most recent work by Vittore Baroni is *Post-cards, Cartoline d'artista* [Post-cards, Artist Postcards] (2006), published by Coniglio Editore, Rome. The AAA Edizioni webiste is <www.aaa-edizioni.it>

15   An interesting reconstruction of mail art, written by Vittore Baroni, is found in the first issue of the independent e-zine "Ah!", under the direction of Bruno Capatti (net director) and Attilio Fortini (webmaster). The on-line magazine "Ah!" published, unfortunately, only two issues (September 2000 and March 2001), can be found at <http://digilander.libero.it/wwwart/AH/>. The introductory editorial of the magazine's issue revealed a simultaneously critical and ironic spirit. "An interviewer asking Marcel Duchamp about his famous painting *Nudo che scende le scale* [Nude walking down stairs] asked him whether it depicted a woman or a man. For me? For you? For the sake of a quote, the Maestro said that he had never thought about it. In effect, what could have changed... What truth is there in a truth that does not appear? Wanting to reduce, at all costs, a person to his/her knowledge, is more a necessity for control than for understanding. The rest has desirable outcomes, but only for those who are content with just living. We don't have any else to offer but the desire to...AH! Won't you help yourself? A small does of survival... it's not much; but maybe precisely because of this it is undeniably necessary." Quoted from <http://digilander.libero.it/wwwart/AH/ah!/AH!html>

16   Vittore Baroni's description, as quoted from the mail art bulletin "Real Corrispondence", in September 1999. The bulletin, distributed for free by mail (and then distributed by e-mail), was created in 1980.

17 Recently, Vittore Baroni and Piermario Ciano launched the F.U.N. project, Funtastic United Nations (2001), offering a bridge linking creative and imaginative geographic entities. The projects developed giving rise to meetings, individual and group stamp collecting projects dedicated to people and events of the Funstastic nations and to the issue of paper currency produced by the citizens of the F.U.N. and collected in the "Bank of FUN" project (2003).

18 Just as Vittore Baroni explained in a personal letter to me, "Real Corrispondence 6" from 1981, was part of a series of flyers called Real Corrispondence. The sketch was printed again by Ragged Edge Press in 1990, in a postcard entitled "The Evolution of Art", on which the image was inserted in a frame partitioned like a postage stamp.

19 Cfr. the introduction by Simonetta Fadda in Stewart Home's *Neoismo e altri scritti. Idee critiche sull'avanguardia contemporanea* [Neoism and other writings. Critical thoughts of the contemporary Avant-garde.], Genova, Costa & Nolan, 1995.

20 The definition of Neoism on Wikipedia is on-line at <http://www.en.wikipedia.org/wiki/Neoism>.

21 Quoted from the booklet "Centre de recherches Néoistes" [Neoist Research Centre], 1981.

22 Further reading at <http://www.thing.de/projekte/7:9%23/horobin_index_index.html>.

23 Quoted from </www.thing.de/projekte/7:9%23/y_Proletarian_Posturing.html>, that posts a critical essay by John Berndt on the London Festival of Plagiarism.

24 Klaus Maeck is a renowned figure of the German post-punk culture of the 1980s. He managed an independent music label and wrote the official book documenting the life of the band Einstürzende Neubauten (*Hör mit Schmerzen*, 1996),. Maeck is remembered above all for having written and produced the movie *Decoder* (1984). The director and co-writer of the film was Muscha (Jürgen Muschalek), a filmmaker from Düsseldorf who wrote various punk Super-8's. The film's third co-writer was Trini Timpop, a Punk musician from Düsseldorf who was also the lead drummer of the famous band Die Toten Hosen. Among the other many individuals involved as actors in the movie *Decoder*, we should recall William S. Burroughs, Genesis P'Orridge, FM Einheit of the Einstürzende Neubauten and Alexander Hacke. The publication "Decoder Handbuch" [Decoder Handbook] (1984), which accompanied the film, included written works by William S. Burroughs and Brion Gysin, Jean Baudrillard, Genesis P'Orridge, Klaus Maeck and others.

25 An account of the Festival written by the Decoder collective "Decoder on tour – Festival on Plagiarism – Glasgow 4-11 August 1989" in Tozzi, 1991, p. 203, quoted from "Decoder", 5, 1990, Milano.

26 In particular, Guy Debord and Asger Jorn apply the concept of psycho-geography to the practice of *détournement*, realizing the 1957 work *Fin de Copenhague* [The End of Copenhagen]. a publication, of which 200 copies were printed, made up of collages of articles and illustrations clipped from daily Copenhagen newspapers, "dripping" by Asger Jorn, reworkings of the visual understandings of urban living that transform into an emotional map. An effective description of the collaboration between Guy Debord and Asger Jorn is found in the English work by Christian Nolle, *Books of Warfare: The Collaboration between Guy Debord & Asger Jorn from 1957-1959, published by* <http://virose.pt/vector/b_13/nolle.html>.

27 These considerations on the three collective identities are the result of a mail exchange with Florian Cramer, active in the Berlin Neoist circle, as well as the subsequent experiences by Luther Blissett to software art.

28 As Roberto Bui maintains in a private conversation with Florian Cramer.

29 Consideration taken from Luther Blissett, *Rendez-vous coi ribelli: Intervista a Coleman Healy*, on-line at: <www.lutherblissett.net/archive/215-04_it.html>.

30 As it says on: <http://www.lutherblissett.net/archive/228_it.html>.

31 Taken from *The Night Luther Blissett Hijacked a Bus in Rome*, written on: < www.wumingfoundation.com/english/biography.html#nightbus>, July 2007.

32 In the Wu Ming Foundation site it also says that the prank is revealed even in the daily "la Repubblica", in an article that reconstructs the case in detail. The article, *La beffa firmata Luther Blissett*, written by Loredana Lipperini, is found on-line at: <www.repubblica.it/on-line/sessi_stili/blissett/blissett/blissett.html>.

33 To learn more about *Seppuku*, Luther Blissett's collective suicide, read: <http://www.lutherblissett.net/indexes/thematic_it.html#seppuku>

34 The complete list of works is found at: <http://www.wumingfoundation.com/italiano/downloads.shtml>.

35 They are respectively found at <www.wumingfoundation.com/english/giap/giapissues.html> and <www.wumingfoundation.com/italiano/nandro_sezione.html>.

Towards the
Cyber Utopias

Punk and "Do It Yourself"

During the 1960s and 1970s there grew the desire to progressively open art up to everyday life, with the intent of examining the concept of the Avant-garde. The latter was seen as an elitist phenomenon confined within the walls of museums and galleries. The idea was to imagine artistic expression in places other than those with which it had been dialoguing up to that moment, favouring

the escape of paintings from their frames. However, in the artistic practices of the 1960s and 1970s, the elitist, and mercantile, basic concept remained the same, even if it did reclaim spaces and places for the expository dimension which had not been previously designated for this purpose. The intent was revolutionary, but it was quickly reclaimed by the system, for it was art that went down to meet life and not life that was transformed into art [1].

The concept of life that transforms into art is subsequently found in other forms of radical practice which have made the relationship between art/life evermore intimate. Initially, they emerged as independent entities from the world of institutional art, and developing really only on the streets and in the local realities of daily spaces. Practices such as graffiti on city walls, created in New York in the 1970s, demonstrate that it is possible to produce art, going beyond the idea of the work itself. Initially, the *writers* did not write on the walls because they were artists; their "works" could not be categorized on the market and the phenomenon of the art gallery was foreign to them. Often, the TAGs on the walls either had strictly personal meaning, or they followed the dynamics of belonging to one group or another, as a sort of direct communication between communities. Most of the time, they were created simply to go beyond the set limits, in a sort of hacking of walls within the city.

Here, too, there are different techniques that characterize the flow of information; they are mobile signs talking to the city, located in the most unusual places: on lampposts, on traffic lights, on street signs; the visible presence of stickers, self-produced posters, graffiti, stencils (reproductions of images printed on a photocopier), instant and rapid performances, usually taking centre stage at night either on the walls or on the roofs of buildings. In the course of the 1980s and 1990s, the practice of graffiti art intensified and was widely diffused, often abandoning the traditional TAGs in favour of more articulated drawings on the walls: *urban art*, as it is defined by some. Even today in the various non-places of the city, writings and drawings are created and recreated, as if they were the spontaneous voice of cities, especially of those that are constantly changing[2].

At the end of the 1970s, the movement that best distilled the idea of breaking away from the tradition of art and music, was punk, which, in Italy, was most prominent in the early 1980s. A rebellion "made up of intolerance and refusal, but also of urgency for freedom - giving a communicative sense to one's own life" (Gavyna, 1994)[3]. Many people involved in the punk movement came from art schools and certainly the Punk aesthetic has roots in the Dada and Letterist currents, in the Situationist International, and naturally in Fluxus. The point was that punk never declared itself an artistic phenomenon, if anything, it refused "art" in the most traditional sense of the term, and gave life to a different cultural, musical and creative imaginary.

In Italy, the punk movement took on different forms, often aligning itself with movements of radical political practice and self-governance, other times accentuating its "anarchical" and a-political component. The more "politically engaged" point of view (even if at that moment no one would have defined it as such) is found in many publications of the period, such as in the various books produced by the Shake Edizioni Underground publishing house in Milan and in the book *Opposizioni '80*, edited by Tommaso Tozzi (1991). In *Opposizioni '80*,

59

through the collection of writings and testimonials coming from the members of the countercultural era of the 1980s, Tozzi ties their life practices together, which go beyond the realm of Punk to the world of the graffiti artists, to industrial music to reggae and hip hop, to the hacker universe, to that of Mail art, all the way to Cyberpunk and subliminal art, following the thread of self-governance.

The point of departure is the opposition to the idea that the 1980s were to be considered nihilistic and indifferent to every type of antagonistic political practice. The main theme that ties these actions together remains the idea of Do It Yourself (through self-produced magazines, independent labels, radio programs, records, video, movie reviews), making them promoters of concrete actions on the political and social level, with the goal of creating horizontal networks and communities (at least ideally) which give life to a new form of procedural and collective art.

Do It Yourself means to personally create, in an independent manner, outside of the commercial and market environment. Do It Yourself is contrary to the traditional logic of parties, to delegating, to leadership and it offers itself up as a form of direct governance, unconcerned with party leaders, bringing the idea of collectively producing something to the creative level; often thanks to a network of friendly, cultural and political relations. For this reason, whoever has gravitated towards the panorama of Do It Yourself has often had some reservations about joining leftist political movements, even when they were extra-parliamentary formations, due to the rejection of the concept of delegation and leadership, which are instead the products of these contexts.

Music is a very important aspect in the punk movement, especially because of its opposition to the idea of the stage, to the figure of the artist as a diva, to the artificial showiness dictated by commerciality, and to the idea of separation between artist and public. Frequently, young punks expressed themselves by creating musical groups (even without any real professionalism) in which the singers "screamed as if they were possessed" and often they fused with the public, *poguing* together with them, making more noise than music.

In the beginning, in Italy, there was an attempt to imitate Anglo-Saxon Punk with lyrics in English, but afterwards they concentrated on the local reality, composing songs in Italian about rejecting the institution and, above all in the Milanese area, about the rejection of an antagonistic political character.

WE REFUSE THE LOGIC THAT WANTS US TO BE PASSIVE OBJECTS IN FRONT OF A SHOW, WE ARE CREATING ITALIAN MUSIC BORN OUT OF OUR REAL NEEDS: REAL FUN AGAINST THEIR FAKE GAME. WE DO NOT ACCEPT INTERMEDIARIES (...) Those who come to concerts need to understand that the role of the spectator can also be reversed – the great technological changes push us to independent production. We no longer need star business scientists. We no longer want to beg the record labels and the nightclubs: only the best play there, only those who have at least five years of study, everyone will play in our spaces... (Philopat, 1997, p. 64)[4].

Punk was not only something "conceptual", but it had a strong impact at the physical, bodily level. It was a great collective performance of body art. It is enough to think of the dyed hair, the piercings, the tattoos, the clothes which were torn and covered in writing; elements promptly commercialized by the clothing industry and, from then on, diffused in the mainstream, so that even today they are a strong corporal icon.

In punk, the meaning given to the external aspect is central, seen as a mouthpiece for a style and philosophy of life. On one's own body, the punk print their ideas of refusal of a society that wants everyone to be equal and standardized. A new concept is proposed with respect to a life imposed from above and realized in the family, in work, in a certain type of consumption, in the way of dressing, of listening to music, of talking, etc.

Marco Philopat, one of the founders of the Shake Edizioni publishing house in Milan, in his book called *Costretti a sanguinare*[5] [We Must Bleed] brings to life the ideals and the way of life of the young Punks from 1977 to 1984, giving a very incisive split of the Milanese reality of the first 1980s; also because he lived through it.

The point of view of *Costretti a sanguinare* is that Punk is neither a fashion trend, nor a subculture, nor a "spectacular youth band", but a *movement* which brings with it very strong ideals of breaking against the tradition and the rejection of the ideologies of past years. Punks are aware of the death of such utopias, but in spite of this they do not fall victim to nihilism, as much of the information of that time would have us believe. Together they work to build a future and they do it with their means (poor) and their ideas (antagonism and rejection), willingly keeping themselves on the confines of determined environments of *spectacular visibility*, as it is defined in a large part of the more commercial cultural industry. Punks are opposed to the spectre of heroine and to *regular* life, trying to construct new possibilities, independently.

This idea of constructing the transformation with an "opposition" mindset was central to many of the fringes of punk of the 1980s, and in Italy it was especially applied inside the Squatted Social Centres. It should be underlined however that while in Milan the anarchical wing of punk was fused by the experience of the Social Centres, in Rome, for example, punk remained for the most part diffident with regards to all the forms of "political" practice, even though it remained outside of the traditional and the institutional. Above all, many were interested in, the idea of the freedom and the anarchy that were experienced within punk culture; going against the rules and all the theoretical frameworks.

A concrete example of this is the Roman band Bloody Riot, officially formed in 1982, who authored the first completely self-produced record in Rome in 1983. Often finding itself in conflict even with other members of the "scene" for being openly and "happily" *politically incorrect*, it embodies a more "hooligan" aspect of Punk, as we read in the book *Bloody Riot* (Perciballi, 2001). Bloody Riot even played in the Social Centres, like at the *Feste del Non Lavoro* [The Non-Work Festivals] of the *CSOA Forte Prenestino* of Rome, but their approach remains different, well described by the group's lead singer, Roberto Perciballi, in his book *Come se nulla fosse* (1998) [As if Nothing had Happened].

The Squatted Social Centres

Punks brought several ideas into the reality of the Italian CSOA of the 1980s: the refusal of a homologizing reality, trying to give life to the autonomous areas in which to independently experiment and create something new; zones defined as "liberated" (Primo Moroni). This last concept would accompany the adventure of self-governance in the future 1990s. In those years, numerous autonomous spaces were spread throughout Italy: liberated and occupied at the same time; in which the concept of squatting was expressed through "liberated" music, art, language, meanings and bodies.

Living through the contradictions was the characteristic of the different occupants/frequenters of the Social Centres, in which "resistance" behaviours were expressed towards the ratification of the external and the "liberation" from the inside, answering the categories such as work, and family, standardized cultural production with another vision. This attitude has tried to interpret the political and social changes in an "active" manner: to make them one's own, in this way, creating a different world. An attitude of "resistance" that in the 1980s and 1990s was the basis for great experimentation at the creative and cultural level. Perhaps today it risks transforming itself into a closure of opposition toward the external, now already fragmented and no longer interpretable through the direct contraposition and dualisms of opposition. This mechanism runs the risk, in fact, of recreating the dynamics of power that one wants to fight.

In the 1980s, the Social Centres were created to propose an alternative way of "producing culture", organizing Do It Yourself events, such as concerts, films, video projections, artistic and photographic exhibitions, or distributing books, magazines, music CDs, video and other productions at modest prices. During this time, networking zones were born, creating pubs, kitchens, tea houses, places in which to dance and present new music at markedly reduced prices.

The symbol of the Social Centre became a circle with a lightning bolt, a closed reality (as the city reality can be) dilated by a new amalgamating force, which among its various actions is opposed to the use of heroine; a real social evil among the young people of the time. Continuing the tradition of the "sub-proletariat circles" of the 1960s, the Social Centres progressively developed throughout all of Italy as interfaces of an "antagonistic" political movement which would see the height of its development in the 1980s and 1990s, especially in the bigger cities.

An important point of reference for Italian punks in the early 1980s was the Virus in Milan (1982-1984), a squatted house in via Correggio, in which all the major punk groups of the period had played, organized events and produced independent material, among which the "Anti Utopia" punkzine[6].

In a flyer that presents the major points of the Virus project we read:

VIRUS EXPANSION OF ACTIONS IMAGES AND SOUNDS
Virus is a space self-managed by a group of young people in the via Correggio 18 occupied area of Milan.

Virus is a non profit development project of autonomous culture.
Virus is participation – the space belongs to everyone who participates in the project – and it is also open to external situations working towards the same goal.
Virus is activity.
Virus is the negation of drugs.
Virus is now in Milan because there is much boredom and all the other spaces are not available to us – it is our intent to create others.
Virus is not closed off in itself- but it operates/organises even the external level according to current facts/situations.
Virus is a great meeting point for all groups that would like to play or carry out their activities – the meetings are on Tuesday nights.
As a space, Virus is the result of hard-fought battles against the owners. As a structure, it is the result of the fight against the lack of money.
Virus is neither commerce, nor is it marketable – for this reason the shows will be qualitatively more true or real or ... more scarce (depending on the points of view) – in any case the price of the ticket will definitely be lower.

Signed
Collettivo punx anarchici – PUNK/ATTIVI VIRUSIANI (Philopat, 1997, pp. 105-106).

Within self-managed spaces such as Virus, self-produced material circulated including punkzines, the punk magazines produced by punks themselves.

The creation of punkzines becomes a focal point. The presence of photocopy shops mushroomed throughout the labyrinths of cities, therefore the possibility for the "do it yourself" materialized and involved practically all the Punx of the Virus. Bartering became a daily practice. Even solo ventures multiplied in number: editorial projects where the editor is also the graphic artist, the printer, the bookbinder and the distributor. A Virus Diffusion was created; it became a permanent stand for the sale of self-produced records and punkzines (*ivi*, pp. 111-112).

When in the first part of the 1980s the punk movement spread all over Italy, the PUNKamINazione" (1982) was created with a travelling editorial staff managed by the Italian Punk communities. In turn, they each had a page available to them in which to describe the current state of the local punk scene and in which to give information regarding concerts and new self-produced records. As an interesting experiment in punk networking, it followed in the wake of different, other previously diffused punkzines, such as "Dudu" (1977, a self-produced publication of philo-Dadaist subversion which took its name from the combination of Dada+Punk), "Pogo" (1978, the subsequent version of "Dudu"), in which the songs lyrics of The Clash and The Sex Pistols were translated into Italian; "Xerox" (1979); "Attack" (1982, created in Milan, it included radical political content) and immediately after "T.V.O.R (Empty Heads Broken Bones)" on the punk hard core scene; the already mentioned "Anti Utopia" created by the Virus collective, and many others[7].

Inside the same realm that connects music, magazines and places, some independent communication groups formed, such as *Amen*, who starting in 1983 gave life to a real fanzine and to records, videos, books, performances, and for the first time, included computer disks in its productions (*Amen* also published the aforementioned *Opposizioni '80* by Tommaso Tozzi).

The Amen group would gravitate around Helter Skelter, another self-produced space in Milan created as a space for concerts and then opening itself up to new cultural ferments such as industrial art, noise, and electronic experimentation.

With the arrival of the industrial music groups, Einsturzende Neubaten, Test Department and many others, the Milanese punx felt in some way supplanted. Music maintained the Punk grit and velocity, but the instruments were not the classic base, drums, and guitar. One played on instruments stolen from the decadence of the industrial society, such as drums made out of oil drums, drills, grinders, tubes, chains and steel ropes (*ivi*, p. 176).

Around the middle of the 1980s, the punk experience in Italy appeared to be over. Virus was vacated in May 1984 and even in other places the concerts faded away. Even if a few groups continued to play into the early 1990s, surely the most "genuine" soul of punk had died out by the middle of the 1980s and in the years following other forms of free creativity were created, from electronic music, to techno, to raves...

A singular experience which reunited artistic experimentation and punk attitudes in the middle of the 1980s was the *Bang Amen* group (Florence, 1986) and the subsequent *Pat Pat Recorder* (Florence, 1986-88), formed by Tommaso Tozzi, Steve Rozz, Nielsen Gavyna, and Priscila Lena Farias, which Massimo Cittadini joined later. Tommaso Tozzi describes the experience in this way:

At the *Pat Pat Recorder,* in a period of approximately two years a frenetic series of alternative initiatives followed each other such as poetic, sonorous, multimedia performances, shows or Fanzine presentations; groups and individuals; nights of urban graffiti, publications and other things, which in a certain way "moved" the alternative Florentine movement in 1986 and 1987. Some performances that I created in these two spaces were the exact repetition of those created by the Avant-garde artists during this century. The point was to show an academisation of the Avant-garde practices in play, as it was done for Conceptual art. It was a way of also contesting the whole fringe of the so-called Bohemian artists, who during the 1980s, used various alternative cultural modes to present heroes, victims, crazy people and geniuses of the moment, as had been previously done (1991, p. 17).

There would be many experiences to cite in the period of digression between Punk, Cyberpunk and the Hacker movement. Unfortunately it is not possible to re-propose all the multiple experiences here that occurred between Milan, Bologna, Florence, Rome, and Catania in those years of passing between the old and the new media in the network culture[8]. It is necessary to note however, that many of these experiences were created and developed within the Social Centres. In fact, the current state of the Social Centres can be instrumental to understanding why there are politic roots in a large part of the Hacker movement and the artistic experimentation with technology in Italy.

Even if most of the time many DIY experiments were inspired by utopian ideals, once put into practice the Social Centres were the propellers of many networking experiences of in Italy – in spite of the often deterring programmatic slowness which has characterized a great part of the collective projects. During the 1980s and 1990s, in different Italian spaces, editorial, musical, visual, technological and political projects were created, laying down the foundations for a defining conception of "movement" for the experiments that followed, for many individuals and groups (including me, I add) who have tried to give life to their own dreams of "resistance", imagining "another" model of society and economy and promoting self-governed production (even with income).

Unfortunately, most attempts were not successful in concretely producing an alternative political, social and economic model which had continuity over time, large diffusion at the international level, and a long-term economic return. Maybe this is due to the fact that in the Social Centres many of the experiments openly refused any type of "centralization", applying instead the model of fragmentation and decentralization. Consider, for example, the case of the G.R.A., Grande Raccordo Autoproduzioni (Great Self-producing Connection) promoted by Rome's CSOA Forte Prenestino, one of the most "frequented/ participated" and longest lasting Social Centres in Rome - it is active even today, although it has changed, through the years. The G.R.A. was created with the idea of coordinating the production of material of self-governed works, distributed in the various *infoshops* (the Social Centres' bookstores), with the intention of creating a sort of agency that exploits the many fragmented local experiences. Unfortunately, the project did not develop as hoped, especially because of the negative vision with which every attempt of "centralization" was always seen in this arena.

Instead, the network dynamic has given more long-lived results in the realm of the alternative use of new technologies, which even with respect to the "fragmentization" has allowed the generation of a big national network of people, and it coordinated collectives initially through widespread data transmission networks and, later, on the Internet. The Social Centre of the Forte Prenestino of Rome acted in this direction, with the CyberSyn II project, then Forthnet, proposed by the AvANa.net collective <http://avana.forteprenestino. net>[9] which permitted the creation of the computer network within the Social Centre, planning its "cabling" piece by piece.

The Forte Prenestino gave life to other collective experiences which imprinted upon the imaginations of many people at that moment; it is enough to think of the *raves* and of the activities in the musical field, as well as the re-interpretation of *trash* music of the 1970-80s with *Toretta Style* created by Luzy L and Corry X <www.torettastyle.com>. Here, the fantasy of Japanese cartoons and of so much "commercial" music was re-lived in a sort of cut'n'mix which disassembles language and codes, and reassembles them, giving life to new liberated heroes, from Goldrake/Ufo Robot to Capitan Harlock (a hacker of fantastical imaginations, it is enough to simply listen to the cartoon's song...)[10].

During the second half of the 1980s, ideas were starting to spread that would connect those who frequented the Italian Social Centres to new technological instruments, like the first personal computers and the modem. Computer technologies were seen as "an extraordinary opportunity to dilate the sphere of democracy" (Primo Moroni), using as examples the experiments of the American *phone freaks* and the Hackers in the 1970s[11]. The importance of computer instruments was understood: in amplifying interpersonal relations and creating self-governed products even more completely, thereby limiting costs and time, and even improving their quality.

Fundamental concepts of what would be called *etica Cyberpunk* [Cyberpunk ethic] started to emerge in Italy, drawing inspiration from and reinterpreting books of the literary vein of the same name, from William Gibson to Bruce Sterling, and giving life to practices which would materialize in the reality of daily life and in politics. The Social Centres have always been territories of libertarian experimentation with the utopian first phase of diffusion of the technologies, from modems to computers. A large part of art in networking in the 1990s had its origins and development there.

Maybe it is also due to this reason that Cyberpunk in Italy has taken on the connotations of a political movement, influencing a large part of the future Hacker reality and artistic experimentation in digital technology. Certainly, the activities of a few collectives inside the Social Centres, the first among them being the Decoder group from Milan, have contributed to the spread of the idea of a politically-oriented Cyberpunk, sending it in a direction in Italy different from that followed by Cyberpunk in the European and American scene (generally a-political, more of a literary phenomenon than anything else). The discourse returns to the "Italian case", for which the phenomenon of Italian networking is unique in its genre, because of this mixing and penetration among political, artistic, radical and technological areas, which have seen several collectives and individuals remain active through all of the 1980s and 1990s, until today.

Cyberpunk in Italy

The term Cyberpunk was initially created as a journalistic neologism for qualifying the literary activity in the 1980s of a few American writers, from Bruce Sterling and John Shirley to William Gibson. Or, if we want to be more precise, it refers to being inspired by the 1960s and 1970s books written by Philip K. Dick, William S. Burroughs and James G. Ballard, as well as Thomas

Pynchon's imaginative writing and Timothy Leary's visionary and libertarian works.

Certain central themes continuously emerge in Cyberpunk. The theme of bodily invasion: members, prosthetics, implanted circuits, cosmetic surgery, genetic alternation. And the more powerful mental invasion: the brain-computer interface, artificial intelligence, and neurochemistry. All the techniques that radically redefine human nature: one's own nature. (Sterling, 1986, p. 40).

Books like William Burroughs' *The Naked Lunch* (1959), James G. Ballard's, and Philip K. Dick's novels, the works of Allen Ginsberg and the Beat Generation writers, are rediscovered and considered real sources of inspiration for their perturbing and visionary writing. Burroughs' *cut-up* technique puts the writer, perhaps for the first time, in a non-passive condition (as for example will happen later with a book like *TAZ* by Hakim Bey in 1991): amidst an apparent psychedelic delirium, the writer is stimulated to create personal sensory narratives, to construct one's own montage.

The cut-up technique will be considered a point of "aesthetic" departure for the future practices of hacker art and digital artistic experimentations. At the cinematographic level, they become real cult movies like Ridley Scott's *Blade Runner* (1982), David Cronenberg's *Videodrome* (1982) and *The Naked Lunch* (1991) the film version of Burroughs' novel, and Klaus Maeck's movie *Decoder* (1984).

Another source of inspiration is found in Timothy Leary's texts, starting from the 1960s, and his vision of the psychic liberation through the use of psychedelic and "psychoactive" drugs, such as LSD. With the computer affirming itself, Timothy Leary's mysticism arrives at the concept of a perceptive expansion within the computer science data and bits, theorizing an interzone computer-brain hybridization inside a more democratic virtual space; a place of autopiloted practices (fantasies that would be found again in the Virtual Reality of subsequent years). In his words, the visionary use of drugs presents itself like a liberation strategy, with an extreme faith in progress and human evolution, while the image of the "interzone" would become a very prominent icon in the Italian underground area of the 1990s.

In the different Cyberpunk books, such as William Gibson's famous *Neuromancer* (1984), in which the term *cyberspace* appears for the first time, the characters live in a visionary, underground universe populated by monstrous creatures, by drifting, marginalized solitary individuals. They live in a world raging with drugs, guns, machines, artificial creatures, and organic-electronic mutants. The fantasy evoked by the Cyberpunk novels is materialized in the creative environment of those years through the performance of determinant artists, who stage post-futuristic shows in which machines become the principal actors who overthrow the traditional theatrical scenic spaces. Among these the Mutoid Waste Company, the Fura Dels Baus, the SRL group (Survival Research Laboratories), the performer Stelarc.

In the book *Realtà del virtuale*, Pier Luigi Capucci reflects on the links between Science Fiction and art:

It is with electronic art that the connections appear more relevant, in particular when it interrogates itself on the contemporary problematics inherent to the use of technologies and their social impact, when one uses these instruments, these media created for other reasons in an original manner: in this realm there are experiences that are based on Science Fiction in an evident way, actually, that they want to represent it. It is not by chance that these experiments are particularly interesting to the telecommunications sector, to the social mass vocation, to its totalizing and conditioning aspects and that their work often consists of a radical criticism, all the while expressed with a refusal of media technologies of and in itself; of the new nature that it is capable of generating, through an appropriation and a use which is radically different from these (1993, p. 128).

In Italy, between the end of the 1980s and the beginning of the 1990s utopian scenarios began to spread from VR (Virtual Reality) and the reflections on new digital technologies: seen as in the *Virtual* magazine and in the books by Antonio Caronia, such as *Nei labirinti della fantascienza* (1979), *Il Cyborg. Saggio sull'uomo artificiale* (1985) and *Il corpo virtuale* (1996), they are the mirrors of an era. Even if, as a literary phenomenon, Cyberpunk is to be considered over in the first years of the 1990s (as Bruce Sterling, maintains in a 1991 article that appeared in the English magazine "Interzone"), the Cyberpunk fantasies would be brought forward in the following years by many writers. Let's not forget the post 1991 texts, clearly inspired by Cyberpunk, by Neal Stephenson (*Snow Crash*), and Pat Cadigan (*Myndplayers*), Richard Calder and Alexander Besher.

In Italy, Cyberpunk is more than a literary current; it took the form of a radical movement inspired by writers of Science Fiction who created new utopias. The principal action in this direction was the activity of the Decoder collective from Milan, which in 1990 published an Italian anthology on Cyberpunk, called *Cyberpunk. Antologia di testi politici* [An Anthology of Political Texts] published by the Shake publishing house (Scelsi, 1990). Thus interpreted, Cyberpunk became the perfect fantasy through which to transfer certain practices of characters of opposition, gravitating in the political world and brought forth by hackers, in film, and in experimental music and inside the artistic performances which were developed in Italy over the course of the 1990s.

In those years, the conditions developed that produced some libertarian events - pre-announced by the concrete and real literary current - answering the Italian crisis of the post 1977 "reading Science Fiction from the left" (Caronia). The reason why Italian Cyberpunk took this particular direction is explained by referring to the scenario that started to take shape during the preceding years at the political, social and cultural level in the so-called "countercultural" environments.

In the 1980s, in the Social Centres and the activist underground scene, the presence of a book store called Calusca City Lights, should be noted. It was managed by Primo Moroni (a name that reminds us of the San Francisco Beat bookstore) inside the Cox 18 Social Centre, in via Conchetta in Milan. The Calusca, in reality had existed since 1971, managed by Primo Moroni, in a building in Via Calusca in Milan, hence the name of the book store. In 1995, after being evicted, it remained without a building and then found a warm welcome inside the Cox 18 space.

This space is known for its diffusion of material pertaining to the political and countercultural movements of the last decades (dating back to the 1960s) and it is here that the activity of the Shake cooperative originated. The Shake Edizioni had proposed editions and translations of works on Punk, Cyberpunk, Cyberfeminism, psychedelic counter-cultures, and movements, together with some essays on "gurus" like William S. Burroughs, James G. Ballard, Brion Gysin and Hakim Bey.

The Decoder group, which founded the magazine of the same name and the above mentioned Shake Edizioni, was created in 1986 and it was among the promoters of the first debates on the social use of telematics technologies. Formed by Raf "Valvola" Scelsi, Ermanno "Gomma" Guarneri, Gianni "u.v.L.S.I." Mezza, Giampaolo "Ulisse Spinosi" Capitani, Marco Philopat, Rosie Pianeta, Paoletta Nevrosi and others, it was one of the principal diffusers in Italy of the Hacker and Cyberpunk telematics.

Gomma, in an issue of the "Decoder" magazine, reminds us of the birth of the experience inside the Calusca. Explaining how in Italy, the DIY circuits were the main point of diffusion for the Cyberpunk networks, departing from the punk scenario. A guiding thread, therefore, inserted in the context of the radical activism practices of the era. In 1983, Primo Moroni allowed the punks to self-manage an internal room in the Calusca bookstore, in order to autonomously sell their materials outside of the cultural market.

So we started working in the bookstore, during a period when the 1970s experience was ending (badly) (…). But for us the Calusca was so special that we only saw the beauty which remained within the movement: the great quantity of magazine and books by Communists, Anarchists, Libertarians, Heretics, genial types, criminals, crazy people, drug addicts, gays, lesbians, freax and various "artists" (…). At the end of those two years (1985), Primo proposes, to our small group of already "contaminated" punks, to continue with the editing of the "Calusca Newletter", a magazine capable of representing the very diverse components of the bookstore ("Decoder", 1998, p. 929)[12].

And further, regarding the changing of the cultural panorama at the end of the 1980s in Italy, following the diffusion of computer technology, he continues:

The "end of the movement" seemed to correspond with the end of an era in the field of production. Information was becoming valuable merchandise and the technological hammer drill was about to take off. In a few years, especially in Milan, everything seemed to be transformed. A sort of deep-rooted uneasiness, that certain "modernity" theorists indicated was a result of a typical acceleration of our era, was therefore alleviated, and was to be taken on with coolness and a sense of adventure, in order to not be overwhelmed by it. To change one's skin without losing one's identity: transforming the movement, or at least, trying to transform oneself in order to not passively succumb to the transformation. At that point we understood that the game was to be played and the editorial group decided to create its own magazine: *Decoder* (*ivi*, p. 930).

The Decoder group tried to interpret the needs of the moment, starting to create numerous translations of foreign works, among which the publications of San Francisco's Re/Search and many other books from the international anarchical, technological and literary counter-culture. Their editorial operation contributed to diffusing a political and antagonistic vision of Cyberpunk in Italy. Outside of Italy, Cyberpunk was not seen as a political movement and it was considered a strictly literary phenomenon adherent to pop culture, as seen in "Vague" magazine, founded in the early 1980s by Tom Vague. The Cyberpunk-themed issue of Vague (1988) does not in any way hint at a political component of Cyberpunk, even if the anarchical-situationistic approach remained (the *Vague* graphic artists is the situationist Jamie Reid, who is also the designer of the Sex Pistols).

Even Lee Felstenstein, mentioned in *Cyberpunk. Antologia di testi politici* as he who "elaborated the technological concept of cyberpunk", in reality underlines that he does not remember having used cyberpunk with this meaning. Surely Lee Felstenstein was a key figure for an utopian vision of technology and hacking, but he never identified with a real political digital underground movement; which is instead a totally Italian phenomenon[13].

In Italy, Cyberpunk collects all of the libertarian utopias and the radical traditions of the preceding years, giving life to a unique current in its genre for a collective participation. In our country the punk tradition is met with that of Do It Yourself, so the need to create liberated spaces: new open technological possibilities; the attitude to share and to create networks; Cyberpunk and Hacktivism, as we intend it today, converge all in a particular ethic. Cyberpunk entered in our country in a "porous" way, assimilating within it needs and imaginings that already smouldered for many years and taking a totally unique direction, which have then contributed to giving a strong identity to our hacker movement, very different than that in the rest of Europe or North America, which does not have specifically political connotations, except for isolated incidents[14].

The book *Cyberpunk. Antologia di testi politici* includes different texts from different characters and groups, creating a panorama that goes from Cyberpunk literature to psychedelic cyber to the cyber applications to the techno-anarchical to the political Cyberpunk. Not all the reproduced texts are openly ascribable to a "political" discourse. Cyberpunk however is reconnected by "elective affinities" to the preceding antagonistic practices and to the punk phenomena in its more active political component, highlighting that it was shaped by two components: cyber+punk, in a continuity of radical practices created at the end of the 1970s.

This line of conjunction between punk and cyberpunk, seen as an opposition movement, is found clearly delineated in *Mela al Cianuro*, a text written by Raf "Valvola". I chose the following passage from the book:

Today it appears essential to conduct a battle for the right to information, through the construction of alternative networks which are evermore branched out. This is a battle than can be won, if one keeps in mind that the same capital cannot stop, for reasons of political opportunity, an intrinsic economic movement to its same progress. The computer is an instrument, which is potentially extremely democratic; the important thing is to acquire a consciousness at the collective level. Adding to this, Cyberpunk literature seems to be a great Trojan horse, good to interest those contiguous sectors, still not involved today, which gravitate to the furthest orbits of the movements. Today, through Cyberpunk, the opportunity is offered to all the cultural operators of the movement, to pen a new, enormous field of production of a collective imaginary, capable of destroying the tenacious imaginary existent vault from which, for a while we are compressed. (…) The inspirational themes of Cyberpunk belong, because of its history, evocation and future fascinations, to the counter-cultural movements. We must collectively take it back (1990, pp. 32-33).

This is where the "Cyberpunk Legend" is born, which in Italy inspired hackers, artists, intellectuals, creative minds, and young people with a passion for computers who recognized themselves in that vision of the world. Through Bruce Sterling and William Gibson's novels the ideas that the panorama of technology can be a new reality in which to expand and self-determine one's own actions are diffused. It is thought that through the digital and the critical use of technology it is possible to expand the concept of democracy and freedom in a new frank territory which still needs to be explored. The Decoder experience makes us understand how the concept of DIY was fundamental for affirming certain practices which today hope to give a critical sense to the use of the web, and in large part the Hacker ethic in Italy today. It was not however the only experience to have acted in this direction, but it is inserted in a debate born in our country during the 1980s that has involved many individuals and groups. With the idea of combating the institutionalization of an initially free technology such as the Internet, we see, within the Italian panorama, the creation of BBS networks and radical websites that claim the freedom of communication and fight for a real accessibility to all of the computer technologies.

Amateur Computer Networks

In Italy, the Cyberpunk background described earlier has taken shape in an active network with the goal of guaranteeing certain rights (the so-called cyber-rights) to the individual, in order to promote a conscious use of technology and free circulation of data. Between 1980 and 1990 the idea of using computer technology to create horizontal network relationships between individuals was actively supported, with the goal of allowing a *free and uncontrollable communicative flow*[15]. Allowing too the possibility of creating connections between *network islands*, i.e. spaces of free discussion and information flow. These are independent areas whose philosophy is described in one of the texts which have inspired most whoever gravitated in the underground areas of those years such as TAZ, Temporarily Autonomous Zones, by Hakim Bey (1997).

In 1985 Hakim Bey writes:

I believe that by extrapolating the stories of the past and of the future with regards to the "Islands in the Net" we could collect proof to suggest that a certain type of "free enclave" is not only possible in our times, but is also existent. All of my research and speculation is crystallized around the concept of the Temporary Autonomous Zone (from now on abbreviated as TAZ). Despite the synthesizing force which it exerts on my thoughts, I do not want however that TAZ be taken as anything but an *essay* (an attempt), a suggestion, almost a poetic fantasy. Despite the initial enthusiasm of a preacher, I am not trying to construct a political dogma. In fact I deliberately avoided defining TAZ: I go around the topic shooting off exploratory rays. At the end TAZ is almost explained by itself. If the phase were to be commonly used it would be understood without difficulty...even in action (1997, pp. 12-13).

The concept of Cyberspace, between 1980 and 1990, was seen in the radical scene as a territory of reciprocal confrontation and of collective relations in which to share and diffuse knowledge; a metaphor in the neural networks in which information travels according to the reticular, rhizomatic dynamics.

Cyberspace is imagined as a place in which one can act in a global space, but it is not for this reason that it is an informative one: the individual can feel part of a world community, without ever having to renounce his individual informative needs. The term *glocalism* connotes the first utopian phase of on-line communication. Through the many *virtual communities* it is possible to experiment with new associations and at the same time act in a trans-national universe of data and information bringing inside it its individual and "local" experiences.

In Italy, these utopias were created in the middle of the 1980s with a name: FidoNet. But let's take a step back. At the end of the 1970s, the Internet network, as we know it today, was called Arpanet, and in reality it was the privilege of only a select few, such as university and research centres. The first computers available were the *mainframes*, too big and costly for average use, which instead get closer to computer science at the end of the 1970s with Apple I (1976) and at the beginning of the 1980s with the first PC IBM (1981). In reality, the first personal computer in history was the Altair 8800, which was produced by Model Instrumentation Telemetry System (MITS) owned by Ed Roberts in New Mexico and sold in pieces, to be assembled. The Altair took name from the Star Trek series (one of the places where the star ship Enterprise was headed) and appeared for the first time as the "Altair kit" on the cover of the "Popular Electronics" magazine, in 1975.

In Chicago, at the end of the 1970s Ward Christensen created the free distribution of the MODEM program, which allowed two computers to exchange data through a telephone line and "lays down the foundation for a social telematics base, and that which then would become the culture of the electronic bulletin boards" (Gubitosa, 1999).

Ward Christensen used the Altair 8800 computer based on the 8080 Intel processor and circulated the first version of the MODEM inside the Chicago Area Computer Hobbyist's Exchange, creating, together with Keith Peterson the XMODEM model. In this period, many people try to create "collaborative assembling" of this version until Chuck Forsberg gave life to a new ZMODEM protocol written in C for Unix systems. But it was in 1978 that Ward Christensen and Randy Suess created the first BBS, Bulletin Board System, called CBBS at the time.

Most of the time the term BBS was translated into Italian as "bacheca elettronica": in fact it was based on the exchange of messages sent via modem and computer by several different users, in the spheres of different thematic areas of discussion.

The computers of an amateur network were connected through telephone lines via modem and went on to form the "hubs" of the network of many BBSes which, in turn, were connected. The messages circulated through the network mostly at night when the computers were predisposed to receive and send data, which travelled from node to node in a manner much slower than today.

Every computer which is used as a BBS is predisposed to answer the calls coming in, in an automatic way: at every node in the network various users connect in order to take the messages that pertain to them. Contextually to the collection, messages are posted on the "bulletin board": both private messages(electronic mail destined particularly to a particular user) and public messages readable by all the participants of the collective discussion group. (*ivi*, p.14).

In Italy, the BBS were diffused thanks to the FidoNet network. In 1983, Tom Jennings (Boston, Massachusetts, 1955) had given life to the BBS Fido N.1 in San Francisco. In 1984, Jennings connected Fido BBS with Fido2, administered in Baltimore by John Madill giving life to the first FidoNet connection. The FidoNet Network would be diffused in all directions, measuring up to 160 hubs at the beginning of 1985.

Jennings is an interesting character, who besides being interested in technology and science, defines himself as "an artist with a technological background". He acts in the interstice of different disciplines, applying the logic of *problem solving* from 1977 in the computer science, programming and electronics fields, from 1984 in the networking BBS area and from 1992 in that of Internet; transferring all of this in his artistic works: machines realized with obsolete technologies, which refer to "an obscure, technological culture". Jennings' machines are not easily distinguishable by design and materials from those of the early computer makers of the 1950s, fully functional and highly visionary. He ironically calls them products of the "World Power Systems", remembering the period of birth of much of the Web and Technology Culture and reproducing at that time the contradictions that existed from the Cold War to today.

Today's competencies and the libertarian cultures, pop culture, working on the internet, music and communication cultures, trips, intercultural and international commerce: everything started in this period. Surveillance and control culture did the same thing: the world, economic conflict, the loss of anonymity, medical and insurance redlining. Technology is not something which is isolated, which happened in factories, it is an integral part of our Western culture, no longer removed from the daily life of clothes and language; it presents the same ambivalences and tensions between merchandise and culture (<www.wps.com/about-WPS/WPS/index.html>).

Jennings' objects tell the story of aesthetics in design, and their functions highlight a story of political and economic interests. Tom Jennings had a past as a punk and had come out as a homosexual, he was therefore used to going beyond the predictable and seeing things in their multiple perspectives. Only a bright mind could give life to that which was one of the main inputs of the net culture, that which saw the BBS as his launching pad.

1985 is an important year for Web cultures, since we see at that time in California the birth of WELL (Whole Heart 'Lectronic Link), a BBS derived from the "Whole Heart Review" magazine and founded by Stewart Brand and Larry Brilliant. An environment for a "declaredly uninhibited, intelligent and iconoclastic" discussion (the WELL) which collects intellectuals, artists, programmers, journalists, teachers, activists, and all those who wanted to freely express their ideas. Here Howard Rheingold coined the term *virtual community* and numerous web theorists met, including Bruce Sterling. In 1999, WELL was purchased by Salon.com and remains an open and active place for discussion on <www.well.com>. It was in the midst of this scene that the foundations of hacker ethics were diffused.

In 1986, FidoNet arrived in Italy and Giorgio Rutigliano launched the first hub in the city of Potenza, called Fido Potenza. Internationally Jeff Rush created Echomail, a mail programme that allowed the creation of areas of collective discussion from the circulating messages in FidoNet.

George, passionate about computer technology, had written a program to transform his centre of computer services into a BBS during nighttime hours, taking advantage of some of the commutated lines that remained unused at night. When FidoNet was about 100 hubs and several thousand users big, Giorgio came to know about the existence of the Web (Gubitosa, 1999, pp- 21-22).

The first FidoNet hub does not have anything directly to do with the Italian counterculture and DIY scene.

In order to reconstruct the history of the underground digital network in Italy a series of complex factors that took root in the political movements of the 1970s must be considered. The main steps of this intricate journey are well summarized in the text *La nuova comunicazione interattiva e l'antagonismo in Italia* (edited by Tommaso Tozzi, Stefano Sansavini, Ferry Byte and Arturo di Corinto, 2000) which allows the contextualization of the artistic practices of networking that we described in the preceding chapter:

In the second half of the 1960s and in the 1980s in Italy we see the birth of two forms of distinct social protests, with continuous exchanges and comparisons. The first is identifiable in the autonomous movement of the Antinuclear and Anti-imperialist Coordination; it has its roots in the opposition and conflict with the political and economical institutions. This area collects a good part of the reality of the movement in Italy and in many Social Centres. The second can be identified with the punk movement (and around it a network of fanzines and self-managed alternative spaces). It is in individual and collective artistic practices connected with the practices on the street (graffiti art and other), of social and non profit protests and in the mail art sector where the concept of "Networking" is developed. This second area finds its battleground in the counter-cultural, musical, artistic sectors, and in the new experimentation of the new languages of communication. (...) It is around both "zones" that the first forms of social use of media technology are tested, the creation of "virtual communities" and of "rhizomatic" relationships. (...) Even though the social components are much more complex and differentiated, the history of the digital networking in Italy essentially correspond to the history of the two Italian radical networks: the European Counter Network (E.C.N.) and CyberNet. Although other networks exist alongside these, for example, Peacelink and other cultural movements.

The European Counter Network (E.C.N.) was created as a consequence of a proposal of the Danish group TV Stop, who in 1988 proposed the idea of creating a European, countercultural digital network.

The proposal had other groups as contacts in France, England (Class War), Germany (the Autonomen, some groups of occupants of the houses of Hamburg and Berlin, Radio Dreickland in Freiburg bordering with Switzerland), Italy (the area that referred to the Coordinamento Nazionale Antinucleare e Antimperialista). (...) In 1989 the international meetings of the E.C.N. area stopped, and the first debates and experimental connections started in Italy. This is how the E.C.N network was created in Italy. Zero BBS was created from the Cyberaut Oll nuclei, which became E.C.N. Torino (Di Corinto, Tozzi, 2002, p. 205).

In Italy, the first European E.C.N. hubs were created in 1990, in Padova, Bologna, Rome and Milan. In the meantime, inside the FidoNet network, in 1991 we see the creation of an area of messages called Cyberpunk. Inside this area, a new vision of understanding telematics begins to be proposed.
We therefore have

the E.C.N., on one side, who for the moment considers computer technology as a simple tool available to political action; on the other side a more variegated area (including elements of: Decoder, the future AvANa BBS from Rome, the Cayenna by Feltre and others) which sees within computer technology a new rhizomatic modality of communicating a new challenge for human action (Tozzi, Sansavini, Byte, Di Corinto, 2000).

In 1992, the Cyberpunk area detaches itself from FidoNet. The schism occurs due to political and technical reasons, which are, above all, tied to the cryptographic discourse, not permitted in FidoNet and instead promoted by some internal realities in the Cyberpunk arena as a form of tutelage for individual freedom[16]. From this schism, in 1993 an alternative BBS network called CyberNet is born and a few experimental BBSes are created, configured in a way to dialogue between them through the CyberNet network number.
Senza Confine BBS (Macerata) is the national hub and the other three nodes are Hacker Art BBS (Florence), created in 1990 (in 1994 it becomes Virtual Town TV BBS), Lamer Xterminator BBS (Bologna), created in 1991, Bits Against the Empire (Trento) and Decoder BBS (Milan), which was created

especially for the occasion. After a few months other hubs are added, which, within a couple of years, reach about forty BBS within the CyberNet network (among these AvANa Avvisi Ai Naviganti BBS, created in Rome in 1994). This autonomous network offered open *gateways* to all the networks that asked for it and was presented like a transversal zone in several networks (P-Net, FreakNet, E.C.N., ecc.) configuring itself like an exchange circuit between different networks. Great diligence in this "transverse" direction is shown in the actions of the *Senza Confine BBS*, the first hub of the Cybernet network created with the goal of the civil and legal defence of immigrants.

During the birthing phase of the first BBS networks in Italy, even FreakNet took shape. It is an alternative BBS network unhinged from the FidoNet world circuit and similar to the CyberNet and E.C.N. networks, created by Asbesto and Hecatombles in Catania, and soon many other people join. In those years, between FreakNet and the historical anti-mafia magazine *I Siciliani* (created by Giuseppe Fava) a spontaneous collaboration occurred, making the magazine the first publication that used computer instruments for the editing of articles and for the diffusion of the digital version of its contents. "I remember a few meetings in the *I Siciliani* office on how to create CD-ROMs with various content or how to create a BBS on the premises, as a telematics node which could serve for many things: anonymous anti-mafia accusations, collection and sorting of information, anti-mafia database, etc." (Asbesto, <www.freaknet.org>).

Among the active BBS networks in Italy in the first period of the "amatorial" net culture besides FidoNet, CyberNet, FreakNet and E.C.N., we also find OneNet, FirNet, ToscaNet, ScoutNet, ChronosNet, EuroNet, Itax Council Net, LariaNet, LinuxNet, LogosNet, P-Net, RingNet, RpgNet, SatNet, SkyNet, VirNet, ZyxelNet and PeaceLink[17]. This last one, managed by Giovanni Pugliese, was created in 1991 as a BBS inside FidoNet and would then become an autonomous BBS network the following year. It was one of the victims of the Italian crackdown that unleashed in May 1994 against the Italian BBSes.

In the book *Italian Crackdown*, Carlo Gubitosa retraces the events which brought about the first, and major, collapse of the Italian underground digital network that started as an investigation of computer piracy initiated by the Pesaro and Torino Attorneys' offices. On May 11, 1994 several FidoNet Network BBSes were confiscated by the *[Guardia di] Finanza* (Revenue Guard

Corps), and there were accusations of "criminal conspiracy, contraband, illicit software duplication, computer fraud, altering of computer and/or telematics systems".

Dozens of computers which contain freely distributable programs were seized and numerous system operators (sysops) were incriminated on the basis of a simple suspicion, completely ignoring what was actually happening on the amateur BBS networks. A large part of the material seized would lie for many years in the *Guardia di Finanza* [Revenue Guard Corps] warehouse, without ever being examined (Gubitosa, 1999, p. 41).

A different type of confusion ensued between all the Network Operators, who were being hit by the mandates and the propagated seizures that spread in all directions, progressively following all the hubs of the Italian BBS Networks (approximately 300 during the FidoNet era). Predictably, the investigation failed, demonstrating that FidoNet was not used for exchanging pirated software. However, after this episode the Network suffered a hard blow (even Giorgio Rutigliano, of Fido Potenza, resigned with a letter to Oscar Luigi Scalfaro the President of the Republic), even if many other people continued to work to make computer technology a shareable, public commodity.

After the Italian Crackdown at the national level there was a strategy of repression towards established amateur BBSes. On June 3, 1994, the victim of another inquiry, the Central Hub of the PeaceLink network, a network association for the promotion of peace, had its property seized by the Taranto *Guardia di Finanza* [Revenue Guard Corps], accused of selling copyright protected programs. From here, a network of solidarity and support for PeaceLink was formed, fighting to "give voice to those who have no voice", until the full acquittal six years later of Giorgio Rutigliano, the PeaceLink network manager.

The account of censure in Italy does not end here. It is enough to remember the action taken in 1998 against the server of the Isole nella Rete (Island in the Network) association <www.ecn.org>, following the accusation of the Turban Italia Srl, travel agency, instigated by a message sent by a collective on an Isole nella Rete mailing list inviting readers to boycott tourism in Turkey to support the Kurdish population.

Then there is the seizing of the Roman Civic Network's web spaces in July 1998. Even this is on the cusp of absurdity, since the justification was the accusation made by the Sicilian priest Don Fortunato, from Noto, of the *Associazione Telefono Arcobaleno* (Rainbow Telephone Association) of presumed "Satanist content" on the Foro Romano Digitale Association website, hosted by the Comune di Roma. The reason for this is "a quote from a literary piece published in a nationally distributed magazine, which can be purchased in all bookstores. The quotation is taken from *Femminile nella fantascienza: modelli di scrittura* project, which is also a Bachelor's thesis successfully presented at the Facoltà di Lettere in Rome"[18].

There are a series of thought-provoking censure cases which accurately represent the climate that is still seen in Italy today. Many of these cases are found on the *Sotto Accusa* website, which is an archive managed by the Isole nella Rete listing censure cases and attempts to limit the freedom of expression on the Internet at <www.ecn.org/sotto-accusa>. The information found in the archive is circulated in order to evaluate it on the *cyber-rights@ecn.org* mailing list. Founded and managed by Ferry Byte, this mailing list an important point of reference for digital debate in Italy, from censure to privacy, to the possibility of access to on-line information <https://www.ecn.org/wws/arc/cyber-rights>.

In time, the answer of the Italian BBS networks to this type of censure took shape with a series of collective initiatives at the local and national levels to increase awareness surrounding the questions of digital rights such as privacy, anonymity, computer technology literacy, digital divide, etc. One of the first and surely the most indicative at the national level in the period of birth of the BBS and consequently at the Italian Crackdown, was the *Diritto alla comunicazione nello scenario di fine millennio*, event organized by the Strano Network group in Florence. The convention, whose proceedings were published in the book *Nubi all'orizzonte* (1996), took place on February 19, 1995 at the Centro per l'Arte Contemporanea Luigi Pecci in Prato and offered an interesting panoramic view of the situation of Italian networking, with talks presented by different theorists, sysops, artists and networkers of that phase of the digital culture.

In the book *Nubi all'orizzonte* it is possible to relive part of the atmosphere of the period; dense with questions regarding the future use of technology in independent and radical Italian environments.

This is a direct example of how the creation of the BBSes has given life to a network of individuals, projects, and collectives, which in the subsequent years has continued to work in this direction. The follow-up story of these realities is tightly intertwined with the concept of the hacker ethic, synthesized with the term "hacktivism": master of ceremonies of a great part of the future initiatives of the network.

From Cyberpunk to Industrial

The video and cinematographic work of Mariano Equizzi <www.marianoeq uizzi.com> is an example of how the cyber utopias influenced the creativity of many Italian artists and activists at the beginning of the 1990s. Its description allows us to add a new link in the panorama of Italian networking, connecting the "alternative" use of technology and computers with the musical and visual experimentations between cyberpunk and industrial. Mariano Equizzi, an author born and raised in Palermo, currently travels between Rome, New York and Tokyo. Inspired by authors such as William S. Burroughs, James G. Ballard and Philip K. Dick, Equizzi transfers the settings of many Beat Generation and Science Fiction books into his works. He has directed several short films which have now become Italian independent *cult* works such as *Syrena* (1998), *AgentZ* (2000, Premio Italia 2001), *Giubilaeum* (2000), *Ginevra Report* (2001, Premio Italia 2002*)*, *Crash* (2001), *Sign* (2001), *New Order* (2001, Premio Nokia-Wind Contest 2002) *D.N.E.*[19] (2002), *The Mark* (2003), and *R.A.C.H.E.* (2005). Since 1999 he has worked with Luca Liggio (digital video producer) <www.lucaliggio.com> and Paolo Bigazzi (sound designer and audio producer) <www.iter-research.com>. He is currently working on the movie *Revenge*, based on Valerio Evangelisti's story *Gorica tu sia maledetta* (1998) and *Le Bestie di Satana*, a horror piece written with Andrea Colombo.

Mariano Equizzi dedicated himself to video produced with the analogical instruments widely-used in the 1980s, studying at the Centro Sperimentale di Cinematografia of Rome in 1996[20]. It was here that he worked on the production of the school's short films and later worked as assistant producer and *runner* on film sets, becoming Michele Soavi's assistant director. In 2000, together with

Emiliano Farinella, Equizzi created *Next Text TV* (Interact production, Rome), a portal that explored the content of different types of media (text, flash, video and audio), blending them together and creating all the video and flash content <www.ntxt.it>.

Mariano Equizzi narrates; describing his first creative endeavour in technology, together with Luca Liggio and Paolo Bigazzi,

Devoted to Cyberpunk as an operative practice and as an aesthetic verb we are launched into the arena of non linear editing when computers had at the most a MMX 166Mhz processor. It seems that the videophones of today are more powerful. But back then everything was delegated to the legendary Targa 2000 card and to the SCSI II controller, all bought by Luca. We were used to the horrendous Sony operators which they mounted with control L cables and with an avalanche of large boxes to process the creatively filmed material, huge boxes which still work excellently today. The computers were kept open with fans close to them in order to avoid the notorious thermic calibration. In this state of a hardware crisis, which even included audio equipment (midi files instead of non compressed .wav files and a DM80 Roland which Paolo used as if it was a NEVE[21]) we have postulated our guerrilla style[22].

The cinematographic vision of Mariano Equizzi is unique because, even if it was shaped in Italy in the same period of diffusion of many "subversive" Cyberpunk instances, initially it does not have direct contacts with the experiences of the more politicized Italian creative and artistic realities[23]. Equizzi's works, if anything, communicate the cyber fantasies with a point of view that is decidedly "futuristically political" [i.e. unrealistic], proposing the contents as a form of *entertainment,*

working with garbage out of necessity, going around in the evacuation bunkers in the underused warehouses, places which in any case perfectly represent the paranoid processes and the technological decline of which Gibsonismo was the bearer (…) The anomalous journey in video production has allowed us to offer a non "perfect", but an original result, at a very low cost. (…) We have applied the modality to Cyberpunk, that tendency to decodify and make the approach to narration, paranoid, complicated and hackeristic, according to Uncle Bill's motto (William S. Burroughs): *Nothing is real, everything is allowed*[24]. (...) A mosaic of dead and new media, our favourite mix.

Mariano Equizzi, explaining how his video and cinematographic production has been influenced by Cyberpunk fantasies, adds:

For me, Cyberpunk was a system of observing reality, of decoding the ways and possibilities of implementation, independent of the possibilities and of the instruments. Implementation independent of the power that the operator has, be it economic, through media, or political; all the forms of power that are part of the media in a penetrating and castrating way. Cyberpunk created an alibi for us; making the error, the corrupted media, a matrix of *crashed* transmission, the subject, or one of the subjects, of narration. The lack of materials from the time of the analogical video, too deep for our pockets, stimulated us in this sense. My love for garage, work shops and industrial material stores, says a lot about the productive modalities which I still follow today. Bigazzi has a wall of old *vintage synth* and Luca has 16mm camera used by the Chinese during the Mao era (The Canon Scoopic). The use of all types media, for example, from old video cameras to tubes, to video surveillance systems, up until the *cutting edge* of digital, without forgetting the Super 8 is the result of this *melting pot* where every single work must look like a cultural uniform, like the chaotic trend of our medial fluxes.

In particular, the scenes of the short film *Syrena,* according to many is a milestone of Italian independent videos. They were created by recycling pieces of an old Honeywell mainframe found discarded in a warehouse. As Mariano Equizzi narrates,

using only Premiere 2.0, After Effects 2.0 and 3ds Max 1.0 and a very large quantity of video and graphics (more than 250 CD ROMs), we created a Cyberpunk epic which still today, according to many, is unsurpassed in its complexity, originality, a low budget. (...) The indie work that consecrated us is still *Ginevra Report* (2001), which we produced with the Interact Web Streaming distribution and Luca Liggio's (video) and Paolo Bigazzi's (audio) usual patience. It was dedicated to one of our heroes: James G. Ballard, the cantor of *internal* space a very anomalous and venerated Sci-Fi-writer. (...) Once again we had applied an "absurd" productive system; we had sent the webcam with the drivers and Shareware capture program. The audio was recorded with a ribbon audio recorder (I collect these types of recorders). The speeches so recorded were composed on a multi-screen video. There were all kinds of contributors: a Ballard expert, a Cern professor... all on a stereo 7 audio ribbon and separate webcam video. At that time there was no way of getting ADSL and in any case the quality of webcam transmission is still very low for our needs.

At the same time, Mariano Equizzi, Luca Liggio and Paolo Bigazzi's activity were inspired by another creative wave. This time it was the Industrial musical scene that influenced many other artists and creative individuals who were active in Italy from the 1980s to the 1990s[25]. To describe this other fantastical fragment, important in order to understand the situation in Italy during that period, we quote Mariano Equizzi:

Industrial in the proper sense only touched us. It was created in 1975, and Luca and I were born in 1970 and 1971, therefore we missed out on this tsunami wave, but personally we assimilated it subconsciously in its extreme tendency to provoke and to put in artistic discussion, with ferocious liberty, even the worst of humans; something which Punk did not do "too much" of, limiting itself in its more political expressions to take one part instead of another[26]. Instead the Industrial movement shattered everything and that was it, in a process of "exaltation". (…) In this backwards journey through the abyss of the artistic practice and along the obscure horizons of Modern Art, the Industrial movement signals, in my opinion, a much LOWER point and even a questionable/uncivil one. We have been swimming in this "abyss" ever since we started the *Revenge* project, with the approval of foreign operators, especially Western *noise-ofiles*. And I am postulating Anime 28 on the basis of this derivation towards artistic incivility. I definitely believe that this exploration of the more eroded layers (Burriani?) of artistic expression is to be connected to a process that occurs in different fields of media. The tendencies of glitch music and sound-scape, and also of ritual and dark ambient[27] are moments of organized technological derivation that I believe should be coordinated even with the American New Horror of the 1970, which has made a "great" comeback in movies such as *Saw* (James Wan, 2004), *Hostel* (Eli Roth, 2005) and various remakes of extreme films of that period. Works of art that eroded, granulated, worn out and covered with ash, images and documentation of ruins and catastrophes, of *borderline* paranoia and curious hypotheses. I believe that the event which has most significantly derailed my artistic processes in this century is September 11, 2001, with its rubble, its losses and its shadows. We are in the shadows of that event and we construct images and sounds carved out from our conscience surrounded by complex technological sedimentations which appear, as they flow, like burnt plastic.

Technological sedimentations in which punk, Cyberpunk, and industrial movements relive their experiences, as described in these paragraphs. They are that which will constitute the creative substratum for numerous other experiences of Italian artists and activists between 1980 and 1990, as we shall see in the next chapter.

Endnotes

1   Simonetta Fadda, in a private conversation with the author, April 2006.

2   Berlin is a perfect example of the urban art phenomenon. The graffiti artist Voegel/Bird was one of the first to dot the city with his works, bringing messages of a new generation of urban artists to the East Berlin; creating images that were much more articulate than TAGs. Voegel was immediately followed by the Katzen/Cats and by the artist called Sechsen, who for ten years invaded the city of Berlin with the number six: *sechs* in German. Among the most important street-artists in Berlin, one of the most historical, but still current, is the CBS group, which characterizes itself with a yellow closed fist, visible along the path of the S-Bahn, on house walls and in unusual places. CBS is known for their political actions, such as the "kidnapping" of the poster created for the "Kommunikationsstrategien der Werbung" show in the Alexanderplatz subway station. The CBS group literally "kidnapped" the poster art where DDR was written, to put it on the wall of the "Kaufhof" shopping mall in Alexanderplatz, a building in the shape a of a honeycomb, the symbol of Soviet power before the falling of the wall (which, after the recent restructuring, lost its architectural honeycomb motif along with most of its appeal). In place of the poster, CBS put their own work, with the same closed yellow fist, creating a situation which generated much discussion. CBS is known in fact for sabotage, appropriation and communicative guerrilla tactics, carried out with the motto "the city belongs to us", which is reminiscent of the squatters who occupied apartments and buildings in the 1980s and 1990s in Berlin. Every once in a while the nocturnal actions of the graffiti artists cross over into daylight, such as the collective event of several street artists which took place in September 2004 at the Helmholtzplatz Platzhaus (in the Prenzlauer Berg area). Beyond the famous and lesser-known names of the scene, the gathering allowed for anyone who wanted to participate to spontaneously take part. The event was completely self-financed, producing a collective work still visible today on the wall of the Platzhaus. Among the promoters were the street artists Nomad, whose GATA project was able to reciprocally connect the urban art of Berlin, Copenhagen and several cities in Iceland.

3   *Ipertext Fluxus* was created by the Strano Network communication group, who in the same year (1994), curated three other hypertexts: *Testi Caldi*, *Stragi di Stato* and *Metanetwork*, all published by Wide Records, an independent label in Pisa. The hypertexts can be downloaded from <www.strano.net/snhtml/ipertest/ipertest.htm>.

4   Text from a punk flyer that was handed out in front of Studio 54 and at the Odissea 2000 in Milan, as it is reproduced in their book set in Milan between 1977 and 1984. The new 2006 edition of the novel, with a preface by the author and contributions from Stiv Rottame, is published by Einaudi.

5   The title of Philopat's book derives from the song lyrics of the Californian band Germs (*We must bleed*) whose singer, Darby Crash, was one of the most disturbing and at the same time fascinating personalities of that period. Philopat's text also has a literary style which does not follow rules: the traditional way of writing is substituted with sentences that don't present the canonical sequence of a capital letters for the first word, sentence, period, even if they are linked between them with "–" which reminds us of a stream of consciousness or a normal dialogue.

6   A short film about the history of Italian Punk and, in particular, on the Virus of via Correggio in Milan, can be downloaded from the New Global Vision site at: <www.ngvision.org/mediabase/88>. Other material in their video repertoire on the Milan Virus is posted on the Strano Network website at <www.strano.net/town/music/punk.htm>.

7   To read about the birth of the Punk flyer "PUNKamINazione" visit the Acrataz Collective website, which contains many historically informative postings and various materials about Italian Punk in the 1980s. <http://acrataz.oziosi.org/rubrique.php3?id_rubrique=47>. Another useful text in order

to delve deeper into the discussion of punkine and fanzine, even though it was written from a more descriptive point of view, is the excerpt from Susanna Vigoni's dissertation on the history of the Milan Virus, entitled "Virus: Cont-aminazione punk a Milan" published in "Punkadeka" magazine, under the tab: Sezioni>Yesterday Heroes at <www,punkadeka.it/>

8   For a detailed chronological analysis refer back to *Hacktivism, la libertà nelle maglie della rete*, edited by Arturo di Corinto and Tommaso Tozzi, Manifestolibri, Roma, 2002, in particular the chapter "Cronologia e storia", pp. 188-252.

9   For a description of the CyberSyn II and Forthnet project, visit: <www.ecn.org/forte/cybersyn2/index.html>.

10 To get to the heart of this scene, we suggest viewing Goldrake's website <www.goldrake.info> and that of Capitan Harlock at <www.capitanharlock.com>.

11 In order to historically contextualize the techniques envisioned by *phone-freaks*, see chapter 4.

12 Gomma, Editorial in *Decoder* no.12, p.929. It was a long time before the Calusca Newsletter project took off because of the eviction that forced the closure of the bookstore.

13 The reflections are the result of a private email exchange with Lee Felstenstein (in March 2006), who sent me a considerable amount of written material so I could delve more deeply into his approach in dealing with hacking and computer technology subsequent to the experiences of his youth in the student movement at Berkeley (Berkeley Free Speech Movement). Among which was the text of his speech *The Arming of Desire, Counterculture and Computer Revolution* delivered at the Waag in Amsterdam in September 2005, during a conference on "Cyberspace Salvations" in which Lee Felstenstein outlines the origins of the personal computer and the internet starting from the political and social counterculture of San Francisco in 1960 (the video of the speech can be downloaded from <http://connect.waag.org>). One of his autobiographical essays and the text *The Hacker's League* posted on <www.welcomehome.org/hl.html>, an expansion on the article *Real Hackers Don't Rob Banks* commissioned and titled by "Byte Magazine" for the magazine's tenth anniversary. The article remained unedited and was read by Lee Felstenstein in 1985 at a conference about hacking organized by the ACM. More a more in-depth description of Lee Felstenstein's activities, I refer to chapter 4 of this book.

14 The first among them were the CAE (Critical Art Ensemble) and the subsequent Electronic Disturbance Theater in which Ricardo Dominguez was active. Dominguez's political vision of Cyberpunk drew him very close to the idea of Italian hacktivism.

15 Uncontrolled does not mean unregulated: there are rules even in on-line communication (*netiquette*) in order to facilitate the flow of data on the web, and, at the same time, to ensure respectful conduct toward other users. However, they are *unwritten rules*, at the users' discretion, that appeal to their good sense and desire to guarantee a fluid and "correct" data communication.

16 These problems are described well in Luc Pac essay *Il messaggio crittato*, in the Strano Network publication *Nubi all'orizzonte. Diritto alla comunicazione nello scenario di fine millennio*, Rome, Castelvecchi, 1996, pp. 149-154, available on-line at <www.dvara.net/HK/bits.asp>.

17 For a complete list of BBS and many other helpful sources of information regarding the amateur telematics network, consult the text *Digital Guerilla. Guida all'uso alternativo di computer, modem e reti telematiche*, self-produced by Cyberspace, Torino, 1995.

18 To read further, see <www.ecn.org/censura/frd.htm>.

19 *Descrambling Nova Express*, inspired by the story *Nova Express* by Burroughs.

20 In school, he was enrolled in a production course with teachers such as Fernando Ghia (Gold Crest), Giannandrea Pecorelli (Aurora), Dino Di Dionisio (Urania Film), Mario Liggeri, Francesco Ventura.

21 A famous brand name of professional mixers (pointed out by Mariano Equizzi)

22 This and the following citations are drawn from an unedited text by Mariano Equizzi entitled *Dal Cyberpunk all'Industrial, una involuzione crudele di Mariano Equizzi (reflecting on his techno-creative symbiosis with Luca Liggio and Paolo Bigazzi)*. Mariano Equizzi wrote the article in January 2006, when I requested that he tell the story of his artistic activities relative to Cyberpunk, as I had the second publication of this book in mind. The article is a perfect example of the spirit of the era (the 1990s) and of the evolution of the Cyberpunk concept in Italy, especially at the practical level in the visual arts and independent film.

23 The inevitable confrontation with such realities happened a few years later at the Hackmeeting 2000 in the Forte Prenestino in Rome, at which Equizzi screened his short films.

24 From *Naked Lunch*, 1959, by William S. Burroughs, translated by Claudio Gorlier, 1992, SugarCo Edizioni.

25 There is a good definition of the industrial phenomenon on the Italian Wikipedia website: "Born at the end of the 1970s, industrial is certainly one of the most extreme forms of music over produced. Essentially is covers a derivative of Krautrock that is less tied to song form, like that of groups like Faust and New. This genre was influenced by extra musical influences such as the artistic Avant-garde of the early 19th century (like Dadaism, Situationism, and above all, performance art), books by authors like Philip Dick and James Graham Ballard and all those subcultures dedicated to esotericism and/or conspiratorial paranoia. The genre was initiated by the Throbbing Gristle, a British group that grew out of the artistic group COUM Transmission. Their debut Second Annual Report marked the musical boundaries of the scene (which developed in its own right thanks specifically to the incessant work of the group which published Fanzines, maintained contact with similar bands in England and the U.S., and published debut albums of other bands under its own Industrial Records label). The Industrial scene was marked by an almost terroristic use of noise, the total rejection of technical music, the use of pre-recorded tapes and the near-total rejection of any melodic form. Following on their example other groups emerged that, while being similar, developed the genre in very different directions, like the British groups Cabaret Voltaire and Clock DVA, the American Factrix, Boyd Rice and Monte Cazazza, the Australian S.P.K., the German Einstürzende Neubauten, the Italian F.A.R., other than Maurizio Bianchi, and the Slovenian Laibach. Over the course of the 1990s a new draft of musicians, such as Current 93, would take the genre towards the shores of folk music. Meanwhile, in the 1990s, the term 'industrial' would end up being used to define metal-derived bands like Ministry, Skinny Puppy, Godflesh and Nine Inch Nails" (http://it.wikipedia.org/wiki/Industrial). A good book for in-depth reading is *Re/Search. Manuale di cultura industriale*, edited by Paolo Bandera, Milan, Shake, 1998, derived from *RE-SEARCH - Industrial culture handbook*, originally published in 1983.

26 Evidently here Mariano Equizzi refers to the most politicized phase of Italian punk which, in any houses, we saw take on other dimensions, tendentially a-political, as described in the preceding paragraphs.

27 Mariano Equizzi recommends viewing the site: <www.oec.com> in order to better understand the spaces and the sounds of the industrial world and its surroundings.

The Art of Networking: The Pioneers

For a New Cartography of Reality

The concept of a *new cartography of reality* was developed in January 1993 by Mario Canali, Antonio Caronia, Antonio Glessi, Paolo Rosa, Giacomo Verde, Maria Grazia Mattei and Gino di Maggio, at the Mudima Foundation in Milan. The group of artists and scholars produced a document that can be considered the first "manifesto of the virtual era", stressing the affirmation of a new art form that involved all the senses, to "overturn the supremacy of the image, of the tyranny of sight so that a new network of relationships of the body with the world, richer and more problematic, could emerge". This way our body could relate with other "virtual egos" and experience a dematerialised and hybridised, expanded self.

All our practice and research in these years shows how far each of us is from a glorification of technology or from the illusion that electronics can give back a world (real or fictitious) purified of contradictions. In one way or another all of us have taken the marriage between man and machine as a "dirty alliance", as an element displacing contradictions, not as the pacification or realisation of an impossible utopia. None of us wants to "exit the world", even because parallel worlds multiply today, and without redefinition of relationships (maybe even borders) between reality and imagination we risk not knowing where we exited and where we enter. The preliminary condition to be able to start mapping these new territories is certainly the complete assumption of the materiality (or immateriality) of experience, the fragmentation of the body, even its dehumanisation: but without the cynical complacency of whoever seeks an alibi for their impotence in the glorification of the living; and with the worry (which we believe we've always shown) about making theoretical research and communicative practice progress side by side. This ambitious but necessary operation of redefining the categories and reading practices and crossing the world (the worlds), renewing a bond between theory and practice in an action that is increasingly both communicative and aesthetic, is what we propose today. Of course it can fail, but whoever never even attempted will fail more deeply[1].

These reflections, set in the period of maximum affirmation of Virtual Reality in Italy (and therefore are to be inserted in that context), emphasize a fundamental character of the artistic experimentation on the new – at the time – media, meaning that through these latter art becomes *practice* and not just theory, and has an effect on the body of the user, who is a participating *actor*.

In many publications and events of that time there is emphasis that technology in itself isn't important, what is important is its capability of starting up concrete interaction processes between individuals and technological instruments and between the individuals themselves. Attention is moved from the object to the construction process of *performing* communication spaces, as a territory of personal active (and in many cases playful) expression. We point out how the user becomes one of the protagonists of an event that invests him at both a cognitive level and a perceptive one, therefore being able to take the information creation and transmission process in hand, through direct feedback with the medium.

In the early 1990s, the idea of Virtual Reality in Italy was associated with something totally new, revealing new universes in which to amplify one's sensorial sphere. A direct main theme is created between previous experiences, from body art to video art, stressing versatility, transversality and the opening of channels of communication and expression. Concepts such as "multimediality", "interactivity", "new role of the artist and the user" are spoken of to define this emerging trend of artistic experimentation.

The idea is being publicised that with technological and interactive art the artistic product is freed from its *aura*, from its *hic et nunc*, from its *expositive value*, which make the work unique, unrepeatable, far from the individual's direct enjoyment and a sort of fetish to be observed from a distance. The aura, seen as untouchable originality deriving from the manual labour of a single artist, dies, whereas there is the birth, if we wish, of a plurality of as many "auras" as there are direct experiences of the users, who take part in the creative process. The basic theoretical reference becomes the book by Walter Benjamin *The Work of Art in the Age of Its Technical Reproducibility*. In the 1930s, Benjamin analysed the appearance of photography and cinema in the nascent mass society, understanding the importance of the union between art and technique for a massive use of the products of cultural industry.

Mariacristina Cremaschi, one of the most active Italian theorists on these subjects in the nineties[2], describes technological art, in a text she wrote in 1997, as *the art that isn't there*:

The artist is the designer of a work that "isn't" in a concrete materiality and doesn't manifest itself without a user. Through their interactivity with the work, it evolves metamorphically performing the generative project, and the artist, from single author, becomes process activator, while the user becomes co-author of these processes. Indeed, on the one hand the artist entrusts the description of his mental model to the immaterial support of software and on the other hand entrusts creation of the work to the user through interactivity with the environment that has been created (Cremaschi, 1997).

Marcel Duchamp is considered one of the first artists to work on the concept of "interactivity", as the user's physical and not just psychical action. His *Etant donnés* (1946-66) installation contemplates the *concrete action* of the user who, attracted by two holes made in a door, puts his eyes to them, thus being able to surpass the *threshold zone* that initially separates him from the work of art.

When the spectator puts his eyes to the holes made in the *Etant Donnés* door, there is a perspective view, falsely close, of the immobile and desirable body [of a woman] laid down on the ground, as well as the surrounding countryside (Speroni, 1995).

Direct references become the works of the early 1920s, up to the experiments of the Neo-avantgarde of the 1960s, as a stimulus to work on redefining communicative languages and codes. For example, by stressing the "active" character of the user, Nam June Paik suggests the idea of "television as pure significant materiality, of which every spectator can reconfigure its sense in absolute freedom" (Candalino, Gasparini, 1996).

As early as the end of the 1980s installations of digital art via video and CD-rom began to flourish in Italy, nevertheless presenting a program planned by the artist and therefore possibilities of finite enjoyment, whereas on the network the idea of trial enjoyment by multiple subjects will catch on. The concepts of creating collective and interactive works appear more evident within the sphere of the Internet.

Networking art on the Internet is to be seen as networks of relationships that become established among individuals. The artist, creator of network contexts and networking platforms, takes on a lead role in the shoes of the network operator, but does not determine how the artistic process is carried out, which should be free and spontaneous, amenable to the personal creativity of everyone who wants to interact.

Making Networks: the First Festivals and Mailing Lists

In the 1980s the first festivals centred on art and new technologies were set up on an international level. These were attended by many artists and theorists from all over the world; unfortunately in only a few cases there was the active presence of Italian artists who experimented art and digital. This may be another reason why much of our reality has stayed unrelated to various processes that have invested international net culture[3].

In the few festivals organised in Italy in the 1980s, noteworthy experiences were created, many of which in artistic networking, others directed towards computer art, computer graphic and computer animation research, including the production of the first television signatures with graphic subjects (Mario Sasso's videogrammes are an example).

These experiences rank in the emerging phase of a "third culture", as defined by Vittorio Fagone in an article of his describing the Camerino Festival of Electronic Art, the first of the series in Italy. The "third culture" is the electronic one, which should fill the gap between the two macro-cultures, humanistic and scientific (thus defined by Charles Snow in his pamphlet translated in Italy in 1970), and which seemed to be the novelty at that time. Speaking of the "two cultures", Vittorio Fagone writes:

Luckily today there are two cultures with which to face a "third culture", the electronic one where engineers, mathematicians, computer scientists, architects, musicians and artists (or if you wish "visual operators"), graphic designers face off, live and work together, often exchanging models and objectives, if not roles. Electronic art occupies this space, an open area in rapid expansion and development[4].

In this panorama, it is the collaboration of artists and operators of various sectors, where the networking pioneers work via computers and telematic networks.

In July 1985 the first computer art show, named *Il Pulsante Leggero, was organised* in Italy at the 5 X 5 Art Gallery in Rome; at the same time a spontaneous association was set up, with the same name, with the support of artists, photographers, art critics, musicians, computer experts, cultural operators – coordinated by Rinaldo Funari. (...) *Il Pulsante Leggero*, which nearly all Italian computer art artists adhere to, was present in the same year at the only institutional cultural event in Italy, the Camerino Festival of Electronic Art, organised by the Camerino University, by the Comune of Camerino and by the Mountain Community, as well as in subsequent years. *Il Pulsante Leggero* association promotes and participates in numerous manifestations in Italy and abroad, in particular *Imagina* in Monte Carlo, Siggraph in the USA and in many cultural events[5].

During the first respite events in Italy in the field of experimentation between art and new technologies, we mention Planetary Network organised by Roy Ascott, Don Foresta, Robert Adrian, Tom Sherman and by the Italians Maria Grazia Mattei and Tommaso Trini for the Venice Biannual 1986.
In the video "Telematic Art of the 1980s" produced by the Fine Arts Academy, Carrara (2005), Maria Grazia Mattei is interviewed on the Planetary Network and presents the project:

In 1986 the Venice Biennale was centred on the art-science relationship in an unusual way, seeing that our country seems very inattentive to all things that are phenomena of cultural experimentation linked to technology that are not Art with a capital A; yet that year the doors opened to a series of meetings and debates about the use of new technologies in the artistic field. One of the projects at the Corderie was called Planetary Network; we used that large space to create a kind of large laboratory. We put artists on stage with analogue technologies of the time, to give life to a kind of large experimental workshop that connected artists around the world. This project, Planetary Network, was signed by three curators: Roy Ascott from England, Tommaso Trini and myself from Italy and Don Foresta from France. So we can say that there were four corners of the world attempting to structure this project, reasoning on the art of communication, telematic art, furthermore using the electronic mail of the time in the laboratory and planning phase (Bassi B., Bassi D., 2005)[6].

The Planetary Network project lies within the trend of experimentation on remote communication in those years, using fax technology to connect positions in England, Canada and Australia. Planetary Network gave life to an experience of fax art based on the reworking procedure of words and images transmitted in a sort of creative dialogue between sender and receiver. On this aspect, Maria Grazia Mattei adds:

It was very exciting to see the image that came back reworked, to see that there had been communication. There was a communicative dimension with the means we could work with at the time, that made us really experiment this remote action dialogue in real time and action-reaction that was not just voice. To send a visual message, see it return reworked, perceive the presence of the other person, you know and you feel that you're working with others, you live it in real time! (*ibid.*).

Remote artistic experimentation via satellite was the main testing ground for the first artists who worked on technology as networking experience. Among the projects by Kit Galloway and Sherrie Rabinowitz, we mention "Satellite Art Project" (1977), that develops by making dancers located in different places interact with each other. Or the "Hole in Space" (1980) experiment, where a Los Angeles position is put in satellite connection with another in New York and the people taking part in the performance can perceive the space in the same "virtual" place of the people who are physically in other areas of the world.

Other fathers of the networking art via telecommunications are Roy Ascott, Robert Adrian X, Fred Forest and Douglas Davis, who has been producing projects on the transmission of signals ever since the mid 1970s. Bridging the 1980s and 1990s, Richard Kriesche designed Telesculptures, based on the movement of objects triggered by flows of communications and data via the telephone or, in 1993, via the Internet[7].

Even Nam Jun Paik struggled with experiments with the satellite, planning a piano concert between San Francisco and Shanghai (1961-1962), or putting on parallel shows in different places, involving Douglas Davis, Charlotte Moorman and Joseph Beuys, during the inauguration of the Documenta VI show. Or for "Good Morning Mister Orwell", an event that connected New York with Paris, Germany and South Korea, in this case too with the active participation of numerous international artists.

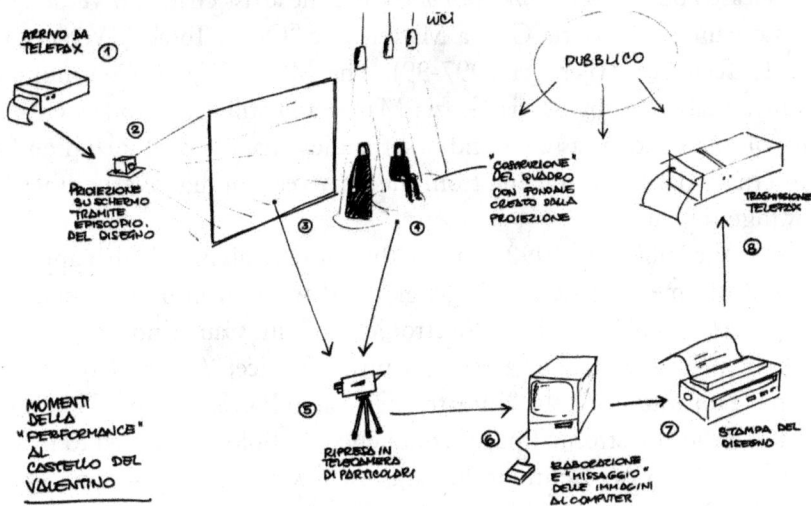

Drawing by Antonio Glessi (GMM). Project diagram which shows the elaboration flux of the images in the fax-performance "Paesaggio della Memoria: il Paradiso" [Landscape of Memory: Paradise] with live fax connections with Cardiff, Melbourne, Boston, Vienna. "Machina", Castello del Valentino, Turin, 1985.

Among the various Italian artists, the Giovanotti Mondani Meccanici (GMM) (*Worldly Mechanical Youngsters*) worked during those years developing the concept of "remote communication" and in the mid 1980s staged a fax performance with real time connection between Italy and positions installed in Cardiff, Melbourne and Vienna in *Memory Landscapes*, an initiative organised by Maria Grazia Mattei for the "Machine, Theatre, Technology Representation" Festival in Ivrea.

In November 1990, at the Palazzo Fortuny in Venice, "Virtual Worlds" took place, the first appointment in Italy dedicated to Virtual Reality (from 1986 to 1990, Maria Grazia Mattei was consultant for the "Video and New Images" sector of the Palazzo Fortuny). Guests were William Gibson, Derrick de Kerckhove, Paul Virilio, Philippe Quéau, Timothy Leary and it was the first appointment in Italy on an "official" level that spoke about cyberpunks and Virtual Reality (also present were the members of Shake Edizioni with their newly released book *Cyberpunk Anthology* and the artist Giacomo Verde). Other reviews organised by Maria Grazia Mattei were "Opera Totale" (Venice, 1996-99) and "Tecnoarte" (Perugia 1997-99). The MGM Digital Communication company, established by Maria Grazia Mattei and still active today, created an archive of 4,500 video cassettes and other audiovisual material including Italian and international works starting from the early years of digital experimentation <www.mgmdigital.com>.

Bridging the 1980s and 1990s, among the few festivals in Italy that approached the world of emerging new technologies and were an important networking platform, are the "Festival of Electronic Art" in Camerino and the work previously mentioned at the Palazzo Fortuny in Venice, "Art and Computers" in Lugano, "Taormina Art", the "Inteatro" festival in Polverigi (AN), "U-Tapes" in Ferrara and the "Electronic Image" conferences in Bologna. Added to this is the work of the Video Art Centre in Ferrara or a few particularly sensitive galleries such as the Diagramma in Milan.

None of these festivals has a tradition similar to the international ones, such as the Ars Electronica Festival in Linz, to mention an example, and no public Italian structure has decided to ride the wave and start up a centre for research on art and the new technologies equal to the Ars Electronica Center. One of the consequences is the total fragmentation of local experiences in those years and the lack of preservation of the historical and artistic memory of the first works of Italian electronic art. It is also extremely difficult to recreate an historical route of those experiences, even on the Internet there are no more materials, except for a few isolated cases, and the only active testimonies are those of the editors who gave life to the events and the artists who participated in them[8].

One further consequence is that few Italian artists drawn to the world of art and new technologies were present in those years of initiatives abroad. For example, in the 1980s and 1990s the renowned Prix Ars Electronica was won by Italian artists only in the first four years, in particular by Mario Canali, Mario Sasso and Nicola Sani, in the computer animation category. Groups such as Studio Azzurro, Correnti Magnetiche and Giovanotti Mondani Meccanici were also present in various international initiatives; but in general there was a certain "void" and in my opinion this sounds an alarm to show the constant delay of the institutional policies in Italy that didn't work towards promoting art and new media, neither inside nor outside Italy.

A singular experience that tries to build a "bridge" with foreign initiatives is the Art of Listening (LADA), a festival that began in 1991, in Rimini, organised by Roberto Paci Dalò/Giardini Pensili, with the collaboration of ORF Kunstradio and RAI Audiobox (the only Italian festival from those days that still has an Internet site: <http://www.giardini.sm/lada>).

Giardini Pensili is a project that began in 1985, organised by Roberto Paci Dalò and Isabella Bordoni. It is based on acoustical and visual experiment promoting a creative relationship between technology, video and theatre. The Giardini Pensili works are staged not only in theatres but also in concert halls, museums and public spaces. LADA, defined as *Radio and Art International Festival-on site | on-line | on-air*, is one of the most uninterrupted experiences that has involved an international nucleus of artist up to 1998. The first appointment, in September 1991, was an international show of acoustical radio and art in electronic space and investigates the use of technology in sound. "A form of acoustical art created specifically for radio, in which any type of text, literary or poetic, is transposed to an acoustic context, thus acquiring new meanings and relations" (Roberto Paci Dalò, 1991).

Various networking projects on the use of public space as a sphere of artistic work have been organised during LADA festivals. Among these, *Publiphono*, an event based on the sound amplification system of the Rimini beach for live diffusion of acoustical environmental performances along twenty kilometres of coastline. In 1995 Giardini Pensili also participated in a telecommunication project, undertaking the artistic management of the Mediterranean network of the Horizontal Radio project, at the Ars Electronica Festival in Linz.

Roberto Paci Dalò actively collaborated in the FutureLab for Ars Electronica (from 1996), proposing various projects including "Atlas Linz" in 1998. Today the Giardini Pensili network has numerous collaborators and is still active in theatre, music and new technologies in Italy and abroad <www.giardini.sm>.

During the 1990s in Italy, initiatives for art and technology increased, even though they were still limited and for experts[9]. On an international level, even after the success of many electronic and digital art festivals, mainly in Northern Europe and the USA, on-line discussion spaces begin to appear on BBS and mailing lists.

The true pioneers are Carl Loeffler and Fred Truck, who started up the Art Com Electronic Network (ACEN), a platform for exchange, sharing and information created in the Whole Earth 'Lectronic Link/WELL.

Inke Arns writes:

ACEN offered its users access to electronic publications, a mail system and, ten years before e-commerce appeared on the web, a (virtual) shopping street with shops regarding art (2004).

Also in that period is the The Thing experience, one of the first platforms of BBS communication <http://bbs.thing.net>, that became a reference point for the debate about art and new media and the subsequent net.art. The Thing was established by the Austrian Wolfgang Staehle and Gisela Ehrenfried in 1991, accessible through the New York telephone network, offering contents via BBS and services as internet provider <www.thing.net>. In 1992 there is the addition of The Thing Cologne and The Thing Vienna and subsequently The Thing Berlin, Amsterdam, Frankfurt and Basil. The Thing Rome, was established later, in 2000.

As reported in the book Net.Art. The Art of Connecting, by Marco Deseriis and Giuseppe Marano (founders of the Rome node of The Thing),

in 1995 the nodes of The Thing New York <bbs.thing.net> and Vienna <www.thing.at> moved to the Web, thanks to an interface written by the young Viennese programmer Max Kossatz, which kept the community characteristics of the BBS, with the possibility for members to chat, post comments and consult discussion lists. Provided with a vast archive of artistic projects, sound documents, radio broadcasts and reviews, articles and interviews, over the years The Thing was to become a necessary reference point both for underground circuits and for those of avant-garde art (2003).

In those same years, between 1994 and 1995, other networking platforms came to life, offering low cost spaces on the Internet and contexts of reflection and criticism of the net culture: De Digitale Stad in Amsterdam, established in January 1994, International City Federation in Berlin, founded on the model of the Digitale Stad in the same year, the Public Netbase in Vienna, 1995, Ljubliana Digital Media Lab in 1995, Backspace in London, 1996.

In 1995, the first international mailing lists for critical discussion and reflection on art and the new media and digital culture are established. Among these "Nettime" <www.nettime.org>, the very first one of them, "Syndicate" moderated by Andreas Broeckmann and Inke Arns <http://www.colossus.v2.nl/syndicate>, "Rhizome", which came about from the work of Mark Tribe in Berlin in 1996 and was then transferred to New York <www.rhizome.org>, "7-11", the first international mailing list dedicated entirely to experiments in net.art founded in 1997 by the Cologne artist Udo Noll and later accommodated by the server of the Slovenian media art centre managed by Vuk Cosic and Luca Frelih <www.ljudmila.org>, "Faces", created by Kathy Rae Huffman, Diana McCarty and Valie Djordjevic in 1997 and focussed on women and new technologies <www.faces-l.net> and many others[10].

The origin of the "Nettime" mailing list undoubtedly deserves more investigation, since over the course of the years it became the most famous international mailing list for comparison and discussion in the net culture panorama. This is exactly where the debate on net.art initially developed, continued then in other international mailing lists, from "7-11" to "Syndicate" and "Rhizome". The origin of Nettime sees, among other things, several artists, theorists and Italian activists at work, who in June 1995 participated in its foundation, in a rare episode in which local net culture stands up to the international net culture in Italy.

Diana McCarty, in one of her writings from 1997, tells that during the Venice Biennale in 1995, a meeting was held among artists, media theorists and European activists[11]. This is the second international meeting of the Medien Zentral Kommittee (ZK), organised by Nils Roeller and Pit Schultz, which

101

began by proposing a critical vision on the media and digital culture (Netz-Kritik) in reply to the all-American line proposed by the magazine WIRED. At the time called "Californian ideology", following the writings of Richard Barbrook and Andy Cameron, this saw the predominance of "a vision of the neo-liberal technology of a white male techno-élite" (Diana McCarty).

The first ZK meeting took place previously near Frankfurt. In the second Venetian meeting, called "Club Berlin", the "Nettime" mailing list came into being. Club Berlin was proposed as an art club event that lasted three evenings in the Malibran Theatre and had the participation of numerous activists, artists, organisers, media theorists and international writers. Among those present were Heath Bunting, Vuk Cosic, David D'heilly, Paul Garrin, Kathy Rae Huffman, Geert Lovink, David Garcia, Pit Schultz, Diana McCarty, Nils Roeller, Gereon Schmitz, Dejan Stretanovic, Siegfried Zielinski and the Italians Roberto Paci Dalò of Giardini Pensili, Alessandro Ludovico of Neural and Tommaso Tozzi of Strano Network, along with other members of Strano Network and the FidoNet network.

The "Nettime" mailing list started up in the summer of 1995, moderated by Pit Schultz and Geert Lovink, initially with twenty members, growing exponentially in the following months and in a short time becoming the model of European avant-garde. In an interview about "Nettime", Pit Schultz states that "Nettime" tried to renew a certain political agenda, generally defined as leftism, which after 1990 became boringly conservative. Over the years the mailing list proposed a critical and not dogmatic vision of the use of new technologies, promoting the network idea as a space for networking and dialogue. Among the subjects for discussion: net.art, public space, digital democracy, mediatic and artistic activism. At the same time, "Nettime" tried to surpass the dualism of an a-critical exhilaration of everyone who welcomed the new virtual worlds and the cynical pessimism of many journalists and intellectuals of what was defined "old media" at the time. "Nettime" action was not exhausted by a mailing list, it gave rise to a network of people, projects and considerations that brought about publications, readers, Internet sites in various languages, putting into circulation the net critique even outside the network.

Subsequent meetings of the ZK took place during the Metaforum II conference in October 1995 in Budapest and during the Next Five Minutes festival in Amsterdam in 1996, in which the first ZK reader was published. The first "official" meeting of the "Nettime" mailing list is dated May 1997 on the occasion of the "Beauty and the East" conference promoted by the Ljudmila platform in Lubiana, Slovenia, that had the participation of more than one hundred international artists and activists and there was the staging of the publication of the ZKP4 reader <www.ljudmila.org/nettime/zkp4>.

The "Nettime" mailing list is also a platform where the first reflections on the term net.art took place. Net.art (with the dot between net and art) was used for the first time by the Slovenian artist Vuk Cosic and refers to a fragment of ASCII characters sent by e-mail to the Slovenian artist in December 1995 by an anonymous remailer, in which appeared, among other indecipherable characters, the word Net.Art. In March 1997, the Russian net artist Alexei Shulgin disseminated in the "Nettime" mailing list the bizarre "legend" attributing the origin of the term Net.art to this episode (on "Net.Art.The Origin", message sent to "Nettime" on 18th March 1997)[12]. Aside from this anecdote and outside its "formal" origin, the term net.art immediately leads back to the particular phase dated 1995-1997 where numerous international artists and theorists were active, who used the "Nettime" mailing list as a space for main confrontation.

A debate that was to have its "institutional" legitimation in 1997, during the Documenta X festival in Kassel, Germany, when net.art entered with full rights in the panorama of contemporary art. During Documenta X, there was also the first attempt to map the network of European digital culture. The *Media Lounge Database* originated from the Hybrid Workspace, and was managed by the Society for Old and New Media in Amsterdam (www.waag.org). The database, called *Hybrid Media Lounge Database* and edited by Laura Martz, Geert Lovink, Thorsten Schilling and Marleen Stikker, became the visibility platform for hundreds of international net culture organisations of the moment <www.medialounge.net>.

Organisations, projects and individuals from all over Europe were invited to contribute by sending information about their work and networks, to create the contents of the database. The Lounge includes all the organisations that work in art and media to promote a critical vision of the network. A CD-ROM shows the contents of the database dated 1st February 1999 and contextualises the various groups and individuals inside the territorial maps, through which one can reflect on the diffusion and development of the net culture of the time.

Simultaneously in Italy, between the end of the 1980s and the first half of the 1990s, net culture development was closely linked to the networking practices and developed mostly within the counterculture artistic and activist realities, near the hacker scene.

From Video to Computer Art

In the first phase of Italian artistic creation with the new media, in the 1980s, several collective practices started up aimed at creating networks that operate mainly in the video sector, and then spread in network during the following decade. The aim that animates the work of many artists at the time, in most cases is to create multi-directional communicational contexts in which the people can freely express themselves and take part in becoming collective processes, the spontaneous evolution of which originates the artistic event. Therefore they act not just on imaginary codes through experimenting and creating new languages, but processes are encouraged that directly touch the system of interpersonal relationships and the interconnection of technologies, from video to the computer. *This happens by collective operations that try to build new means of communication.*

An example of this collectivisation of means of communication is MINIMAL TV, which made its debut in Vince (FI) in July 1996. MINIMAL TV was created by the *Quinta Parete* group[13], made up of the artists Federico Bucalossi, Claudio Parrini, Giacomo Verde and by Vanni Cilluffo, Francesco Galluzzi, Vania Pucci, Alessandro Barbadoro and Renzo Bordini.

Minimal TV is the smallest TV in the world: it broadcasts its programmes by cable to TV sets placed on "streets". Minimal TV is doing TV starting from the bare essentials, nearly zero, because *television doesn't exist, it's only shapes* (Giacomo Verde, from the site <www.verdegiac.com>).

Using a very simple technical instrument set-up (an amateur TV camera, an audio-video mini mixer, a Macintosh for the jingles, two video cameras in S.VHS for recorded reports, a video box to dialogue with the host, the Internet connection to create and send texts and images), people in a given location can build their own TV, directing themselves and their desire to communicate something.

Therefore the video experiment is associated to a "theatre experience" that leads to transmitting contents in a spontaneous way, overtaking the traditional way the generalist media make communications, based on coded rules. We arrive at a *personalised* television, that favours the *spontaneous construction of collective imagination*, starting from an alternative use of the media. A little like the closed circuit video experiments of the video artists from the 1960s and 1970s, with the difference that this time manipulating the communication codes isn't just the artists, who want to offer only *contexts*, it is the people in certain cities, countries, squares.

Giacomo Verde again stresses, in the *Documedia Percorsi Multimediali* convention held at RAI in Rome in May 1998, that at the beginning of the MINIMAL TV broadcasts the people involved initially tend to imitate the traditional manners of television communication and the specific types of generalist TV; then later they begin to create new communications and representation codes, more similar to those of ballad singers, folk theatre, street theatre. Hence TV is *spontaneously self-run and created,* thus acquiring a new collective sense, certainly more real in its *obvious* pretence. In this way there occurs the *revelation of the communicative hidden events* that in much generalist TV are concealed to obtain a greater reality effect: that is the reason for Giacomo Verde's phrase *television doesn't exist, it's only shapes.* A similar approach was later carried forward by the Telestreets, as we will see in later chapters.

Another collective audio visual experiment was carried out by the Pigreca group (Flavia Alman and Sabine Reiff) and by Giacomo Verde, in contact with the Hamburg group Van Gogh TV, in the "Virtual Square" event (1992), for the Documenta IX manifestation in Kassel. Using a satellite connection with Van Gogh TV, several Italian squares ("the little squares") were put in contact (again via satellite) with the squares of Hamburg, Tokyo, Moscow, etc. (the experiment took place in Italy in the Cox 18 Social Centre, Milan). This way the people who participate in the interactive TV manifestation can exchange opinions and information with other individuals living in distant cities and thus exploit the television medium to create horizontal and bidirectional dialogue.

Speaking of "Virtual Square", Giacomo Verde adds:

The spectacular level has nothing to do with it here. It is another level of communication that cannot be understood by anyone who has the mono-directional *forma mentis* of communication. If you hang out on the web you realise that after a while the essence of communication is not what we are accustomed to being *subjected to* with television; the traditional parameters of communications flow transmission collapse and have no more sense: the models of *interpersonal communication*, the *sensorial relationship*, the *sharing of communicative hidden details* become important (1998).

Therefore the reference parameters are others; they are those that come from the true spontaneity of people in the squares, inserted in their life contexts and not in the specially built television studios. Whoever interacts in these networking platforms can try making television by putting their own scenario on stage, giving life to an activity that is much more similar to experimental theatre, where the division between audience and actors is no longer so obvious.

Giacomo Verde calls himself a tekno-artist. He has been working in theatre and visual arts since the 1970s. Starting in the 1980s he created *oper'azioni* connected to the creative use of "poor" technology: video art, techno-performances, theatre shows, installations, educational laboratories. He is the inventor of Tele-Racconto – theatrical performance that combines narration, micro-theatre and macro direct shooting – a technique used also for live video backdrops in concerts and poetry recitals. He is among the first Italians to create works of interactive art and net.art. His constant is to reflect while playfully experimenting with the ongoing techno-anthropo-logico mutations and create connections between the various artistic types <www.verdegiac.org>.

Giacomo Verde's path, starting from the street theatre, led him to create the Tele-Racconto by first experimenting with video, then with digital. In connection with the Tele-Racconto practice, but in a different expressive context, in 1998 he developed the Mandalic Stories hypertext narrative, created from a proposal by Giacomo Verde to the Zone Gemma group, initially formed by the artist Massimo Contrasto (pseudonym of Massimo Cittadini), dramatist Andrea

Balzola, composer Mauro Lupone, critic Anna Maria Monteverdi and Giacomo Verde. The Zone Gemma association is a laboratory of biotechnological culture, coming from the idea of having theatrical research interact with tekno-artistic research (i.e. the use and experimentation of audiovisual and digital technologies), to create interactive events and areas of communication and entertainment <www.zonegemma.org>. Actions beyond performances, as Giacomo Verde writes again in 1997[14].

Mandalic Stories is a dramatic hypertext that takes place in seven episodes, written by Andrea Balzola, connected to each other by a narrative thread and developed with the interaction of video-backdrops in 2D and 3D, placed at the four corners of the scenic space. The cyber-narrator, Giacomo Verde, is in the centre of the scene and the audience at the four sides, surrounding him. Narration execution is defined by the narrator through dialogue with the audience and by interaction with the video-backgrounds. The final version of Mandalic Stories is the central plan (in Sanscrit, Mandala means "magic circle") and implies the graphic use of FlashMX, evolution of the version with the Mandala System created by Massimo Cittadini. Thus, in Mandalic Stories 3.0 the navigation of the interactive depths (reworked in Flash by Lucia Paolini and Francesco Menconi) takes place on network too, via the site <www.zonegemma.org>.

Scenic interaction with the video backgrounds that we find in Mandalic Stories was initially developed by Giacomo Verde with the Tele-Racconto, even though with different means of expression, narration and language. In Tele-Racconto, created in 1989, very simple daily life objects (such as mints, nut shells, spaghetti, crackers) and body parts (fingers, hands) put on stage and filmed with a TV camera are transmitted via video, taking on new meanings following a narrative track and once again revealing the hidden details of television communication pretence. Body performance therefore becomes *social meta-comment*: through body action a critical reflection takes place about the manners of television communication and representation. From body *experience* we reflect on our imagination, stimulating the mind to pause on uncommon associations.

The same margin of fiction/reality is made obvious in the virtual character of the Euclide program, animated by Giacomo Verde and technically produced by Stefano Roveda (Pi Greco group, Milan) with the collaboration of the artist

Flavia Alman, who at the time (1994) was a member of the Correnti Magnetiche group.

The synthetic interactive character Euclide is visualised by a computer and whereas at the beginning his capability for dialogue may seem the result of a computer program, it is soon seen during the interaction that he is animated by Giacomo Verde using a glove of Virtual Reality (a kind of cybernetic marionette). The artificial and the real blend in this bio-cybernetic individual, but also in this case the staging is made obvious and more space is given to the process of dialogue than technology in a strict sense.

The man-machine marriage seen as territory for critical experimentation and active communication interface is even more obvious in the Mandalic Stories show, in which the Tele-Racconto is produced through the Mandala System, the interface device used by Massimo Contrasto Cittadini to create *virtual interaction contexts.*

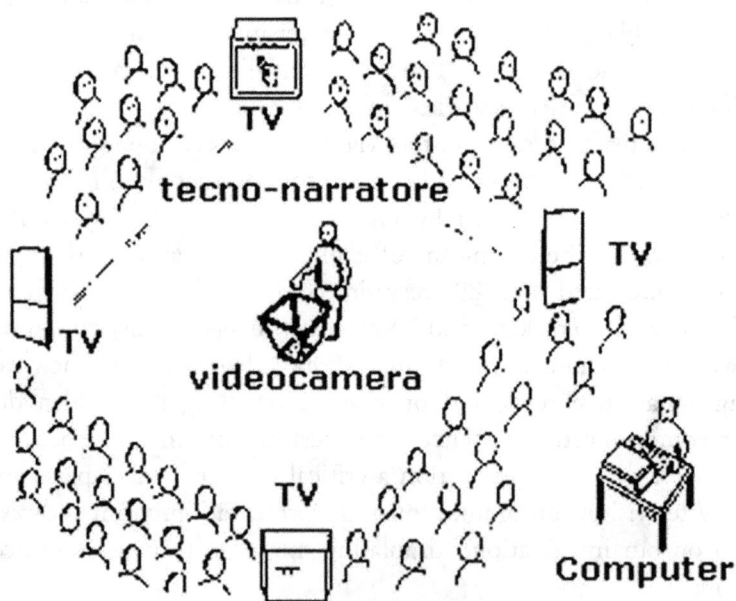

ZoneGemma, Teno-Racconto "Storie Mandaliche", diagram of the performance designed by Giacomo Verde, 1999.

In the Mandalic Stories show by the Zone Gemma cultural association, theatrical practice is referred to digital by creating performances-actions through the gestures of a *virtual double*. More precisely, the Tele-Racconto practice is implemented in the artificial settings of the Mandala System: body parts (for example the hands) by Giacomo Verde are digitalised and are visible on a screen where they can interact with artificial icons created with Mandala. Action isn't done artistically to create finished products, but to give life to open communication contexts.

In the panorama on video, computers and networking in the 1980s, we must mention the experience of Correnti Magnetiche. The group was set up in 1985, organised by Mario Canali, Riccardo Sinigaglia and Adriano Abbado, to explore the potential of video and, above all, computer graphics. Soon other artistic contributions joined in on many different levels, giving life to a network of collaboration, with work by Flavia Alman, Sabine Reiff, Leonardo Aurelio, Marcello Campione and Elio Massarini, in addition to the three founders.

Maria Grazia Mattei, wrote in 1996:

Correnti Magnetiche expresses one big tension: pushing artistic expression towards new dimensions mixing languages and technologies, creating common paths between images, forms, colours and sounds. And then there is the great goal of interactivity, of role reversals between audience, work and artist. A dream once cherished by historical vanguards but only today, with recourse to new digital technologies, seems fully realised (Mattei, 1996)15.

Correnti Magnetiche is one of the first groups, along with very few others, who try to use the computer not just for work but to give life to computer graphic works that are recognised internationally, such as the Ars Electronica Festival in Linz. They began by considering a centre for research on Virtual Reality, use of multimedia and interactivity. In the various Correnti Magnetiche videos, collected in the video DVD "Correnti Magnetiche 1985-1996", there is experimentation with video and with 3D computer graphics, coming to progressive aesthetic research in the elaboration of synthetic images.

The idea is to work with "virtual" materials, studying the manners of man-machine interaction and writing programs directly to elaborate abstract dynamic forms, 3D creations that can easily be made automatically today, but at the time were the result of complex research in the aesthetic, visual, perceptive and programming sector. After the first videos on three-dimensional images that covered all of the second half of the 1980s, with the 1990s the Correnti Magnetiche group began working with Virtual Reality, producing various installations that allowed the audience to interact and feel "involved", through navigation and sensorial immersion devices. Among these are *Satori* (1993-1994), *Ulisse* (1995), *Inside* (1996), *Ritmi* (1997), *Neuronde* (1997), *E.mx* (1999), *Scribble-Test* (2002)[16].

Other artists who since the 1980s had been experimenting with digital, creating videos and computer art works are GMM, *Giovanotti Mondani Meccanici*, a group founded in 1984 by Antonio Glessi and Andrea Zingoni in Florence, soon making a name for itself as one of the main Italian groups in this sector <www.gmm.fi.it>.

A multidisciplinary laboratory, it had the participation of artists, designers, videomakers, musicians, computer scientists and science philosophers, becoming a concrete expression of what is called the 'third culture', to use the words of Vittorio Fagone. In an interview for the Taormina Arte Festival (1992), Antonio Glessi, Andrea Zingoni and Roberto Davini presented their artistic work, present in various expressive fields from the beginning:

> We are interested in searching for a "place of absence" where communication can develop its possibilities, its presences. We believe in dialogue and want to bow to its demands. (…) In the early works the Mystery theme was quite present, which is directly connected with the communications theme. It is clear to us how, without this curiosity towards what is not standard, towards what cannot be explained, and is the force that commands communication, it is impossible to exchange any information. I never communicate with myself, I always communicate with what I don't know. The rest is just conquest and horror. (…) It is a matter, in general, of using the means suited to building that place of global crowding that allows everyone to communicate with everything. In our case it is a matter of adapting techniques to the curiosity of the mystery. We are attracted by what is Perturbing and, properly speaking, this is not the aim of the mystic, but rather the aim and interest towards life[17].

Beyond the mystery and the perturbing, the ironic component has always been important in the GMM's artistic research, accompanied by a certain desecrating scepticism towards the present, creating a con-fusion of the tragic with the comical. This is seen also in their likeable "creation", Gino the Chicken, the first chicken lost on the network, preaching philosophy about the contemporary age lost in cyberspace and later in various satirical-critical clips, "GinoTG", visible on the portal my-tv.it that made history[18].

In many of the GMM's creations, daily life encounters surreal and visionary settings, nearly grotesque, yet through which there can be a critical reflection about reality and about human attitudes.

The name Giovanotti Mondani Meccanici comes from the characters in their first works (dated 1983) who took life in the form of the cartoon computer. These strips, created graphically on an Apple II by Antonio Glessi and dramatised by Andrea Zingoni, initially published in the magazine "Frigidaire", were later adapted to the video formula, staged as brief "theatrical works". The images were artistically worked by Antonio Glessi, and mounted on a sound track perfected by Maurizio Dami, while the voices of the characters are based on a poetic text written by Andrea Zingoni. This how the actual dramas were made, like the "modern nocturne melodrama" titled *Giovanotti Mondani Meccanici* (1984), or the "gothic tragedy" *Giovanotti Mondani Meccanici against Dracula* (1984), where the Giovanotti Mondani Meccanici act in ironic-tragic contexts; they are "three cybernetic hooligans, a bit punk, a bit dark, a bit dandy, a bit Huey, Dewey, Louie" (Giovanotti Mondani Meccanici).

In short this is the content of the first theatrical-digital works[19]:

Giovanotti Mondani Meccanici
Modern Nocturne Melodrama
by Andrea Zingoni
Computer Art: Antonio Glessi
Computer Music: Maurizio Dami
Voices: Victor Beard, Eva Ciucci, Andrea Zingoni, Maurizio Dami
June 1984 – Runtime 12' – Format: 3/4' U-Matic

Content: Projected on a metropolitan lunar scenario, Ella's evening twists sadly, beginning and ending at the Tabù bar. Behind her appear the GMM, Giovanotti Mondani Meccanici, subspecies of replicants, very efficient and almost unpleasant. They trick her and she believes them; drunk on dreams, whisky and amphetamines all she can do is let herself be robbed and raped. The amorous disappointment, tiredness, violence, could all be a joke. It is 0h30 in the morning on the 1st of April with the story begins…

Giovanotti Mondani Meccanici against Dracula
Gothic Tragedy
by Andrea Zingoni
Computer Art: Antonio Glessi
Sound Editor: Maurizio Dami
Music: Verdi, "Forza del Destino", Overture, Alexander Robotnik, "Dance Boy Dance" (Maso Records) – Bach, "St. John Passion"
Voices: Alessandro Benvenuti (Dracula), Rolando Mugnai, Roberto Nistri, Paola Pacifico (the GMM)
July 1984 – Runtime 13' – Format: 3/4' U-Matic

Content: ironic revisitation of the famous myth of the Prince of Darkness. Dracula, a disenchanted vampire in a senile crisis, receives the Giovanotti in his lugubrious castle. The three of them offer him their jugular veins so he can take a colossal drink. The prince, tempted, just can't refuse and gulps down a deadly dose of blood … with hepatitis.

This video and the later ones (in which the theatre performance encounters the digital images and the digital sound treatment), such as *The Colour of Darkness* (1985), *Marionetti* (1985), *In-A-Gadda-Da-Vida* (1985), *Drum* (1985) and *Movements in the background* (1986), give life to imaginative worlds located on the borderline between reality and desire, classical myths and fiction, settings that are ordinary and surreal, real and synthetic.

A journey is undertaken in the imaginary world of Aguares, the Grand Duke of the oriental part of Hades, who falls hopelessly in love with a little girl and "who, for the inhabitants of the Infinite night, becomes the seduced demon who talks of colours" (*The Colour of Darkness*). Or the adventures of Marionetti ensue, "a kind, ironic character, always hovering between situations of plain comedy (Marionetti/marionettes) or sophisticated futuristic atmospheres (Marionetti/Marinetti)" (*Marionetti*, video from 1985). Or there is participation in an experiment of theatre "without body", "a testimony of those Indian eyes through which the English saw India, an India that was both physical and metaphysical" (*In-A-Gadda-Da-Vida*). There is revisitation in an ironical key to the tragedy of Orlando, "with his calculator spillage that allows him to change the ending of the story, interacting with reality" (*Drum*). We dive into the poetic reconstruction of "a marine landscape populated by fish-men, castaways, derelicts, imaginary marine compositions, wild seabeds" *(Movimenti sul fondo/ Movements in the background).*

The GMM's path is an artistic one that uses various techniques and media to communicate the becoming of what exists, without putting themselves in an educational position, but leaving the possibility for an interpretation that is open and free of transmitted contents. In 1991, at the Pecci Museum of Contemporary Art in Prato, the GMM organised an exhibition called *Tecnomaya in Infotown,* bringing the video installations inside a museum structure: the *Electronic Mandala,* "electronic creatures" with giddy colours that cause the GMM to be defined as *hackers of the imagination.*

The exhibition was divided into two areas: in the first one (IN/OUT) a pyramid of monitors transmitted data that was selected and processed at high speed by a program (the data came from video disks about the Florentine artistic heritage, subliminal messages – among them the subliminal virus RIBELLATI! by Tommaso Tozzi, images of current affairs, communications from hackers, key words, virus), in the second wall/interface two large vertical 'X's formed by monitors project the synthesis of this data, that appear as so many visual splinters. At the centre of the X monitors were two Electronic Mandalas, psychoactive circles formed by energetic colours. The Electronic Mandala came from the elaborations of interfaced computers, consequent to sending starting inputs and, in the words of Andrea Zingoni, *they take life almost by themselves, giving life to the universes hidden in the digital circuits.*

The Man-Machine Interface

In the early 1990s, there was remarkable interest in Italy for everything that was Virtual Reality. Already in the mid 1980s various artists began working on interconnections between video and computers. Many of them entered in contact, collaborated and gave life to a network of experiences. This networking component was even more alive in the independent art circuits, which more often than not was shown inside self-run spaces or social centres. Many artists, among them the Correnti Magnetiche *(Magnetic Currents)* group and the GMM too, were interested in the possibilities of interaction in virtual settings. These studies join with the experiments carried forward previously on "tele-presence" and on the simultaneous connection via satellite of people in different locations, of which we wrote above.

Even though it's difficult to attribute absolute authorship in this field where the most varied scholars interact and continuous applications follow one another, the artistic works of Myron Krueger - the person who coined the term Artificial Reality - can be considered a starting point for experimentation in artificial settings.

Krueger's models from the 1960s-1970s, such as *Glowflow* (1969), *Metaplay* (1970), do not require the use of stereoscopic glasses, gloves or overalls, typical of immersive AR, but allow the user to enter an environment where images generated by the calculator are projected on the walls, while the gestures of interaction are perceived by the machine through the TV camera rather than through sensors. Thus the individual ends up participating in an event that stakes the basic mechanisms with which he perceives physical reality, producing his body and experiencing behaviours outside the rules[20].

In Italy, the direct consequence of these reflections comes with the experiments on the Mandala System. The Mandala System, similarly to Myron Krueger's experiences, allows taping the shapes of the users and mixing them with the program graphics, interfacing a computer with a TV camera through a digitalising card. Thus the shapes of the users appear on a TV (or on a screen) connected to the computer with a video genlock, whereas the movements of the user interact with the graphic animations created previously with the program.

The Mandala System software, a device for the Commodore Amiga Personal Computer created in 1986 by John Vincent and the other members of the Canadian Vivid Group <www.vividgroup.com>, has bi-directional optical-sound but not tactile interaction, even if the contact effect is extremely noticed since the individual sees himself moving in a virtual environment that is sensitive to his movement, which he can transform according to his creative instinct. With the Mandala System, whoever interacts becomes a kind of living mouse whose silhouette, in the virtual settings of the installation, can transform objects, change the background and build a virtual hypertext. There is no need for "immersive" helmets or gloves, movement is done in a two dimensional reality.

This *reality effect* therefore favours a progressive "adaptation" of the individual to the synthetic environment, while at the same time the system responds to the impulses received, progressively altering its aspect. Hence a work-user feedback relationship is created that makes it possible to set up a *dialogic* but not *transmission* communication between individual and medium.

Time by time the artist creates interaction contexts that help man and machine to interface. At the same time, seeing oneself reflected in an artificial world encourages reflection on the manner of perception and relationship with reality, and on the option of feeling and interacting. Antonio Glessi, in a 1998 interview, sustains:

In 1991-92 I launched a theory about Cyber-Transcendence. It was an idea, a little extreme and provocative, about digital seen as the last stage. Just as certain drugs can lead to altered states of awareness that come closer to one's inner life, and therefore since chemical formulas exist that allow it, there is probably a numerical formula that can lead to the discovery of its own "doubles". After all, the Mandala System is an experience with its own double that is seen to live inside a screen. The purpose of the Mandala is to be seen as a first level experience. This gives awareness of the possibility of another own double that can act in another way, therefore by expansion of the concept it can give many people the idea of what it means to "live on the network". This way we can experience what it means to act remotely in a digital world where certain manners of relationship are presented in a way that is different to reality[21].

The GMM, with the collaboration of Massimo Contrasto (Cittadini) and Tommaso Tozzi, presented *Buddha Vision,* their first interactive installation with the Mandala System, in 1991 at the "Art and Computer" review in Lugano. In *Buddha Vision* the user has the possibility to interact with "mystic" scenarios divided into episodes. This time it isn't the characters created at the computer, like the cartoon Giovanotti Mondani Meccanici, to adventure into imaginary worlds, it is the very individuals who can personally build their own trails of body experimentation (clearly within the limits of the possibilities offered by the program). Again in the 1998 interview, Antonio Glessi adds:

This installation, staked on the four elements – water, air, earth and fire – proposed situations that, starting from an Indian graphic, created scenarios for interacting above all on a musical level. It acted on pentatonic type of harmonic scales that offered various

115

combinations of sounds. For example, putting oneself before the image of Buddha, lotus flowers fell and sounds were made when they were picked up. Or before a table depicting the Tantric calendar, it could be considered a keyboard and generate the rhythmic sound of drums or ambient atmospheres depending on the type of scene and keys pressed. When the Buddha Vision was presented in small art galleries with little attendance and in situations that were not particularly crowded, the presupposition was created so that it worked as a personal meditation system. There was also the situation where people came and left right away because they didn't understand, but if they entered the game they stayed at length.

Another GMM installation was *Contacts of First Mutation*, presented at "Remote Future" (Naples) in l993. This time the work with Mandala, playing ping-pong, is enjoyed by several people in various rooms, who interact with each other on the screen by playing with the virtual ball. Again, Antonio Glessi writes in 1995: "Taking a good look, all of this is not much different to what happens habitually in the amateur BBS network, where all they do is exchange virtual information-objects in an immaterial common territory"[22]. Artistic experimentation in this sense becomes a vehicle of communication, dialogue process, bidirectional exchange, network.

Massimo Contrasto (Cittadini) is another Italian artist who, after having worked with video in the 1980s in the Florentine field, experimented in the early 1990s with the concept of bidirectional interaction and man-machine interface <www.strano.net/contrasto>. After an interval in Milan in 2000-2003, when Contrasto taught courses on virtual communities, digital video and interactive interfaces at the IED (European Institute of Design), he moved to Levanto, Liguria, where, after managing an Internet point for a year (which became a small networking centre for the Ligurian and Milanese independent scene) he began an experience as lecturer at the Fine Arts Academy of Carrara[23]. At present he follows a thread of experimentation that unites the experiences of the Mandala System in the 1990s with the possibilities for interaction offered on the Internet by Flash technology <www.mutoto.org>[24].

His first installation created with the Mandala System was in 1992, called *Real Virtual Choice*, followed by *Man-Machine* in 1993. This too was based on the Mandala System device. In an interview in 1998, Contrasto described the works he produced in the 1990s:

We interpret a work of art with our filters and our knowledge, yet the work remains finished, as is shown, yet with the possibilities offered by interactive technology, we are able to continue it. For example in Man-Machine, entering in Jackson Pollock's painting we can take colours and continue to do "action painting"; or passing by Yves Klein monochrome we can be stained with paint or our hair can be burned; in the same way, passing in front of the letters by Kurt Schwitters the arrangement can be changed, or sentences can be made with Giuseppe Chiari's words. Another possibility is moving Kazimir Malevich's squares. In our imagination we connect, for example, abstract art with Malevich's red and black squares, yet they can even become objects that can be moved, played ball with, by changing the configuration of the painting. The painting is still Malevich's, but it turns into a likely road to continue Malevich (personal interview, December 1998).

The playful component acquires special importance, since we have the impression of being inside a video game. This aspect is developed further by Massimo Contrasto in Mr. Regular (1997-1999), that comes alive in the imaginative cartoon of the characters of the Robert Crumb cartoons. Mr. Regular is actually *Fritz the Cat* and is a virtual character everyone can identify in by joining in the "game". During interaction we live through structured experiences in various episodes, such as an animated cartoon, or a video game. The participants see their image reflected in the video and can interact with virtual objects, making the narration continue and overcoming various "visual" obstacles, until the end of the game, arriving at the last level.

In Mr. Regular the concept of reality is linked to the imaginative world of animated cartoons and reminds us of those films such as *Roger Rabbit* where real characters were associated to cartoons. In Mr. Regular we realise that the computer isn't real, but we have fun looking like a cat that plays with it. Reality is lost because we are clearly fidgeting with air, we don't interact with real objects, yet in another sense reality is acquired: it's the same that happens with the phone, which on the one hand has us experience a reduced version of real dialogue with the other person, but from a certain point of view increases our communication capabilities and can be considered Marshall McLuhan's metaphor as a prosthesis of the ear and voice (Contrasto, 1998).

The Mandala System device is used by Massimo Contrasto not only to create interactive installations, but also in theatrical performances, such as in the staging of Mandalic Stories with Giacomo Verde, who we spoke about, and interactive dance (starting from 1995), called EXP, in collaboration with Ariella

Vidach and Claudio Prati, then later on in collaboration with the Art Mouv group in Corsica (2000).

In these performances the actors can interact with the virtual bodies created with the Mandala System, using a mixture between material and immaterial.

In Massimo Contrasto's works, art becomes action, play, perceptive experimentation and wants to put the user in a condition to build his worlds personally, like the player of the adventure game Myst who has to build his life on a desert island, discovering the secrets stage by stage. An art that wants to encourage contact with the machine and the possibilities for enjoyment and interaction: even though these possibilities are clearly not infinite (in fact everything is guided by the program), the possibilities for user reaction in the various settings become manifold.

The work becomes a personal path and offers the possibility to experience the relationship freely with the tool of communication, allowing the user to become the interaction pilot. We touch the dynamics of the relationship between artist and user, between mass media and spectator, the problems regarding greater independence offered by digital, set against the risk of greater machine control of human creativity. The user is invited to test his means of perception and he is offered the chance for new body experiences, even though they are simulated.

In this setting that had its maximum affirmation in Italy during the first half of the 1990s, various artists got in touch with each other and started to collaborate, above all the ones who were interested in computer art and hung out in what at the time were called 'counter-culture' spaces, which actually contributed in shaping the present media culture. Many artists came from punk experience and began to experiment with technology bringing into it the "DIY", self-management, "doing art" from low down. Many artists active on the network of Italian digital culture initially moved within the Social Centres, which proved to be creative terrain *par excellence* in the sphere of networking practices. Among these is Federico Bucalossi, who tells us of his experience:

I've always tried to test new concepts and new artistic practices. In the beginning with small groups of people, because it was very difficult to find people in Italy with your same interests. In 1988 the Social Centres began. In my small town in the province of Empoli (Ponte a Elsa) we occupied a place where we created a rehearsal room for music, a stage for concerts, a library, a space for painting, and new aggregations started up in this centre. Then links were established with the other Social Centres in Florence and the Tuscan region, until we had created links with the national ones. We travelled a lot to test firsthand the experiences of the other Social Centres. (...) Coming from punk experience, I rejected the term artist. Now I have succeeded in understanding that it remains the only plausible definition. The words "doing art" leaves a rather wide margin of action and in my opinion what we carry forth cannot be enrolled in too rigid confines. For me "doing art" means producing ideas and stimulating new thoughts to whoever interacts with my works, thoughts that they would otherwise not have had. I define myself an "artist" because in my opinion there is no other definition, even though I'm not drawn to conventional artistic fields (galleries, museums, etc.) (personal interview in December 1998).

Federico Bucalossi uses different art media in his works (video, painting, installations, computer generated art, music, theatrical performances). His approach to artistic productions is minimalist/reductionist. Both within the Strano Network communications group of Florence <www.strano.net>, and individually, in recent years he has worked on abstracting signs and information using bichromias, clear elementary forms, immediate social/emotive concepts. In his latest works everything revolved around the new concepts of "Human". *The end of contemporary Human* (1998), *Thinking Different Humans* (1999/ 2000), *NotHuman* (2001/2006) <www.nothuman.net>[25].

In one of his first works, *Sensualzone*, created in 1995 as a video, then as a video-installation and finally as software on a CD-rom, he fine tunes a kind of *brain machine*[26], through which to choose and experiment the desired sensations (choice can be joy, relaxation, fear, depression, meditation, external peripherals, casual, escape paths). *Sensualzone* was inspired by Philip K. Dick's book *Do Androids Dream of Electric Sheep? (Blade Runner)*, which began with the reawakening of Rick Decard and his wife Iran stimulated by the "Penfield" mood modulator, a machine, once programmed, capable of inducing in its users the desired sensation for that day or that given time. Entering a predefined code in the machine, various sensations are experienced obtaining the necessary mood for the various situations. Therefore by programming a machine, interior emotions can be managed at will. In Federico Bucalossi's interactive installation, with the interaction of the user, the machine is stimulated to produce sounds and minimal luminous impulses.

Using the video-loop technique, the mind of the person interacting interfaces in real time with digitalised colours and signs in order to perform cerebral processes otherwise numbed. A stimulus to "open the doors of perception", in the words of Timothy Leary (1994), as a means to produce psychoactive bodily practices. The flat and violent shades of the colours contaminate our perceptive universe, eliminating the mass of information that does not belong to us.

Technology becomes a means for carrying forward liberation strategies, a point of view that places Federico Bucalossi very close to the rave culture of the 1990s, experiences he himself took an active part in with Spartaco Cortesi, in the sector of sound performances and video-loops of the Yellowcake group <www.nothuman.net/bucalossi/yellowcake>. Therefore it is not a matter of a technology that bombards the mind with useless excessive information, but a technology to support emotional desires, turning one's own emotional baggage into the guide for participating in a kind of psychic videogame. A technology that is to be a means of introspection, a way to live again the interior experience starting from its recovery, an invitation to look into what already lives in our emotional world, with the possibility to manage the relationship with the machine in a completely personal way and escape from the visual blockage of contemporary society[27].

In the years from 1989 to 1997, another group first made videos and then interactive installations, centred on identity topics with special attention to the subversion of social, cultural and rigid sexual categories: the Pigreca Associates group made up of Flavia Alman and Sabine Reiff.

The Pigreca group was formally established in 1993, but Flavia Alman and Sabine Reiff have been working with it since 1986 and both of them were previously part of the Correnti Magnetiche group. Today Pigreca is a company with twenty years of experience in the sectors of communications, didactics and entertainment, specialised above all in 'edutainment' (education plus entertainment), with their base in Milan <www.pigreca.com>.

Experimenting the 1990s interactive installations of Flavia Alman and Sabine Reiff, we immediately have the sensation that our identity is a construction, based mainly on body-mind forms of communication. Their works became animated entities that made irony with the strict mental configurations, playing with our exterior being. They became animated in real time, giving life to creative processes that were always different.

The interactive portraits of Flavia Alman and Sabine Reiff appear as openings for experimenting the condition of seeing oneself in the plural, fragmented, crossbreeding our identity with that of the other person.

The body becomes something to play with, it is used to experiment with our "alpha" element, the non tameable that lives inside us. Our culture has accustomed us to give excessive weight to sight, so seeing ourselves as an image, an external appearance, therefore interactive portraits are directly *felt* on our body, becoming a *second skin* (Pigreca, 1998).

In their video works, Flavia Alman and Sabine Reiff had decided to become a metamorphosis and dreamlike universes, but with the interactive installations the user ends up participating directly in the process, putting himself at stake. For example, with *Telespecchio* (1992) the observer can match and combine his mirror image, joining the right and left halves of his face in an unusual way, reconstructing his own features by emphasizing the proportions, making eccentric pictorial creations. At the same time the machine seems to play independently with our body, giving creative answers to our commands.

With *Identimix* (1994), acting with another person on some of the installation commands at the same time, the image of our face blends with the other person's face, so we can see a "hybrid" version of ourselves. A synthesis is created from the dialectic of the two faces, but it doesn't eliminate the reciprocal differences. This is how a dialectic entity is created that doesn't crush the diversity, making itself syncretic.

Anamorfic Generator (1995), on the other hand, lets us play with the perspective illusions of anamorphosis, and the images of our body, reflected on reflective solids, are distorted and are perceivable only if seen from a certain angle. Using a TV camera, the image of the user is captured and is elaborated in real time with the laws of reflection; then the user can see on an inclined column the phenomenon of the distorted picture around a reflecting cone. To interact with one's own image and, with the same work, the user must move, must become a nomad, must continuously move his point of view and hearing, constructing a personal perceptive map.

Lastly, in the interactive installation of *Audio-portrait, the colour of the voice* (1996), by using one's voice and resonance frequencies, the user sees himself as a colour, shown by an animated hand (*hand* with *finger*) inviting him to talk. "The hand" identifies the timbre of the voice inside the colour spectrum, and when the voice changes so does the colour.

All of this artist's works have in common not just the experimental approach on video or computer, but also the fact of being the result of networking relationships, meaning a circuit of collective projects and ideas that sees "doing art" as a chance for exchange and sharing. The work of art is considered an opportunity to overcome the idea of a single signature (and a single form), bringing about a collective entity where the process, the backstage, the context, the relational system that created this work acquire more importance than the artistic product in itself.

The artist Claudio Parrini <www.parrini.net> also works in this direction, once a member of the Minimal TV group and the Strano Network collective of Florence <www.strano.net> and, subsequently, the Undo.net group in Milan <www.undo.net>. Parrini too, coming from video and painting experience, produced interactive works for manipulating old and new media. Among these, *Etere-Arte-Rete* (1995), where the user can intervene with various tools (temperas, felt tip pens, sprays, digital graphic programs) on photos printed or digitalised from TV programmes, that can then be placed on the Internet. At the same time other materials can be downloaded from the Internet and manipulated with an inverse procedure, in order to reflect on the mediatic/aesthetic dynamics that wind their way through the videosphere and the network environments, activating a continuous flow of reciprocity and contamination among all the possible distribution and production channels.

Other works of his consist in creating contexts to exhibit the artistic products of others, therefore Claudio Parrini introduces himself more as a "networker" than as a traditional artist. As in his work *Proiezioni* in 1991, a frame of enamelled sheet metal with the videos of Alessia Lucchetta appearing inside it. In this sense, with a collective work defined by Claudio Parrini as *un-far-sì-che-si-crei-insieme (let's-make-it-happen-together)*, work is done to highlight the content of the communication and not who communicates, following the idea of art as network. Therefore, through neutral, anonymous, undetermined, open work in which the "I/Artist is gradually rounded off until it becomes so small that it disappears" (Parrini, 1998). At the same, according to Claudio Parrini, the dissolution process of "I dominant and despotic", can take place even in the relationship of an individual work (such as a painting), in which the ego of the author is so "expanded" that it can no longer be perceived by the audience, who can thus experience the work mainly in relationship to themselves. In this sense, for the users, the work becomes a void to be filled personally, and the ego of the author, when it expands, disappears. In 1998, Claudio Parrini explains what networking is for him:

I am not much interested in distinguishing whether or not something is a work of art; for me it is important to create the situations where people can express themselves freely, and the most important thing is that they decide for themselves what a work of art is. I define myself a networker and a painter. The fact of working on the network, where my painting can convey the same as a painting by Picasso, can mean that everyone can decide if this is a work or art or not, and the task is not assigned only to the market circuit, as happens within the traditional art system. This system presents specialised magazines, critics who confer authority to works, or presupposes a network of galleries so that the validity of the artist is not a consequence of his work, but is due to the fact that he has exhibited in certain places and not in others. At times it becomes more important where an artist has exhibited rather than what he has exhibited. In talking with art critics, the first thing they want to see are résumés, personal catalogues, and this could be useful, but it is placed in an economic dimension of art that has little to do with the art-life relationship (personal interview, December 1998).

Consistent with his view of art as network, Claudio Parrini has directed attention to all the forms of "minor" painting (café art, votive offerings, small antique dealer paintings), experimenting the possibility of contact and contamination between the two systems, the "private" painting system and the collective one of electronic projects. He has recently turned to doing paintings: landscapes, self portraits and still life, giving a "farewell" to doing art on the network, as can be read in his site <www.parrini.net>.

Hacker Art

In the artistic conception proposed by Tommaso Tozzi at the end of the 1980s, with theorization in his booklet *Subliminal Interactive Happenings* (1989), Hacker Art is realised by free diffusion, creation, manipulation of information determining an uncontrolled flow of digital data. Anyone who participates in this process enters a network of creative contaminations, originating the artistic event with their own spontaneous action. Hacker art is comparable to a virus that develops dynamically using the network nodes, causing the progressive contamination of the elements involved in the creative process. Hacker art is proposed as a form of open exchange between people, who are all simultaneously users and producers of information.

In the 1980s and 1990s, Tommaso Tozzi's artistic activity places in the forefront the matter of creating contexts of "horizontal interaction" between people. The media are used, working on their capability to create relationships between several people, putting into practice the concepts of self-management and networking.

Starting in 1982, Tommaso Tozzi collaborated in this direction with the musician Giuseppe Chiari, a Fluxus member, setting up numerous happenings and, from 1986, preparing alternative spaces for presenting performances, graffiti, shows, fanzines, groups and singles, publications, etc. The spaces animated part of the Florentine underground scene until 1988: Bang Amen (1986), set up in a small garage and Pat Pat Recorder (1986-1988), established and managed with Steve Rozz, Nielsen Gavyna, Priscila Lena Farias and Massimo Contrasto.

In the 1980s, more precisely in the 1987-1989 period, Tommaso Tozzi used his telephone answering machine according to the hacker art principle, giving life to the *419695 – Art Fanzine for an Answering Machine* project. His answering machine was open to everyone for a year and a half; anyone could record any kind of sound presence – musical, poetic, philosophic – giving space to improvisation skills. Like fanzines and punkzines, people could freely express their thoughts (from home, from the street, from the workplace, etc.) autonomously running a technological medium spontaneously: the answering machine. The messages recorded were retransmitted the following month at certain times of day to be listened to on the answering machine. Several copies of the programme "schedule" were then printed by Tommaso Tozzi and subsequently sent to various alternative spaces, art galleries, magazines, fanzines and museums – among them the Museum of Modern Art in New York.

The same project was later adapted to information technology using the Hacker Art BBS (1990), a home-made data bank (since 1992 a node of the Cyberpunk amateur telematic network) that everyone could access by connecting to Tommaso Tozzi's computer through the modem, with the aim of reading, leaving, manipulating data, philosophy, sundry texts, images, individual or collective creations. In his no-copyright book *Oppositions '80*, Tommaso Tozzi defines it an "exhibition open to everyone, evidently continuing to have the characteristic of the electronic and interactive fanzine" (1991a, p. 30).

The book *Oppositions '80. Some of the facts that have shaken up the global village* was published in 1991 by the independent publisher Amen, in Milan, and quotes most of the experiences of the punks, cyberpunks and hacktivism of those years, including texts, images of flyers and individual and collective writings of many people who were active in that period.

In the new Hacker Art vision presented by Tozzi, with the possibility to manipulate and reproduce images with digital means, art becomes a temporary flow and an open process, left to the spontaneous improvisation of the participants. Through the telematic networks everyone simultaneously becomes a user and producer of information.

Tommaso Tozzi defines Hacker Art thus in 1989:

Hacker Art as a proposal and non destructive form of democracy of information and communication.

Hacker Art as the definition of a threshold within which the virtual operation and the real operation interchange roles indistinctly, keeping stable the management and purpose of the transgressive act.

Hacker Art as a form of struggle for social freedom.

Hacker Art or Subliminal Art as a struggle against definitions, against the roles and labels of official culture, against advertising practices about appearances, against the manipulation of things and facts through language.

Hacker Art or Subliminal Art as an anonymous practice, not to be mentioned when used as a tool of economic interests of the multinationals; against the very definitions of Hacker Art and Subliminal Art exploited by official culture.

What is interesting is just the clandestine "practice", the rest will be just trading goods or noise in favour of everything that moves against the system of cultural power (Tozzi, 1991b).

Therefore Hacker Art is not made by the creation of artistic object products, it takes origin from individual and collective *actual practices*, aimed at giving life to networks of relationships between people, thus connected by a form of communication defined "horizontal".

In 1998, Tommaso Tozzi told of how his vision of Hacker Art and Subliminal Art came about:

I used the term Hacker Art for the first time in 1989, when I was working on experiences in the artistic field that I define Subliminal Art. This type of research of mine started from reflection on communication forms of entertainment society and consequently on the search for communication forms that were not comparable to goods. Quite to the contrary, these artistic forms were to appear as a VIRUS and be capable of spreading anywhere in ways transversal to media systems, or else find fertile ground in them. The existence of people capable of producing and writing a VIRUS on a data disk seemed to me an excellent metaphor to define the operative model that I was carrying forward in art, which was to produce actions capable of being transmitted, communicated and contaminated in the most widespread way possible without necessarily being recognisable as artistic actions, but capable of acting in transversal sectors. These artistic forms were called *subliminal* because they consisted in subliminal messages that I made act inside several exhibitions, pretending I wasn't the artist but the curator of the show that usually contained artistic objects by other people. Therefore it was also a reflection on the artist's role. I thought it was much more useful to act inside the context of the exhibition rather than by producing an artistic object. I presented a monitor at the exhibition entrance in which I entered all the names of the participating artists, or the floor-plan of the exhibition where I illustrated the path to follow in order to see the works. Subliminal messages appeared inside this monitor, such as REBEL, ART CONDITIONS YOU, etc., that were unconsciously enjoyed by the public (personal interview, December 1998).

In 1989, the "REBEL! Virus.asm" virus originated as a Subliminal Art work, contrived by Tommaso Tozzi and created by Andrea Ricci. The virus had no destructive purposes, but came about as an artistic experiment without ever being widespread and appears on the screens of users with the subliminal word "Rebel!".

126

At the beginning of the 1990s, Tommaso Tozzi upheld that it wasn't the possibility to act in the "interactive" and "multimedia" media that determined the horizontal aspect of communications, it was maintaining and conserving free communications, guaranteeing everyone the chance to create and present structures, no matter what they were, to others. In his idea of Hacker Art free choice and creation must be protected and the redistribution of the *power of presentation* must be considered the primary goal to achieve a real communicative democracy. "True interactivity is in the power of presentation. In *being able* to present to others, more than being able to participate in performances" (Tozzi, 1992c).

In the beginning Tommaso Tozzi's artistic work headed in this direction, manifesting itself as a *creation of networks* open to participant interventions and manipulations, such as the *Digital Interactive Happenings* project (1992). This project developed in the collective, self-managed creation of music, texts and images created and interactively manipulable by using a computer. In the project presentation flyer, Tozzi wrote:

Digital Interactive Happenings is an anthology of music, texts and images that were produced in group by several people following methodological and creative criteria that made it possible to manipulate in succession the works done by others, thus creating an enormous collective cut-up. At the requests of Tommaso Tozzi, all over Italy chains were formed of musicians, writers and artists who produced their pieces, texts and images reworking them from the ideas created by each one of them in rotation. In most cases the means used for creation was a computer. In any case everything was saved in digital form so that anyone who had a computer could continue the chains and participate in creating never-finished artistic products. Some of the creations were made and exchanged taking advantage of the Hacker Art BBS, a digital data bank that can be connected to with a computer and modem.

Digital Interactive Happenings comes in a boxed set (reminiscent of George Maciunas' *Fluxboxes*) containing a booklet, a floppy disk and a CD-rom: a futuristic project at the time – 1992 – when in Italy only a limited group of people spoke of multimedia art. The large quantity of musical pieces, texts and images collected were saved on the CD-rom and floppy disk as digital files. Specifically, the CD-rom was a "mix-mode" compact disk.

As Tommaso Tozzi writes,

this particular compact disk is organised so that there are 35 audio tracks in it that contain the musical pieces and can be listened to using an ordinary audio compact disk player. Furthermore, on a single track of the CD-rom (to be precise, track 1), the "digital" files corresponding to the music are recorded in a MIDI standard. This means that when a CD-drive is available, you can not only listen to the music on your own computer, but you can also make modifications to it. (...) The music files are also recorded on floppy disks so that they are available to anyone who has a computer but not a CD-rom player. (...) The same criterion adopted for musicians was used at my request also for producing written texts. Several writers united in a group preparing texts with the usual chain method. The text files were then saved on the first CD-rom track so that they could be used again in turn; in addition their content was printed in this book in the section "Texts written in group interactively" (1992b).

In Tozzi's idea of collective interaction proposed in the 1980s and 1990s, both with individual artistic projects and in the sphere of the Florentine group Strano Network[28], we find the fundamental principles for understanding a networking art, where the artist becomes the creator of exchange contexts and the people in the "audience" become co-authors actively co-involved in the creative process. As Tozzi points out, "the context of improvisation: build a neutral context. Black square on white context. Something inside which there is no need to feel part of a specific identity, but inside which there is the maximum freedom to build (and leave traces of) multiple identities"[29].

In the *Cotropy: Lifeware and Mutual Co-evolution*[30] text, Tommaso Tozzi stresses that a work of art in its object form is the result of the artist's state of mind caused by a series of factors, each one with equal dignity in determining this interior emotion. He maintains that value is in the object only in relationship to what the above mentioned state has caused and to the context it is inserted in Therefore the profound meaning of the work is not to be searched for in its object manifestation, which is only the exterior shell, but in the networks of relationships, in the collective processes, in the emotional components that contributed in forging the material of what is inside the shell and the shell itself. The artistic aspect is therefore in life, in the rizomatic connection of creative units, in the construction process of a relational context, in the free and self-regulated activity of people, in the system of relationships in *co-evolution*.

The work of art has a collective nature, in which the parts that make up the whole cooperate interactively, determining the evolution of the global context, in order to guarantee local benefit in relationship to the more general context, which is equally benefited. In the same text, Tommaso Tozzi adds that as the single cell is the owner of its neural system and as at the same time it is the evolutionary result of a symbiosis between various organisms, thus the work of art that is created from the spontaneous relationships of individuals preserves its independence from the art system and has its origin from the chaotic (but conscious) action of the single parties participating in the process.

Hence, the *co-evolution* system that is created does not contemplate a ratifying fusion of the parts, but the placing in relationship of so many critical self-organised entities, that preserve their individuality in the collective relationship. At the same time, a non permanent organism is determined from their interaction, with its own characteristics (and therefore independent in this sense too), therefore the statement that the whole is greater than its single parts is valid.

So the work of art originated from the spontaneous, independent action of individuals who, interfacing with each other and collaborating, brought about an ongoing process that developed as an organism in becoming chaotic and not casual (*lifeware*). The *mutual co-evolution* offered by networks must be open to cooperative situations, such as for example the Social Centres, the antagonist counterculture, in general to all those movements and individuals who act in view of a autonomous, collective use, liberated and critical of it. Consequently what is collectively and critically grassroots generated becomes art, the group of autonomous practices that use multiple languages and constitute relational standards by themselves, reinventing and deconstructing those made by the official culture, giving life to collective behaviours that are not a specific patrimony of any subject concerned.

Following this point of view, which is the one of much art in that period and well represents the visionary phase of the first experiments with digital, the concept of art work is dematerialised in the practices of life, in movements, in collectives, in self-organised situations, in spontaneous, improvised performances, in horizontal social relationships, in all those events that put cooperation from below in the foreground.

Even museums should become open containers of elements and entities that encourage the circulation, distribution, evolution, interaction and contamination of knowledge in order to give rise to networks of social and individual relationships. Artistic information should not be something fixed and permanent; it should be capable of self-replication, like a virus, contaminating other entities in its process of spontaneous and free propagation. Following these orientations, the objective of Tommaso Tozzi's activity in the following years continued to be creating *networks*. Towards the end of the 1990s, the main objective was to "transfer resources" from an institutional field to a non-institutional one.

In the non-institutional fields new forms of social languages are being built spontaneously. I think the existence of non-institutional places is fundamental for society, places that have workshops for experimenting new feasible forms of communication, and it is necessary to guarantee this possibility of redistribution of the social forces, which are usually managed by the institutions. When institutions redistribute the social forces so that the self-management fields are also involved, we should think about a transfer of resources that does not contemplate the constraint of reciprocation by the non-institutional forces, i.e. the self-management forces are not forced to respond by legitimating any institutional values which may at the moment be in rebellion and where new ones are taking over. Therefore if receiving resources from institutions should implicate for a self-managed model the return of the gift by recognising a value at the criticised moment, this mechanism would not work. The work must be the filter system so as to transfer resources from the institution to the self-managed systems, so that these latter are not obliged to respond according to fixed rigid standards, but can then take part in the process simply by receiving these resources. It is clear that the non-institutional systems, such as the social centres and the non-profit associations, being part of society, nevertheless participate in building certain social fabrics and can make their contribution in this way (Tozzi, personal interview, December 1998).

Following this line, Tommaso Tozzi applied the concept of "resource transfer" in 1997, when he decided to relinquish the 19th National Prize for Visual Arts, City of Gallarate, to donate the total amount of the prize (three million lire) to the Isole nella Rete (Islands in the Net) association <www.ecn.org>, legendary site of Italian movement, source of coordination for antagonist events in the country[31].

As is read in the communication,

the artist Tommaso Tozzi relinquished receiving the money for the "Città di Gallarate" National Visual Arts Prize since it implicated creating an "art object" for the "Signals of Work – Art and Digital Culture in Italy" exhibition that would take place starting on Sunday 19th October 1997 in the Civic Modern Art Gallery in Gallarate. For Tozzi, documenting the artistic work that individuals or groups carry out on the telematic networks has no need for an aesthetic "surplus" that takes concrete form in a real presence in an art gallery. It is sufficient (in the case of his work done with the Strano Network group) to guarantee the existence of public positions that in a "permanent" way (and not just for the exhibition) give anyone the possibility of free access to these telematic networks. In this sense Tozzi decided not to enter any artistic "object" in the above mentioned exhibition, but to donate the prize money as an "artistic operation" (...). "Work" and "artistic" is any activity carried out in the field of science, culture, volunteering with and just ordinary daily life, that encourages the existence of virtual and real communities where each person has the same opportunities as all the others. Since examples of individual or collective social initiatives already exist in this direction, Tozzi's work confirms the need for such entities to be considered "artistic" and that their work (meaning an inseparable complexity of actions, relationships and materials produced by these entities) be considered a work of art without the need for making "fetishes" within the art galleries that involve additional and unnecessary expenses for the institutions that organise them. (...) The separation between "operative" moment of art and "celebrative" moment must be abandoned forever. It must be abandoned in the sense that there must be no more art places and events that reduce it to rhetoric moments and in so doing weigh on the collective finances, and their transformation must be strengthened in areas that truly weigh on the construction of *mutual co-evolution* patterns[32].

These considerations, that view the work of art as a pattern of relationships and "resource transfers" between persons, collective projects and institutions, have developed today in Tommaso Tozzi's activity on historical documentation of the hacktivism practices and new media art, over the Hacker Art site <www.hackerart.org> and the WikiArtPedia project, the Free Encyclopaedia of Art and Cultures of the Networks, produced with the contributions of students in his courses at the Fine Arts Academy in Carrara (where Tozzi is the Director of the Department of Multimedia Arts), the Faculty of Formation Sciences, University of Florence and RAI Master course in Multimedia <www.wikiartpedia.org>.

Endnotes

1 The text of the document was sent to me by Giacomo Verde when I was writing my thesis for my degree in Sociology of Mass Communications "Real practices for virtual bodies in Italian interactive digital art" in 1998-1999, on-line at: www.strano.net/bazzichelli/tesi.htm .

2 In the 1990s, Mariacristina Cremaschi fought on an institutional level to promote Italian digital art and tried to propose a vision of art as a network. Among the initiatives she organised, we mention a workshop of young theorists and artists called <.net art>:<Anywhere><Everywhere>, organised in April 1999 in Modena. Promoted by the Emilia Romagna Region and taking place in the Modena Comune halls, the workshop was held by Massimo Cittadini, Giacomo Verde and Tommaso Tozzi and its aim was *the study of methods inherent to the realisation of art works that make the best use of Internet potentials* and intended to create *an interactive work/process during a workshop*. Everything was imagined with an eye to creating a virtual collection dedicated to emerging Italian net.art, hosted on the site <www.stradanove.net>. While the workshop was going on and the participants created collective works, still visible on <www.stradanove.net/netart/undermagma>, Mariacristina Cremaschi's proposal to the net.art on-line gallery didn't have sufficient support, showing that in this case too the incapability of an institution to manage innovative topics even though they showed interest in the beginning. Mariacristina Cremaschi was the curator of the "Art of Virtual Reality" section for the "La Coscienza Luccicante, dalla videoarte all'arte interattiva" (The Shimmering Conscience, from video art to interactive art) exhibit, the last "official" great respite event on the topic during the nineties, at the Exhibition Palace in Rome (September-October 1998).

3 Among the main international festivals, we would like to mention: *Ars Electronica Festival* in Linz, Austria (active since1979 and annually since 1986 <www.aec.at>), *Siggraph Art Show* in Chicago, USA (active since the early 1970s <www.siggraph.org>), *Multimediale* in Karlsruhe, Germany (in 1989, before the ZKM was established as permanent headquarters <www.zkm.de>), *ISEA International Symposium on Electronic Art* in Holland and Canada (since 1988 <www.isea-web.org>), *EMAF European Media Art Festival* in Osnabruck, Germany (since 1988 <www.emaf.de>), *VIPER International Festival for Film Video and New Media* in Basel, Switzerland (since 1981 <www.viper.ch>), *Imagina* in Monte Carlo, Principality of Monaco (since 1982 <www.imagina.mc>), *Next Five Minutes* in Amsterdam, Holland (since 1993 <www.next5minutes.org>), *DEAF Duch Electronic Art Festival* in Rotterdam, Holland (since 1994 <www.deaf04.nl> promoted by the V2 research centre <www.v2.nl>), *Transmediale Festival* in Berlin, Germany (since 1997 <www.transmediale.de>).

4 *Vittorio Fagone, from "VideoMagazine", 1986.*

5 Text from the Notes area of *"the Critique. Telematic review of art, design and new media"*, directed by Enrico Cocuccioni, one of the foremost Italian critics who reflects on the relationship between art and technology. In 1983, he wrote the text published by 50x70 Rome Pub., where the possible uses of the personal computer were investigated and compared as a new technological tool for elaborating new artistic forms, such as computer art. In the site "the Critique. Telematic review of art, design and new media", that presents a vast archive of articles by sector experts (many of them gravitating in the creative areas of RAI, Rome), the "Tangential" event began in 2004, an open on-line space for collecting free contributions (texts, photos, videos, etc.) inspired by the ongoing debate in Rome about the plans to demolish the imposing structures of the San Lorenzo overhead road. A creative work in progress that will end once the overhead road is demolished. Among the various contributions already published, a presentation of Luigi Ciorciolini's project, another legendary character in the field of art critique and technology, a video contribution from Enrico Cocuccioni, a video by David del Bufalo and other texts and visual materials made by scholars and artists in the field *<www.lacritica.net>*.

6   Interview with Maria Grazia Mattei. From: Bassi Bruno, Bassi Dora, Biagini Giselda, D'Antongiovanni Silvia, "Telematic Art in the 1980s", video, Academy of Fine Arts, Carrara, Course in Mas Media Theory and Method, Prof. Tommaso Tozzi, 2004-2005 Academic Year. On the Internet, the text of the interview can be found at: <www.wikiartpedia/index.php/Intervista_a_Maria_Grazia_Mattei>. The video can be downloaded from the New Global Vision site: <www.ngvision.org/mediabase/513>.

7   For more information about art via satellite and telecommunication, consult the text *Interaction, Participation, Networking. Art and Telecommunication* (2004) written by Inke Arns for: <www.medienkunstnetz.de/themes/overview_of_media_art/communication/1/>.

8   For reconstruction, consult the sites in the on-line magazine already mentioned: "la Critica" by Enrico Cocuccioni <www.lacritica.net>, the site by the critic Franco Zeri <www.francozeri.com/digitale/storiadigi.htm>, the publications edited by the critic Lorenzo Taiuti, that include *Arte e Media. Avanguardie e comunicazione di massa*, Genoa, Costa & Nolan, 1996, *Corpi sognanti. L'Arte nell'epoca delle tecnologie digitali*, Milan, Feltrinelli, 2001 and the latest *Multimedia. L'incrocio dei linguaggi comunicativi*, Rome, Meltemi, 2004. Another site for possible reconstruction of part of this history is LuxFlux, the site of the Rome Contemporary Art Laboratory Museum, directress Simonetta Lux and coordinator Domenico Scudero <www.luxflux.net>, and in the WikiArtPedia site edited by Tommaso Tozzi and the students of the Carrara Academy of Fine Arts <www.wikiartpedia.org>. Furthermore, within the field of artistic networking is the Teo Museum experience, established in 1990 by Giovanni Bai and Teo Telloli, a museum with no headquarters and no works, that is expressed in the magazine "Museo Teo Artfanzine" and through periodic events of video art, performances and reflections on society and contemporary art <http://utenti.lycos.it/MUSEO_TEO>.

9   There are interesting experiences, again following the networking thread, with "Cybernauts, an upside-down world" in the Palazzo Re Enzo, Bologna, July 1993, prepared by Pier Luigi Capucci and Carlo Terrosi, organised by the cultural association "The Mirror of Dionysus", under the patronage of the Comune of Bologna. Here we reflect on the new experiments via video and computer and many of the more acrtive Italian artists of the time were present (among them Massimo Contrasto, Piero Gilardi, Ale Guzzetti, GMM, Sabine Reiff, Tommaso Tozzi and Giacomo Verde). Another avant-garde initiative for the Italian situation at the "Virtual Light, new frontiers in communication and in art" event, set up in Bari in March 1996, at the Palazzo Fizzarotti, prepared by Gabriele Perretta, Antonella Marino, Aurelio Cianciotta Mendizza, Patrizia Marino and organised by the Multilink Association and under the patronage of the Comune of Bari. Historical names appear here too in the installations section, among them Tullio Brunone, Massimo Contrasto, Correnti Magnetiche, Marcello Pecchioli, Mario Sasso, Studio Azzurro, Tommaso Tozzi, Giorgio Vaccarino, Giacomo Verde, Orlan and there is also talk of cyber-feminism. Among the initiatives trying to catch on in new technology research of Italian digital on an institutional level, we mention "Segnali d'Opera, Arte e digitale in Italia", promoted by the Gallarate Civic Modern Art Gallery in November 1997, under the patronage of the Lombardy Region and the Varese Province. This review has proven to be a valid attempt to promote local digital art. The Councillor for Culture Carmelo Todoverto sustains that the manifestation "intends proposing, with strong commitment, an authentic historical, social and therefore cultural happening of our existence" (1997).

10 For a more in depth history in Italian of networking platforms and mailing lists on an international level, see the chapter "Connection policies" in the book by Deseriis and Marano, 2003, pp. 189-210.

11 The origin of the "Nettime" mailing list is described by Diana McCarty in the text *Nettime: the legend and the myth*, July 1997, published in: <www.medialounge.net/lounge/workspace/nettime/DOCS/1/info3.html>.

12 We will examine the topic net.art in the next chapter.

13 Giacomo Verde at the *Documedia. Percorsi Multimediali* convention held at RAI, Rome, in 1998, defined *Quinta Parete* as *the imaginative wall.*

14 Giacomo Verde in "Actions Beyone Performances" extracted from the message of 21st November 1997 to the Arti-Party mailing list. Federico Bucalossi, Claudio Parrini, Tommaso Tozzi, Giacomo Verde, along with Antonio Caronia, in 1997 started the Arti-Party mailing list in order to give life to (and to abort, writes Claudio Parrini) debates on art (in the *open* meaning of the word).

15 Maria Grazia Mattei, in "Correnti Magnetiche Immagini virtuali e Installazioni interattive", Arnaud pub.- Gramma 1996, on the Internet at: <www.geocities.com/SunsetStrip/Backstage/3166/correnti.html>.

16 Mario Canali is still active today in Milan in the Arcnaut centre, set up in 2003, an important testimony to the applications of virtual reality (immersive and non) in Italy, where encounters and events are organised on art, science, technology and philosophy. In the Arcnaut space the installations of the 1990s are still visible and can be used. Among the various events organised are a *Laboratory of the Imagination* to set up research and reflection groups, courses and seminars, philosophic appointments and debates open to the public <www.arcnaut.it>.

17 From *Intervista ai Giovanotti Mondani Meccanici* – Taormina Arte, 1992. Andrea Zingoni, Antonio Glessi and Roberto Davini answer. Document sent to me by Antonio Glessi by e-mail in 1998.

18 The memoirs of Gino the Chicken are found in the book by Andrea Zingoni *Gino the Chicken – The amazing adventures of the first chicken lost on the net,* Rome, Castelvecchi, 1999. Later, the character was extraordinarily successful in its new twice-weekly web-cartoon version: *Gino week-end,* designed by Joshua Held. In November 2001, with the fortieth episode, musical parody of "tu vo' fa' l'americano" by Renato Carosone which, in homage to the news of the moment, becomes "Tu vò fa' o' Talebano", Gino comes to the news forefront as a national web phenomenon <www.gmm.fi.it>.

19 Texts taken from "Giovanotti Mondani Meccanici, video production 84/96", a document sent to me by Antonio Glessi in 1998.

20 Cf. Myron Krueger, *Realtà Artificiale*, Milan, Italia Editoriale, 1992.

21 Antonio Glessi, personal interview, December 1998.

22 Antonio Glessi "Antenna Cinema Media – Conegliano 27/3 – 2/4/1995".

23 At the Academy of Fine Arts in Carrara, he taught Computer Art and today teaches Multimedia Installations in the Department of Multimedia Arts.

24 His latest creations are the interactive keyboards and various videos, always interactive, based on detecting movement in front of a webcam (therefore usable through this device). They are found online at: <www.mutoto.org/CA0405/playsoundzcamindex.htm> and <www.mutoto.org/webcamlabs.htm>).

25 Today, in addition to carrying forward his activity and artistic research, Federico Bucalossi is a Web Design lecturer and Multimedia Assistant at the Academy of Fine Arts in Carrara and lecturer in a European Master course "Multimedia directing applied to the theatre" in Empoli.

26 William Burroughs had previously spoken of the *Dream Machine*, a psychedelic machine causing altered states of awareness. In 1998, Federico Bucalossi in *Brain Machine, how to build it and use it,* a text written for the Strano Network *Bioenciclopedia*, wrote: "I would like to clarify right away that the Brain Machine is not a toy, even though it can entertain and amuse anyone. It's main intention is to help people achieve altered states of awareness. These altered states are translatable towards the various waves of frequency (measured in cycles per second), for example: using the Theta waves with the relative program the mind will be stimulated towards imagination and creativity. I need to specify that 'altered states' does not mean a 'buzz', but any alteration outside the ordinary towards the expansion of one's own creativity, imagination or simply to 'get away' for a few minutes or relax".

27   The end motto of many of Federico Bucalossi's works was: *SWITCH OFF YOUR MONITORS... EXTERMINATE US ALL.*

28   We will dedicate more time to the artistic activity of the Strano Network collective in the next chapter. In particular, Tommaso Tozzi's path is described in the section of the site <http://www.strano.net/tozzi.htm>, where one can find a selection of the works, writings and biography of the artist.

29   Tommaso Tozzi's text taken from *Notes on the relationship between identity, improvisation and telematic networks* found on the Strano Network site <www.strano.net>.

30   Conference organised by Tommaso Tozzi for the project "Art, Media and Communication", 1997. The text was read by Tommaso Tozzi during the "The Shadow of Networks" seminar, at the Modern Art Gallery, Turin, 12th April 1997. It was later published in "La Stanza Rossa", 25, year 6, July-September 1997, Ortica Editions, Bologna.

31   The whole matter is described at: <www.strano.net/town/arte/freeart/tozzi/relation/gallarat/index.htm>. As we will see in the next chapter, along with the donation of the Islands in the Net prize, Tommaso Tozzi would present as a non-object work of art the Strano Network site, made up of collective actions of all those who worked and interacted on it, calling this project "Cotropia".

32   Text taken from the e-mail with subject line "Tozzi gives up the money of the National Visual Arts, City of Gallarate", sent by Tommaso Tozzi to the Arti-party mailing list, 16th October 1997. Online at: <www.strano.net/town/arte/freeart/tozzi/relation/gallarat/001.htm>.

Hacker Ethics and Shared Networks

Social Hacking

With the Hacker Art concept, we directed our attention to the relational components, the exchange networks and the collective processes that originate a work of art, making use of technology to reproduce itself, spread and be transformed. So if we consider the path of the Avant-gardes and Neo-avant-gardes up to the phenomena of the 1980s, according to the Italian declination (from punk to cyberpunk) described previously, it is clear how the idea of art can be attributed to many networking practices on BBSes or the Internet. The term "hacker" must be contextualised, opening the issue on a series of practices, events and actions that have animated part of the Italian underground scene since the end of the 1980s, and above all from the 1990s up to today.

There are many ways to be a hacker and also many possible definitions of this term. In Italy most of the official media have associated the word hacker with information pirate. This is a false, simplistic and negative conception that doesn't do justice to complex and variegated actions of groups and individuals on an international level, from the USA to Europe.

In the 1980s Steven Levy described the hacker's condition, more or less unchanged today:

Unfortunately for many true hackers [...] the popularization of the term was a disaster. Why? The word hacker had acquired a specific and negative connotation. The trouble began with some well-publicized arrests of teenagers who electronically ventured into forbidden digital grounds, like government computer systems. It was understandable that the journalists covering these stories would refer to the young perps as hackers – after all, that's what the kids called *themselves*. But the word quickly became synonymous with "digital trespasser". [...]

According to this definition a hacker is at best benign, an innocent who doesn't realize his true powers. At worst, he is a terrorist. In the past few years, with the emergence of computer viruses, the hacker has been literally transformed into a virulent force.

True, some of the most righteous hackers in history have been known to sneer at details such as property rights or the legal code in order to pursue the Hands-On Imperative. And pranks have always been part of hacking. But the inference that such high jinks were the essence of hacking was not just wrong, it was offensive to true hackers, whose work had changed the world, and whose methods could change the way one viewed the world (Levy, 2001, pp. 432-433).

Today hacking is immediately connected to computer technology, yet the first hacking practices date back to when calculators still used punch cards. In general, the origin of hacker culture is set in the early 1960s, when the first PDP-1s began circulating in MIT laboratories in Boston, and a research committee was set up at the Tech Model Railroad Club which then created the Artificial Intelligence Laboratory. In the 1970s hacker practices acquired identity thanks to the use of ARPANET, the first high speed transcontinental computer network, to the point of intervening in the creation of the Silicon Valley phenomenon, paving the way for those who would later build empires, taking advantage of the institutions that emerged from down low.

In various texts we can read the history of hackers at length and reconstruct this path. The most reliable source for correct definition of the term hacker is "Jargon File" <www.catb.org/~esr/jargon/>, the most famous hacker dictionary (recognised as such by them), originally written by Raphael Finkel (Stanford University) and currently maintained by Eric S. Raymond. In The Jargon File (the first version dated 1973) eight definitions are given for the term hacker.

hacker: n.[1]

[originally, someone who makes furniture with an axe]

[1] A person who enjoys exploring the details of programmable systems and how to stretch their capabilities, as opposed to most users, who prefer to learn only the minimum necessary. RFC1392, the *Internet Users' Glossary*, usefully amplifies this as: A person who delights in having an intimate understanding of the internal workings of a system, computers and computer networks in particular.

[2] One who programs enthusiastically (even obsessively) or who enjoys programming rather than just theorizing about programming;
[3] A person capable of appreciating *hack value*[2];
[4] A person who is good at programming quickly;
[5] An expert at a particular program, or one who frequently does work using it or on it; as in 'a Unix hacker'. [Definitions 1 through 5 are correlated, and people who fit them congregate.];
[6] An expert or enthusiast of any kind. One might be an astronomy hacker, for example;
[7] One who enjoys the intellectual challenge of creatively overcoming or circumventing limitations;
[8] (deprecated) A malicious meddler who tries to discover sensitive information by poking around. Hence password hacker, network hacker. The correct term for this sense is *cracker*.

As Florian Cramer observed in his text *Social Hacking, Revisited* (2003), quoting in turn the text of the intervention by artist and cyberfeminist Cornelia Sollfrank for the "next Cyberfeminist International" convention (1999), "definitions [6] and [7] of The Jargon File are not restricted to computer technology; they expand the meaning of the term, including every type of system" (Cramer, 2004)[3].

The more properly "social" sense offered by points [6] and [7] was underlined several times by that area of the Italian hacker community that sees itself in a collective and political vision of hacking and reconnects directly to the experiences already described in the previous chapters. However we must make a specification, in order to better identify the "Italian case" this time too, which takes on various characteristics with respect to international experiences. In Florian Cramer's text, following the thread of the discourse on social hacking, a "hack" is defined as "a trick or deception, as an efficacious but conceptually unclean intervention (like a 'patch' or a 'bugfix'), or as a solution that is at once ingeniously simple and elegant, absorbing an abundance of issues in the most dense possible form." (*ibid*).

A social hack is therefore a trick, a fake, a prank, that plays with shared social and cultural belongings, having its main "playing" territory as the *status quo*, which is altered and overthrown, showing the "faults" in people's common sense. According to Florian Cramer, starting from the analysis of Cornelia Sollfrank's works, a *social hack* is a *hack* in social issues, a hack in the interpersonal communication medium rather than in the programming code medium. Social structures become the main target for operations. An approach that sees for example, on the front line, in addition to Cornelia Sollfrank[4], the experience of Luther Blissett or the net.artist Netchoka Nezvanova (Florian Cramer, 2003).

Yet there is a second point of view for defining social hacking, that sheds light on the networks of individual relationships, the idea of collective participation, exchange and sharing resources and knowledge: in short hacking seen as a networking practice. This is the approach of most of the Italian hacker community, which doesn't exclude the idea of social hacking as social *hack*, but develops it from another angle, pausing on the "community" idea of hacking.

Tommaso Tozzi and Arturo di Corinto, in the book *Hacktivism. La libertà nelle maglie della rete (Hacktivism. Freedom in the mesh of the network)*, describe these two possible visions of social hacking.

In the 1980s the actual social hackings in computer networks presumably were relatively few, if by this we mean raids, sabotage and campaigns with actually positive effects from a social point of view. They were few and done by a very limited number of groups. If we consider social hacking to be the creation of virtual communities with a strong critical sense towards new technologies or the more or less legal diffusion of knowledge, skills and digital tools, or the demand for cyber rights and the diffusion of protest towards new communication technologies and its motivations, then the 1980s were a real explosion that spread by exponential multiplication of fanzines and paper magazines, BBS and electronic magazines, that circulated proposals of new technological and community models (2002).

This conception of social hacking is particular to a broad community of people in Italy who use computers and technology as channels for sharing knowledge, opening up more free and open communications possibilities and tools of critical reflection.

Most of the international net culture scene has associated the concept of social hacking to that of "social hack", as we have seen in Florian Cramer's text, at least throughout the 1980s and 1990s. An exception is the Chaos Computer Club in Berlin and Hamburg in the 1980s, where Wau Holland stands out, known in Italy above all in the Decoder group's publications, which tightened relationships with the CCC in 1989[5]. Wau Holland was co-founder of the CCC, a group established in Berlin, Germany, in 1981, carrying forward the demands for freedom of information and communication, struggling for greater transparency in governments and supporting the principles of the hacker ethic, such as free access to technological infrastructures and computers for everybody[6].

In an interview with "Decoder" in 1989, Wau Holland told about the actions of the CCC in the 1980s and speaks, in this sense, about social hacking:

In 1981, in Berlin there was a meeting of various people in the rooms of the "Die Tageszeitung" newspaper. That is where we began to talk about the possibilities of the computer and I must say that when we left we were enthusiastic. For example we saw that there was the possibility to exactly determine the electrical energy consumption of a city like Berlin, or do a census of the vacant houses and distribute this data to occupation movements. In essence, we understood that the people who have the power in this society derive part of this power from data processing, and that not only the police or "power" could use the databases, but we could do it too. (...) This is how hacking began, which I would define as a practice that lets you be inside a situation as soon as it happens and be able to create new meanings from it. The tools that let you do these things are technological, and I already realised it when I went to school and was involved in the movement. (...) Certainly, collective work must be done to realise this and we moved in this direction, regularly organising meetings and practice exercises on the media. (...) Our main activity developed on computers and on the relative forms of hacking. With this training you enter databases, go around, take a look at what's there and collect information. The spirit we enter with is a community type, meaning that we take information for the social use that can be made of it, in essence we do social hacking. (...) Our philosophy is only one: 'freedom' and we try to work in this perspective by exchanging social ideas and social inventions with other people. Learning from them and teaching them what we know. And remember that information is also deformation, it is like making a bottle starting from raw melted material: with your hands, using the information process, you give a specific shape to what had no shape before, and by deforming it you get your bottle, so you get a tool for exchanging ideas[7].

In Wau Holland's vision, a component of hacking co-exists as "social hack" (the same underlined in Florian Cramer's text mentioned above), and a more communal one that emphasizes networking, collective meetings and sharing experiences. This second idea of social hacking as a habit of sharing resources and collectivisation of information tools, was the strong point of the CCC's activity in the 1980s, whereas today it no longer seems to be the group's priority aim[8].

Among the operations implemented by the CCC in the 1980s for greater socialisation of tools and information knowledge, the episode of the BTX hack in 1984 should certainly be mentioned; this was the Telebox telecommunications service, elaborated by the German post office in collaboration with IBM. The CCC immediately criticised this computerised service, through which registered users could receive personal communications or send them to another subscriber, or even book goods or services. During the same period the German government launched the initiative of a digital census of all Germans. Consequently the telecommunications service was immediately perceived as an attempt to check on citizens and create databases with their personal and consumption habits. The operation took place in perfect hacker style, for which "all information must be free" (Levy, 1994).

To defeat the BTX project, the CCC invented an enormous hoax to reveal the flaws of a Hamburg savings bank, HASPA, where at first it paid them 135,000 Marks. Then with a hack the CCC succeeded in obtaining the password to enter HASPA's central computer, where it left in memory the order to call continuously the service offered by the CCC in the BTX. So HASPA called the service in question 13,500 times in about twelve hours. The 135,000 marks were thus calculated and paid to the Chaos Computer Club with the telephone bill of November 1984. The bill really exists and so does the rebate, but the CCC made the matter public immediately, stating that they didn't want to withdraw the money, considering that the purpose of the action was just to make known the serious gaps in the BTX. Furthermore the CCC affirmed they received the password from the bank through an error of the BTX system. More precisely through the uncontrolled issue of decoding pages (Scelsi, 1991, pp. 25-26).

This episode reminds us of phone phreaking in the 1950s, aimed at free use of technology. Phone phreakers such as the Americans Captain Crunch (John T. Draper's nickname <www.webcrunchers.com/crunch>) and Richard Cheshire,

141

started up hacking activities to allow everyone to phone free unconditionally. Captain Crunch and Richard Cheshire realised that the telephone switchboards at the time automatically decoded the signals sent by phones and that, discovering the right frequency of the signal (2,600 Hertz), and reproducing it correctly, it was possible to phone everywhere for free. Captain Crunch realised that this frequency could be reproduced by blowing in one of the free toy whistles in the "Cap'n Crunch" cereal boxes (hence his nickname), and put his "discovery" into use becoming a legendary symbol of the underground computing world (and today, a consultant for information security)[9].

Even though phone phreaking kept its anarchic spirit that characterises most hacking, it is different from the vision of social hacking where technology is seen as a means to create community types of actions and, in this sense, networking. They are not animated by "political" objectives and can't even be called "social hacks", because actually they don't want to show the faults in any system, either cultural or technological. They want to make communication open and they do it by cheating Ma Bell, letting everyone phone for free unconditionally.

In the idea of social hacking that caught on in Italy on an activist and political level, the hacker isn't someone who shows his skill in entering information systems (more properly called a *cracker*), he is someone who shares his knowledge, who fights for communication that is free and accessible to everyone, creating and spreading knowledge, letting it be manipulated. In brief, someone who shares a particular ethic with others.

Steven Levy describes "hacker ethics" in a chapter of the text *Hackers. Heroes of the Computer Revolution* (1984), which precedes by seventeen years *The Hacker Ethic and the Spirit of the Information Age* by Pekka Himanen (2001). Hacker ethics is intended as a model of life and action dictated by deep principles of collectivism and horizontality, opposing the destructive meaning that a term such as information pirate wanted to spread. Steven Levy proposes six basic principles of hacker ethics:

[1] Access to computers – and anything which might teach you something about the way the world works – should be unlimited and total. Always yield to the Hands-On Imperative!;
[2] All information should be free;
[3] Mistrust authority, promote decentralization;

[4] Hackers should be judged by their hacking, not bogus criteria such as degrees, age, race or position;
[5] You can create art and beauty on a computer;
[6] Computers can change your life for the better (1984, pp. 45-46).

In Italy, the idea of hacker ethics is closely linked to social hacking, proposing "hacking for social and political purposes"[10]. The more "political" Italian hacker scene operates a combination between counterculture activism and use of technology (computer science), following a tradition that sees as important international references: on the one hand the CCC's work with Wau Holland, as we have already said, and on the other hand the event, International Conference of the Alternative use of Technology (ICATA '89), mentioned several times on Italian sites and movement publications as one of the first hacker meetings on an international level, and which will become the model for hackmeetings <www.hackmeeting.org>.

ICATA '89 was also called a "Galactic Hacker Party", a collective meeting held in Amsterdam in 1989 that gave rise to a Final Declaration that did the rounds of alternative groups in Italy[11]. Among those present at the meeting, in addition to Rop Gonggrijp and Paul Jongsma, promoters of the initiative and founders that same year of the Dutch magazine HackTic <www.hacktic.nl>, Wau Holland and other members of the CCC, there were Steven Levy, John Draper "Captain Crunch", MIT professor Joseph Weizenbaum and Lee Felsenstein (whose opening speech at ICATA '89 made him famous in Italy)[12].

ITACA '89 was widespread mainly in Italy by the Decoder group, and the "ethic principles" were inserted in the *Cyberpunk* anthology published by Shake, which we wrote about before. It was already the mid 1980s when the future Decoder group was the prime mover of the *political cyberpunk* issue and the *social hacking* issue, speculating on a social use of telematics that would then be implemented thanks to foreign contacts, in particular Hamburg's CCC and the Dutch HackTic[13].

The Decoder collective spreads these experiences, but does it through the filter of their background in the Italian punk movement and within the alternative self-run spaces. Therefore *political cyberpunk* and *social hacking* develop in Italy within a more radical and activist context, as shown by the *Cyberpunk* anthology. The Italian movement will embrace this vision, personalising it and transforming

143

it, and in the Italy of the nineties it will contribute to forming an imagination based on an idea of alternative computer technology.

Numerous Italian publications often mention Lee Felsenstein, a character who seems to have become a sort of myth for all of the Italian hacker community, above all concerning social hacking. Actually Lee Felsenstein doesn't use this term in any of his publications, nor the term cyberpunk, which in Italy is often associated with his work.

On the site <www.fonlyinstitute.com> of the Fonly Institute, Palo Alto, California, where Lee Felsenstein works, we can read that he is recognised as one of the pioneers in creating the design of the first personal computers and in developing the first computer science industry starting from an amateur past. In this connection, the legendary Homebrew Computer Club (1975-1986) in Silicon Valley is often mentioned, which gave rise to twenty-three of the Valley's major computer companies, even prompted by the idea of opening the technology to everyone (*computer power to the people*) of which Felsenstein was one of the utmost promoters. Felsenstein created the design of the first complete personal computer with video display and the first commercially successful portable computer.

Another interesting aspect for our reconstruction of Felsenstein's career leads him to associate the idea of computer science with counterculture movements, above all through his experience in the 1970s at the University of California at Berkeley and within the Free Speech Movement (FSM) <www.fsm-a.org>. In "The Arming of Desire, Counterculture and Computer Revolution", an intervention carried out at the Waag in Amsterdam in September 2005, Felsenstein retraces most of the experience that led him to unite his passion for computer technology and the fight for civil rights[14].

Felsenstein notes that

neither the drug culture [referring to the hippies' experiences with psychedelic drugs and LSD] nor the youth political culture of the 1960s [referring to the civil rights movement of the 1960s called "New Left" which then converged in the battles against the Vietnam war] nor the unrelenting technological development were directly responsible for the development of the personal computer and the Internet. Yet while there is no direct connection, all these factors were actually responsible indirectly. My point of view is that human passion, thought and interactions are much more complex than oversimplified linear models and that the personal computer and Internet were the result of a human process made by men.

To support his hypothesis, Felsenstein resorts to the Nietzschean metaphor of the Apollonian character and the Dionysiac character. The Apollonians (from Apollo) are guided by logic, reason and self-control. The Dionysiacs (from Dionysus) are guided by body, libido and sensuality. The former follow the motto "I think, therefore I am" and for Felsenstein are referable to the New Left political activists; the latter act according to the motto "I feel, therefore I am" and are referable to the members of the hippie culture. Then there are also the Ephesians who take their name from Ephesto, the god of fire and smithy of the gods, son of Zeus and Hera. Ephesto was never accepted by the gods of the Olympus because of his ungainly, malformed appearance, and at birth his mother threw him from Mount Olympus and he was later raised by Thetis and Eurynome. Because of his skill in forging precious materials he was accepted on Mount Olympus, but he always felt excluded, then he finally left it for good taking refuge on Mount Etna in the company of the Cyclops. For Felsenstein, the Ephesians act according to the motto "I do, therefore I am" and succeed in feeling themselves part of society, deploying their practical virtues. This tendency for "doing", which I would define with the expression "hacker attitude", is typical of many people who work in the technology sector, as is confirmed furthermore by the first principle of Steven Levy's hacker ethics: "Always give precedence to the Hands-On imperative "[15].

In his experience within the FSM, Felsenstein tells about the revolts at the University of California that began in 1964 at the Berkeley campus to guarantee more rights to students, above all in freedom of communication and expression against an authoritarian, centralising management. During the 1965-1975 decade, students, engineers and scientists began to build ARPANET, which then became the Internet, putting into practice the principle of informal cooperation between highly skilled individuals and trying to substantiate the *Zeitgeist* (spirit of time) of the revolt against institutions, applying the Ephesians' awareness. This is translated into the motto "management by participation" (Lee Felsenstein, 2005)[16].

Within this course, in 1973 Lee Felsenstein and a group of computer science researchers who were part of the community called Computer Group One started the "Community Memory" project, a kind of BBS made up of four computers based in Berkeley and San Francisco that implied open use for anyone. This project was followed by many and was one of the first attempts to make the technology usable by many people.

Networking and human attitudes therefore seem to have been a substantial impulse for the development of technology. Felsenstein also mentions the proto-computer, launched in 1973 by Don Lancaster with the name "TV Typewriter", imagining a TV one could write on by using a keyboard. The idea was launched by a magazine for computerised do-it-yourself lovers and immediately 10,000 readers sent two dollars each to produce the plan. People wanted a TV to use in order to start up a new life with electronics, "they wanted to write words on a TV screen". According to Felsenstein, this episode was the beginning of the personal computer revolution. An episode where it is clear that the desires and human relationships control the development of technology[17]. Felsenstein adds that "a court of people, mostly Ephesians, began cooperative work in the open source movement, continuing to build tools to compensate for the *zero-sum logic* of traditional economy" (*ibid*).

And here another world opens up, which sees other characters who have made the history of hacker ethics, from Richard Stallman to Linus Torvalds, showing with their work that the computer is by definition a democratic tool, open to use by everyone.

In the book written by Milan's Ippolita collective titled *Open non è free* (*Open Is Not Free*) (2005), in the "Computer Stories" chapter the birth of the hacker community is described up to the experience of the Free Software Foundation (FSF) by Richard Stallman, reporting the development of hacker ethics through the work of the FSF <www.fsf.org>. After leaving the AI (Artificial Intelligence) laboratories of MIT where he worked, in 1984 Stallman began the GNU project, devoting himself with a team of collaborators to writing a code for an operative system based on Unix, but free (GNU's Not Unix!). The following year, 1985, he founded the FSF. The key discourse, on which the FSF work is based, is opening the source code of an operating system, something that does not happen with Microsoft's Windows, and the consequent issue of a GNU GPL (General Public License), which offers the possibility

Inherent to the concept of free software is a political vision of using technology as a vehicle of freedom, with the possibility to exchange, modify and distribute a software without restrictions, therefore fighting the copyright logic, which thanks to the FSF action becomes Copyleft.

While Stallman was working on creating a kernel (called HURD) - the software engine for every computer that was to make the GNU operative system complete - in 1991 Finnish Linus Torvalds began to produce another kernel based on the Minix code, a Unix-based language for the 386 computer, which was created by Andrew S. Tanenbaum as a teaching tool. The GNU/Linux operating system originated from a collective network work.

As the authors of *Open Is Not Free* write, referring to the text *The Cathedral and the Bazaar* (1998) by Eric S. Raymond,

Linus spontaneously showed that to obtain better performance, when you are released by prize-awarding institutions (...) adherence to a group of values capable of combining community involvement and technical passion is necessary (2005, p. 33).

To describe this rhizomatic model, Raymond proposes the term *bazaar method*.

With the entry of the "bazaar" method used for the Linux kernel, the community took on a completely different configuration. The role of the developers was joined by that of a myriad of peripheral functions aimed at testing, documentation, translation. (...) Torvalds' bazaar had marked the final passage of hackers from the closed place of the universities and networks of only developers to the endless space of the Internet network. (...) The networks encouraged deterritorialisation of development, therefore an unambiguous physical place – the laboratory – was no longer (*herein*, p. 33-34).

In spite of the fact that it is considered controversial by many hackers, above all for its obvious support of the open source "cause" and the idea of greater involvement on the free market (Raymond is co-founder of the Open Source Initiative), in contrast with the Free Software Foundation work that promotes the idea of free software and puts an accent on the concept of freedom, *The*

Cathedral and the Bazaar is certainly interesting in its description of the *bazaar method*[18].

Raymond, writes:

Here, I think, is the core difference underlying the cathedral-builder and bazaar styles. In the cathedral-builder view of programming, bugs and development problems are tricky, insidious, deep phenomena. It takes months of scrutiny by a dedicated few to develop confidence that you've winkled them all out. Thus the long release intervals, and the inevitable disappointment when long-awaited releases are not perfect.
In the bazaar view, on the other hand, you assume that bugs are generally shallow phenomena - or, at least, that they turn shallow pretty quick when exposed to a thousand eager co-developers pounding on every single new release. Accordingly you release often in order to get more corrections, and as a beneficial side effect you have less to lose if an occasional botch gets out the door.[19].

The idea of the "bazaar method" brings us directly back to the idea of networking and the capability to create software and other products of intelligence and creativity through the collaboration of a community of individuals acting to make communication channels open. A model of *rhizomatic* research and development, to use the words of Gilles Deleuze and Felix Guattari (1997), that promotes an interactive, reticular vision of communication, enabling the diffusion of knowledge in a horizontal way, without a centre that acts as a privileged transmitter. According to this idea of networking, everyone can potentially be transmitters and receivers and the communication must take place across a flow of data free from distortions of official mediations. In the *rhizomatic* model everyone counts equally and no one can feel authorised to impose oneself on the others. There are various communication nodes that cannot be controlled or managed by a single apparatus, even because limiting one of them does not automatically generate a block of the others, who are of equal importance in the network communications structure.

These libertarian principles take us directly back to the idea of hacker ethics brought forward by various members of the Italian hacker community. In 1999, the meeting of the promoters of the second national Hackmeeting (the first was in Florence in 1998), held at the Laboratorio Studentesco Deposito Bulk in Milan, writes:

The hacker idea of communication is the opposite to that underlying the television medium: horizontal, rhizomatic, decentralised, not hierarchical or authoritarian, not controlled or censored, where a peer to peer exchange of knowledge is possible;

The hacker idea of communication is also a different, critical vision of technology: no longer thought of as for a few "priests", but understandable, dismountable and put back together again to adapt it to individual and collective purposes;

The hacker idea of communication also foresees sharing knowledge and technologies: the great opportunity of free software programs, created collectively on the network already today allow millions of users to evade the economic burden of commercial software and can become an opportunity for occupation and new organisation of the production;

The hacker idea of communication lays the foundations for shared practices of collective intelligence, that know how to amplify the resources of individuals towards goals of common good;

The hacker idea of communication is at the basis of the Networking concept, a practice that has no borders, nor does it know ethnic groups, so for its very nature it can do nothing other than actively oppose any logic of war.

Meeting of the promoters of the Hack IT 1999
(Laboratorio Studentesco Deposito Bulk - Milan)

Independent Magazines and Radical Websites

Networking and critical reflection on technologies in Italy has taken shape with success in creating underground websites and independent magazines, which were the most important vehicles for spreading hacker ethics from the 1990s up to today. The antagonist sites followed the tradition of the amateur BBSes of the late 1980s, as the independent magazines followed that of the fanzines and punkzines of the first half of the 1980s, becoming the mouthpiece of artistic and creative experimentation of the period. Many sites and magazines, managed by collectives and groups more than by single individuals, were important vehicles for the self-management ideas and the "opposition" culture of many Italian Social Centres and the politico-activist requests for protection of the computer science rights of social hacking.

Various experiences have flourished which are practically impossible to list completely here, therefore I will just mention the most long-lasting in time, most participated and known on a national and international level.

As we said before, when Italian amateur telematic networks were being created, various BBSes were being set up all over Italy. During this phase there was collective action to create open communicative contexts in which people could express themselves freely. Therefore it was not just experimentation and creation of new languages directed at the diffusion of computer science technologies; collective operations were also encouraged to try to build various means of communication and processes that touch directly on the system of relationships among those involved in the network and technologies.

What is wanted is to claim, through collective and individual action, freedom of communication and visibility for everyone, and action is being taken to create real accessibility to computerised infrastructures, trying to give a concrete reply to the increasingly frequent attempts at regulation (the *Italian Crackdown* in 1994 is an obvious example). In this scenario, there have been some significant experiences for the history of underground digital culture. Most of the people already active in BBSes give rise to groups and collectives, each one with a specific identity. Many of them, in later years, transferred their experience in BBSes to the Internet, creating different websites as an interface to their own on-line editorial activities and experiences, which replace the earlier digital "information bulletins".

We have already mentioned the experience of the Decoder collective. Among other activities, Decoder started the magazine "*Decoder. International Underground Magazine*", active from 1987 to 1998, one of the best known independent publications in the Italian underground scene of the period. In its "manifesto of intentions" we read: "the goal is to create new counter-information spaces, participate in debates on activism, cyber information and in social hacking, computer networks, communications, new technologies and Virtual Realities" (from WikiArtPedia). The founders of the group come from various backgrounds, from anarchy to punk to amateur telematics, working in the publishing or communications field – music, video, radio, graphics, literature, computers – either on their own or, later, for more "institutional" publishing houses (1992 saw the start of the Interzone series published by Feltrinelli, edited by Raf "Valvola" Scelsi and Ermanno "Gomma" Guarneri, who are still working with the Milanese publisher).

Independently the group founded the Shake Edizioni Underground publishing association <www.shake.it>, which distributed books, VHS and magazines of the Italian underground scene and translated various international publications (among them several texts of the Re-Search series). The first book published by Shake was the *Cyberpunk* anthology edited by Raf "Valvola" Scelsi, presented in July 1990 at the Sant'Arcangelo di Romagna Festival, about which we have spoken at length. Among the people active in Decoder/Shake over the years, we mention Ermanno "Gomma" Guarneri, Gianni "u.v.L.S.I." Mezza, Giampaolo "Ulisse Spinosi" Capisani, Marco Philopat, Rosie Pianeta, Paoletta Nevrosi, Adelino Zanini, Sandrone Dazieri, Kix and many others. Today Decoder exists in an on-line version (in Italian) and continues giving information about the underground universe and much more <www.decoder.it>.

Another magazine deeply committed to disseminating cultural and creative experiments in the cultural panorama of the network, in the 1980s and 1990s, is "Neural, Hacktivism, E-Music, New Media Art". It began in December 1993 in Bari and made a name for itself over the years as one of the main Italian magazines dedicated to the culture and art of the new media and to electronic musical experimentation. "Neural" may well be the Italian publishing phenomenon that was best "contaminated" with the net.art and international media panorama, popularising abroad many of the Italian experimentations and also informing Italy about what was going on outside. The "Neural" point of view has always given great attention to emerging phenomena in the fields of art and technology, placing itself as an Italian alternative to magazines such as "Wired", with tones that were too emphatic towards technological development.

As the founder of "Neural", Alessandro Ludovico, tells us,

to fully understand the origin of the Neural experience, we must consider the Italian context of the period it was formed in. In Italy there were three basic interrelated scenes: the "cyberpunk political" movement, carried forward by the various collectives and independent publishing houses that understood the importance of the political and social aspects of digital, fighting to keep cyberspace a zone of free expression; the Italian electronic musical scene, which developed quickly from Detriot's techno acid using computers and samplers to produce "house" music; lastly, the scene of the Bulletin Board Systems (BBS), which started

151

up international networked communities animated by the enthusiasm of sharing opinions and files on a worldwide scale for the first time. In 1991, I worked as graphic designer for Minus Habens Records, an independent electronic music label and we published a small guide to virtual reality, the "Virtual Reality Handbook", released with a music CD, a real success[20]. Then, with the owner of Minus Habens Records, I decided to establish a magazine about digital culture. That's how "Neural" started and we printed the first issue in November 1993, exactly five months after the release of the first issue of "Wired". Our main themes were cyberpunks, electronics and BBS, but we have also carried forward special graphic research in order to show correctly the electronic culture of the moment. For example, the page numbering was strictly in binary code, only zero and one, in spite of the printer's protests (only after three years did we decide to associate the binary numbers to the decimal ones). Another "sensory experience" was creating the double centre-page with references directed to optical art, to offer readers a little dynamic mental trip as a pause in their reading. In issue 18, we replaced this technique with a hacktivist fake, printing fake stickers created by the Italian hackers' labs. These stickers were the sarcastic copy of the SIAE (Italian Authors' and Publishers' Association) seals that appear in every Italian book or CD, stating "duplication recommended on every media, hack productions, Italian HackLabs"[21].

Initially based on Virtual Realities, networks, media, future sounds, Science Fiction and UFOs, in 1998 "Neural" aimed at developing a critical discourse on the hacktivism, e-music and new media art panorama, following the current evolution of Italian and international digital culture. After the experience in 1994 of a network column based on culture and technology, in 1997 "Neural" became an Internet site in addition to being a paper magazine. Neural Online, initially updated every two weeks, as of 2000 presents news every day at <www.neural.it>. Since 2001 the magazine also has an English version to appear directly on the international panorama that shows increasing interest in Italian hacktivism and media arts, distributing the magazine in the United States and in Europe and with subscribers all over the world. Today it is printed every four months in two different editions: Italian and English, as Neural Online.

What makes "Neural" even more interesting is the fact that it originated as a reality to inform about the various Italian communities "by putting in connection ideas and information to give people the tools to develop their projects, comparing them with others, giving life to a kind of info-node, free for everyone" (Ludovico, 2006, cf. note 22). In a certain sense, Neural Online can be considered a work of art, and in 2004 the English version of the magazine on the web received the Honorary Mention for the Net Vision category of the Prix Ars Electronica (of the Ars Electronica Festival in Linz, Austria, <www.aec.at>), important recognition for a professional Italian work that has survived independently for more than ten years.

Another successful experience in the art and media sector was "La Stanza Rossa" *(The Red Room)* (1991-1998), the first magazine in Italy to deal programmatically with the relationship between art and new technologies[22]. "La Stanza Rossa" magazine takes its name from the novel *Röda Rummet (The Red Room)* written in 1879 by Johann August Strindberg and describes the Italian scene that in the early 1990s united artistic and technological experimentation, critically analysing the advance of Virtual Reality and the emergence of artistic practices in the network world. Nevertheless "La Stanza Rossa" is also an important networking work because it involves numerous artists and theorists of the period and is the mirror image of that very vital Italian phase in which many artists and theoreticians endorsed the origin of experimentation and criticism on the media.

As is told by Francesco Galluzzi, editor-in-chief of the magazine and former member of the Strano Network communications group in Florence,

ever since the first issue in 1992, the magazine that declared being dedicated to "young artists" (… the rhetoric of the "young artist" that marked the 1990s…), was characterised as "interdisciplinary", giving space also to cinema, literature and architecture. The year following the launch of the magazine, a more experimental character was defined (in the convictions of what could be considered the "editorial group"[23]) thanks to the meeting of hot topics that began in the last decade of the past century, computer technology and Virtual Reality (…). Our work concentrated above all (…) on finding a group of accompaniers and recognised predecessors so that we could outline a line of descent and a tribal boundary for the community we felt we were a part of. So starting from number 8 (I mention a few names at random, with no intention to exclude or privilege anyone) there appeared the voices of artists such as Giacomo Verde, Tommaso Tozzi, Massimo Contrasto, the GMM, Michele Mariano, Claudio Parrini, Correnti Magnetiche, Norman T. White, Federico D'Orazio, Studio Azzurro, Pascal Dombis, Nello Teodori or Simonetta Fadda: artists who place reflections on the social or aesthetic relapses of the technological transformation, and who were more or less part of the horizon of our present; and, along with Giuseppe Chiari, Paul Sharits, John Cage, Luca Maria Patella, Carlos Ginzburg, General Idea, Fred Forrest, Franco Vaccari or Pietro Gilardi, in the research where we believed we recognised a kind of root for the spirit with which we wanted to animate our work. In this sense interventions of social hacking should be remembered, such as those alongside the movement, very active especially at that time – an exemplary place of coincidence between attempts to renew the very conception of "art" and libertarian movements (Finelli, Galluzzi, Righetti, 2005, pp. 19-21).

Added to these experiences is the theoretical reflection on the emerging thematics such as cyberpunk, virtual communities, computer networks, electronic arts, net art and on the new models of thought and behaviour linked to the technological developments in progress at the time. "La Stanza Rossa" marks an important chapter for the development of criticism of art and media in Italy and becomes a reference point for many other subsequent publishing experiences, both paper and on-line. It ended its work in 1998, with the progressive change of the Italian artistic scene and as the topics dealt with by the magazine became outdated, by then "metabolised in common sentiment" (Galluzzi, 2005, p. 23).

In the publishing field of reflection on art and new technologies, we find more recent experiences such as "Cut-up, magazine dell'immaginario" (first issue of 1998) directed by Andrea Campanella, an unparalleled expert of underground comic strips and hardcore films who combines cyber imaginaries, comics, electronic music and reflections on the new media and the theatre in an interesting creative mix (these latter two themes organised by Anna Maria Monteverdi) <www.cut-up.net>. In Rome we remember "Simultaneità, New Media Arts Magazine", edited by Giulio Lotti, the first issue of which is dated 1997, whereas from 2003 it was published in English <www.simultaneita.net>. The "Simultaneità" magazine, with graphic design and pagination by Giulio Lotti, offered an original combination of artistic, technological and "movement" themes, in both the first issue and the following ones, involving many members of collectives active in the Roman counterculture circuit (such as AvANa.net, Infoxoa, etc.), demonstrating another valid relational platform between 1990 and 2000.

As we mentioned earlier, the Italian networking dynamics that combine artistic experimentation and technological activism also find expression in the production of independent web sites, which more often than not reflect the activity of collectives working in research and criticism on the cyberpunk themes, Virtual Reality and computer networks in the 1990s.

In 1993 the Strano Network collective was founded in Florence, its activity being of great importance concerning the development of networking art in Italy[24]. On the Strano Network site we read:

Strano Network inaugurates the 22nd of April 1993 at the CSA Ex-Emerson in Florence as research on communication territories. By comparison and interaction of experiences and research carried out in different areas, from technology to social problems, from visual arts to experimental music, Strano Network declares its aim is to safeguard the real possibility to communicate freely and democratically for everyone. (...) Since 1993 debates have been promoted with interventions and reflections on topics of contemporary art (radical and network art), on the use and abuse of communication (copyright and social hacking), electronic music concerts, installations of Virtual Reality and hypertexts, exhibitions about mutations of western customs with an ironic background, projections of unpublished videos (<www.strano.net>).

The work of the Strano Network group originated to promote the possibility of creating direct, horizontal dialogue through technology, increasing the level of awareness in using media. This is aided by the struggle for protecting the "rights of electronic citizens" (the *cyber-rights*) to guarantee the free, uncontrolled and universal diffusion of digital communication and the active social participation through implementing practices such as the Netstrikes (we will talk about *cyber-rights* and Netstrikes later). Among the first Strano Network projects, we find the creation of four hypertexts: *Testi Caldi* (1994), *Stragi di Stato* (1994, <www.strano.net/stragi>), *Fluxus* (1994) and *Metanetwork* (1992-1994), issued by the independent Wide Records label, in Pisa.

The Strano Network group operators present themselves as networkers, creators of interactive contexts and, in this direction, they debug the metaphor of the *fluctuating interface*. "The interface of a communications model is not simply a technological standard, it invests (and must take care of resolving) matters concerning quite varied sectors: politics, legislative economics, social" (Strano Network, 1996a, p. 98).

The *fluctuating interface* must not be considered a simple technological means for decoding computer information and interface, it must put various interfaced entities in relationship with each other. It must not reflect the intentions of the programmer or the system operator, however it must be the changeable expression of the virtual community's intentions. The interface is *fluctuating* in the sense that it can be manipulated by people, it can be contaminated, reproduced and in continuous evolution according to various personal inclinations. The users are the ones who contribute to its creation and its growth.

Various Strano Network projects actually show what a *fluctuating interface* is. Such as the Virtual Town T.V. (V.T.T.V.) BBS originated in 1994 (no longer active today), in which each user could interact directly with the graphic interface of the virtual city shown, and at the same time communicate with other people connected to the BBS. In Virtual Town (reminiscent of the interface of the video game *SimCity*) the user could manipulate and create texts, videos and music and participate in on-line interactive multi-chats about various topics (politics, cyber-rights, art, networks, culture, education, counterculture) and personally build their own building in the city, using it to organise public conferences with the other BBS users or to create personal archives. In turn, V.T.T.V. was a node of other BBS networks, among them CyberNet, Peacelink, European Counter Network (E.C.N.), FidoNet, FirNet, ToscaNet and One Net Italia.

This same concept of a *fluctuating interface* can be applied to the *Virtual Body* (or *Telematic Identity*) collective performance[25] in 1996. The graphic interface, which can be shown on a computer screen or video screen (or projection), is formed through the users' digitalised bodies, creating a collective organism. Each individual inserts a part of their own body into the virtual organism, capturing it with a webcam and sending it via e-mail, or by being filmed on video in the case of public events. The resulting work is a body made up of many bodies with no hierarchy among the parts which grows as a collective flow.

In 1997, Strano Network started the Web-Disk bio-encyclopaedia, a network encyclopaedia created collectively by the users <www.strano.net/wd/indice.htm>, which may be considered the proto-version of the subsequent projects by Tommaso Tozzi: *Archivio Hacker Art* <www.hackerart.org> and *WikiArtPedia* <www.wikiartpedia.org>. When the Web-Disk was developed, Tommaso Tozzi presented the *Cotropia* project (1997) at the "Digital Art in Italy" exhibition at the Civic Gallery of Modern Art in Gallarate, and, as we wrote in the preceding chapter, the Strano Network site was presented as a net-artwork, along with the collective works of everyone who worked and interacted with it.

The work is dematerialised and resolved in relationships, dynamics, potentials, behaviours and collective imaginaries carried out not exclusively by the actions produced for the show, but by the pre-existing or emerging systems inside of which the actions on show are used for an ulterior co-evolutionary flow (press announcement sent from Tozzi on 16th October 1997 to the Arti-Party mailing list, on-line at <www.strano.net/town/arte/frreart/tozzi/relation/gallarat/001.htm>).

Art goes beyond the physical object to become a strategy in progress and the museum gives direct visibility to networking interventions.

In this networking scenario the experience of Isole nella Rete (Islands in the Net) must be mentioned, which will assert itself over the years as the most long lived movement server and provider. Originated in 1996 with the idea of coupling the DIY practices and the Social Centres scene, it transfers the main contents circulating in the ECN (European Counter Network) to the Internet, along with the areas of BBS platforms, which become mailing lists: Movement (on the political initiatives of the Italian movement), CS-list (on the initiatives of the Social Centres), International (with news from abroad), ECN News (a newsletter published by Ecn.org), Cyber-Rights (on rights for information communication and accessibility) to which are added later EZLN.it (on news and initiatives of the movement in Chapas), AHA, Activism-Hacking-Artivism (on artistic activism, hacktivism and net art).

In brief, this is the story of Isole nella Rete:

In 1989 the Danish independent television TV Stop announced a public meeting among the European movement organisations and proposed creating a BBS network called European Counter Network (ECN). But the time wasn't ripe yet, the project started up only in a few countries and would never become truly European. In Holland it was called XS4all, in Germany Spinnenetz (Spidernet). In Italy it would see its most significant realisation. In 1991, some of the movement radios (Sherwood, BlackOut, OndaRossa) sparked the first nodes of a network – created with amateur technologies – which in a year's time achieved national dimensions and became a proper alternative agency to the Social Centres' movement that characterised the political initiative of the radical left of all the 1990s. Afterwards, the coming of the Internet as a means of mass communication prompted not only the collectives that gave life to the nodes of that first network but also many other movements accustomed to technology, such as most of the cyberpunk scene, to join in the *islands in the net*. The aim was to create a "movement server" capable of providing and promoting services of digital communication and web visibility – based on Internet technology – for all the antagonist movement: the website <www.ecn.org> was launched on the 1st of August 1996. Today the political and social scenario, where this project was born and founded, has changed; yet Ecn.org continues to be an inalienable tool of communication for the fragmented galaxy of the Italian counterculture. And it needs support in order to continue to guarantee a truly free space of expression, meaning outside the rigid control to which all the means of communication, individual and collective, are subjected today (Isole nella Rete, 2005)[26].

Today the Isole nella Rete project still carries forth the will to build a space of visibility on the Internet that joins people active in the world of self-management, maintaining free and independent access to means of communication as a priority goal (this is also why the log files of the users are not generated or maintained on the server, making it impossible to trace their path and on-line operations, safeguarding everyone's right to privacy and anonymity).

Creating the first Italian *anonymous remailer* was another work of the Isole nella Rete, in 1998, another tool of digital self defence put into practice by the collective and added to their other resources, first among others the cryptography, whose problems were condensed at the time in the book *Kryptonite, Escape from global control. Cryptography, anonymity and privacy in telematic networks* (1998) edited by Luc Pac and Marta McKenzie and in the Isole nella Rete directory <www.ecn.org/crypto>. *Kryptonite*, edited by Nautilus and since 2003 reprinted for Marco Valerio publishers, is the first book in Italian about cryptography, anonymity and other privacy techniques; it can be downloaded from <www.ecn.org/kriptonite>. Another site with a critical and practical point of view on the use of information and privacy technologies is *Postaxion Mutante*, created by Ferry Byte on Strano Network in 1999. An early version is found today on the Isole nella Rete server <www.ecn.org/mutante> with a mirror on <www.infoaccessibile.com/mutante>.

In the meantime the Roman underground scene has been very active, and the year when the site of Islands in the Net started up (1996) was the same year as the sites Tactical Media Crew <www.tmcrew.org> and Malcom X <www.malcolmx.it> (at first a BBS of the Cybernet network). In the presentation of Tactical Media Crew in 1996, we read:

Tactical Media Crew originated from the need to give various basic social realities access to the Internet, with special attention to what is generally defined as the "antagonist

158

movement". And [it originated to] transform and evolve the information/communication system the movement has used for years. (...) The subjects we turn our attention to, starting from our experience, are Social Centres, movement radios, feminist collectives, independent trade unions and many others who decide to make use of the potentials offered by this further means of communication. (...) Thus creating a further possibility for diffusion/ retrieval of information for a public scene, yet with the logic of the "banchetto" (info-desk) at underground events, of the infoshop or the radio broadcast, "structures" we are part of and support, but which have obvious limits. The photocopier was a fundamental invention, copy/reproduce, but there is no auto-distribution and we manage only to cover our city taking a very long time. Personally we think that the spirit that carries us away is obvious, not the longing of storing more and more information, but the search for meaning. Meaning, replies, understanding/reading and communication keys. All this could signify which alternatives are possible but above all, in a state of manifest discontent and hidden anger, understand which tactics to use to transform ourselves from unproductive to productive, (...) where producing means realising. For now realising (probably) means fighting the enemy with equal weapons: more and more "fragile points" are discovered in current capitalism. (...) If most of the strength of the capital is expressed today through information/communication channels, then we can say that its fragility is in information itself (www.tmcrew.org/tacticalmedia/tmcrew.html).

The Tactical Media Crew actions and reflections came several years before the ones realised by several activists working on "media guerrilla" topics in the net.artistic field,.

Again in Rome, in 1994 in the Forte Prenestino Social Centre in the Centocelle quarter, the AvANa, Avvisi Ai Naviganti (literally Warning to Sailors) collective started up, from 1995 a BBS, then an Internet site <avana.forteprenestino.net>. AvANa originated inside a Social Centre and with its activity shows how the reality of the social centres is linked to the experimentation of new information technologies. Then through the *Forthnet* project, AvANa put the "digitalisation" of Forte Prenestino into action, creating a LAN inside it, independently building the cabling over the years, with the idea of developing a computer network among the Social Centre rooms so that each laboratory could share their experiences and resources with the others (the beer hall, cinema, tea room, music room, graphics laboratory and infoshop, and the machine room).

Around 1999, many AvANa.net resources converged in creating a networking project called *CyberSyn II*, which started up as a technological platform to encourage cooperative work on the net, both inside and outside the Italian social centres. On the project's website we read:

> *CyberSyn II* refers to the original Cybersyn Project developed in Chile by Salvador Allende to provide new tools of democratic government for the area of social ownership, evading the alternatives of the free market and planning. That project, almost unknown because it was cancelled by Pinochet's coup d'état in 1973, proved functional beyond all expectations (especially if we consider it had only been operating for 18 months). Cybersyn foretold many of the organisational and technological concepts generally known today, such as net organisation, distributed processing, workflow and knowledge management. (<www.ecn.org/forte/cybersyn2>).

CyberSyn II originated with the idea of connecting three projects: *Forthnet,* the free net of the Forte described above, *Brain Workers Network* (BWN), a project for a public cooperation platform for the brainworkers, brought forward by a group inside AvANa and later independently, and the Observatory on communication rights, i.e. information and consultancy service for cyber-rights, a training tool on conscious action on the Internet and a platform of confrontation on censorship, privacy and access to information (topics partly disclosed by the preceding Agency project of cyber-rights, created during the first Italian Hackmeeting in 1998).

Over the years the AvANa group has worked with computer technology regarding electronic democracy and informatics citizenship (no-copyright, social networking, DIY, local civic networks), with creative production activities in relationship with other experiences such as the Electrosophic Church collective, one of the first experiences of underground video art connected to the Roman underground environments, the Sciatto Produzie collective <www.ecn.org/sciattoproduzie>, creator of perceptive installations and underground comic strips, and later the Candida TV independent media collective <candida.thing.net>, in addition to the already mentioned The Thing Roma <www.thething.it>. From 2001 to 2003, AvANa organised *Jet-Net* at the Forte Prenestino, "technological Thursdays" of DIY sharing knowledge, with free participation meetings and seminars on various topics, both technical and theoretical, with the idea of using technology consciously and learning to assemble it by themselves, at the same time sharing their own knowledge on-line with the hacker Habd-On attitude.

Before and after *Jet-Net*, AvANa promoted events about the new technologies, always inside the Forte Prenestino, among them *PsycoSurf e Media Trips* (1994), *CyberSyn II* (1999), *Not in My Number* (2001).

On the other hand, speaking of environments closer to the world of pop counterculture, with its excesses on the body, between identities, altered codes and expanded radicalism, the experience of the "Torazine" magazine to this cut-up (Rome, 1999) is worth mentioning.

"Torazine, Polychrome Capsules of Pop Counterculture" is a "chemical literature" magazine, as it is defined by co-founder Francesco "Warbear" Macarone Palmieri, which

is based on the discarding, destruction and radical questioning of all narrative models. (...) Terminal narrative diseases that wisely seize, dismantle, modify and reassemble, the body/brain of the reader/customer, acting in neuronal depth on the linguistic/narrative code that sets up the mechanisms of self-representation. (...) The post-modern youthful panorama fades/blossoms racing through poetry beyond boundaries. This is again the imaginary of Torazine that starts out as a package, as a product, as a brand, as a logo and therefore can't help flirting with the definitions, brutalising them as carrier of that iconoclast, ironic-nihilist, politically incorrect and critical production in its extreme exaggerations, touching lightly every frontier of experience. Chemical literature is as seductive and deviant as Torazine is[27].

Torazine magazine is close to the experience of the Roman collective Ordanomade <ordanomade.kyuzz.org/tora.htm>. Ordanomade began in 1997 and was housed by the Kyuzz server (independent platform committed to hosting many members and collectives of the hacktivist movement), gravitating in the scene of illegal techno-raves and offered a "liberated" vision in the mixture of body, smart drugs, identities, technology, videos, music, porn and networking. In the 1990s, all over Italy there were expanded experiences in music, perception and body in many rave parties, such as those organised in Rome in abandoned factories, called FIN*TECH (1998).

FIN*TECHKLAN INFINITEK*DESIRE is a

multiconnection of people who, by mixing their experiences implemented in recent years on targets such as music, free creative expression, self-productions and performances have given life to a single force, determined accomplice and aware in its complexity (<ordanoma de.kyuzz.org>).

The independent publishing house Venerea Edizioni (<http://ordanomade.kyuzz.org/toravener/venerea.htm>) was also close to the Rome "Torazine"; together they created the magazine Catastrophe, with the first issue dated 2005 <www.catastrophe.it>.

Then in 1995, the first issue of the magazine "CyberZone" came out in Palermo; this experience was close to that of "Torazine" in terms of style and subject.

CyberZone originated to map the changes within contemporary imagination and put together the most visionary philosophical hypotheses of our age. The CyberZone style is something that resists media taming, encompassing all scriptures and experiences that resist the dominant routine of converting themselves in the predictable. Its ethic emerges in this particular stylistic part: CyberZone exists as an indomitable negativity that denounces the lie of the new world economic order. Philosophers, sociologists, communication experts, literary, cinema and art critics, as well as a great number of artists (painters, illustrators, cartoonists) collaborated with the magazine (text freely revised from the CyberZone site <www.cyberzone.it>).

Another Sicilian experience, which began in the early 1980s during the experimentation with new technologies was FreakNet Medialab, mentioned before when talking about the amateur BBS networks. It was an independent network with respect to FidoNet, and an alternative to CyberNet and E.C.N., even though politically similar. FreakNet is a laboratory for experimenting with communications technologies, which for several years proposed free, shared use of technology, creating the first Italian HackLab and carrying forward their activity over the years with courses, seminars and events, an actual forerunner in the Sicilian information panorama <www.freaknet.org>.

In the beginning, the FreakNet MediaLab originated within the Auro Social Centre in Catania, with various participants who brought hardware equipment (rare pieces today!) to get the project started. The first service was the "Freaknet Bulletins" for the public, made with a simple 286 computer that had only one floppy drive. Later Linux was installed in a 386 machine with 40 Mb of hard disk and 4 Mb of RAM and the activity began. This included various initiatives in the Auro Social Centre and in the Italian hacker movement, participating and organising cultural, political and, above all, hacktivist events, helping the Social Centre and everyone else who wanted to use computers, the BBS network and e-mail at the Medialab, organising cyberpunk fund-raising parties, creating radio broadcasts (RadioCybernet), carrying forth hack-poetry projects <http://poetry.freaknet.org>.

Unfortunately the work done by FreakNet, openly anarchic-libertarian and critical, often had a hard life in the Catania setting, above all because of the heated contrast with the members of the right wing Forza Nuova[28]. FreakNet is still active today, even though no longer in the Auro Social Centre; it has found hospitality at Arci Catania.

Hackmeetings and Hacklabs

The Italian underground hacktivist network gave rise to Hackmeetings <www.hackmeeting.org>, an important point of arrival for the collective process of Italian networking, which began in the 1980s with the construction of amateur computer networks and BBSes. The first Hackmeeting came from an initial proposal by the Isole nella Rete collective and took place in Florence, in the CPA Social Centre (5-7 June 1998), at the time risking eviction.

The idea was to consider technology as a platform for sharing, a moment of exchange and relationship between people, involving many activists known so far on the web only by their nickname. An important moment of socialisation, as is shown by the manifesto of the first Hackmeeting in Florence in 1998, but above all an occasion for self-education and critical reflection. Below is the introductory communication that circulated in the Italian and international mailing lists to launch the initiative.

A Hackmeeting.
This is what will take place in Florence from the 5th to the 7th of June 1998, inside a squatted social centre that risks eviction. A Hackmeeting in Italy is something new compared to the rest of Europe and the United States. Just what is a Hackmeeting?
Basically it is a non-profit self-organised social event. A moment of intense exchange during which numerous fanatics of horizontal computer technology and communication gather

around a totem of connectivity and hardware to experiment and discuss the social, technical and political use of modems and things similar.

Then if we want to go further into detail – or simply be more practical – a Hackmeeting is three days of camp, three days of self-organised, self-run seminars, three days of 24-hour a day connectivity for those who bring their computer, three days of competition, challenges and games concerning everything that we know or we can play with, three days of face to face meetings for people who know each other so well but only through e-mail or chat rooms.

An enormous industrial area readapted as a social centre – the CPA (Centro Popolare Autogestito) of south Florence – will host Hack-IT '98. Dozens and dozens of people, collectives, BBSes, user groups, systems analysts, webmasters, lovers of privacy and freedom of information are heading for a meeting in order to check out the status quo of the network citizens.

A virtual organising committee, reachable in the <hackmeeting@kyuzz.org> mailing list, coordinates the physical organisation and the event programme.

Anyone who wants to share their knowledge and skills is invited to come forward and propose a seminar, a meeting, a performance or anything else they have in mind, for the use of everyone participating in Hack-IT '98. Anyone who wants to get involved in the organisation is welcome.

Hackmeeting Promoters 1998

Therefore the Italian Hackmeeting is three days of sharing collective information and knowledge about everything that concerns technology, from the computer to the radio, to video, to artistic experimentation, through free courses offered by anyone who wants to share their knowledge, and events that involve everyone whose prime objective is freedom of information and the critical use of technological tools.

Each year, a promoter collective, who is always someone different but always part of the hacker movement, spontaneously decides to host a crowd of computer enthusiasts in his/her home city, also inviting anyone who is interested in understanding something about it, starting from scratch. As is written in the later manifesto, "a hacker can even be someone who has never seen a computer in their life". The promoting group isn't actually the organiser, since the event is organised collectively using a public mailing list, which today is hosted by the server of Autistici/Inventati <hackmeeting@inventati.org>.

With respect to other foreign initiatives, such as the Chaos Communication Camp, <www.ccc.de/camp> (1999, 2003, 2007, Berlin), the Italian Hackmeeting has no entrance fee and is totally self-financed, with a strong political character regarding digital freedom. This is also why Hackmeetings are usually organised in self-run spaces and social centres.

Furthermore, the aspect of sharing technology is central, and this is why it is preferable to create an internal LAN so that all the participants' computers can network, rather than giving them the possibility to connect externally. The idea isn't to spend three days downloading all kinds of material from the web, it is to exchange knowledge with people who are going through the same experience, playing and learning at the same time.

Workshops, seminars and meetings are organised dealing with various subjects from cryptography to artificial intelligence, digital divide, free software, Freenet, GNU/Linux operative system, basic HTML, accessibility to network information, cyber-rights, networking art, hacker art, hacktivism and net.art.

The second Hackmeeting was organised at the C.S.O.A. Deposito Bulk in Milan (18-20 June 1999), the third at the C.S.O.A. Forte Prenestino in Rome (16-18 June 2000), the fourth at the Auro Social Centre in Catania (22-24 June 2001), the fifth in Bologna at the Polyvalent Occupied Theatre (21-23 June 2002), the sixth in Turin at the El Barrio youth centre (20-22 June 2003), the seventh in Genoa at the Buridda Occupied Social Laboratory (2-4 April 2004), the eighth in Naples at the C.S.O.A. Terra Terra (17-19 June 2005), the ninth in Parma (1-3 September 2006) in a space occupied for the occasion along with various other social groups from the Parma activist area. Information about future and past Hackmeetings can be found at <www.hackmeeting.org>, where there is logistic information, press releases and a Wiki for suggesting seminars. In Pula, Croatia, from 25 to 27 July 2004 there was a meeting of the international hacker community, called TransHackmeeting, with a site <www.transhackmeeti ng.org> and mailing list <thk@autistici.org>.

At the end of each Hackmeeting there is an assembly of all the participants where they share their experience and draw conclusions. Usually, but not always, this is when the promoting group for the following year's Hackmeeting comes forward, which will arrange locations and technical resources for the future event. The final assembly is useful for coordination, and as a platform for launching new projects and suggestions. It is also a humorous chance for irony about what has taken place in the preceding days and to feel "part of the group" after three days of courses, seminars, sleepless nights and lots of code.

On an international level, the country that may be closest to Italy in organizing Hackmeetings is Spain, thanks to the work of the Sindominio collective and the Nodo50 group, promoters of the first Spanish Hackmeeting in 2000, which took inspiration from the previous Italian one[29]. Recently even new projects emerging in Argentina seem to embrace the conception of networking and technology that approaches our own, surely because of the country's socio-political situation, where it is increasingly urgent to fight for rights to information and communication[30].

It was the people active in the Spanish hacktivism who created the site <www.hacklabs.org>, a useful coordination platform between all the Hacklabs worldwide, in particular Spanish and Italian. At the end of the second Italian Hackmeeting, held in Milan at the Deposito Bulk in 1999, there was the proposal to create numerous HackLabs all over Italy, many nodes in a network of contacts and experience to distribute nationally the principles of hacker ethics and a particular critical, libertarian and experimental attitude towards technology. This proposal aims at giving continuity to experiences already active throughout the years (which we have already described) and an extra chance for networking beyond the Hackmeeting event, which takes place only once a year, even though the coordination mailing list is always active.

In a short time many local HackLabs started up: HackLab Florence, LOA HackLab, HackLab Verona, HackLab Savona, Reload, HMN HackLab, Neapolis HackLab, BugsLab, Hackaserta, ZK_Warez, Area51, HackLab Asti, SpinHacker 404, F-HackLab, Underscore_To, Hacktung, HackLab Bologna, HackLab Pisa, Synusia, which the "older" FreakNet MediaLab and AvAnA.net connect to and to which others were added during the years to come.

The presence of numerous local HackLabs, joined in a national network, contributed to reinforcing the experiences of many technological laboratories in the Social Centres and created new ones; the same mailing list <hackmeeting@in ventati.org> also served as coordination for the various HackLabs. They created important training grounds for technological self-formation and spaces for reflection and battle on the right to communication, privacy and anonymity, as well as territory for sharing acquaintances and knowledge, software development and second-hand hardware exchange (through areas ironically called *organ banks*).

The results of this participated networking were clearly seen in 2001, a particularly florid year for creating new network projects. In June, the same month as the Hackmeeting in Catania, there was the first experience of the collective Autistici/Inventati <www.autistici.org> and <www.inventati.org>. The Autistici presented a more technical imprint: the term "autism" was used ironically to describe the visceral passion for the computer and the technology that leads to it being used indiscriminately. The Inventati, had a more cultural imprint and present themselves as a place for developing libertarian and critical projects on a social and informative level.

Autistici/Inventati began as a production place for projects without censorship, circulation of practices, materials and hacktivism, the use of digital knowledge as a conscious conflict instrument. It soon became a project parallel with Islands in the Net in terms of offering web spaces, mailing lists and mail accounts, radio, chat rooms, IRCs and forums, anonymizer services to surf the web anonymously and remailers to send e-mail anonymously. Like Isole nella Rete, Autistici/Inventati survives thanks to the donations of participants and members, according to the logic of self-management.

As is printed in the Manifesto about Autistici.org:

Inventati is the area that tries to digitally reproduce the matters that belong to reality, through web sites, or creating discussion areas that already exist but are placed in a daily physical space (for example an assembly can be reproduced by creating a mailing list that makes it permanent and omnipresent). Autistici, on the other hand, starts from a technical base and the passion for knowing the means used to gut the politicalness implicit in computer tools; these tools are purely digital, but this doesn't mean that they have no political impact. We start from the tools, but we arrive at quite precise political vindications in digital terrain and from there up the real sphere. (...) We feel that communication media should not only belong to IT professionals. We believe in the value of DIY practices (<www.autistici.org/it/manifesto.html>).

Nevertheless, as we have seen in the past for many amateur digital initiatives, even for Autistici/Inventati the control measures on this independent activity didn't take long to appear. A new *Italian Crackdown* happened, as we can read in the website telling what happened: "The cryptographic services offered by the Autistici/Inventati server, housed in the Aruba web farm, have been compromised on the 15th of June 2004. We discovered the fact on the 21st of June 2005. One year later. During an enquiry on a single mailbox, the Postal Police may have tapped every user's private communication going through the server Autistici.org/Inventati.org for a whole year" <autistici.org/ai/crackdown/>. As is written on the site, the Postal Police – at the orders of the Bologna prosecutor – went to the office of the Aruba provider housing one of the Autistici/Inventati (formally, Associazione Investici) servers and for one whole year retrieved information and sensitive data concerning a considerable number of users, without informing Associazione Investici, who found out about the situation only one year later almost by chance. The server was immediately shut down and replaced with a new "clean" machine and placed somewhere more reliable, and today the Associazione is still fighting to have the fact recognised as damaging to user privacy.

To react to what happened, the members of the Autistici/Inventati collective started up "Plan R*: A network of resistant communication". This foresaw the services offered deployed to several servers, located in different places. This way, they responded with a "network" strategy, according to which if a machine is forced to interrupt its work, there will always be others active, ready to continue the work.

The idea was to

create a reticular structure between the servers, like a ring network. Different access rules correspond to each ring, based on the type of services offered. The rings are built on the basis of the critical aspect of the service, the quantity of available connectivity, the server's physical location and the type of hardware. (...) One of the fundamental goals of Plan R* is to guarantee that the services are not interrupted if one or more nodes are forced to be placed off-line (if, for example, a node has been compromised). This meant it was necessary to structure a synchronisation mechanism of the materials, making it easy to redirect all the requests made to the compromised server towards a new server (<http://onenetbeyond.org>).

Here we see how it is practically possible to use the networking logic to protect the users' rights to privacy.

As we said, in 2001 various projects originated within the Italian movement. In the same period the CopyDown project also started up, with "Download a Copy – Upload an Idea", housed first on Strano Network <www.strano.net/copydown> and later on Inventati <copydown.inventati.org>[31]. CopyDown deals with giving information about free access and free circulation of knowledge and about copyright, no-copyright, copyleft, free licenses and hacking. The project immediately appears with the idea of building an extended community on the topic of free circulation of information, giving space to no-copyright projects, in both text and musical formats. One of the first initiatives of CopyDown was the opportunity to download the complete concert of the hip-hop Mano Negra act , which took place at the CSA Ex-Emerson in Florence, in July 1991 <www.autistici.org/muchocalor>.

Today CopyDown offers regularly updated news about freedom of communication and free licenses, it allows publishing articles with an open-publishing system and sharing knowledge on a public mailing list <copydown@inventati.org>.

Other projects that have followed the experience of the independent servers and originated within HackLab, offering services in the logic of knowledge sharing, are Indivia <www.indivia.net>, Diciannove <www.diciannove.net>, Oziosi <www.oziosi.org> and Ippolita <www.ippolita.net>. This latter, in particular, is an independent server for publishing projects: the members of Ippolita.net collectively wrote the book *Open is not Free* (2005), <www.ippolita.net/~ippolita>, the book *Laser, il sapere libertario* (2005), <http://www.ippolita.net/?editoria/2> and other texts are scheduled, always written by several hands, released under the Creative Commons license.

In the Ippolita site, we read:

Ippolita is a server and a community of "writers", a crossroads for sharing instruments and skills in the digital languages and the "writing" languages. The sharing of knowledge, skills and their flow into the magma of the web – digital and otherwise, the will to probe and research the manifold connections between real and virtual, between technique and philosophy, between reflection and direct action, even through a work that is published and digital, are the main ingredients that led to the origin of ippolita.net. (...) Ippolita.net is a free virtual place, based on sharing knowledge and the opportunity to equip oneself with tools for developing projects and sharing information. Ippolita.net offers services for self-productions, books, pamphlets or publishing projects on the web, by activating mailing lists and Wikis, as well as information about everything that concerns free and independent communication. (...) Ippolita.net is not just services: we would like the projects, that later become books which can be bought or downloaded for free, to continue to live on the web in a way that allows not just reproduction but also modification, additions and enrichment of the project through interaction with other communities and other subjectivities (<www.ippolita.net/?chi+siamo/>).

The Netstrike

The Netstrike is an on-line strike, a means of collective participation for web surfers, aimed at carrying forth demonstrative actions on, but not only on, the Internet, a way to make the most of the network's social and political potential. The first Netstrike took place on the 21st of December 1995, conceived and promoted by the Strano Network group, against the nuclear experiments by the French government in the Pacific Ocean, at Mururoa. The operation of ten of the French government's sites was considerably slowed down thanks to the joint action of various net-demonstrators who simultaneously concentrated the activity of their browser on the Internet addresses that were the object of the protest, repeatedly reloading the pages and clearing the cache so that the pages had to be completely reloaded every time. Participation was good and connection to the server of the "incriminated" sites was slowed down considerably, making clear the social and political protest action of the net-demonstrators.

Tommaso Tozzi, at the time member of Strano Network, described the Netstrike practice this way:

The Netstrike mechanism is similar to a demonstration. The dynamics of a street demonstration entail the need to create a traffic jam to get the attention of the population and the media to whom their protest message is aimed at. Similarly, a web demonstration will try to paralyse the activity of a certain server or the connection it relies on for a certain period of time, and at the same time will promote circulation of the reasons for the strike through the streets of cyberspace. This paralysis will be the effect of the thousands of users entering in mass, at the same time, in the same server. Since only a certain number of calls can pass through the phone cable used for Internet connections at the same time, the cable traffic will have to tail back and will clog the same way as it does on streets, slowing the operations of the server connected to that cable as well as the pace of every user travelling that section, until the path is blocked. Therefore the success of a Netstrike is proportional to the number of users connected, and this is how one can establish representation. The strength of the Netstrike will naturally result from its success in worldwide circulation of the announcement motivating the strike (1996, pp. 15-16).

The first Netstrike in 1995 was followed by many others: in 1996 a Netstrike for Chiapas and later against the American legal system for the cases of Mumia Abu Jamal and Silvia Baraldini (the White House site was blocked for twelve hours); in 1998 the Electronic Disturbance Theatre promoted a global Netstrike against Zedillo, the Pentagon and the Frankfurt stock market; again in 1998 there was a Netstrike in Italy against the clearance of the CPA Social Center in Florence; in 1999 a Netstrike was organised against the war in ex-Yugoslavia; in 2000 there was a protest against the OECD and a few months later against the site of the Comune of Milan because of the clearance of many Milanese social centres and the site was blocked for more than three hours. This action also uncovered that on the Comune site much private information about citizens is "exposed", contrary to the protection of privacy, and the Netstrike succeeded in causing a great stir in the local press; again in 2000 a Netstrike was promoted against the death penalty; in 2001 a Netstrike for free access and free circulation of knowledge, and later a Netstrike against the reforms of the Ministry of Public Education, the rise in university fees and temporary employment; again in 2001, a Nestrike against the G8 site during the Genoa events, consequent to Carlo Giuliani's death.

Tommaso Tozzi and Arturo Di Corinto write about whether or not a Netstrike is legal:

Since a Netstrike uses the same tools the surfers usually use to surf, it is hardly interpretable as sabotage. The techniques to be considered "in conformity" with the original spirit of the Netstrike are those in which, during the Netstrike, there cannot be proof and capability of distinguishing between anyone downloading a site to consult it and anyone doing the same to block it. (...) The Nestrike takes shape as a protest in which the strength is directly proportional to the participation of *cyber-citizens*: the strike is carried forward on the level of bandwidth occupation, and the bandwidth available to surfers, no matter what software is used to join in the protest, is reduced to the capacity of a normal modem, similar to the

171

presence of an individual demonstrator on the street, and as such not punishable by law (2002, p. 127).

Despite these considerations that show how the Netstrike began as a form of pacific sit-in, Netstrike legality remains a "thorny" matter and a debate is still ongoing that, somehow, shows the divide between those who have the computer skills to understand the technical functioning and consequently the social and political legitimacy, and those who consider it an illegal activity. In fact, there is still not a clear, comprehensive response on the matter at a legal level.

The consequences that such a situation can lead to was already shown in 2001 when, during the Genoa demonstration against the G8A, the Netstrike site was isolated and removed from the web by the Bologna police department at the request of the Genoa Postal Police department following the investigations by the Magistracy on the events of those days. After Carlo Giuliani's death during the demonstration, a group of activists spontaneously decided to make a Netstrike against the G8 site. The Netstrike succeeded in slowing down site action but it didn't block it (in fact this rarely happens), yet the information site <www.netstrike.it> was seized by the Magistracy anyway, appealing to a penal code article dealing with the divulgation of programs aimed at damaging computer services.

The Netstrike.it work group and many other movement groups reacted and got moving, considering the seizure of the site an act of censorship dictated by the climate of repression of the moment, and the response was to create various "mirror sites" – such as <http://netstrike.ipv7.net/> - in Italy and abroad that put the seized site back on-line. Contrary to the magistrates' intentions, the seizure brought about solidarity towards Netstrike by various associations and individuals on the web[32].

Actually, until then no one so far had so openly considered a Netstrike as a cyber crime and many people today blame the climate of tension in the air in Italy at that time for what happened, meantime the lawsuit is still going on. Anyone with a thorough knowledge of the history of Italian underground digital network, and hence also the context in which a practice such as Netstrike originated, knows it is obvious that it is a form of pacific virtual protest, a tool to make one's voice heard on the web as well.

Netstrike is an immaterial practice that began as a proposal by a group of individuals, but when it is practiced on the web it can no longer be closely connected to the individuals and the sites that launched it. Netstrike is now a global practice, that involves all web citizens, just like street demonstrations involve all the citizens of the world. Netstrike is a networking practice that operates "locally" towards certain sites, yet is functional for starting a debate on topics of public interest, involving various media and uses various platforms. The "call to Netstrike" announcements are circulated on mailing lists, websites, fliers, newspapers and magazines, so that everyone can be at the web rendezvous at the set moment, starting their protest simultaneously.

The meaning of the operation isn't so much flooding the server as it is to circulate the reasons for the protest as widely as possible, stimulating a debate. The same holds for demonstrations: the aim isn't to block city traffic, but to focus attention on certain problems, make them visible and reach as many people as possible.

As a consequence to the Italian Netstrike activities, in 1997 the Critical Art Ensemble (CAE), founded in 1987, speculated on the idea of *electronic civil disobedience*. This was accomplished by the Electronic Disturbance Theater (EDT) collective, established by Ricardo Dominguez (earlier, part of the CAE), Brett Stalbaum, Carmin Karasic and Stefan Wray in the United States. The EDT gave life to its own version of Netstrike, at first calling it Virtual Sit-in and later, creating a special tool, Floodnet. Floodnet is an application (java applet) that automatically reloads the sites being protested, making the attack on their servers more massive.

The first Netstrike organised by the EDT is dated 1998, with various actions against several sites, among them that of President Zedillo to protest in favour of the Zapatist cause, that of the Pentagon and that of the Frankfurt stock exchange. In the September 1998 action, presented during the Ars Electronica Festival in Linz (Austria) that year, the Pentagon responded by building a hostile applet, neutralising the Floodnet action and giving life to a virtual battle in cyberspace[33].

As of 1999 the Floodnet code is issued with an open source license and since 2001 it is also in the form of a graphic tool, a software where it is possible to draw and simultaneously activate the java application to repeatedly call the server of the protest object, thus creating a Netstrike through a drawing. Even for EDT, Floodnet is placed inside a broader dynamic, like a tool to catalyse attention on certain social and political matters. In this sense, whether or not Netstrike succeeds is of secondary importance and consequently, in my opinion, even using a java application that makes the action easier is secondary. What are more important are the reasons of the protest and its effects on the dynamics of on-line networking and on a socio-political level.

In fact, over the years Netstrike has become a widespread practice on the web to combat various forms of oppression. Along with the fight for protecting cyber-rights, this enters in the group of practices that see the web as a territory for carrying forward libertarian strategies and social battles.

The battle for cyber-rights in Italy started mainly with the BBSes and radical websites. So in 1998 Ferry Byte started the Cyber-Rights mailing list on Isole nella Rete <www.ecn.org>, since 1993 a BBS discussion area. In the 1990s certain electronic citizens rights were placed as priority: the right to interactivity of a communications system, the right to anonymity and privacy of the end user, the right to information reproduction, the right to communicative infrastructures to guarantee that everyone has access to information and communication.

The importance of the cyber-rights battle, visibility for everyone on the Internet, accessibility of network information and the need for reaction to censorship attempts on the web, are topics that find ample space in the book *Search Engines in the Chaos of the Net* (2001), by Ferry Byte and Claudio Parrini, where the techniques for making information more visible on the Internet are outlined, reflecting on the power dynamics that control the index-linking of on-line contents, hence analysing how the search engines really work and who they are controlled by.

As the authors stress,

the network search mechanism is moved by double dynamics. On the one hand we have saturation of information due to the material received, examined and readymade (work done by the search engines), on the other hand we must not underestimate the need that urges the user to know the "truth" about what he receives. But searching for a definition of "truth" within the information technological chaos leads to squaring things up with oxymorons, such as *chaotic truth*. The truth is in the operational moment, in the patient sequence of the creative process of the search, in the awareness of the complexity of experiences. (...) So web search doesn't concern just an abstract form of knowledge, it is a form of experience and knowledge that comprises the strong will to discover something new. Being happy with pot luck or looking elsewhere? (pp. 17-18).

This critical attitude to "search elsewhere", as we have seen, unites not just many experiences in the Italian hacktivism sphere, but also the artistic search that works on the new media to give life to creative projects and to forms of expression that are not limited to the brief representation of virtual objects: they act to question concretely the means of communication on the web and to give life to new forms of relationship between individuals. Practices that originate from the search for a *chaotic truth*, as Ferry Byte and Parrini uphold, generating new revolutionary models of behaviour and thought.

Endnotes

1 From The Jargon File at: <www.catb.org/~esr/jargon/html/H/hacker.html>..

2 In The Jargon File: "Often adduced as the reason or motivation for expending effort toward a seemingly useless goal, the point being that the accomplished goal is a hack. For example, MacLISP had features for reading and printing Roman numerals, which were installed purely for hack value. See display hack for one method of computing hack value, but this cannot really be explained, only experienced. As Louis Armstrong once said when asked to explain jazz: 'Man, if you gotta ask you'll never know.' (Feminists please note Fats Waller's explanation of rhythm: 'Lady, if you got to ask, you ain't got it.')". From: <www.catb.org/~esr/jargon/html/H/hack-value.html>.

3 Florian Cramer, *Social Hacking, Revisited*, April 2003, <http://cramer.plaintext.cc/all/social_hacking_revisited_sollfrank/>. Cornelia Sollfrank's text is *Women Hackers – a report from the mission to locate subversive women on the net*, in: "next Cyberfeminist International", Rotterdam 1999, <www.obn.org/hackers/text1.htm>.

4 In the case of Cornelia Sollfrank's works, *social hacks* originate in the art and computer culture systems. Florian Cramer mentions various pranks she played, among them the video interview of the woman hacker she invented, Clara S0pht, an intervention that caused chaos in the CCC Congress in 1999 <www.artwarez.org/aw/content/rot{_}clara.html> and the *Female Extension* work of 1997, where hundreds of women artists (they too non-existent) participated in the first net.art competition promoted by a museum, the Galerie der Gegenwart (Gallery of Contemporary Art) of the Hamburger Kunsthalle <www.artwarez.org/femext>.

5 For a more in-depth explanation see the Italian text written by Gomma in 2001, the year of Wau Holland's death. <www.decoder.it/approfondimenti.php?task=view&articleID=47>.

6 The CCC history is published on Wikipedia: <http://en.wikipedia.org/wiki/Chaos_Computer_Club>.

7 *Interview with Wau Holland*, from Cyberpunk Anthology, and in video on Videozine 1, Shake publications. Chaos Computer Club, Hamburg, 1989. On-line on the Decoder site at: <www.decoder.it/radio.php?task=view&articleID=46>.

8 After Wau Holland's death in 2001, the Chaos Computer Club took a different direction, strongly a-political and more oriented to technological research than to social matters. I was able to attend

the Chaos Communication Camp in Berlin in 2003 and participate in the subsequent international congress in December that same year, as well as follow the programmes of the successive congresses, and I realised that the idea of "being a hacker" of the most political fringes of the Italian movement is a phenomenon indigenous to us. During the "Wau Holland era" the vision of the Italian movement and that of the Chaos Computer Club had moments of contact; today the point of view is quite different. In the CCC Camp I participated in many high level technical seminars, yet none oriented to a political vision of hacking as happens in the Italian Hackmeetings. For some people, who have always challenged this Italian political aspect of being a hacker – because it is seen as too ideological – it can be an advantage. For others, Wau Holland's death meant an impoverishment of the critical aspect of the group. The current CCC projects that seem to have greater success are oriented towards technical and graphic experiments, such as *Blinkenlights* <www.blinkenlights.de>, with high impact but also quite far from the hacking idea as a source of social and cultural criticism. At the same time, the idea of making art actively is completely alien to the thinking of today's CCC, which is reticent towards everything that is "artistic" in the technological field, unless inserted in an "Art & Beauty" category. In brief, today the CCC seems to have a "hard and true" vision of what the hacker's job is: not political, not artistic, very technical, even though there are few occasions of applicative and formative comparison on systems such as GNU/Linux <www.ccc.de>. The women's collective of the CCC has shown attention to more social and cultural topics: they are called Haecksen <www.haecksen.org>.

9   For the history of Captain Crunch's activity, see: <http://en.wikipedia.org/wiki/John_Draper>.

10 On the Decoder site there is the combination between these two aspects: social hacking and hacker ethics. <www.decoder.it/archivio/cybcult/politico/hacksoc.htm>.

11 The text of the final ICATA declaration is on line at: <www.ecn.org/settorecyb/txt/icata1989.html>.

12 The ICATA '89 episode is told also in the text by Arturo Di Corinto and Tommaso Tozzi, *Hackeraggio Sociale e Cyberpunk* in the book *Hacktivism. La libertà nelle maglie della rete*, Rome, Manifestolibri, 2002, pp. 205-206. On line at: <www.hackerart.org/storia/hacktivism/3_4_2.htm>.

13 As Tozzi and Di Corinto write, "The synthesis of the main interventions [of ICATA '89] is shown in the *Cyberpunk* anthology that the Decoder group created the following year, causing an acceleration in the diffusion of hacker ethics in Italy", *idem*, p. 206.

14 The text of the intervention was sent to me by Lee Felsenstein personally and is not found on-line.

15 *Lee Felsenstein doesn't use the word hacker directly to describe these people, he speaks of "personality in and around the technology sector".*

16 *In this context, Felsenstein mentions Stewart Brand's experience and the creation of the Whole Earth Catalog, as well as his past in psychedelic counterculture and his studies on the co-evolution of biological systems.*

17 In an exchange of personal e-mails, Felsenstein writes: "My vision of the likely future of hacktivism presumes a synthesis in which the gap between work organisation and the organisation of people (a phrase that evokes images of cynical manipulation) is filled and the activities built by individuals become an integrating part of human society. This should make us understand that the work that leads to create technology is the same that leads to create human society, with all the uncertainties and hopes that emerge; for example, raising a child. I would like to see people observe prototypes in the same way they look at their children's faces, as a promise of a future that is both difficult and stimulating and as a challenge to our individual and social capability of being better than what we can allow ourselves to be" (Lee Felsenstein, personal e-mail, 7th March 2006).

18 *Eric S. Raymond refers expressly to Linus' capability to "use the whole world as a breeding ground of minds" in the viewpoint of free market development – a consideration that leads him to assert at the end of the essay that "maybe in the end open source culture will triumph", bringing grist to his mill.* On Eric S. Raymond's text, many people read between the lines that the metaphor of the Cathedral and the Bazaar was actually the

research method applied by Richard Stallman and the Free Software Foundation versus the method that enabled Linus Torvalds to create Linux, judged a winner by Raymond. Stallman's work was criticised several times by Raymond and judged not open enough towards the market, which promotes open source, taking as example the creation of the Linux kernel. From Stallman's point of view, he observes that calling software open source is just a marketing operation that actually aims at tarnishing the very conception of freedom, FSF's main battle, since software can be open, but not free. This is why, when the book *The Cathedral and the Bazaar* was released, it created great controversy within the international hacker community. Eric S. Raymond's figure is controversial also because he is admittedly right-wing, in favour of the war in Iraq and has been accused of supporting racist ideas, such as blaming the Africans in America for a high number of crimes because they have a lower IQ. Much more about this and about the "controversial" figure of Eric S. Raymond can be found in Wikipedia <http://en.wikipedia.org/wiki/Eric_S._Raymond>.

19 Eric S. Raymond, "The Cathedral and the Bazaar", 1998, original English text: <www.catb.org/~esr/writings/cathedral-bazaar/>.

20 Among the various publications, in addition to writing the *Virtual Reality Handbook* (1991), Ludovico wrote the *Internet Underground Guide* (1995), an exploration of the network underground with the first musical collection put together by e-mail, and the book *Suoni Futuri Digitali* (2000, Apogeo Edizioni), research on the production and digital enjoyment of sounds. The first two were written with Ivan Iusco, owner of the Minus Habens Records, with whom Ludovico also founded the "Neural" magazine. In 2001 Ludovico formed the n.a.m.e. (normal audio media environment) group, an artistic collective that developed the sound art Sonic Genoma project.

21 The "Neural" story was sent to me via e-mail by Alessandro Ludovico and is the presentation text of the magazine in an international context (2006).

22 Issues of the "La Stanza Rossa" magazine are no longer available in bookstores, but the experience is revived in the book *Stanza Rossa. Trasversalità artistiche e realtà virtuale negli anni Novanta*, edited by Finelli, Galluzzi, Righetti, epilogue by Antonio Caronia, San Lazzaro di Savegna (Bologna), Fabula O, 2005, <www.fabula.it>. The book is a collection of essays and interviews that involve numerous theorists and artists of today, providing important testimony of the 1990s in the art and new media sector.

23 In addition to Francesco Galluzzi, Alessandro Finelli and Stefano Righetti, many other people are involved in the editorial staff of "La Stanza Rossa". The complete list (three pages) is in Finelli, Galluzzi, Righetti, 2005, pp. 32-34. This group of people clearly offers a reliable illustration of the characters involved on the Italian artistic and media panorama of the 1990s.

24 Participating in the Strano Network were the artists Tommaso Tozzi (sysop and co-founder of the group), Federico Bucalossi and Claudio Parrini, Ferry Byte (co-founder of the group) who takes care of cyber-rights and accessibility of the web sites, Lobo (co-sysop of the VTTV BBS), Carla Maltinti (co-founder of the group) who takes care of formation and usability, Francesca Storai (co-founder of the group) who takes care of art, education and technology, Positive Mind close to the Italian counter-culture and cyberpunk environment, Stefano Sansavini (co-founder of the group), always committed to political and social battles in the sphere of telematic counter-information; Luca Scarlini (co-founder of the group), cultural organiser, and many others (including myself since 1999).

25 Created by Tommaso Tozzi with Claudio Parrini and Federico Bucalossi.

26 Text written by Snd, and subsequently integrated by Ferry Byte, for a flyer to be distributed during an initiative supporting the Islands in the Net project in Livorno on 11th February 2005. The e-mail, with subject "[ECN] Storia di ECN x Volantino", reached the [ECN] list on the 6th of February 2005. Islands in the Net is alive today thanks to the subscriptions of the association members and all those who share

the objectives and principles. This is the very reason why the server continuously risks being shut down, but has held on for ten years so far.

27 Taken from the article "Letteratura chimica. Scritti di infamia e marciume postmoderno" ("Chemical Literature. Writings of post-modern infamy and rot"), by Francesco "Warbear" Macarone Palmieri, published on <www.euromovements.info/html/letteratura.htm>.

28 The FreakNet history is found on the collective's site at: <www.freaknet.org/hacklab/history>.

29   On the website of the Nodo50 collective, www.nodo50.org, we read: "Organización dedicada a la telemática antagonista ya la organización de proyectos digitales alternativos". Sindominio too, whose experience refers directly to that of the Italian ECN collective, is a place of visibility and diffusion for many Spanish collectives: <www.sindominio.net>.

30 See for example the site <www.hackingballz.com> or the initiative by Piquete Virtual (Netstrike) against the site <www.ambitoweb.com>, an important Argentinean right-wing newspaper, promoted in 2002. Information at: <www.nodo50.org/piquetevirtual>.

31 CopyDown was conceived by Oedipa_m, with whom Pinna began collaborating immediately and who keeps the site alive today.

32 A good reconstruction of that seizure is found in Maria Teresa Paoli's graduation thesis, "New Media and Independent Communications Policy. Indymedia between Hacktivism and No Global Activism", University of Siena, Faculty of Letters and Philosophy, Degree Course in Communications Sciences, academic year 2000-2001. A downloadable on-line version in Italian in pdf format is found at: <http://italy.peacelink.org/mediawatch/docs/1248-14954_tesi.pdf>.

33 This episode is narrated by Ricardo Dominguez in the "Electronic Disturbance Theatre" video produced by Candida TV and inserted in the "Reality Hacking" video collection <www.candidatv.tv>.

Art on the Net and for the Net

Net.art and Hacktivism

From the second half of the 1990s up to today, there have been three basic passages in net art practices: the mass diffusion of the Internet as a chance to make the preceding computer utopias real, the progressive identification of networking practices inside well defined communities and the use of the Internet as a reinforcement platform for everyone's own artistic work.

These passages are quite evident if we consider the difficulty in finding definitions for the practices of networking art that took shape in the second half of the 1990s and today already begin being inserted in a historical context through various curatorial or publishing initiatives.

The communities that have taken shape in the first half of the 1990s, by creating BBSes and mailing lists, start feeling the need to give themselves an appearance, recognise themselves in a definition so that the members feel they are part of a community. A process certainly accelerated by the widespread of the Internet and electronic mail, seen as a launching pad for the immediate divulgation, without filters, of one's own ideas and, above all, an effective ground of visibility for everyone. As we have already seen, on an international level mailing lists such as "Nettime" were fundamental for creating a community of artists working on the web and for the web. And in the period between 1995 and

1997 this is where projects, actions, festivals and spontaneous interconnections start up, mainly organised independently by artists and activists who have identified themselves in the term "net.art"[1].

In 1997, after Documenta X (Kassel, Germany) - the first institutional festival to internationally accredit net.art art practices - the first mailing list expressly dedicated to the 7-11 (seven-eleven) topic started up. Founded by the German artist Udo Noll, in later years it became an important ground for comparison for everything that happened in the most experimental net.art panorama, after the "Nettime" mailing list became more moderate and many artists preferred a more open and free work channel. Before 7-11, there was a more fragmented and variegated net.art scene. The 7-11 mailing list was later hosted by the Ljudmila.org server, today the media art laboratory in Ljubliana founded by the Slovenian artist Vuk Cosic, with the active collaboration of Luka Frelih[2].

Going back to the origins of net.art, the "legend" publicised on "Nettime" by the Russian artist *Alexei Shulgin in March 1997,* shows that the term net.art was "found" for the first time by Vuk Cosic in an e-mail he received in December 1995 through an *anonymous remailer,* where the word "Net.Art" stood out in the text, made in undecipherable ASCII characters, referring to the fragment that made history:

(...) J8~g#|\;Net. Art{-^s1 (...)

So it's a real *ready-made,* as Alexei Shulgin writes in his e-mail sent to "Nettime". Shulgin tells how

the net itself gave Vuk Cosic a name for activity he was involved in! He immediately started to use this term. After a few months he forwarded the mysterious message to Igor Markovic, who managed to correctly decode it. The text [author's note: converted to a legible form] appeared rather controversial and a vague manifesto in which its author blamed traditional art institutions (...) and declared freedom of self-expression and independence for an artist on the Internet. The part of the text with the above mentioned fragment so strangely converted by Vuk's software was: "All this becomes possible only with emergence of the Net. Art as a notion becomes obsolete"[3].

Therefore the term net.art arises from the very guts of the net, as if a world incomprehensible for humans took light all by itself, ending its function as soon as it was converted to normality (once decoded, the text sent to Cosic doesn't look all that interesting).

This fragment of software was actually premonitory. The "golden days" of net.art were actually the second half of the 1990s, when numerous artists and activists gave life to events, works, debates on an international level, recognising themselves (and being recognised) as part of a new *Avant-garde?*. A network of projects and sparkling actions that fuelled Internet's utopian vision as a free uncontrolled means, applying "*hacking, social engineering and open source* from the digital practice; actions, ready-made, situation tactics and pranksters from the twentieth century tradition" (Lampo, 2005).

The first debates about net.art took place on the web, showing how networking was functional in sharing new aesthetics and objectives. Running through the "Nettime" on-line archive again, the first message on the list that puts the accent on the topic is shown by Pit Schultz on the 31st of May 1996, quoting Vuk Cosic with the subject line "The net.artists". Here, with reference to the 1995 works of Heath Bunting <www.irational.org>, light is shed on the nature of net.art in relationship to the first media art experiments, and it reflects on an audience not yet used to considering net.art as art[4].

Among other things, Heath Bunting was actually the first net.artist to send a message in the "Nettime" mailing list in December 1995. In that period, Heath Bunting, Vuk Cosic <www.ljudmila.org>, Olia Lialina <art.teleportacia.org>, Alexei Shulgin <www.easylife.org> and Jodi <www.jodi.org> were the first artists who worked expressly on the web recognising themselves in the "net.art" label, later involving a vaster scene, and thanks to networking done on "Nettime"[5].

In the following years, in addition to the above mentioned artists, activists and theorists, many others began experimenting on and with the web: among them Etoy <www.etoy.com>, Ubermorgen <www.ubermorgen.com>, ®TMark <www.rtmark.com>, The Yes Men <www.theyesmen.org>, Natalie Bookchin <www.calarts.edu/~bookchin>, Graham Harwood of the Mongrel Project <www.mongrelx.org>, Joan Leandre of retroYou <www.retroyou.org>, Mark Napier <www.potatoland.org>, Surveillance Camera Players <www.notbored.org/the-scp.html>, Matthew Fuller, Colin Green, Simon Pope of the collective I/O/D <www.backspace.org/iod>, Ricardo Dominguez of the Electronic Disturbance Theater <www.thing.net/~rdom/ecd/ecd.html>,

181

Cornelia Sollfrank <www.artwarez.org>, Amy Alexander <http://plagiarist.org>, Alexander R. Galloway <http://itserve.cc.ed.nyu.edu/galloway>, Adrian Ward <www.adeward.com>, Florian Cramer <http://cramer.plaintext.cc:70> and the Italians Jaromil <www.dyne.org>, [epidemiC] <http://epidemic.ws> and 0100101110101101.ORG (cf. Deseriis, Marano, 2003).

Hence the networking dynamics seem to have been fundamental for the net.art development, so much so that the Dutch duo Jodi, that began a real aesthetic of the programming code, created an online interactive map as artwork, showing the connections between the various servers of the net.art projects, still visible at <map.jodi.org>[6].

As Marco Deseriis and Giuseppe Marano write, speaking of the net.art network,

the construction of networks and shared contexts doesn't take place only in virtual space, it passes mainly through a dense succession of "physical events": meetings, exhibitions and festivals, that allow the various souls of net.culture to share ongoing experiences, and to deepen personal contacts and construct social moments. The events function as "accumulators and accelerators" for the initiatives that are sorted out on a translocal scale. (...) The chain among various cultural ambiences is produced concretely through festivals and meetings, where the net.artists meet and share their knowledge with hackers, political activists, cultural workers and others (*ivi*, p. 200).

Connections that involve artists, programmers and critics, carrying forward works and practices that live on the net and are created for the net, as the legendary debate on "Nettime" witnesses, where the concept of net.art (art as a net flow and process) is in contrast with *art on the net* (art exhibited on the net, but which does not exploit its intrinsic components, using it only as a showcase for works that already exist in real life)[7].

An intense networking activity that does not exhaust itself just on the Internet, causing the artist Vuk Cosic to declare:

I go to the conferences. In fact, net.art is this: an artistic practice that has much to do with the web. You come to the conference, you meet a hundred and more foreign people. This is a net. (...) When you're having fun, it's as if you were creative and you're producing something. When you have a good argument, when you're stimulated to create new subjects, new ideas, for me this is creativity, and therefore it is art[8].

There are numerous festivals and opportunities for sharing that over the years have involved international artists active in net.art and media art[9]. The spirit that gives life to the 1995-2005 period is well described in the catalogue of the *Connessioni Leggendarie* exhibit (2005) by Luca Lampo of the [epidemiC] group:

The net.art scene was not produced by strategies or money, but by people with special enthusiasm and attention to momentous change. People who, to discredit a legend, move and meet in the physical as well as the virtual world. Homes and hospitality, parties and dinners, trains and planes towards cities where someone, out of nowhere, invented a festival, a rendezvous... thousands of kilometres to present their own mailing list, a fake site, a small program or an idea, or maybe just to be there; being there was quite enough to be respected, no matter what for. Artist, author, promoter, editor, nuisance, were often the same person in different places (p. 17)[10].

A form of networking that is very similar to the one described in the preceding chapter on Hackmeetings. Yet it is singular how the live, flourishing network of Italian artists and activists whose origin and development we have told, seldom had anything directly to do with the net.art network. Many of the net practices made in Italy have remained mostly unknown on the international scene, except for a few instances. Among these, Jaromil, [epidemiC] and 0100101110101101.ORG, who from the very beginning got in touch with the other net.artists and today are usually considered part of the net.art phenomenon.

Marco Deseriis and Giuseppe Marano try to answer this question:

For us, net.art is above all a connector, a neuron, a syntagm among the billions of inert objects that make up the Web. It is the opportunity to turn the banal surfing experience into a narration where the characters and authors continually redesign the pathways we walk on. This is another reason why the 'Italian scene' stays in second place. Beyond the doubtful existence (and need) of a true national scene, the characteristics of the groups and the Italian practices closest to net.art lend themselves to little contamination. Added to the persistent techno-linguistic gap is the peculiarity of Italian movements, ever directed to an expansion of the inclusion and participation mechanisms, to the detriment of the speed of execution and interference (2003, pp. 10-11).

Actually, as the practices described here show, an Italian scene has certainly existed and has produced fertile connections and numerous projects. Such a scene, particularly the more politically oriented one, has never been defined with the term "net.art" and acted mainly on a national level. The reason was not just a linguistic problem, even though this was undoubtedly an obstacle (note that many sites of the groups described here are only in Italian). The determining factor was a different manner of perceiving its artistic work, often directly connected to the movement practices (with all the derived benefits and problems).

As Tommaso Tozzi, Stefano Sansavini, Ferry Byte and Arturo Di Corinto wrote in 2000:

> The history of underground digital culture in Italy is also a history of Italian media art. This means that to speak of art we must not be forced to speak of acts that present themselves as art, otherwise we end up in confusion that seems latent in the way the "net.art" label is used. If for example one of the characteristics of net art is to operate collectively, to build relationships, etc., describing those counterculture practices that spread this collective attitude is the same as describing artistic works[11].

It appears understandable because, according to this vision embraced by various artists and activists in Italy, net art practices and mainly the networking dynamics were first defined as hacker art and later spread to the concept of hacktivism. Using these definitions, the direct reference to the medium is abandoned, giving greater importance to the collective dynamics of political-activist orientation that can occur on the Internet, as well as through other media. But then even the net.art practices don't take place solely on-line, as we have seen; yet in the definition of "net.art" there is explicit reference to the Internet.

Concerning the definition of hacktivism, Tozzi and Di Corinto write:

> The term hacktivism comes from combining the words hacking and activism. *Hacking* is putting into practice a particular attitude towards information machines that presumes the study of computers to improve operation – through cooperation and free exchange of information between programmers – and sharing the knowledge that comes from it in order to give everyone unlimited access to knowledge. *Activism* in a strict sense is the American term indicating the means of organisation and political propaganda of the

184

grassroots movements, and in particular indicates the forms of direct action such as sit-ins, demonstrations, picketing, boycotting goods and consumption, squatting buildings and streets, self-management of spaces and self-production of goods and services (Di Corinto, Tozzi, 2002, p. 13).

The term hacktivism has been widely accepted in Italy since the 1990s (following the political cyberpunk tradition) and includes those activist and artistic practices in favour of freedom of expression and communication, in particular but not limited to the web. Outside Italy there is not a long tradition of the term hacktivism, and many hackers - for example the present members of the CCC in Berlin - do not recognise hacking as making politics and much less creating art. But in the context of American activism, another cyber-activist and artist, Ricardo Dominguez of the Electronic Disturbance Theatre (EDT), refers directly to the same term, as well as to the Netstrike practice, to describe his actions supporting the Zapatista cause. The idea of hacktivism as a networking practice is particularly recognised in Italy, above all by the presence of a vast network of movement that includes artists, hackers and digital activists, alive since the 1980s.

Therefore the term net.art seems little "used" in the 1990s by Italian "movement" artists, but the definition is not unknown, because many artists and theorists are enrolled in the international lists such as Nettime, even though not participating actively in the discussions (and here the linguistic limit returns), and because some of the independent magazines, as we have already described, publicise in Italy what happens across the border. An example is the fact that, during the 1990s and 2000s, the artist Giacomo Verde expressly uses the term "net-art" to define his more recent works on the web. This happens, in particular, for the *Qwertyu* project:

Qwertyu is the first seven letters on the PC keyboard, it could be the work of an ancient language, it makes us wonder what it means, thus opening up to many feasible answers. Qwertyu is a net-art work: a meeting place among the web's immateriality, the lightness of poetry, the materiality of architecture and the transience of sound; an encounter between their various specifics in a context 'mined' by the fear of the "information bomb" that at each step will blast the concepts of material, space, time and place (<www.qwertyu.net/qwertyu/>)[12].

Removing the "." (from net.art to net art) the borders are less defined and in Italy the practice is attributed to projects and works that are not necessarily part of the net.art international network. Evidence of this phenomenon from the end of the 1990s is the workshop for young theorists and artists <.net art>: <Anywhere><Everywhere> described previously, organised in April 1999 in Modena by the critic Mariacristina Cremaschi (it is not by chance that the workshop is called .net art and not net.art).

In the early 2000s, due a little to the influence of international practices, which were nearly at their peak, due a little to the reawakening of the academic environments oblivious of the phenomenon, a second wave of young theorists and editors began to use the term net art to define media art practices. There is distribution in Italy of the international works that have become "historical" and the Italian works by emerging artists who see themselves in the term net.art and who gravitate mainly in institutional environments, outside the movement circuits[13].

The use of the term net art (without a dot) moves the field of use towards less politicised settings, which after many years of net criticism "invent the wheel", but surely are worthy of spreading a series of media art practices in the more traditional circuits of art, known until then only by a close circle of people. We must also say that most of the Italian artists who worked in the 1980s and 1990s with a computer and the web have intentionally kept away from the "art system", proposing a no-copyright artistic vision in opposition to the market dynamics and the normal power mechanisms that often influence certain artistic circles.

This kind of separation was a factor that allowed the development of spontaneous creative projects that were strongly precursory because animated by actual utopias, but it was also the cause of the lack of recognition of work by various artists. It also could have been that the artists themselves never wanted to circumscribe it in particular artistic currents, experiencing it as a form of rebellion to the hierarchic and client dynamics, as well as political opposition.

In November 2002, the art critic Francesco Galluzzi and the artist Claudio Parrini, during the "Making Art on the Web" (Pistoletto Foundation, Biella) convention, gave a critical vision of the net art matter, starting from the networking dynamics of the 1980s, passing through mass Internet diffusion in the 1990s and consequently reflecting on the dynamics of net art at the beginning of the 2000s. Referring to the situation of the 1990s, with the diffusion of the Internet model of communication, they write:

The Internet myth spreads like a new frontier of total communication, horizontal and global, capable of guaranteeing everyone a moment of glory, or at least visibility and exiting anonymity. Appearing on the Internet (whatever this means) creates an illusion of dizzy amplification of the effects of participation in a television talk show. Thus a curious phenomenon of artist site proliferation takes place, which does not tackle the problems put forth by computer technology. Amateur artists and sculptors hope to be lucky – intended as the chance that an influential critic, struck by their work (never before encountered in a gallery or museum) while surfing the web, becomes the master of their luck. Or more modestly, that at least someone looks at their work. They establish themselves again (vanguard of the new economy!) in the telematic world of deterritorialisation and desubjectivation, the models of individuality and authoriality. With a difference that is not slight. Network territory is still unexplored, web life is experimental, lawless. It is not yet regulated by hierarchisation models (Galluzzi, Parrini, 2002).

Continuing, Francesco Galluzzi and Claudio Parrini describe the situation at the beginning of the twenty-first century, during the new economy boom. Even though not excluding the innovative and shattering component of Community projects such as the development of Linux, Gnutella and Freenet, they point out the emergence of more and more individual works on the web, which consist in direct sales and on-line auctions of their works. We quote a long citation, still indicative of our present, though after the collapse of the new economy:

The Internet has become an instrument among others, even if it preserves (especially for artists) a certain suggestion, though it seems linked to its "neophiliac" character rather than to the social potentials that web practice could set off. Even the "traditionalist" artists (the term must be intended in relation to the manners of participation in the art system, it is not a judgement of evaluation about work quality) plan on-line operations, yet they generally propose again, on a new support, the problems and attitudes already present in offline art. For example, many artists propose exhibition videos, which doesn't mean this makes them video artists. Therefore the web stops being a problematic "place", and is simply a new kind of "place". For the web, as for video, the impelling force of the "specific of the means" (to use a definition borrowed from cinema critics of the 1970s) is used up, to the extent that many discourses about net art compared to the present "state of the art" run the risk of appearing anachronistic and tautological. (...) The origin of conventional artist sites, and the logic of portals such as the indexing of search engines on parameters functional to the logics of the new economy, as a first effect deprived the horizontality and heterogeneity that characterised the early periods of popularising art on the Internet. Paradoxically (but maybe not too much), the new economy of art achieved the effect of forcing a system of relations and values on web life, which finds its legitimation, its discipline outside the web – that in this sense becomes a mere container (*ibidem*).

As Galluzzi and Parrini write, on the one hand there is sharing of material through files, the peer-to-peer philosophy, peer-to-peer exchange, both of them essential prerogatives of networking and hacker ethics; on the other hand many individual artists display their works on the Internet, selling them to whoever makes the best offer. At present, in my opinion, it is no longer possible to make art and activism without confronting certain market dynamics. The secret may be in finding new strategies to bend these dynamics to the best advantage, acting like creative viruses within a system that is always in need of new sap, yet without losing freshness and identity.

Today it is more intelligent to try to stand face to face rather than crash. Once it has been ascertained that the dynamics of profit will repeat themselves over and over, the winning strategy may be to succeed in stepping into this process as determinant players rather than as impotent spectators or as opponents who often act in favour of what was supposed to be destroyed.

The Craftsmen of the Code

In 2003, during an interview for the CyberZone magazine, I asked Jaromil (Denis Rojo's nickname), an Italian GNU/Linux programmer resident in Amsterdam, what the words "hacker ethics" meant for him:

I would talk about attitude rather than ethics. It is the desire to go hands-on, not be resigned to using without understanding, throwing out without repairing, passively accepting the rules that can often be disproved, broken and violated, generating new attractive possibilities. A hacker is curious and irreverent, sceptical and cerebral, rational enough to delight in the unachievable irrationality of the occasion (or chaos, if we wish), ecstatic admirer of fractals and eloquent minister of the entropy representing the web. The awareness of the value of information in today's world that leads the hacker to organise his revolution on the basis of sharing knowledge, an ideal experiment of power redistribution without precedents and that makes up the most visionary, equalitarian and deliciously chaotic response to Hobbes's theorem in which knowledge is power: information wants to be free! (2003, pp. 42-46)[14].

In Jaromil's works the ideas of networking, artistic experimentation, hacking and political activism live together in harmony. His activity is the concrete example of what we described in the previous chapter, speaking about social hacking: as a programmer he intentionally uses free software, and as artist (better, craftsman, as he points out) he creates projects and works where the central theme is sharing resources and accessibility to technology. Jaromil calls himself a Rasta Coder <http://rastasoft.org> and this title conceals a philosophy that isn't only involved with the exterior aspect, it highlights an attitude of thought and action that Jaromil applies to his programming and defines himself a "code craftsman".

As Armin Medosch writes in *Roots Culture, Free Software Vibrations "inna Babylon"* (2005), a direct comparison can be made between hacker's *culture roots* and the *reggae roots* that originated in Jamaica. The *culture roots* represents the hacker's pride of being the root of a Unix system (including the GNU/Linux operating system), which is the super-user who has all the access "privileges" to the machine and manages other accounts. Reggae roots is a subgenre of reggae music with rhythmic African influence. This is closely linked to the Rastafarian basic movement that originated in Jamaica in the 1930s. Rastafarian was the expression and struggle movement of the Jamaican workers of African origin, opposing racism, colonialism and capitalist exploitation. It is a "hybrid" movement, influenced by the drumming style, by agricultural tradition and by African social and food organisation and by the R&B, soul and American black music sounds. Rastafarian became quite popular in the 1970s with the reggae music of Bob Marley and the Wailers, with the consequent widespread of dreadlocks, a status symbol for many young people who identified themselves with a certain lifestyle and way of thinking.

Armin Medosch stresses the similarities between the Rastafarian movement - seen as political resistance and struggle for freedom, peace and justice from oppression - and hacker ethics - belonging to the international hacker community, working to open channels of communication and code sharing, proposing a constructive approach regarding computers and networks.

In Jaromil's work, an open supporter (and member) of the Rastafarian style, the approach to technology is targeted in giving life to open processes and the use of the computer becomes a means of freedom and not an ultimate end.

rastasoft.org

Jaromil, "Rastasoft Lion", 2003.

All his creations are freely available on the web under GNU General Public License (promoted by the Free Software Foundation <www.fsf.org>). And not in vain, his work has been on the web since 1991, through the CyberNet network, and his first experience with a computer was during the period of Italian counterculture BBSes. As is read on his site, Jaromil was co-founder in 1994 of the non-profit association Metro Olografix, for computer technology diffusion with base in Pescara, Abruzzo <http://olografix.org>. Metro Olografix is a virtual community founded on the free circulation of information, on the global village

190

concept, on the possibility of taking decisions democratically and it started in 1994 as a BBS[15].

In the same period, Jaromil participated actively in the FreakNet Medialab experience in Catania and collaborated with the Giardini Pensili company since 1998. His roots are therefore in Italy, yet his activity continued first in Vienna, Austria, where in 2000 he founded the DIY network Dyne.org <http://dyne.org> and then in Amsterdam, Holland, where he collaborated with the Montevideo/Time Based Arts institute <www.montevideo.nl> and he has always been active in the self-management environments. Jaromil is also part of the ASCII collective, Amsterdam Subversive Center for Information Interchange, a communications laboratory in the style of the Italian HackLab, with its base in a squatted city building (http://scii.nl).

As Jaromil explains:

Accessibility is a keystone for two of my projects, in the attempt to develop useful tools for the less expert, for those who are less interested in learning contorted computer formulas, and simply want to make the best use of its most recent potentials. The first one is *MuSE*: software for online network radio that offers a predictive graphic interface <http://muse.dyne.org>; the second one is *dyne:bolic* GNU/Linux[16], an entire operating system that runs directly from a CD-rom, no need to install anything, it too is configured to suggest its operability and make interaction as natural as possible (http://dynebolic.org) (*ibidem*).

Among Jaromil's other projects, *FreeJ*, for veejays and mixing videos in real time (http://freej.dyne.org), and *HasciiCam*, to allow ASCII video streaming by converting the video signal into ASCII characters using the Aalibs, Linux libraries, and giving life to a visual aesthetic of the programming code (http://ascii.dyne.org). Furthermore, Jaromil is normally considered part of the international net.art community, because he has collaborated directly with many people, such as Future Lab of the Ars Electronica Center in Linz, and because he has personally created net.art works while he lived in Vienna and Amsterdam.

Returning to the fifth point of Steven Levy's principles of hacker ethics described before, *you can create art and beauty on a computer*, "hackers enormously appreciated those innovative techniques allowing programs to perform complicated operations with very few instructions. The shorter the program, the more space available for other programs and everything ran faster"

(1984). From this reflection it emerges that the program code has its own beauty and even the programming style has its aesthetics. Jaromil is the person who puts this principle into practice, creating his *Unix Shell Forkbomb* (2002):

:(){ :|:& };:

The Unix Shell Forkbomb is defined "the most elegant forkbomb ever written" (Cramer, 2004). An apparently simple string code that is actually a virus for a Unix system: as soon as it is run, it replicates cyclically causing the machine to crash. Nevertheless, as Josephine Boxma writes, the fact that the machine is stopped isn't as important as the philosophy behind the work. The Unix Shell Forkbomb was selected for the "I Love You" show at the MAK, Museum of Applied Arts, Frankfurt, in 2002 (www.digitalcraft.org) and for the "P0es1s, Digital Poetry" event at Berlin's Kulturforum in 2004 (www.p0es1s.net). As Jaromil sustains, the forkbomb was created for all the people who sell off the web as a safe zone for middle-class society, showing how chaotic viruses must be considered spontaneous compositions, poems that cause imperfections in machines, a mirror of digital rebellion.

Among Jaromil's other works of art, the *Farah* net.art project, arising from the need to document, through the voices of the people, what is still left uncontaminated of Palestinian life and culture after years of wars and violence (http://farah.dyne.org), and the *Tubocatodico* collective theatrical performance, where an actor interacts with audio sounds and video images, putting on stage the daily use of television by any spectator <tubocatodico.dyne.org>[17].

Jaromil recently collaborated with Giacomo Verde in the "T&T Zone-laboratory for Technologies&Theatre" workshop, encounters on theatre and visual technologies at the Metarock Live Club in Florence <www.lacittadelteatro. it> (2005). Jaromil and Giacomo Verde's creative work presents various points of contact, above all concerning the artistic use of the video camera, the HasciiCam for Jaromil and the web-cam for Giacomo Verde <www.verdegiac.org>.

Also Giacomo Verde can be considered a true artisan of the code and the visual sign, always having worked with poor materials and worked at decomposing and recomposing video images, consistent with the computer hacker "attitude". In particular, his *Web-Cam-Theatre* (2001) project proposes using the web-cam through the Internet to connect and see distant places and people in real time <www.webcamtheatre.org>.

The idea was producing short theatrical events with a web-cam, using the small frame of the scenes that were filmed as if it was a stage, or better yet a "small planetary stage".

The artistic work of Giacomo Verde, as I mentioned before, is aimed at encouraging the development of collective relationships starting from the staging of web contexts, in which the *performatory* component plays a central role.

For example, in one of his previous projects, *Con-Tatto* (1998), in the forefront he places touching by hand, experiencing directly through technology. The interactive installation contemplates setting up a con-tact with the media, exploiting the *video-loop* technique, thus interfacing with a TV set and a video camera, generating luminous pulsations, corridor effects, rotating snail spirals. Hands or small objects can be inserted between the video camera and the TV to create visual effects (a kind of self-taught *TV-story*). In the second place, the installation enables con-tact with a touch-screen connected to a computer and a video projector, in order to navigate web sites based on aesthetic-political topics.

Giacomo Verde, describing the *Con-Tatto* work, maintains:

I intend pointing out that the various experiences of social activity, amplified by the web's connection possibilities, can be understood as the art works that have surpassed the limits of critical representation of the world and its problems, for a politically aesthetic action aimed at directly improving the state of affairs[18].

Of late, Giacomo Verde has been involved in the *EutopiE*, an artistic communication project on the new possible derivations of utopia.

The old social utopias are dead, but the new ways of "imagining" and creating "better worlds" are taking shape "here and now" without postponing the solution of injustices to a distant hypothetical future. Eutopia means a "happy place" and it is one of the "roots" used by Thomas More to coin the term utopia, in his book in 1516. The EutopiE website contains proposals of artistic operations and materials on the topic of the new Possible Utopias and also contemplates being space for giving notice of events and experiences concerning utopia, as a place for exchanging and sharing materials and ideas. Anyone who has information about events, materials, hypotheses, signs, dreams to report is asked to do so by writing to: info@eutopie.net (<www.verdegiac.org/eutopie>).

As Giacomo Verde points out, Eutopia is also a root of utopia.

Returning to the discussion of artistic, critical and creative use of software and its interconnections with net.art, Florian Cramer maintains that "software is something aesthetically, politically and culturally oriented" (2003, p.6), regarding recent projects that use the programming code not so much for developing generative processes, but as a game and experimental tool.

Again in 2003, Florian Cramer writes on the "Nettime" mailing list:

I see one important difference between early conceptual art and contemporary software art in that the former strived, as Lucy Lippard called it, for "dematerialization" and, where it actually used the term software (as in Jack Burnham's 1970s concept of software exhibition or in the "Radical Software" magazine), understood it as a puristic intellectual laboratory construct. In contrast, contemporary software art treats software as an unclean material (involving bugs, crashes, incompatibilities) which is not purely syntactical, but loaded with cultural semantics, aesthetic associations and even politics; experimental web browsers and game modifications are cheap but still good examples.[19].

The "viral" operations of the Italian group [epidemiC] <http://epidemic.ws> are placed in this context. These unite creative experimentation on the code and on the web, irony about language constructions and détournements of communication mechanisms, plagiarism and pranks, disorientation for unaware users, customers and curators who take too many things for granted. The [epidemiC] is "a group of about ten people who from various professional and cultural points of view analyse and speculate on aspects, dynamics and paradoxes produced by the mass diffusion of information networks" (Lampo, 2006).

As Luca Lampo tells, in the phase before the group's formation in the mid 1990s, one of the [epidemiC] members, MacumbaDigital – an anonymous post-cyber label with Blissett sympathies – began producing various works-in-progress, among them the *dis-educational* CD-rom of various plagiarisms and recycling titled *AnalFabestia* <www.analfabestia.com>.

A review appeared in 1999 on Neural Online:

Rapid images, messages inoculated by pausing on the retina only as long as strictly necessary, apparently infinite repetitions. Almost a home version of the disturbing pathway undertaken by the irregular CD-rom "Blam!" produced in New York a few years ago, this "diseducational digital microwriting" allows itself a little megalomania, trendy for these times, rambling among erotic perversions, frames of little-known films, and animation made of successive shots, in a continuous loop it settles in its tones like a deliberate visual/sound aggression. A narrative pattern that is current, disturbing and a necessary virus to create antibodies to the TV-induced addiction and drowsiness (<www.neural.it/no19/no19.htm>).

This was [epidemiC]'s entry in net culture, even though the group's name comes later "officially". Subsequently [epidemiC] gave life to the *Ribaltatore* <http://ilribaltatore.net>, "a casual generator of Italian grammar that at first is used to spread 'viral' misunderstandings in 'fashionable' forums/mailing lists/chat rooms" (Lampo, 2006).

The urban legend that a "bizarre group of hacker-poets is writing a new computer virus" reaches 0100101110101101.ORG in 2001, who propose that the project participate in the D.I.N.A., Digital Is Not Analog, festival in Bologna in 2001: thus [epidemiC] is born formally. Luca Lampo tells about the spirit with which the group was formed, which well shows the reason for the irreverent ironic character of many of his works: "The only requirement for participating was to have a well-paid job – to avoid ambitions dictated by hunger or self-referential attempts of the group's promotion. After three years of work only one press release was sent. Just for fun!"[20].

During the D.I.N.A. Festival in 2001, [epidemiC] present the *Virii Virus Viren Viry* manifesto about the beauty of the computer virus source code. Here the artists commission Franco Berardi (Bifo) to read *Love Letter*, vocal interpretation of the *I Love You* virus source code (<www.kinakuta.it/[epidemiC]/loveletter2001.mpg>). A similar experience of reading literary, textual and poetic codes was repeated in Frankfurt during the inauguration of the "I Love You, Computer Viruses Hacker Culture", (Digitalkraft, 2002, MAK) show mentioned previously. Florian Cramer was present at this reading event, called *Code Slam*, and he selected the texts of [epidemiC], Jaromil and 0100101110101101.ORG. Experimentation on artistic viruses by [epidemiC] later finds a prestigious showcase during the 49th Venice Biennial (2001) with the production of *Biennale.py*, along with 0100101110101101.ORG, written in Python language.

The virus manifests itself in various media: the code is shown on a poster in the Biennial's Slovenian pavilion, printed on T-shirts and distributed on a CD-rom. In *Biennale.py* the code becomes "animated" and, using the programming language, tells about a virus that goes to a party, meets people and in the end copulates, driven by the uncontrollable desire to duplicate himself: *party...my body...fornicate...(guest)*.

When *Biennale.py* infects a computer, it carries out the intentions already declared metaphorically. It multiplies itself, infecting all the Python type programs. Following its diffusion, the Symanthec Corporation, world leader in computer security, identifies *Biennale.py* and starts the hunt. From this moment on, if a computer is protected by an antivirus, *Biennale.py* is immediately identified, recognised as an enemy and eliminated (Lampo, 2005, p. 68)[21].

In 2002, [epidemiC] move on to creating a creative program that plays with one of the most intimate means of computer users: electronic mail. "Since viruses continued being seen as 'damaging' to information or to computers, we began thinking about a type of program that could directly damage the person using the computer and the digital information," says Luca Lampo. So they created *downJones sendMail*, a program that doesn't cause visible damage in the computer, but is subtly conceptual: it enriches e-mails by slipping short phrases into the body of any e-mail, completely changing the meaning, without the sender noticing it and even the recipient doesn't notice any sign of "intrusion".

Phrases such as "I'm not sure", "I think I love you", "you give me dysentery", "even if I lied the last time", "by the way, can you loan me your stockings?", slip into the e-mails, playing with the language. As Domenico Quaranta writes describing *downJones sendMail* "the maximum damage is the one that eats into human relations, whether it is a work, personal or diplomatic relationship. If this kind of virus were to spread, we would no longer be sure of anything we received. Putting in doubt our trust in the unalterability of data, *downJones* makes communication centrality evident, and the dangers derived from an alteration of its flow" (*ivi*, p. 51).

The viral art of [epidemiC] continues with the creation of the "Brand Virus" *Bocconi.vbs*, a *worm* that, once it is carried out, multiplies by e-mail spreading the name "Bocconi" to the joy of the university that, as Luca Lampe ironically

196

tells, doesn't seem to be very happy but nevertheless consigns the compensation to the artists... <http://epidemic.ws/bocconi/version.html>.

Subsequently, the group gives life to the program *AntiMafia –Action Sharing* that, in our opinion, concretely epitomises the concept of software art as a culturally and socially oriented artistic expression and refers to many social hacking practices described in the preceding chapters <http://epidemic.ws/ antimafia>[22].

AntiMafia appeared as a commercial software for Windows (but the code was under GPL license). Its aim was to unite experiences of dissent and protest such as Netstrike and Floodnet to an architecture more in keeping with the digital networks: the peer-to-peer, which at that time started to become widely used by "File Sharing". With AntiMafia, instead of sharing documents, actions could be shared or offered; in this case, disturbance towards web or e-mail servers. The program would do the rest, the "dirty work" :-). Anyone could protest about anything. The support rankings would multiply the effectiveness, the range of the protest, exponentially. The leader figure would disappear, in a very anarchic and democratic way. Obviously it was a provocation. Yet the software was real and its source code was public. The only thing missing was a function: an ordinary denial of service. Thirty lines of code that any programmer could have written. No one wrote them. AntiMafia was based on the Gnutella protocol. Now it is old, but maybe one day someone will write it again on more advanced protocols, such as eMule or Torrent, and the digital protests will become fashionable again... (Luca Lampo's personal e-mail, January 2006).

After participating in "CODeDOC" at the Ars Electronica Festival 2003, where the [epidemiC] presented a programme called *Double-Blind Invitation* <http://epidemic.ws/double-blind> causing invitations to the Festival to be unwittingly sent to equally unwitting programmers, the project was to be considered concluded, even though several of its members remained active singularly[23].

Beyond the Limits of the Net

As we have seen, describing the work of *viral art* by [epidemiC], networking doesn't always mean being politically correct, in fact at times by playing, social hacking can be done on the "system errors" (not just by the machine). As we have already seen, social hacking comes from two main needs: making networking the central idea, sharing collectively, using technology according to politically oriented means, and creating a prompt social hack, revealing the backstage in its ordinary sense and playing with the media and communications strategies.

In the second case, we still speak of hackers, or rather of *cultural hackers*. Hacker ethics, if considered without moralism and value judgements, are directed towards network action seen as a disclosure and, according to what Steven Levy teaches in the third fundamental principle of hacker ethics, as a criticism of the authority to promote decentralisation. Therefore a hacker is always a hacker even if, to show that information must be free and decentralised, he uses "borderline" actions. This doesn't mean that senseless destructive acts should be legitimised; it promotes critical, aware actions, that in order to be truly constructive and actually dismantle the logics of power, they can happily (and effectively) be "amoral". Or give rise to a new "moral", that of having no moral, above all in the case of appropriating other people's works if protected by copyright or by a closed, unmodifiable system.

In this sense, "the only responsibility of an artist is to be irresponsible" (<http://0100101110101101.org/texts/cyberzone_generic-it.html>).

Cultural hackers can initially act on the quiet, but once the hack is done, they make it totally transparent, quite often to shed light on the social and media bugs that until then were unknown or commonly accepted.

As Luther Blissett teaches, one can take possession of the logics the "mediasphere" feeds off of, reveal its mechanisms and find new means for reply and protest, playing with the dynamics of a society that speaks through images and expresses itself through formal memberships and immaterial codes. The web and other media, from printed paper to television, are functional platform for spreading "viral" practices, giving life to media prank and widespread telltale press releases.

An extremely significant example is the activity of 0100101110101101.ORG, a rebel cyber-entity, author of numerous media hits. In fact, the Bologna duo Eva and Franco Mattes comes from the Luther Blissett experience, putting into concrete practice the concept of "having the maximum visibility with the minimum effort" <http://0100101110101101.org>.

Known initially thanks to the Darko Maver hoax, they subsequently brought forth actions aimed at unmasking the media and art system strategies, working with plagiarism and *détournement*.

In particular, in the Darko Maver case, dated 1998-1999, 0100101110101101.ORG spread the story of a Slovenian artist, during the war author of works considered unpatriotic, and later persecuted and jailed in 1997. As reported in the announcements publicising the case, Darko Maver is a Slovenian artist who created murder scenarios in abandoned houses, exhibiting slashed mannequins to demonstrate the violence of the tortures during the conflict in ex-Yugoslavia. The artist's event found great solidarity in Italy, above all after the news of his death in a Kosovo prison; various commemorative shows were organised at the 48th Venice Biennial, at Level 57 in Bologna and at Rome's Forte Prenestino. The problem is that Darko Maver never existed, but no one thought of searching for the origins of the "legend", so the case was publicised as an episode of censorship and abuse of power <http://0100101110101101.org/home/darko_maver>.

At the beginning of 2000, 0100101110101101.ORG wrote a long press release and the hoax was revealed to the whole world through the web, stating that they invented Darko Maver's total existence. Newspaper headlines cry out: "We exposed the tricks of the critics" (Caronia in l'Unità, 14 February 2000). Indeed 0100101110101101.ORG showed how, in many institutional (as well as movement) fields, much news was accepted giving rise to myths, legends and famous artists.

Again in 1999, 0100101110101101.ORG organised the "theft" of the Hell.com art gallery, an art site accessible only by a limited nucleus of users, with password and protected by copyright. Thus begins the series of *fakes*, which will directly "attack" the sites of the principal artists of net.art, making copies, perfectly identical to the originals, of their works.

A "cut-paste strategy", as 0100101110101101.ORG defines it, which after Hell.com hits the sites of Art.Teleportacia.org and Jodi.org, recognised pillars of international net.art <http://0100101110101101.org/home/copies>. Hell.com immediately starts a lawsuit for copyright violation and the international press begins discussing topics such as authenticity and copyright in relationship to network art.

Actually there is no sense in talking about originality on the Internet: any file can be reproduced to the infinite with no loss of quality, and every copy is identical to the original. Furthermore, while surfing the web everything that is displayed is immediately saved on the hard disk and, consequently, become one's own.

As 0100101110101101.ORG sustains,

the fact that the figure of the author is no longer so important does not condition either the quality of cultural production or artistic creativity. This should make us reflect on the social nature of culture: no one has ideas that have not been influenced, directly or indirectly, by their social relations, by the community they are part of. No genius exists who is isolated form the world and inspired by a muse; there are only people who exchange information and re-elaborate what they have been told in the past. It has always been like that. Culture is enormous plagiarism.

The answer to this type of reflection isn't long in coming, and in 2001 Florian Cramer creates "the plagiarism of plagiarists", publishing on-line a copy of 0100101110101101.ORG's original site[24] and a self-interview of the authors, which later turned out to be a fake.

Again in 1999, 0100101110101101.ORG carries out *cyber-squatting* (unauthorised occupation of Internet addresses) buying the *vaticano.org* dominion and keeping it for a whole year as the official information organ of the Holy See (no one notices the difference). Actually, even though the site is formally identical to the original one, the contents presented are modified into something quite different: song lyrics, encyclicals revised and corrected, cut-up of the official site contents, but assembled in an unusual manner. After a battle with the religious authorities, 0100101110101101.ORG didn't obtain renewal of the dominion, but the cloned site still exists at <http://0100101110101101.org/home/vaticano.org>.

Later they made the virus-artwork *Biennale.py* created with [epidemiC] we have already written about, then in 2002 they originated the *Vopos* project. The idea was to reflect on the global control we are always subjected to: from the start of the project and for one year both of them wore a GPS transmitter that, by sending signals via satellite, showed the artists' exact geographical position on their site. Therefore 0100101110101101.ORG is constantly "tracked" physically, and, with the *Life Sharing* project (2000-2003), even virtually <http: //0100101110101101.org/home/vopos>.

Life Sharing is a digital portrait in real time that for two years was the mirror of 0100101110101101.ORG's activity. Their computer became an open sharing system and everyone had direct visibility on the artists' hard disk, including private correspondence. The artists sustain that privacy nowadays is "stupid" and apply their idea of hacktivism by opening themselves in a transparent manner, through a platform based on Linux <http://0100101110101101.org/home/ life_sharing>.

The work that would cause greater discussion on an international level was *Nike Ground* <www.nikeground.com>. Keeping abreast of the times, the project reflected on how brands pervaded urban spaces, creating a fake-info-point in the city of Vienna, Austria, in which passers-by are informed about a new futuristic project by Nike, the famous gym shoe multinational. At the same time, the duo create an Internet site in perfect Nike style, which explains the operation and presents itself perfectly in line with the corporation's official sites. *Nike Ground* proposes substituting the name of various important city squares with "Nike" and putting an impressive monument right in the middle with their "swoosh" (Nike's logo worldwide). For example, Karlsplatz, one of the most famous Viennese squares, is renamed Nikeplatz and 0100101110101101.ORG informs curious citizens about the upcoming event with a very credible info-point placed in the "incriminated" square.

Obviously in this case too everything is false, but the month-long campaign provokes an indignant reaction from the Vienna citizens, who want to save their square, and, naturally from the Nike Group, who declare they are extraneous to the whole operation and start a legal battle…

The interesting aspect is that this time the duo don't work in isolation; the entire performance is produced directly by Public Netbase, a Vienna *netculture* institution directed by Konrad Becker, who states clearly that *Nike Ground* is an artistic intervention and that its presence in the square must be seen as a creative appropriation, aimed at artistically manipulating the symbols of daily life. In a certain sense *Nike Ground* is also a turnabout by 0100101110101101.ORG, who decides to play the game supported by an artistic institution. The "opponents" become the Corporations, whereas art world is the playfellow.

In reality we should wonder how much of an "opponent" the multinationals are in operations like these, since everything could be seen as a source of indirect advertising for Nike and as the mirror of a new creativity that could benefit the multinational's image. The question that remains unanswered is whether the members of Nike are sharp enough to understand it... maybe the answer is yes, since the sports giant's lawsuit comes to nothing.

One thing for sure is that, with its new operation, 0100101110101101.ORG has made fun of the whole city of Vienna and everyone who fell for it completely, whether for or against Nike.

In the most recent artistic operation by 0100101110101101.ORG, the two levels, artistic experimentation and institutional prank, remain in synch. By now 0100101110101101.ORG is known in the art world and somehow the art system has become its "ally". But the mega-corporations and new business horizons are still a playing field. In the duo's last operation, this horizon took shape with a word: cinema.

United We Stand, Europe has a Mission is the new *fake-movie* by the pair of artists, who include movie stars in their cast, from Penelope Cruz to Ewan McGregor. The idea is to present, for the first time on the screen, United Europe as a champion of justice, in a scenario that sees the United States struggling against China, incarnating one of the most ingrained fears of overseas power. The film appears in perfect Blockbuster style, it books appealing actors and naturally starts the media chatting. But the film doesn't exist, obviously, even if on a media level it has all the attributes of being real: posters in all the main cities in the world and an official Internet site <www.unitedwestandmovie.com>.

In the 0100101110101101.ORG site the film is clearly stated as being a fake, false, but we know well that this information will reach only an "Internetized" audience, while everyone else will believe that the film really exists. Let's hope that a producer believes it soon too, since at this point the film could be interesting to see. It would be the latest hit of the duo of clairvoyant tricksters...

Actually one of the qualities of 0100101110101101.ORG has always been being more farsighted than the others and knowing how to "obtain maximum visibility with the least effort" (Eva and Franco Mattes, 2000). So much so that today "Flash Art", the Italian magazine of contemporary art best known in the institution spheres and most hated in the movement ones, placed

0100101110101101.ORG in the one hundred and second place of the "Top 100: the new classification according to Cattelan" (yet it contains 134 artists), based on the opinions of the top Italian critics. This classification appears rather debatable (even because the names of the critics that decided it are not shown), but it is useful as an expression of current trends in the artistic market circuits, in particular the galleries.

0100101110101101.ORG, which originated critically revealing the underhand work of this world (see the Darko Maver operation), appear in a good position in the classification, after they started showing the digital prints of their works and other productions reminiscent of them in the Fabio Paris Gallery in Brescia. Among these is the *Macchina Perpetua Auto Dis/Infettante* installation (2003) where the *Biennale.py* virus stands out. These operations start being highly rated for all the late-coming lovers of the cyber-rebellion that was. We are waiting for someone who at this point makes a theft in true Lupin III style, to continue the tradition…

The present artistic path of 0100101110101101.ORG may seem a contradiction compared to its previous experiences, but in my opinion it should be interpreted as the achievement of an awareness, mixed with a good dose of cynicism, that doesn't escape from the market mechanisms and therefore it is more strategic to bend them to our advantage. Or simply it is all another hoax in the art system, demonstrating that the rule of obtaining maximum visibility with the least effort is always valid. So instead of creating works from scratch, the previous artistic operations are exhibited in a gallery, taking advantage of the same market circuits that once "fell into the trap". Of course the prank remains, but the critical element that was found in the first works signed by 0100101110101101.ORG is lost, which, with tactical irony, irritated and confused various circuits of power, from the artistic one to the ecclesiastic one.

Network vs. Network

It is the year Two Thousand, and because of a classification of the best artists based on the judgement of critics and gallery managers in the magazine "Flash Art", the magazine editor, Giancarlo Politi, received an inflamed, colourful e-mail from the artist Oliviero Toscani, protesting about his not flattering position among the "Top 100". A thick exchange of inflamed e-mails begins (among them "Dear Editor, your newspaper makes me vomit." signed Oliviero Toscani) and in the course of correspondence, in spite of the ranting, Giancarlo Politi offers to edit a section of the infant Tirana Biennial for the photographer. A biennial exhibition that the editor of "Flash Art" is starting to organise in Tirana, Albania, involving numerous artists who for the occasion become editors, among them Maurizio Cattelan, Vanessa Beecroft, Nicolas Bourriaud, Francesco Bonami and many others for a total of twenty editors. The icing on the cake seems to be the photographer Oliviero Toscani, by now acclaimed on an international level for his photos in the transgressive advertising for Benetton, who accepts the proposal promising sponsorship from his friend Luciano (Benetton). Is this the real Oliviero Toscani? Politi doesn't seem to have any doubts.

This is the beginning of the famous "Tirana Conspiracy", maybe the best Italian media hoax pulled off so far, which was spoken of at the time by numerous local and international dailies, and fully involved the so-called "first art magazine in Europe" and its editor[25].

Authors of the legendary Conspiracy are the mysterious Marcelo Gavotta & Olivier Kamping, pseudonyms of two unknown persons who pass themselves off as Oliviero Toscani, signatories of a press dossier sent to all the major Italian and international newspapers. The envelope, containing the thick e-mail exchange between the fake Oliviero Toscani and the real editor of "Flash Art" is worthy of the best mystery films, accompanied by a treatise explaining the artistic-theoretic motivations of the hoax.

The (fake) photographer proposes four still unknown artists to make the Tirana Biennial unforgettable. Four characters who actually were ahead of the times, but who unfortunately are perfectly inexistent!

The first one, Dimitri Bioy, from Miami, is a confessed paedophile and makes amateur hard core videos accompanied by teenagers travelling from one hotel to the other. For the Tirana Biennial he proposed a series of nude young girls and teenagers; the Nigerian artist Bola Ecua, tells about the horrors in her country, fighting for human rights through photocopied photos; the Italian Carmelo Gavotta, proprietor of a Milan kiosk, produces self-made pornographic videos in perfect trash style; lastly, the real pearl of the four, the fundamentalist Hamid Piccardo, is appreciated by Bin Laden himself and by Al Qaeda.

Oliviero Toscani (the fake one) describes his (fake) creations in a long sincere article published in the July 2001 edition of "Flash Art Italia" and this same text is published in the Tirana Biennial catalogue, along with the texts of the other editors. Here is an indicative extract:

My fantastic four (allow me the analogy), have not had esoteric consent. To get to know them better I went on trips that took me from Morocco to Nigeria, from Florida to Piemonte. How can I introduce them to you here in just a few lines? I'm sure that in spire of appearances, Dimitri Bioy loves mankind as maybe only did Keats– the poet whose name was written in water. His photos were often misunderstood (as were mine, for that matter), therefore some prominent American judge pointed out that it is just rubbish... But I know that he really loves them and can't stop taking them; I'm not a transgressive quirk of an artist in search of vainglory; I am a vital function for him. For years Bola Ecua has been committed in the protest against capital punishment that still exists in her country and it appears that her works are a further tough testimony of the legal murders that persist in Africa, as well as in Asia and in the Americas. Bola always refused the typically local techniques of expression, such as sculpture or painting that often result in Afrokitsch, and I think she was the first African artist to use the photocopy as a means of revelation/delation, a kind of Yoruba Andy Warhol who, with the force of monotone images, denounces the crimes of Nigeria's militarist government. Carmelo Gavotta is Italian for all intents and purposes, and today this seems almost a fault. Right, an Italian artist should at least be required to be famous. In any case I don't think he is less interesting than Phil Collins or Maurizio Cattelan. Gavotta's short-video reminds us, with honest simplicity, that pornography can be produced today by anyone who has something to record images that each one of us can experience and investigate at will. It's too bad that he didn't let me present the series of his Lovelysecam videos, which he defines "unfinished masterpieces of a chronic voyeur". Lastly, a few words are more than enough to introduce Hamid Piccardo, who can't be called just an "artist": his Islamic fundamentalism places him one step higher; his burial shrouds (kafans) inscribed with phrases from the Koran about the apocalypse are pure acts of faith and they are not less conceptual than the religion he confesses. Osama Bin-Laden proposed him as Jihad spokesman in art[26].

We must remember that when this text was written the attack on the Twin Towers in New York (September 11, 2001) hadn't happened yet, and Oliviero Toscani (actually Marcelo Gavotta & Olivier Kamping) quotes Osama Bin Laden expressly. We also remember that the Tirana Biennial was inaugurated on

September 14, 2001, three days after the New York attack and presents an artist supported by Osama Bin Laden in the front line. For the same reason, the artist Maurizio Cattelan will decide not to participate, displaying only his silence. For Oliviero Toscani (the fake one) participation is an opportunity not to be lost, because it is as false as the four exhibiting artists and, after September 11th, is even more grotesque.

But the hoax doesn't stop at the presentation of the four artists invited to the Tirana Biennial; even more outstanding is the creation of its manifesto, which Oliviero Toscani (the fake one) takes responsibility for preparing it free of charge, after Giancarlo Politi proposes it to Fabrica, the graphics 'factory' founded by Toscani (the real one). None of this, just like the shipment of the works by the artists, is ever agreed over the phone and Marcelo Gavotta & Olivier Kamping send the poster by e-mail. This is, naturally, another provocation: the image is a distorted Albanian flag, with a two-headed eagle like the KLA eagle. In a country like Albania, ravaged by wars and surrounded by countries at war where people die for a flag, Toscani's proposal rings paradoxical and dangerous, and is opposed by the local authorities.

But thanks to the pressure by (the fake) Oliviero Toscani and the threats to foul things up, the poster passes and the symbol of the review becomes the flag, crooked, with the words "Tirana Biennial". At the same time even the invitation postcards are the fruit of the tricks of Oliviero Toscani (the fake one): presented as being created by Rocco, his son, actually they came from the imagination of Marcelo Gavotta & Olivier Kamping and were sent to various members of art and critics. Among them, one has a photo of a smiling Osama Bin Laden, here too cynically foreboding (it is 2000 - 2001, before Bin Laden's name is on everyone's lips).

As can be seen in the various articles on the topic, the matter lasted a year and a half with Giancarlo Politi never having felt the need to call the real Oliviero Toscani on the phone, and Toscani never knew about his organisational role in the Tirana Biennial. The knot unravels only at the end, when the hoax is complete. As soon at the catalogue is ready, the editor of "Flash Art" sends it to the address of the real Oliviero Toscani and naturally the photographer is flabbergasted.

But the Biennial has now been inaugurated, the catalogue distributed and the works of the (false) artists exhibited. All of this a few days after the fateful 11th of September! Oliviero Toscani doesn't want to take into account the genius of the organised conspiracy, which in our opinion says a lot about how the system of Italian and international art functions. So, assisted by two lawyers, he reports an unknown person who pretends to be him, but even today it isn't clear who Marcelo Gavotta & Olivier Kamping are. Giancarlo Politi, impotent before this hoax, writes in the October-November 2001 issue of "Flash Art" that the pair are geniuses and offers them a desk at "Flash Art", maintaining that the works sent are real artworks of great value. Marcelo Gavotta & Olivier Kamping don't turn up, naturally.

If we want to find the "moral" of this story, the answer is that it doesn't exist, but as in the fairy tale "The Emperor's New Clothes" by Hans Christian Andersen, the Conspiracy clearly turns the cards of the players of the art system face up and shows how games function in the art system and in our vacuous society of patronage and always putting in an appearance. Luther Blissett teaches, and some have learned the lesson better than the teacher, above all because they have shown they not only know how to keep playing the game but they can also pull the marionettes' strings in an exemplary manner.

This episode shows us that Orson Welles' Martian attack in the end isn't so unreal and above all it makes us wonder: what is real? What does art propose today? If all of us can make art, like Marcelo Gavotta & Olivier Kamping show with their action, where two nonexistent people create four just as nonexistent artists, whose even more nonexistent works are acclaimed by art and by critics and upheld by the "most famous art magazine in Europe", what is the sense in perpetuating a system like this? If anyone, urged by the right person, succeeds in reaching the highest goals, is there still any sense in taking the artistic market seriously?

The Tirana conspiracy shows that making art today is decidedly, and heavily, conditioned by the market, in turn monopolised by traders-collectors who influence the very market, triggering a vicious circle that decides who can be an artist and who can't. Marcelo Gavotta & Olivier Kamping turn market strategies into aesthetic rules, demonstrating that in today's art world these latter are equal to nothing, they don't exist, just like the four imaginary artists proposed for the Tirana Biennial.

In a certain sense the Tirana conspiracy also shows that making art today is conditioned by networking, meant as the ability to create relations that keep alive the market strategies described above and therefore endorse the mechanisms that decree certain people to be artists.

A networking naturally different from the one in this book, two forms of network creation that end up coexisting and clashing with each other at the same time: one dictated by the business networks, by the power relations, by "upper floor" friendships, that steps heavily in a Jurassic territory, always putting in an appearance, superficial, of slight substance, that continually needs life blood to self-replicate always the same; the other one knowing how to exploit the networks, critically dominates them and knows how to use them to its best advantage, because it understands the fluid, global, viral range, it knows the system's strong points and weaknesses.

As shown by the fake Oliviero Toscani, his fake son Rocco, the four fake artists and the fake Albanian flag, the "Tirana Conspiracy" is only the reflection of a period that stopped asking itself questions and can substitute one face for another, all that's needed are the right contacts and the right arrogance when necessary. Cynically, in this case too the real art was the network, the net of relationships (between Giancarlo Politi and Oliviero Toscani; between Oliviero Toscani and Benetton; between Marcelo Gavotta, Olivier Kamping and Giancarlo Politi; between Marcelo Gavotta, Olivier Kamping and the four fake artists), whether horizontal or vertical. The works of the artists (actually nonexistent) were not determining factors for planning the Tirana Biennial, it was the people behind them, the commercial image of Oliviero Toscani and behind him economic support from Benetton that Giancarlo Politi evidently hoped for.

The validity of Marcelo Gavotta & Olivier Kamping's action is in having claimed responsibility for their "conspiracy" to the various newspapers *anonymously*, and then disappear totally in the web flow. At the time they claimed responsibility in the press, the two cyber-ghosts refused to reveal their true identity, to avoid a successive "appearance" effect, thwarting all the action of complaint perpetuated by entering the artistic system. It may be for this very reason that the Tirana Conspiracy was so quickly forgotten and the protagonists who were the actors and victims of it have gone back to their usual routine.

In spite of newspapers with good credibility, such as "Sole 24 Ore", having spoken about it and the editor of "Flash Art" discussing it publicly in the "Letters to the Editor" column of his magazine, the news was not long-lived and the virus didn't actually take root. Even though the "conspiracy" was a legendary hit that somehow made many cathedrals tremble, and was a very successful net.art work, in Italy the event soon sank into oblivion.

A system of art made of friendly relationships surely played its part, not wanting too much exposure and preferring to forget, and also the part of a media mechanism that makes artists be stars only if they can be associated to specific faces to put on the front page, or if there are certain critics who will talk about it, struggling with each other to give visibility to their works. Furthermore, what Italian critic could have spoken about it without siding against a system that is worthwhile for everyone (including critics), possibly risking to reveal having participated in a phoney Biennial? And on the other hand, who in the movement linked to hacktivism visits the more "traditional" network environments of the art system and reads magazines such as "Flash Art", or dailies such as "Il Giornale", to actually become aware of these kinds of actions and, above all, intervenes "getting their hands dirty" with the institutional art system?

In this sense, even though Marcelo Gavotta & Olivier Kamping simulated an artistic networking operation, presenting four artists and organising a section of a Biennial, they subsequently did not take advantage of the network that could have supported them: hacktivism and net.art. They worked like viruses in the official art network, but they did not try to gain benefit by participating in the countercultural network.

The fact that Marcelo Gavotta & Olivier Kamping did not immediately reveal their identity in a press release, showing themselves as stars in the various art events and international festivals, contributed in actually making them ghosts, for the artistic network of gallery managers and critics, and for the of net.art network and for hacker art.

Two networks somehow incommensurable, which for once are confronting each other, yet they have neutralised each other, answering with silence to a perfect work of art. This might be because Marcelo Gavotta & Olivier Kamping did not belong to either of the two, so no network "recognised" them.

Marcelo Gavotta & Olivier Kamping played in a true non-place on the web that embarrassed everyone.

The "Tirana Conspiracy" was a strong artistic operation because, among other things, it sunk the knife in the system's weak point: the market strategies and the collector-market-artist relationships. Unlike the hoaxes, such as those by artist Maurizio Cattelan, who in reality winks an eye at the system, or those of 0100101110101101.ORG, who acted on détournement of communications mechanisms, plagiarism and pranks, the conspiracies like the Tirana one were carried forth with a different severity that brings them closer to the political-radical type of subversive actions. This means staying "masked" once it has been released to the press and the legal complaint has begun.

Paradoxically, even though the conspiracies are much more assertive than the spoofs in terms of criticising the system, they can be forgotten more easily for the very reason that they are not immediately associable to an "author" and because they are not functional to any network, even though based on the networking relational dynamics.

Therefore the "Tirana Conspiracy" shows us, on the one hand, that today's artistic challenge is in the invention of new means of action and new contents, as long as someone is still interested; on the other hand this action cynically demonstrates that neither the network of art critics nor the one of net artists are interested.

Endnotes

1   The "Nettime" mailing list archive of that period and later can be consulted on-line at: <www.nettime.org/Lists-Archives/>.

2   Unfortunately, today 7-11 no longer exists, since its domain was bought by an English corporation that intimated the removal of the archive because of copyright violation. Information about this case are found at <www.irational.org/7-11>.

3   Alexei Shulgin "Net.Art. The origin", message sent to "Nettime" on the 18th of March 1997, <www.nettime.org/Lists-Archives/nettime-l-9703/msg00094.html>.

4   Cf. Schultz, *The net.artists (Fwd)*, text written by Vuk Cosic, 31st May 1996 <www.nettime.org/Lists-Archives/nettime-l-9606/msg00011.html>.

5   The message sent by Heath Bunting is an ironic text titled "pickin up nettime" that describes the network the artist is part of, showing the e-mail addresses of the various characters it is made up of in a kind of celebrative punk-rock piece, optimistic about the future of the web practices to come and about the presence of a network capable of supplying them. "Pickin up nettime" was sent on the Nettime mailing list on the 27th December 1995 <www.nettime.org/Lists-Archives/nettime-l-9601/msg00051.html>. In the 1980s Heath Bunting began working on building networks that were social and open, originating from the street, graffiti, performances, pirate radios, fax and e- mail art, BBS and becoming one of the most active participants during the Internet boom. He created various web projects, many of them highly recognised internationally and he was one of the net.art pioneers. Today Bunting works in biotechnology, which he considers today's "new media" and he creates network performances that make active use of the body <www.irational.org/heath>. For experience with pirate radios, as *Heath Bunting suggested to me in a personal e-mail, see*: <http://scanner.irational.org/> and <http://67.19.211.178:8004/ >.

6   The same map was *detourned* by me in 2004, showing a split in the Italian net.culture. Collectives and authors of projects are present in <www.ecn.org/aha/map.htm> in the hacktivism sphere up to net.art. The Jodi map was *detourned* also by Marco Deseriis and Giuseppe Marano to show the connections between various international net.art projects.

7   See the minutes of the ZKP4 meeting, The Nettime Spring Conf, Lubiana, 23-25 May 1997, Beauty and the East <www.ljudmila.org/nettime/zkp4/>, in particular the text by Joachim Blank *What is net.art? :-)*, published on <www.ljudmila.org/nettime/zkp4/toc.htm> taken from a message sent by Blank to "Nettime" on the 22nd of April 1997.

8   The quotation is taken from Deseeriis, Marano, 2003, p. 200. The original text is on the "Nettime" mailing list, Josephine Bosma's e-mail, "Vuk Cosic interview: net.art per se", 27 September 1997, interview with *Josephine Bosma for the net.art.per.se event in Trieste (1997)* <www.nettime.org/Lists-Archives/nettime-l-9709/msg00053.html>. From 1997 to 2006, Josephine Bosma gave various interviews to the main network members of net.art, publishing them on the "Nettime" <www.nettime.org> and Rhizome <www.rhizome.org> mailing lists. The database of these interviews, along with many essays, articles and conference texts is found in Josephine Bosma's Database: <http://laudanum.net/cgi-bin/media.cgi?action=frontpage>. Another mail art critic very active in the period is the German Tilman Baumgärtel, who among the various texts on the subject, wrote the books: *net.art – Materialien zur Netzkunst*, Verlag für moderne Kunst, Nürnberg, 1999 and *net.art 2.0 – Neue Materialien zur Netzkunst*, Verlag für moderne Kust, Nürnberg, 2001. Website <www.thing.de/tilman>. Again in Germany, active as critics are Inke Arns, now artistic director of the Hartware MedienKunstVereins in Dortmund, author of the book *Netzkulturen*, Hamburg, Europäische Verlagsanstalt, 2002 <www.projects.v2.nl/~arns> and the Transmediale director Andreas Breockmann <www.v2.nl/abroeck>.

9   Consider festivals such as *Next Five Minutes* in Amsterdam and *DEAF Festival for Unstable Media* in Rotterdam, *Transmediale* and *Wizards of OS* in Berlin, *Ars Electronica* Festival in Linz, *Read_me Festival* in Eastern and Northern Europe, *Backspace* in London, *World-information.org* and *Public Netbase* in Vienna, *Beauty and the East* and *City of Women* in Ljubliana, *Metaforum* in Budapest, *net.art.per.se* in Trieste and *Digital is not Analog* in Bologna and *Campobasso* (now *The Influencers* in Barcelona) and the Nettime mailing lists, 7-11, Syndicate, Spectre, Rizhome, Faces, Roulx, Xchange, Rohrpost, Old Boys Network, to mention only the main ones.

10 The review "Connessioni Leggendarie, Net.Art 1995-2005" retraced the work of net.art artists and activists over the last decade. It took place at the Mediateca di Santa Teresa, Milan, 20 October -10 November 2005, Ready-Made Editions, 2005. The exhibit was managed by Luca Lampo, with the scientific committee composed of 0100101110101101.ORG, Marco Deseriis and Domenico Quaranta.

website: <www.connessionileggendarie.it>. The text is taken from the catalogue at Acknowledgements, p. 117.

11 Text from *La nuova comunicazione interattiva e l'antagonismo in Italia* edited by Tommaso Tozzi Stefano Sansavini, Ferry Byte and Arturo Di Corinto, with the collaboration of Avana (Rome), Decoder (Milan), Lamer Xterminator BBS (Bologna), Luther Blissett, Senza Confini BBS (Macerata), Zero BBS (Turin), F. Innocenti and M. Tognoni. It is published on the web at: <www.hackerart.org/storia/cybstory.htm>.

12 Giacomo Verde and Lello Voce, promotion flyer of *Qwertyu* distributed in 2000 during the Hackmeeting in Rome at Forte Prenestino.

13 An initiative that stands out in terms of diffusion, care and visibility of content is the "ExiWebArt" section, founded by Valentina Tanni in 2000, hosted by the artistic portal Exibart.com. Valentina Tanni received her degree from the Rome La Sapienza University in 2001 with a thesis titled "Net Art, 1993-2001" and that same year started the on-line column *Random, notiziario quotidiano sulla new media art* <www.random-magazine.net>, still active. Another young Italian critic recently attentive to the net.art phenomenon is Domenico Quaranta, also active in Exibart and in 2004 author of the previously mentioned *Net.Art 1994-1998. La vicenda di Àda'web*, Vita e Pensiero Publications, Milan. The book comes from the same thesis in Modern Literature at the Catholic University, Brescia.

14 Jaromil, in Tatiana Bazzichelli, "Artivism, quando l'arte diventa consapevole", interview with 0100101110101101.ORG Jaromil and Giacomo Verde, published in "CyberZone", number 18, year 8, 2003, pp. 42-46. The interview is on-line at: <http://0100101110101101.org/texts/cyberzone_generic-it.html>.

15 Among the many members of Metro Olografix I point out Stefano "Neuro" Chiccarelli, author with Andrea Monti of the book *Spaghetti Hacker. Storie, tecniche e aspetti giuridici dell'hacking in Italia* <www.spaghettihacker.it>. Stefano Chiccarelli was initially sysop of the Neuromante BBS in Pescara, a node of the CyberNet network. Among the various events organised by Metro Olografix, the Metro Olografix Crypto Meeting (MOCM) began with the aim of presenting the principles of cryptography in a popular way so as to make the importance and means of application understood <mocm.olografix.org>.

16 Dyne:bolic was created in perfect hacker style with the collaboration of various people, among them many activists of the Italian code such as Smilzo, Bomboclat and c1cc10. For a complete list of the co-authors, see <http://dynebolic.org/index.php?show=authors>.

17 The performance was prepared with many Italians, among them DinDon, Lele, Mag-One, MikyRy, Pinna, Shezzan, Maresa and GradoZero.

18 The text is taken from Verde *Presentazione installazione interattiva CON-TATTO (polittico interattivo)*, April 1998.

19 Florian Cramer, message "Re: <nettime> Don't Call it Art: Ars Electronica 2003", September 2003, on-line at: <www.nettime.org/Lists-Archives/nettime-l-0309/msg00119.html>. The message arrived on the list due to a thread started by Lev Manovich with the theme "Don't Call it Art: Ars Electronica 2003" referring to the Ars Electronica Festival that year with the theme being "Code" (Linz, Austria, 2003).

20 Luca Lampo, personal e-mail, subject: "Various info about the epidemic", received in January 2006.

21 *Then one year later the virus was "exposed" in Frankfurt and Symanthec was among the sponsors of the show!*

22 An unpublished video of the *AntiMafia – The Action Sharing* project is found at: <http://epidemic.ws/antimafia/AntiMafia.rm>

23 Luca Lampo, for example, organised the "Connessioni Leggendarie, Net.Art 1995-2005" review, at the Mediateca in Santa Teresa, Milan, 20 October-10 November 2005, already mentioned several times before.

24 Found at <http://0100101110101101.org/other_projects/01vs10> is the description of the plagiarism of plagiarism from Florian Cramer during an interview organised by Snafu.

25 Here is a list of the magazines that dealt with the "Tirana Conspiracy". Il "Sole 24 Ore", 6 January 2002, titled *Vittime del Complotto di Tirana*, article by Manuela Gandini; "Il Giorno", 27 October 2002, titled *Beffa firmata Toscani*, article by Marinella Rossi on-line at: <http://ilgiorno.quotidiano.net/chan/80/7:2670692:/2001/10/27>; *Rekombinant*, 8 January 2001, which quotes the article in "Sole 24 Ore", on-line at <www.rekombinant.org/old/article.html.sid=1421>; "ExibArt", 24 October 2001, titled *Numero 230, Ottobre/Novembre 2001, Flash Art*, review by "Flash Art" by Massimiliano Tonelli, visible at: <www.exibart.com/notizia.asp?IDNotizia=3319&IDCategoria=81>; "Artforum", 23 March 2002, titled *Tirana*, by Francesco Bonami on-line at: <www.artforum.com/talkback/id=1677>; "Raster", titled *Biennale Tirana* at: <raster.art.pl/prezentacje/tirana/tirana.htm#moni>; the Derive Approdi publishers, with the book not on sale commercially by Marcelo Gavotta (!) at: <www.unilibro.it/find_buy/product.asp?sku=1931445>, "Artnet", 4 September 2001, titled *Tirana "Biennale Opens"*, at: <www.artnet.com/Magazine/news/artnetnews/artnetnews9-4-01.asp> (who seem to be aware of the conspiracy); Yahoo! News on 16 January 2002 *Beffa Informatica, artisti inesistenti alla Biennale di Tirana*, by Roberto Buonzio <it.news.yahoo.com>, and naturally in the Letters column of "Flash Art" in October and November 2001, where Giancarlo Politi wrote a letter figuratively sent to the artist Maurizio Cattelan.

26 Signed by Oliviero Toscani, but actually written by Marcelo Gavotta & Olivier Kamping, published in "Flash Art Italia", July 2001.

Becoming Media

A Movement of Images

From the 20th to the 22nd of July 2001, during the three days of the G8 in Genoa, the media focused their attention on a new political and social subject and immediately labelled it "Anti-Globalisation". This term was used by many journalists to identify an anticapitalist battle and opposition movement against the main world powers, increasingly pervasive on the political and economic level. Actually the term "Anti-Globalisation" is an approximate construction to find a name for practices that are hard to define with just two words and to superficially lump together different social and political practices, with very different histories, going from pacifism to battling for human rights, from militancy in the basic organisations to anarchy. These subjects have in common the will to resist the capitalist interests of industrialised countries that decide for the rest of the world and oppose the consequent economic and political levelling of the planet dictated by the dynamics of power.

The actions of these collectives, groups and individuals, closely join and intersect during various world events, the first one in Seattle in 1999. The World Trade Organization meeting took place here and for the first time a global movement took on international visibility to the extent that journalists called it "the Anti-Globalisation movement", and later in Italy, "the movement of movements".

There would be a lot to say about this, and much has been said. In particular, if we pause on the networking dynamics that interest us in this context, and that relate to the practices described in the previous chapters, one factor seems to characterise these experiences strongly: the capability of developing media strategies, acquiring visibility starting from grassroots and, in particular, the "tactical" use of information and the Internet as a networking platform. Various associations are starting to use the web to distribute information and coordinate protests, and the Internet becomes one of the main media platforms to describe the Genoa events. "Don't hate the media, become the media", becomes the slogan of one of the most highly participated events at the end of the 1900s and the early 2000s, which was to be a very important information tool in that enflamed July 2001 in Genoa: Indymedia <www.indymedia.org>.

On an international level, Indymedia was founded in 1999 in Seattle during the WTO protests. The collective that started the first Indymedia node, named Indymedia Seattle <http://seattle.indymedia.org>, comes from the experience of a group of Chicago activists called Countermedia and the tradition of the London project Reclaim the Streets[1]. Indymedia then spread from Boston to Washington in the US, later involving many other countries from Europe to Australia[2].

Indymedia soon made a name for itself as the "activists medium". It is still a broad platform where one can read information directly from the activists and demonstrators during the protests, get daily updates on world events described from "another" point of view, display videos, images, photos, listen to audio files and create networking. This is possible locally, using the site's newswire, the open publishing space where anyone can post, and internationally in connection with the other Indymedia sites shown in the links of each national site.

Indymedia's web platform is flexible, it has an automated database that organises the contents posted, it presents a constantly updated news flow and audio/video streaming services. Anyone can join Indymedia, all that's necessary is a computer connected to the Internet and knowing how to load and edit audio recordings and video images, photographs and texts on the collective on-line platform. The site guide makes the operation easy even for non-experts and the coordination between the members of each node is done through a public mailing list and IRC channels.

Indymedia does not act only on line: the Independent Media Centers (IMC), are local hubs run by people who embrace the cause - collecting and publishing amateur videos, photos and texts and organizing activism on a grassroots level.

Between the 1990s and the year 2000, Indymedia progressively acquired visibility, above all as a "amplifier" of the world protests that took place before Seattle (1999) and then in Nice (2000), Prague (2000), Gothenburg (2001) and Genoa (2001), to mention just a few of them. The platform started to become a source of information for many, even for the official media who saw Indymedia's sites as a direct, heterogeneous voice of the demonstrators. The network of the territorial Independent Media Centers has been managed with the principle of decentralisation and has been based on the self-management of locally active independent collectives and on the principles of free exchange and free access to information, typical of hacker ethics.

Indymedia's history in Italy is strictly connected with the ones of the underground digital network, becoming a further piece in the counterculture scenario and the DIY tradition. A path which began by using pirate radios and BBS networks, that led to the scene of hacktivism and networking.

The Indymedia Italia site, <www.italy.indymedia.org>, was launched in Italy with the following text (this is an extract of a longer announcement):

Indymedia represented a split-up in the North American mediascape and is now getting ready to do the same also in Italy, the last node to join its international network. Originated due to the need for media coverage of an event that the official media risked deforming - the Seattle protests against the WTO - thanks to the Internet Indymedia showed that it was possible to create grassroots mass media, self-managed, non profit and independent of institutional and commercial media. Nothing was any longer like it was before: from that moment mass media had to compete with a voice that public opinion considered reliable, and this forced them to greater objectivity. The real strong point of Indymedia is lastly the capability of influencing the official mass media, forcing them to collaborate with grassroots information, to watch their behaviour. Indymedia is the splitting wedge in the gears of the mass media industry and forces it to start up again in a new way. (...) Indymedia Italia developed strategically considering its history and the current state of Italian media scenario, and it wants to win its own visibility on the television, radio, press, Internet. (...) Indymedia Italia looks for editors, journalists, organisers, technicians, activists, videomakers, photographers and above all web designers, system analysts, Linuxists and hackers sensitive to free information and available to work at Indymedia Italia. Indymedia appeals in particular to all those Italian collectives that in these years have already tested forms of grassroots information, independent and self-managed, with the hope of best developing the wealth of this network (<http://italy.indymedia.org/process/about.php>, 10th of June 2000).

The creation of an Italian section of Indymedia started in the Italian underground movement in June 2000. The "Net_Institute" mailing list, managed by a Bolognese collective set up in 1999, gave particular attention to the subject on its website <http://net-i.zkm.de/indymedia>. Here, the collective initially decided to be responsible for creating the Italian node and coordination between Indymedia Italia and Indymedia International on a technical level. Indymedia Italia became operative on the occasion of the OECD summit in Bologna, planned for the 12th to 15th June 2000[3]. The first announcement was published on the "Net_Institute" site, asking people to get in contact to collaborate on building the Italian node. The first organisation meetings took place in Bologna, before the OECD summer, and in Rome in the conference on net.art and hacktivism at the Hackmeeting 2000 at the Forte Prenestino[4].

Among the founders of "Net_Institute" are Franco Berardi "Bifo" and Matteo Pasquinelli. It originated as a mailing list in February 2000. The "Net_Institute" project was created in order to spread network culture and criticism in the Mediterranean area, relating directly on the international experience of the middle European netculture, among them the "Nettime" mailing list.

As Franco Berardi "Bifo" writes,

on the one hand "Net_Institute" proposes attacking the Wired ideology of virtualisation with criticism tools, which systematically removes the physical dimension (the territory-planet, the sensitive body) and tends to see the future as a pure and simple development of the disembodied web. On the other hand, "Net_Institute" leads its theoretical/practical battle against the instrumental vision of the web, against the simplism of those who (in the political formations of institutional left or extreme left) believe that the Internet is merely an instrument. Internet is not an instrument, it is a cosmos. *Netculture* does not at all mean using the Internet to carry out a political traditional type of battle, replace fliers or branch meetings with electronic lists and nicely coloured sites. This instrumental vision is dominant in the Italian dimension of the web. And "Net_Institute" originated to criticise it, defeat it, sweep it away[5].

The "Net_Institute" experience obtained national and international participation and visibility, but it ended in January 2002, transforming and blending with the Rekombinant project, mailing list and relative website <www.rekombinant.org>. The Rekombinant project was launched in "Net_Institute" on the 16th of July 2000 by Franco Berardi "Bifo" and Matteo Pasquinelli, preparing a conference in Bologna planned for the following September, at the time of preparation for the Prague protests against the International Monetary Fund and the World Bank. Rekombinant presented itself as the instrument of *dissolution/recombination of politics and network of cognitive work*. The initial manifesto claimed:

In September 2000, in Bologna, we intend organising a meeting about these subjects: cognitive net workers, virtualisation of politics and emergence of the global movement. (...) It is our intention to understand how the web is dissolving the very forms of modern politics, and how alternative perspectives take shape on the web. September will be an important month for the global movement. The World Economic Forum will meet in Melbourne, Australia; the International Monetary Fund and World Bank joint meeting will be held in Prague on the 26th of September. On both occasions we will see the global movement return to the squares, in unpredictable and original forms, fighting against the vampires of globalisation, against the illegitimate organisms who claim to decide the life and death of millions of people without having any mandate other than that of the multinationals that make a profit from the knowledge of others. Rekombinant wants a better understanding of the problematic scenario of the global movement, starting from the awareness of the fact that cognitive work on the web cannot be recognised in the forms of modern politics, and only by the dissolution of the existing political forms we can start the social recombination capable of opening prospects of humanity[6].

The main interlocutor is a global movement in progressive growth, the same one that television and newspapers paradoxically defined "anti-global", a movement that started using the web strategically during street demonstrations and creating networking between one event and the other. In this context, the Indymedia Italia project acquired central importance in terms of diffusion and coordination of this network. It developed by spontaneously embracing various practices, individuals and objectives, with various backgrounds and training, both political and non-political, but with the common idea of freedom and criticism of information.

Indymedia had greater visibility in Italy during the three day protest at the G8 in Genoa (2001). Here, many complex events took place, from the death of Carlo Giuliani to the violence to the demonstrators, from the police raid in the Pertini-Diaz school to the intimidations in the Bolzaneto jail. The reporting and networking between the persons involved and the active collectives took on a central value. During the days against the G8 summit, members of the Indymedia collective, lawyers for the Genoa Social Forum, demonstrators and activists of various associations involved in the protest, many foreigners who came to Genoa to collaborate, interacted spontaneously in the Media Center located in the Pascoli school, opposite the Pertini-Diaz school. The Indymedia Center was set up there, on the top floor of the building.

Indymedia became a vital reality in the circulation of photos, texts and videos of the counter-summit, and it is through the action of many volunteers active in the Indymedia Center and others scattered around the city with video and photo cameras that information about the events of those days becomes worldwide in real time. Above all, the official media realised that they were dealing with a very combative interlocutor, grassroots, and not depending on governmental or commercial institutions, determined to circulate the events quickly and without censorship. The Indymedia Center became the reference point for many independent media activists spread around the city filming what took place during the demonstrations, using their own digital video cameras and then delivering what they filmed for uploading on the site available to all the web users. The same was done by photographers and editors writing news in real time.

The Pascoli school, headquarters of the Genoa Social Forum, became the press centre not only for the movement but also for the official media. A true network is generated between the various activists and operators, networking the computers and radios to produce information. Set up inside the Media Center was the editing office of Radio GAP <www.radiogap.net>, another successful experiment of Genoa's three days, that continued its action in later demonstrations. Radio GAP (Global Audio Project) is a network made up of seven Italian free radios (Radio Onda Rossa, Milan; Radio Onda d'Urto, Brescia and Milan; Radio Black Out, Turin; Radio K Centrale, Radio Città Fujiko and Radio Città 103, Bologna) and by a press agency (AmisNet). Radio GAP produced the live streaming of the Genoa events, to give information about the events taking place[7]. Lastly, the legal aid office of the Genoa Social Forum was in the Media Center.

For these very reasons it appears obvious why the Media Center and the nearby Pertini-Diaz school became strategic "targets": during the sudden police raid in the evening between 21-22 July, the hard disk of the GSF lawyers' computer was seized along with other video material. The violent scenes of the blitz, spread initially on the Indymedia Italia site, travelled around the world and were used even by commercial TV networks.

In Italy there was a strong climate of tension that, combined with turning the violence into a show perpetrated by the media, contributed in putting the real reasons for the protest in second place, causing the obvious and consequent political and mass media exploitation of most of the happenings during those three days. Even though it was surely important and necessary to film certain scenes of violence and circulate them without censorship, the doubt is whether at a certain point the guerrilla warfare on the streets had become just show material for the TV stations and used to start reciprocal accusations. In spite of the validity of the protest contents and the normal reaction in a climate of tension such as in those three days, one wonders up to what point it was a battle for planetary rights or if it was a game planned by others, becoming instruments of an actual *infowar*. And one wonders if the conflict experienced in that inflamed end of July could have actually been one of the many scripts already written of Italian and world political history.

Genoa's counter-G8 was not, therefore, just a territory of violence and clashes, as most of the media highlighted. The experience was an incredibly successful platform from the point of view of grassroots networking, which gave the starting signal for many other counterinformation projects in the following months. Never as then the network of so many individuals and collectives was active for the same cause, showing to be so capillary and efficient, immediate and forceful, giving proof of great validity and fluidity. Genoa's three days were an important experience for whoever constructs grassroots information, using amateur video cameras, independent radios and Internet sites[8]. A chance to put the strength of the network model into practice, by then proven valid in the more underground circuits and finally coming out in the "overground".

Like all self-organised situations, the experience got out of hand several times and improvised "media-activists" didn't always bring real benefits to the movement. Undoubtedly the massive use of amateur video cameras, photo cameras, mobile phones and the Internet allowed a powerful spreading of information, giving voice to the events just as they happened on the streets. Yet on the other hand the spontaneity of many who became improvised "media activists" has been advantageous for the police. By seizing the filmed material the police later succeeded in identifying and accusing some of the demonstrators who were filmed unmasked. The urgency for spreading news, if not regulated by a common line of behaviour, risks encouraging the "enemy".

This is why the Indymedia collective felt the need to reformulate the principles of an ethic in media activism, reflecting critically on the actual effectiveness of decentralisation. The lack of direct control on the contents of projects such as Indymedia, open to anyone's intervention, can actually be problematic when the Internet platform (or the video material) falls into the hands of someone who doesn't have an adequate critical conscience or political awareness and can easily be manipulated.

This type of problem occurred even later, during the events of the 11th of September 2001, when following an anti-American message (arbitrarily signed "Anti-Global movement") written anonymously in the Indymedia newsware, the whole movement was negatively judged in the Italian TV show "Porta a Porta" hosted by the journalist Bruno Vespa. During the broadcast they showed Indymedia's "incriminated" page. The collective naturally reacted by taking their distance from the message, stating that in Indymedia anyone is free to express their opinions, but that the contents "do not represent anyone except the people who write them"[9]. Once more we see how the lack of moderation of the contents can become controversial if exploited by people who do not have a very critical background, a problem that turns up daily in many mailing lists that decide not to be moderated in order to privilege freedom of expression.

Today the Genoa events are still an open chapter, and in 2004 a team started a new initiative: Legal Support, to give technical and economic aid to Genoa's Legal Forum – and to circulate information about the lawsuits after the counter-G8 days. As we read in the Legal Support website,

Legal Support is a network of people who follow the Genoa and Cosenza trials: the ones involving the people who went there to demonstrate, and the ones involving public officials accused of violence, torture, abuse of power. Legal Support transcribes the hearings, turns them into understandable syntheses, publishes and circulates them; it invents projects, information campaigns and fund raising. Legal Support, which began thanks to the initiative of a few media activists participating in the Indymedia network, works in information and communication, technical support and financing, with a series of fund raising campaigns, depositing all the proceeds for administrative work and court costs. Because memory is a collective mechanism (<https://www.supportolegale.org>).

Networks of Videos and Telestreets

The Genoa events were an important platform for mass media coordination of the movement and for creating independent video projects, but video experimentation as network sank its roots a long time before.

As early as 1970 the Radical Software project has gained international reputation. Founded by a group of journalists, experts and video makers in New York, it was the first magazine about video emphasizing the critical analysis of television, using the networking model for distribution. Around Radical Software, a real community was created, developing until the mid 1970s. Among its members are Nam June Paik, Frank Gilette, Michael Schamberg, Ira Schneider, Beryl Korot, Phyllis Gershuny and others <www.radicalsoftware.org >[10].

An interesting analysis of the political and social use of video in the 1960s and 1970s is provided by the book *Definition Zero*, by Simonetta Fadda (1999), in which creating video is described as an artistic practice and as an instrument of cultural and political information. Simonetta Fadda works with video since the end of the 1980s, creating CCTV information installations in public spaces and art galleries; then in the 1990s using the video camera as an expressive and artistic vehicle to describe what exists in society[11].

This second phase of Simonetta Fadda's career is central to our reflection on networking as a form of social activism and critic. In her video works, the use of low definition critically sheds light on the inherent hierarchies in the field of art and communication. A central issue is the power structure arising from a particular use of technology which defines a certain way of understanding reality. The reflections that have animated Simonetta Fadda's video production since the 1990s are precious today for anyone who wants to create videos critically, not only for actively documenting certain events of reality, but most of all for experimenting artistically on the visual image, whether singularly or collectively.

As Simonetta Fadda writes, reasoning on the difference between high and low definition and on the implications in using this hierarchy,

an expression such as "high definition" evokes per se an improvement, a perfecting certainly referred to the image produced, but also to what that image reproduces, i.e. the outside world. The process of definition, intended in these terms, appears as a long path starting from raw shapeless material (reality), little by little reworked and refined (the image of reality). In this type of context, the social duty of replacing the very reality that this image reproduces, in itself dirty and contradictory or, in a word, unpresentable, would hence be entrusted to the image of reality with its clearness. Therefore the attitude that defends high definition is actually prompted by the desire to cleanse and sweeten the world and from this viewpoint "low definition" is necessarily unacceptable and it couldn't be otherwise. (...) The high/low definition division into departments, turns out explicitly as a way of offering again those hierarchical separations in the television area that separate the professional from the amateur, the artist from his public or the producer from the consumer, on which the general economic order is based. (...) Today's technology allows relaunching the utopia of the first artistic Avant-gardes into more constructive terms: the conquest of freedom through the beauty that constituted their program can be turned into a practice of freedom today, through communication and its tools (1999, pp. 49-50).

Therefore Simonetta Fadda considers low definition the index of an artistic, critical "stance" where the use of a video camera is not presented as falsely objective and merely documentaristic, but rather succeeds in revealing the backstage through which reality is encoded and presented to the public with all its symbolic apparatus, vehicles of power structures. This is why the point of view of the author is not absent in Simonetta Fadda's videos, it is an element of active construction of daily life with all its contradictions and critical aspects. At the same time the "dirty", non glossy visual aesthetics enables you to go beyond the image itself, showing the elements which have formed it, "i.e. how the image is processed, how it is constructed through technology. (...) Thus my videos

223

show mediated reality and at the same time, on a visual level, allow perception of how much and how this reality is turned into an image" (Fadda, 1999).

In her videos, the expressive work is not so much in the narrative construction in hindsight as much as it is in experimentation on language and on the low definition aesthetics. The visuals are shaped as if they were colours on a canvas and appear as evident as a brush stroke. Since 1992 Simonetta Fadda has given life to the use of *telecronaca* (running commentary), filming cross-sections of "ordinary" life on the borderline between public and private, and directly observing people in their daily habits, their life seen subjectively with emotional participation. In her video works, apparently "neutral" elements of daily life become situations that always refer to something deeper, leading the spectator to reflect critically on the meaning and reliability of the media images according to their experience as world spectators.

For example, in the *Genova ora zero* video (1993) a correspondence is created between the Baghdad of 1991, theatre of the Gulf war, the first strongly "mass media" conflict, and almost immaterial for a distant audience, and the Genoa of New Years 1992, with its historical centre "in flames" from the fireworks. This cross reference is presented by "dirty", "contaminated" video scenes in the various passages of copies starting from the original, transforming the initial scene until its material becomes more and more indistinct. As Simonetta Fadda writes, "close to the abstract meaning of porno, which is made of boredom and repetition, but just when it becomes visible in the acts, viewing is denied, making what is depicted paradoxically invisible and leaving it only to the imagination (Gariazzo, *Tutto fuorché alta definizione* (interview), in "Filmcritica", 451-452, November 1995).

The porno-graphic topic of the city returns in *Genova Pissing* (1993), modelled in the visual terms of surveillance and oppression, again according to Simonetta Fadda, in which a hidden corner of a Genoese street becomes the literally releasing place for many male pedestrians passing by, a ritual territory always the same with an incredible power of attraction. Also in *Pulizia* (1994), with a further stimulus to reveal the symbolic manifestations of power, Genoa's historical centre appears as a "kind of Mediterranean Belfast, held under siege by public 'safety' stations, as countless as they are useless" (Fadda, 1994).

Or again, in *Still Life* (1996) the fixed gaze of a drug addict staring at the video camera, and back to the spectator watching the video, presents an urban landscape built from the strategies of seeing and being seen, during a silent performance made of gazes, real and virtual. Simonetta Fadda responds "to the crisis of symbolic order with a pornography of things that replaces their experience, returning emotions that normally remain in the invisibility of language"[12].

Simonetta Fadda's videos are attentive "to hard facts, to the banality of what is real, to its filth, to the noise and total quality of the scenes; by and large she brings out elements considered obscene for television viewing, disturbing for television order" (Fadda, 1999-2000). The visuals in low definition are central for her expressive work, to take what is real into consideration with all its contradictions, without wanting to build a world that is virtual, perfect and in "high" definition.

As the artist underlines,

using low definition to use videos that circulate in the art contexts is not a casual expedient by me, but a precise choice of field. Visual habits induced by the consumption of images with which television has made us become familiar with, belong to live, even trivial, reality. Revealing and identifying our visual habits is possible only with a grassroots approach to live reality. A high level of technical knowledge is no longer necessary today and it will be even less necessary in the future. Instead of being passive consumers of images, we can become *talking subjects, producers of meaning, active participants*. The production of meaning is the high stake of communication[13].

Another independent video project that creates art and experimentation together and makes low definition a mission is the Church of Electrosophy. Established in Rome in 1990, the group is made up of young experimenters who grew up in the field of audio, video and performance.

"The main activity of these young people was to play at making improvised music, disguises, video and film footage, photos and painting. The aim was the creative exploration of randomness, the engine of DIY procedure, the models, the non-school of artistic forefronts (from futurism to pop-art) and the punk music of the 77's" (Link Project, 2000, p. 56)[14]. In particular, "on the technological level, in the first place the electrosophic method turned into a quantity of small handmade inventions and solutions that could make up for the lack of means. In the second place, the forced restriction of (technological) quality of the products forced the electrosophists to accept low definition, and actually use it as an ensign... At the limits of abstraction, chaos, noise. From here, mysticism." (*ivi*, pp. 56-57).

The members of the Church of Electrosophy, whose experience ended in December 1994, produce an effective mixture between underground environment and the art and audiovisual market, working on and off in the broadcast area and giving life to the "electrostatic method". Based on low definition, this allows creating works capable of "translating the free flow of thought into practice, with all the restraints of the contingent ("little money in the pocket, hence limited means and instrumentation." (*ivi*, pp. 56). An attitude in using video as DIY that in the approach to technology becomes a form of activism and criticism of the hierarchical model of communication, found again later in the Italian hacktivism scene.

The Church of Electrosophy is tangent to the Roman counterculture scenario, in particular the underground digital networks (AvANa.net) and video experimentation, which established the Candida TV collective[15] in 1999. Candida TV came about from the experience of a group of people working independently for several years on video and on the web: many of them came from the AvANa.net collective, others from the Ordanomade collective, others were near the rave and techno scene of the 1990s. They all had experience in using the media in a subversive way in raves, live sets, parties in the Social Centres (such as OFF, the Overdose Fiction Festival, later scheduled every year in the summer at Rome's Forte Prenestino). Candida TV, defined "the household appliance television", began broadcasting on the 18th of December 1999 on Teleambiente, a Lazio television broadcaster, starting a cycle of Saturday evening episodes lasting nine weeks.

As early as June 1999 the Candida TV collective had produced two pilot broadcasts, during the Festival OFF at Forte Prenestino, following Teleambiente's interest in the Overdose Fiction Festival. The episodes took place live from the studio with tape-broadcast contributions from the Forte[16]. Agnese Trocchi, one of the Candida TV members, describes here the group's experience on Telemabiente (1999):

Candida will enter the kitchens of Roman families, offering everyone the pleasure of "hands on", because television can be made at home, with everyday tools. Fetishist television technology discard. *Do your own television* makes connective reality for doubting authority and promoting information decentralisation. A new territory to penetrate, invade and mess up the debris of the social spectacle, product of the cultural industry. Candida is a toy idea of the cathode tube and candour is the perverse aspiration of domesticity. Candida happens now, live: the whole technical apparatus of the evident, visible organisation, as shaky as a blender or a washing machine, but active at full speed (...). A strategic delirium, calculated by someone who grew up in front of the television. (...) Television beyond television, instrument of transition in the infinite encoding of reality. Candida contemplates advertising space but, while it feeds itself, it conspires to reveal the magnetism of advertising itself, it decodes, breaks up and remixes the seduction of the image. Candida is not outspoken but has metallic extensions, it is candid and immediate, meaning that it has a non mediated relationship with the media. It is the moment of experience, of television for everyone to the television by everyone. Candida is a community television, everyone can do it[17].

From the very beginning, Candida TV appeared as a poly-media experience: even though the central means of expression remains video, the "household appliance television" doesn't work only in this format. The collective created a website, hosted today by the server of The Thing <candida.thing.net>, a mailing list <candida@inventati.org>, and organises live shows, parties and live sets in independent spaces.

We feel that no one media is more important than another or should be paid more attention; they must all be seen to take their contents and to take those infections that Candida is interested in spreading around itself as much as possible, to touch users and the most varied interactions. It is important to succeed in transforming one's own expression by intersecting it and hybridizing it with each of the various means of communication (personal interview published in "Neural", 2000).

So what links the members of the collective from the beginning is not just knowing how to work on one medium or the other, it is the idea that even with little means it is possible to transmit an attitude, the fact that there are no "interactive" or "passive" media: everything depends on how they are used and by the possibility of making a collective exploitation.

We don't want to imitate the great national shows, we want to create an interchange through nodes, human situations, that decide to communicate through images. We aim at lowering the singularity of means, approaching daily reality, without the need for something really big to happen in the broadcasts, or that there has to be an event with a capital E (*ibidem*).

From the very beginning the members of Candida TV experimented with the idea of creating a community television and they soon became the independent TV most present in the collective situations of Italian hacker community. It is the Candida TV members who filmed from the Hackmeeting 2000 inwards all the main happenings of the hackers' three days, later inserted in the *Reality Hacking* video collection (2003), and the same happens in other movement contexts, from Prague 2000 to the Genoa protests in 2001. Here, the Supervideo character, an imaginative superhero, appears active in the *Supervideo>>>G8* video (2001) and in other Candida TV productions, among them the one based on Netstrike, titled *Electronic Disturbance Theatre, interview with Ricardo Dominguez* (2001)[18]. Producing independent videos, the Candida TV collective translates the hacker spirit of information, "a spirit of playful intelligence, which doesn't apply just to computer science, but to every aspect of reality: it means exploring the limits of what is possible, knowing what we are, what surrounds us in order to change it according to the stimulus of our imagination..."[19].

Candida TV became a cooperative in 2001, specialised in audiovisual production. In addition to producing videos and TV soaps and documentaries made by the people and for the people, Candida TV organised events and workshops about using technology to make audiovisual language accessible to everyone, with the motto "make your own TV". The Candida TV video productions, again according to the hacker ethic of creating information, can be freely downloaded from the New Global Vision site <candida.thing.net/pages/video.html>. Recognition, even international, didn't take long in arriving and in 2004 Candida TV participated first in Amsterdam's *Next Five Minutes* festival and later in the Berlin *Transmediale* festival of art and new media. Among the numerous collaborations was the link with the London project and review "Mute, Culture and Politics after the Net" <www.metamute.org>, followed by hosting in the Openmute server, for the new English version of the Candida TV site <candida.omweb.org>.

The latest video made by Candida TV, together with D Media (a non-profit organisation in Cluj, Romania, involved in promoting free knowledge technologies and in the fusion between art and social activism <www.dmedia.ro), is titled *Made in Italy* (2006). This is an inquiry-documentary about Romanian women labourers, who after the fall of the communist government and the promises of joining Europe, work for low wages in many companies, most of them Italian, and try to move abroad. This is why today Romania is called the eighth Triveneto province and has become one of the main territories of production delocalisation. The video retraces a trip through greater Europe seen through the eyes of Romanian women and leaves many questions open about labour transformations in global society. The project, developed with financial support by the European Community, opens one of the many unresolved knots of our present, which sees the women of the former communist block become a strategic social and economic subject for many companies.

Since 2002, the Candida TV experience is tangent to another circuit of independent video channels that caused much talk about itself in Italy and abroad: the Telestreet phenomenon. This transferred to a national network many of the utopias previously practised by laboratories working on closed circuit video experiments in the 1960s and 1970s and, subsequently, in creating independent televisions, from Pratello TV (Bologna, 1996) to Minimal TV (Vinci, 1996), and to Candida TV itself (Rome, 1999).

Telestreets are micro-broadcasters for the city street, the neighbourhood, covering a range of limited metres (a few hundred, if not less), grassroots and generally built with little money. Their strategy is to take advantage of the shadow losses of the Italian patchy television frequencies to start transmitting their schedule. The idea is to imagine a Telestreet for each television shadow loss, giving rise to a large network for all of Italy, a national network of street broadcasters.

Fabrizio Manizza who until 2006 was involved in Senigallia's Telestreet Disco Volante, explains the birth process of the Telestreets[20]:

It was a matter of exploiting the "holes" in the control apparatus of the mass media and television power, to start up practices that were alternative and absolutely free from control. This strategy is implemented today, in different forms every time, in various fields of knowledge and production/reproduction of material life. Concerning the telestreets, the "holes" that could be exploited were at least of a double nature: technical "holes" and legislative "holes". The technical "hole" consisted in the fact that territorial coverage by the radio signal of the traditional TV broadcasters, according to the geographical conformation of the territory, originates shadow losses inside the single frequencies, i.e. to circumscribed areas of the territory in which the radio signal doesn't reach on a certain frequency. That is why such frequency appears "free" in that circumscribed area, even if formally the frequency appears actually occupied, and owned by a traditional television broadcaster who has paid the State for use and concession. In these "holes" or shadow losses a very low power signal of a street TV could enter, with a very circumscribed broadcast range, typically that of a city neighbourhood and exploiting a frequency that on a regional or national extension was owned by a medium or large television station, but was free locally and hence causing no type of interference[21].

At the same time, as Manizza adds when speaking of the legislative situation that regulates Italian television broadcasting,

> there was a corresponding "hole" on the legislative level, regarding laws in force, since the law in force for television broadcasting defined the rules for the concession and possession of one or more frequencies of the radio range, thinking obviously about television broadcasters of at least provincial or regional dimensions and scale. No one foresaw that micro-TVs could be created on a neighbourhood scale, that didn't need a whole frequency to transmit but just a shadow loss of it, an area so small that it needed a simple unused leftover of a larger broadcaster, a kind of air "waste", "trash", yet susceptible to being used profitably by intelligent independent operators. Since the "shadow loss" is not a "frequency", nor can it be likened to it, a law conceived to regulate the use of frequencies could not, in the strict sense, be applied to the street TVs (*ibidem*).

The Telestreets started up formally in 2002, in a situation of democratic emergency in the country, to respond to the growing Italian television monopoly arising from the conquest of political power by the largest manager of private television, in order to politically control even the national public television company. The Telestreets, in conflict with the Berlusconi monopoly, try to go to the source and directly oppose forced regulation of the television frequencies legitimated by the Mammì law of the 1980s, which established a limited number of frequencies in the Italian territory. The Telestreet phenomenon is seen as an attempt to oppose the Italian television monopoly that appears even more evident in the Berlusconi era, taking on the form of a network of projects

230

that use article 21 of the Italian Constitution as their stronghold, showing that a concrete, practical commitment is necessary for freedom of speech and expression.

Political strategy is what unites many of the hacktivist practices described so far:

The pervasiveness and invasiveness of systems of control generate an apparent monolithness, but when this monolithness is observed from close up it is full of bugs, fractures, interstices, inside which exists a proliferation of new practices as the result of continual reinvention of daily life effected by concrete subjects, groups, individuals, communities. (...) Contemporary society that continuously recreates new bonds and barriers to individual freedom for the very economic law that governs it, can not do without inventing and distributing ever new tools with which people can then regain their lost freedom. And this is the same also for intangible goods such as knowledge and awareness. The university system, it too governed by the same economic structure, can't do without distributing more knowledge and awareness than is necessary, which can then be reinvested in the production and consumer cycle (*ibidem*).

Over the years the Telestreet experience shows that it is possible to give voice directly to the ordinary people with the idea that freedom of expression derives from decentralisation and self-management. At the same time they show how the union between reinventing the mass media imaginary and putting technical capabilities into practice is the paradigm that makes today's hacktivism capable of actively entering the production and consumption cycle, responding to economic dynamics with the same weapons, but with quite different social and political aims.

The Telestreets became a real network of neighbourhood micro-televisions, coordinating mainly through the site <www.telestreet.it>, the mailing list <telestreet@telestreet.it>, the New Global Vision sharing video platform <www.ngvision.org>, and by periodic collective meetings, such as "Eterea" (Bologna, 2002) and "Eterea2" (Senigallia, 2004).

In many and various Italian cities, street TV projects took the challenge to make their own grassroots television, such as Orfeo TV, the first free television of the Telestreet network originated in Bologna in 2002, which with a direct line we could reconnect with the experience of the 1970s of Radio Alice[22]. Other Telestreets are: TeleImmagini (Bologna), Gli Anelli Mancanti TV (Florence),

Ottolina TV (Pisa), Spegnilatv, NowarTv and TeleAUT (Rome), CTV (Brescia), IsolaTv (Milan), Disco Volante (Senigallia), TeleMonteOrlando (Gaeta), TeleRobbinud (Squillace), Telefermento (Savona), RosaGhettoTv (Genoa), InsuTv (Naples), Telecitofono (Reggio Emilia), Telecerini (Pistoia), to mention just a few of them. A network of subjects spread throughout the national territory and a large community netlike structure, which we could theoretically reconnect to the mail art network, so that "every Telestreet exponent could easily move to any city where a street TV was active and be practically sure of finding hospitality with the colleagues-friends there, with room and board nearly free of charge (obviously within reasonable limits)" (*ibidem*).

Yet the range of the Telestreet phenomenon is not so much in the creation of local micro-TVs and in the production of certain grassroots "alternatives", as much as their powerful symbolic value in being a network that expresses overall much more than what the single nodes communicate. A particularity that once again Fabrizio Manizza describes well in his reflections on the Telestreet phenomenon, relating in turn to the reflections developed by Giancarlo "Ambrogio" Vitali, from Orfeo TV:

The strength of the street TV movement was in the symbolic challenge to the general system of telecommunications, proclaiming itself illegal but constitutional, hence *de facto* legal on the basis of the fundamental law of the Republic; the movement claimed a fundamental principle: the inalienable right of any citizen to freedom of expression with the means that present-day technology (including the hackers' "tricks") makes available. So the stake was not simply practical, but symbolic and, in principle, much more important than the simple authorisation to make neighbourhood TV. It was claimed that the right, and therefore the power, to act as active communication subjects, as producers of information, was to be returned to the social unit in its complex, to civil society and its complex, after having been expropriated by the large bureaucratic, economic apparatus, legal of course with respect to the Constitution since they were centralisers and monopolistic by vocation (*ibidem*).

In this sense the Telestreets worked at making their symbolic strength concrete and effective, and one of the proposals indicated by the movement – in particular Orfeo TV – became the one stating "the principle that a 10% share of the new frequencies made usable by digital should be subtracted from market strategies and made available free of charge to society and those who are its expression, associations, NGOs and non-profit organisations, local administrations, social centres, etc. In short, it was a matter of using the symbolic challenge brought by the Telestreet movement to obtain a result on a higher and wider reaching organisational level, and not simply to demand the legitimacy of telestreet's pure and simple practice just as it was" (*ibidem*).

The Telestreets became the object of numerous debates in Italy and abroad, even when two projects were seized – Telefabbrica in Sicily and Disco Volante TV in Senigallia – by the Ministry of Telecommunications that appealed to the Mammì law to block their broadcasts.

In this case too Disco Volante's reaction took place above all by acting on a collective imagination level, a tactic that made the Telestreets network so penetrating:

Disco Volante TV, a street TV located in a relatively low populated neighbourhood in a small town, Senigallia, succeeded in becoming a national and international affair by virtue of the symbolic strength of its event, not by virtue of the strength of the programmes it broadcast: it was the image of a tiny TV station with a staff of four or five people, furthermore half of them disabled, penniless, no sponsors, minimal means, yet in spite of everything succeeded in demonstrating their capability to control the whole flow of television production, from scripting to videotaping to editing to broadcasting, an undertaking considered possible only for systems with considerable capital and adequate human resources – and all this was done only with social and service aims, totally non-profit, against market rules, against the law, against its very logic – we could say. This image, this Disco Volante identity, which was so widespread following the lawsuit that involved us, showed strength on the symbolic and moral level that led us to win several important national prizes and, in the end, win the legal battle with preliminary acquittal. Our weakness was our strength, and in a certain sense one could say that they were afraid to put us on trial because even if they convicted us, moral victory would have been ours in any case, our reasons on the symbolic and moral level were too many and too strong (*ibidem*)[23].

The Telestreet turmoil is soon felt abroad as well, where the Italian television monopoly is seen with great chagrin: in 2004, the Bundeszentrale für politische Bildung/bpb, German national organisation of political education, supported an exhibition, "MediaDemocracy and Telestreet, Networking Free TV", organised in Munich within a show centred on Italian culture and art[24]. The following year the Telestreet and New Global Vision projects received the Award of Distinction at the 19th Prix Ars Electronica in Linz, Austria, in the "Digital Communities" category, jointly with Richard Stallman's Free Software Foundation.

The Telestreet and New Global Vision projects demonstrated that it was possible to oppose the monopoly of the Italian major television channels, and this could take place by creating grassroots communities integrating videos and Internet technologies

Over the years the New Global Vision project became a very useful tool for the Telestreets as an archive of independent videos downloadable from the web at zero cost, allowing all the movements to create a connection point to share their video material <www.ngvision.org>. There are various topics in the on-line archive of the videos: from anti-Fascism and anti-prohibition to Hacktivism and net.art, all of them issued under Creative Commons license, allowing non commercial redistribution[25].

New Global Vision originated from the experiences coming from collectives such as Isole nella Rete, Indymedia and from the Social Centres, and today it is still a very useful resource for orientation in the panorama of independent video production that appears in all its widespread network aspects. NGV allows the Telestreets to build a zero cost TV programming, using for their shows many of the videos archived in the New Global Vision platform.

Whereas the New Global Vision project is still active and alive, the Telestreet network seems to be a little drowsy. It may be due to the scarceness of collective resources, which on the one hand was decisive for developing the whole experience, but on the other hand seems to obstruct the production and realisation of contents to show to the public.

A year ago there was news of more and more new street TVs starting up, but there was also no more news of many of them who had notified us that they had begun, therefore it seemed to me that the dynamics within the movement had taken on a stationary form based on which, for the many new street TVs that opened up, there were just as many that shut down and disappeared. This could be the first phase of a trend where mortality exceeded natality, leading the movement to extinction. The symbolic challenge brought by the movement (the national television giants move in with micro-TVs) was charming and attractive, especially for the groups of young people. But after a while, in contact with the objective difficulties of carrying forth such an undertaking and making the machine work, so to say, many were forced to admit that they didn't have enough energy and resources to last, and they abandoned (*ibidem*).

Furthermore, as often happens, it seems that the internal community dynamics are the strength on the one hand, and on the other hand the source of slowdown for a concrete affirmation of the Telestreet network on a political and social level, to avoid running the risk of being manipulated (as Minister Gasparri's invitation in Rome for the members of Disco Volante's Telestreet could lead to believe), or to avoid becoming part of the ordinary mainstream television (which was followed by the refusal of showmen such as Maurizio Costanzo or Pippo Baudo to become involved in the matter). At the same time, to privilege the Telestreet network's decentralised, libertarian nature, there was always opposition to the idea of creating a national association of the telestreets, which may have entailed the formation of likely leaderships, though it would probably have been a useful coordination tool.

In any case, in spite of the problem of finding resources for the survival of street TVs and the difficulties laid down by internal political dynamics, the Telestreet phenomenon has not at all faded.

Various Telestreets were still active in 2006, among them the positive experience of Insu TV in Naples, active in the Forcella neighbourhood, reaching 35-40,000 people, given the density of the area. The people who created Insu TV gave life to a remote programmable control system to automatically manage the street TV scheduling, created on the GNU/Linux operative system and available for all the other Telestreets that want to adopt it. This work won them a prize, and showed how the presence of a street TV in a neighbourhood with heavy social problems could still be a strong creative input for activism.

Among the various Telestreet network initiatives still in progress, as Giancarlo "Ambrogio" Vitali from Orfeo TV stresses in June 2006, "as producers of Community contents, today we asked the Ministry for authorisation to broadcast in digital terrestrial technique and we obtained it: we are missing the band and the money, nevertheless it is a symptom of how far we could go…" (personal e-mail).

The permit obtained from the Ministry of Telecommunications to broadcast public contents via digital cable is definitely an interesting development in Telestreet's battle and, as Fabrizio Manizza adds, it might be able to lead to the creation of an Italian Open Channel.

The battle that determined achieving this permit is connected to another possible development of the Telestreet network, based on a project promoted by Orfeo TV in 2004. Named T.CAP (Public Access Community Televisions), the project provides for passing from ordinary neighbourhood "pirate" televisions to Community televisions safeguarded by the local authorities (such as the municipal administrations), hence perfectly legal.

As Giancarlo "Ambrogio" Vitali writes:

Orfeo TV and Ottolina TV first of all concentrated their work mainly in promoting the Telestreet project totally and in the likelihood of it expanding to the institutions (civic or Community TVs for example), considering such expansion a politically decisive and strategically promising prospect. In this sense a pathway was identified that gave concrete results in the experience of the municipality of Peccioli (PI): the street TV closest to the municipality of Peccioli – Ottolina TV-Telestreet – kept the contacts and followed the municipality in defining every phase of the project, while Orfeo TV-Telestreet collaborated with the technologies, legal assistance and promotion. About 74% of the Italian population lives in small or medium sized towns (between 250 and 50,000 population). Such sizes can consider television broadcasters that are low cost and absolutely effective; Telestreet is still the model, even if in this case everything is done according to EC standards and with approved equipment, therefore relatively more costly (obviously this is also valid for more important cities). (...) It would be a novelty for many, a curiosity, a chance for socialisation, a way to give voice to people basically excluded from communication circuits. (...) Today Peccioli TV (as we said, the first T.CAP born in Italy starting from the Telestreet experience), obtained authorisation from the Ministry of Telecommunications that will allow it to enter the world as a public access Community television (...). The contents of that TV will be provided partially by street televisions already operating in the area and by an editorial office being created directly in the territory thanks to the training created by Ottolina TV-Telestreet. Peccioli TV will also have a website (created once again by Ottolina TV-Telestreet) so that citizens can converse with it and soon it will contain the more significant productions, so that they are visible and downloadable all over the world. In order not to miss the digital train, there are thoughts of setting up a couple of advertising spaces, in municipal territory, with a broadband connection for the air signal[26].

The widespread of broadband seems to be a promise of the future, so that Internet TVs can be built quickly, overcoming the obstacle of legitimacy of air frequencies. Broadband can receive excellent quality television broadcasts on TV and computer screens, equal in quality to current broadcasts; costs are minimum and the target is widespread. With broadband, TV service is associated to the reception of other multimedia contents, from films to photos, and at the same time one can surf the web and make phone calls[27].

Yet this may be how the community element that made the Telestreets a "street" experience was lost and made it a more competent target in the Internet and technology field, cutting off many others. This is why it appears more convincing and useful to associate the path of Internet TVs to the public access Community TVs, proposed with the T.CAP project.

The merit of the T.CAP project is to directly involve all citizens, not just those technically prepared or those who belong to the independent circuit of the communications production that started up the Telestreet network. The T.CAPs, if circulated on a wide scale, could mark the beginning of a new form of public service in which the Telestreets would play a leading role, because they are a source that has already been "tested" for technical and content solutions. Furthermore, anyone who has participated in the Telestreet experience could start up an editorial T.CAP office, thus solving the problem of finding the resources for street TV survival.

The collateral effect could be no longer making evident the radical nature that accompanied the initial experience of the Telestreet network, whose field of action went beyond mere information, touching the raw nerves in the Italian political and social context in the period of maximum debate on Italian television monopoly.

One further step to take forward along with the construction of Community televisions for all citizens could be finding a way to reinvent and relaunch the symbolic strategies that made the Telestreets a strong movement, even if weak in means and resources.

There may be the preparations for another attempt to exploit the social, legislative and political "holes" for recreating new forms of creativity and activism capable of weighing not only on a symbolic level but also concretely as they would deserve. In any case the true meaning of the movement is in the fact that it dies and comes to life again many times, always inventing new ways to act, with new resources and energies.

Precarious Creativity

The Telestreets' experience tried to act directly on the national scale, applying the principles of freedom of information in television broadcasting. Yet the Telestreets are not the only protest and criticism attempt towards centralising mass media, political and cultural system. In the early years of the 2000s, something new entered the Italian scene at full speed, calling itself "precarious" and, with a grassroots organisation, gives rise to the ChainWorkers collective, <www.chainworkers.org>.

The ChainWorkers are the young children of the New Economy and of all those global economic processes that make a bastion of flexibility. They are the ones where an open-ended contract (and even an ended time contract!) has become a pipe-dream, where there will probably never be a pension, they live with their parents forever but not because they are "mama's kids", who work part-time at all kinds of odd jobs, a "chance to get used to working". They are the young people in uniform at the large shopping centres or multinationals (McDonald's, Burger King, Kentucky Fried Chicken - KFC, Pizza Hut, Ikea, Esselunga, Spizzico, Blockbuster, Media World, Auchan, Tipico, etc.), who work as phone operators in the call centers or in the motorway restaurants, so the rule is rhythm, discipline, hierarchy and an ever-ready smile. They are the young people hired in the magical world of brands or franchising companies, many of them emigrated from their hometowns, and paid 5 euros per hour.

They are also those who work (or have worked) in the "New Economy" companies, paid more but always with weak flexible contracts, as well as the work hours that often exceed eight hours a day, considered by the unions to be "atypical workers", therefore with little protection because not regulated by any law. The problem is that for many young people today this is the standard, whereas the unions seem to defend only those with a permanent job, dealing with a minimum part of current workers or in a nearly pensionable age range.

At the end of the 1990s, Italy too had the flexibility boom, a system that a few years later would show its faults by leaving various "creative" young people by the wayside. At the same time, various young people looking for their first job, start entering the world of the multinational chains or call centers. Flexible workers, temporaries, on rental, are some terms that start showing this reality.

As we can read in the MayDay Parade call of actions (the temporary workers' alternative to the First of May holiday for those working):

Today we're back at square one. The Capital has gone back to being global, total. We work more and more, they saturate our lifetime to the max, we have less and less contract rights, less income certainties, little protection from abuse. We're precarious, atypical, parasubordinate, temporaries. We are in training-work, term contract, apprentices. We are on rental and with an expiry date. The companies swallow us up, intimidate us, they upset our affections and living rhythms, they occupy our minds and then they spit us out when financial advantages require it. We are the majority of those who enter the job market. But we have no voice. We don't exist. Our condition is invisible, it is suffered in silence, alone. The job market is going well today, very well. There are always new offices and shopping centers and executive centres to fill with new slaves of the service and communication industry. We are in full employment. But temporary employment advances and income stagnates. A new generation in the factories and in the commercial chains has started to go on strike. The time is ripe to launch a campaign to rebalance the relationships of work power and massive income redistribution. The coffers are full of capital accumulated in fifteen years of stock market growth, with mergers and acquisitions. It's the right time to stop the blackmail, it's the right time to use conflict to build collectively clear and due rights. More money, less hours: this is the flexibility we demand (Chaincrew, 2001, pp. 111-112)[28].

The ChainWorkers were established in the 1970s in the USA, to protest against the spreading of large franchising chains, from McDonald's to Pizza Hut, and started organising strikes or protests, such as McStrike for example, triggering huge conflicts between unions and multinationals (such as San Francisco in 1973 and Mason City, Iowa, from 1971 to 1975). The large multinationals tried in every way to oppose unionisation and a lot of people lost their jobs because often the reaction to protest attempts was to close down the whole shopping centre, and open one just like it a little farther away. Yet on the other hand the young people fired in the commercial chains became increasingly aware that they had become part of a "family" that is difficult to leave. Nevertheless many young people claim they stay in certain conditions only for a short time, so mobility is still high, flexible work is not always easy to leave, since they no longer have the time necessary to train for a more qualified job.

In Italy, the ChainWorkers began in 1999 from these reflections: the collective came from the area of media activism and the Social Centres and moved "their strong agitation capabilities on the media and society inside the shopping centres, supermarkets and fast foods of the cities", inspired by the experiences of the American ChainWorkers of the 1970s and media activism projects such as Adbusters <www.adbusters.org> and RTmark <www.rtmark.com>.

The ChainWorkers experience initially originated from an idea of Milan's Deposito Bulk <www.ecn.org/bulk>, the Infospaccio and LOA collectives (coming from the Italian hacktivism area), RASC and Smokers, ex-occupants of Metropolix, all of them involved in Milanese activism. The ChainWorkers site, launched in 2000, was hosted by the Isole nella Rete server, the historical Italian "movement provider".

One of the first actions by the ChainWorkers took place in Milan, in the "Metropoli" shopping centre at Quarto Oggiaro, the largest in the city at the time.

A caravan of ten cars parked on the roof. We loaded sound systems and generators on trolleys and went down to the first floor where we occupied the balustrade that overlooks the heart of the centre. To the sounds of Bob Marley and anti-precarious speeches, police beating (taken from the national TV) and resistance, we succeeded in moving people's attention from consumerism to action, to the extent that management announced that it was necessary to evacuate the shopping centre. Seeing how we had parked up on the roof, it took us forever to get out of there (*ivi*, pp. 50-51).

This was the beginning of a series of "actions" that led to the MayDay Parade in 2001 in Milan and to the "Reclaim the Money" campaign for guaranteed income, carried out by the Rome scene around the "Infoxoa" magazine, to local demonstrations in the streets and shopping centres against temporary work (for example, in October 2000 Bulk organised a demonstration against the Milan Council distributing flyers inside all the commercial chains along the demonstration route), etc. The motto became: "We want a minimum of 10 (euros) for every hour of work PLUS 50% overtime for evenings and Saturdays, 100% for nights and Sundays" (Chaincrew, 2000).

Over the years the network of temporary workers has taken on a European dimension "to cast the premises for new welfare and a more horizontal democratic society, where immaterial work, care-giving, services, flexible work is no longer devalued and subjected to exploitation, temporary work blackmail, the impossibility to express oneself and live" (<www.euromayday.org>, 2005).

Various initiatives start up around the MayDay Parade. On May 1, 2005, MayDay in Milan, for example, the deeds of the Unbeatables (Imbattibili) were presented. The Unbeatables are precarious super-heroes, sprouting from the minds of various Italian collectives coordinated in networks, such as ChainWorkers, Reload, Sexyshock, Serpica Naro, Pornflakes, Resistenza Universitaria, CSA Paci Paciana, CSA Magazzino 47, in collaboration with other "precarious" experiences, such as the Teatro Piccolo and Milan's La Scala workers, the people's outpatient clinic in Milan, the workers in the Omnitel-Vodafone call center and the Feltrinelli book stores, and many others for a total of twenty-one Unbeatables.

Actually, as we read on the ChainWorkers site,

the Unbeatables are not super-heroes: they are small gems of experience, capability and relationships, who will find their expression before and during MayDay. They are superheroic: if not as unique and unapproachable as the heroes, these figures are nevertheless heroic because each one of them reflects a way of opposing that destruction of our existence that business profit requirements need. They hold a thousand tricks, subterfuges, that each one of us invents to redeem our dignity, our desires, from the burden of labour and social conditions that always demand maximum availability, versatility and patience and give us in return the minimum in terms of income, security and affirmation of our capabilities and our desires[29].

Each Unbeatable is the protagonist of a sticker to add to an album especially created for the MayDay. The sticker presents the life story of the Unbeatable and his/her super-power details, taken from the experiences settled over the years by the collective representing him/her. For example, "The Peer", the Unbeatable of the Reload collective of Milan, a hacking expert, "accumulated bile so as to act on objects by thinking, creating wireless positions, computers, CD burners, photocopiers" (Reload, 2005); or, "Superflex", the ChainWorkers heroine, after the stress derived from experimenting every type of contract, became "able to mentally communicate with all superflexs, starting the universal precarious conspiracy" (ChainWorkers, 2005); or, "SpiderMom", the Unbeatable of the

Sexyshock collective in Bologna[30], has a «mutant body capable of simultaneously immobilising all the enemies of laity and free "looove"» (Sexyshock, 2005).

These stickers, as is read on the website, don't concern precariousness just as a work condition, they more generally represent its social dimension. They are the result of multiple relationships between the various Italian collectives, each one present at MayDay 2005 with a theme float, with the aim of informing passers-by of their activity and, consequently, distributing the stickers. The Unbeatable's initiative encourages the formation of new relationship networks, generating connections between the people who run from one float to the next, trying to find the missing stickers so that they can complete their collection.

A playful aspect of activism and the social battle against temporary employment is also found at MayDay 2006, Milan, playing the lottery <www.imbattibili.org/lotteria>. From the collective floats, "precarious survival kits" are handed out: the more kits and lottery tickets that are collected – searching for the Unbeatable floats – the more chances there are to win the lottery, hence finally realising the dream of escaping from precariousness.

The precarious survival kits represent the four aces of precariousness: affection, mobility, knowledge and income, and they are produced by the Italian collective that act in the respective areas of intervention (such as Sexyshock, Serpica Naro, Reload and many others). The prizes are even more interesting, provided by all the self-organisation groups participating in the initiative, making available the tools to "overthrow" the precarious condition (7 bicycles from the Anarchocyclists, a 1-year supply of condoms, 6 bottles of Precario Rouge wine, 10 super-cocktails, etc.).

In 2004, the Italian precarious workers proclaimed their own saint, Saint Precarious, the champion protector of all temporary, flexible workers <www.sanprecario.info>. Saint Precarious became the star of holy pictures, stickers, flyers and processions in shopping centers, where the saint was carried on people's shoulders as a symbol of capitalistic oppression. The "Saint Precarious Points" started up, where young precarious workers could obtain the "Precarious Pious Job Assistance" (individual legal-union advice), "Precarious First Aid" (solidarity for collective claims: agitations, pickets and strike organisation), and legal-contractual analysis.

Again in Milan, an original creative project started up from the imaginative world of Saint Precarious, already mentioned above in describing the Milan MayDay initiatives: Serpica Naro, the imaginari designer <www.serpicanaro.com>. Serpica Naro combines mass media strategy, opposition to precariousness, artistic activism, cyberfeminism and social hacking, and makes its debut in 2005 at the Fashion Week, the important Milanese fair.

Serpica Naro, the name is actually the anagram of San Precario (which is Saint Precarious in Italian), became the star of a subliminal action aimed against the fashion business, mass media superficiality and the star system, finally denouncing the precarious job conditions of young people today. The Anglo-Japanese designer, whose face appears in the project logo, is a kind of female Luther Blissett. She doesn't exist but she lives in the sphere of mass media actions, ready to insinuate herself like a virus in the business folds, proposing a new means of artistic production and creation, where sharing knowledge is central. As can be read on the Milanese collective website: "Serpica Naro is the stylish defender of the precarious, the haywire gear that can block the whole machine. Serpica Naro proposes, don't just interfere."

During the Fashion Week in Milan, February 2005, the Serpica Naro nomination was accepted directly by the Fashion Chamber, the central institution that decides who can or cannot participate in the Milan fair. The young Anglo-Japanese designer appears like a promise of international fashion, complete with an Internet site, a collection, two showrooms – London and Tokyo, customer portfolio and accredited press review. Everything is false: Serpica Naro is actually an invention of the young Milanese precarious workers near the area of the hacker movement and the DIY scene, who have already proclaimed Saint Precarious as their protector. Here too, as in many instances described in this book, none of those who accept the Serpica Naro nomination seem to think about making a more in depth investigation to comprehend the hoax.

The Serpica Naro authors enquire about how a designer must appear, what "credentials" are needed to enter the upper crust of international fashion and the whole mass media apparatus that must be built in order to become a star. This takes place in collaboration with the precarious workers in the fashion sector, who help the group in the conspiracy of providing the right information. Yet this action doesn't stop at the presence of Serpica Naro in the Milan fair.

In order to have the necessary notoriety in an event that shows one hundred brands from all over the world, the people who created the Serpica Naro meta-brand developed a strategy. They decided to stage a media conflict: Serpica Naro vs. Saint Precarious, two figures that are the symbols, respectively, of the international fashion world and Milanese activism. From the Milan opposing area, in particular the queer and pink scene, there were protests against the designer. The accusation was having unacceptable behaviour back in 2001, during collaboration with the Japanese gay and lesbian movement. Furthermore there was the accusation of using the imaginary underground for business purposes, issuing disputable declarations against the independent scene and the Social Centres. The news was quickly sent in the pink mailing lists and reached many other activists through the network of various collectives. Consequently it was decided to take action against the stylist on the third day of the Fashion Week.

Simultaneously, the collective registered the dominion <www.settimanadella moda.it> that was still free, and between ad hoc informative announcements produced by temporary workers who actually worked in the fashion world, the site was used as a megaphone for the Serpica Naro declarations and activities. It began being used concretely by many journalists who looked for news by registering in the site's reserved area.

Other precarious men and women, accompanied by Saint Precarious, gathered at the entrance of the Prada fashion show and spread their communications, denouncing several stylists for vampire attitudes towards social issues. Others appeared on the catwalk of the Laura Biagiotti fashion show at the Teatro Piccolo, "denouncing the worsening conditions of their work and stating that the communicative and symbolic demonstration would be followed by a less demonstrative one on Saturday with that Serpica Naro turd" <http://serpicanar o.realityhacking.org/il-progetto/?c=1_La-storia>.

This was all window dressing, and the people who organise the Serpica protest were the same ones who revealed the truth of the events to journalists and onlookers ready to watch the "clash". The people who paraded the Serpica Naro catwalk were very normal, young precarious workers who showed how it was possible to penetrate the superficiality of media information and fashion business. The Serpica Naro activists showed off "new trend" clothes created and sewn by them, actually a sarcastic parody of the conditions of the present precarious job panorama: "Mobbing Style", "Call Donald/Mc Center", "Pregnant Lady", etc. This was followed by the creations of those who actually worked in the fashion system, yet it remained outside the more official manifestations, and to conclude, there was the parade of the Yo Mango Spanish activists <www.yomango.org> and the Conscious Fashion Week collective.

The epilogue of the whole event, which explains the motivations of the Serpica Naro collective, is described in the website of the fake stylist:

Registration in the Fashion Week event must not lead to errors of interpretation. Above all we do not demand the right or merit of participation. We don't care about it. We also know that a presentation is not a fashion show and therefore Serpica Naro's registration on the official calendar of the fashion week must be considered relative. It is just as clear that if a certain number of precarious and creatives succeed in entering the fashion circuit in one week, this circuit is obviously not as valuable as it would like to appear. We are much more proud of the fact of our success in involving a very high number of precarious and creatives, which through active collaboration or concealed complicities allowed the creation of all this. And that 'all this' is the fundamental point for us. We are the ones who produce imagination, culture, conflict and radicalism starting from ourselves, from our desires, from our job and living condition and from the anger that inevitably stems from the social misery that englobes us. And we succeed in doing it, with great effort, in our spare time, within acrobatic employment and with ridiculous budgets. This interests us, of course! To each one his own imagination (*ibidem*).

From curious journalists, to indignant supervisors and the foreign public confused between reality and fiction, Serpica Naro marked a checkmate in the world of Milanese fashion. So much so that, later, the (real) stylist Enrico Coveri will use the (virtual) Serpica Naro logo "without permission", for which the imaginative stylist decided today to register his mark, making its use open to anyone working precariously in the fashion world.

As we can read on the Serpica Naro site,

share means change, sharing knowledge, ideas, information, as well as pleasure, capabilities and talents. Does it have anything to do with piracy? Not at all. Sharing doesn't produce marketable capital and does not use workers as though they were an ordinary renewable resource. Sharing means gratis content in exchange for gratis content. Serpica Naro, the simulacrum of the Japanese stylist champion of the precarious workers, who is capable of using fashion to put on the catwalk the unease imposed by the new job models, decided to become a brand to overturn its philosophy and make as many labels as possible tremble. Serpica Naro is a Metabrand, a Community and an innovative Production Method. The Serpica Naro license makes available, through sharing, creativity and ability, and also the capability and decision not to use practices of work exploitation in the production/ distribution chain (<www.serpicanaro.com>).

This sends us back to the hacker ethic, a tradition which inspired also the young stylists of imagination, the inventers of Serpica Naro. At the same time, precarious infowars, struggles against the multinational centralisers and MayDay Parades inspired other creative young people[31].

Among these the Molleindustria Collective, which presents political and subversive videogames created in Flash on the <www.molleindustria.it> site. Paolo Pedercini tells about the reasons that animate the Molleindustria creativity:

In recent years *video games* have frequently exceeded the limits they had been confined in for decades. The phenomenon of *advergames* has exploded, the Pentagon has ordered "shoot 'em ups" with the professed purpose of recruiting young people, *religious video games* have been created. All this has happened and still happens in a context such as the entertainment industry that is in strong convergence with the other cultural production compartments: it is not by change that we talk about *infotainment* or *edutainment*, that video games are made about films and vice versa, that the "Pokemon" or "Star Wars" brands mark the vast subcultures and not a series of homogenous products. When a large movement crossed the squares of the whole world criticising the neo-liberalist order, it began to relate differently with the mass communication means. Media centralisation was opposed by a grassroots proliferation of the proclaiming agents, in view of the network's democratic utopias. The combination of these two trends prompted us to consider video games as means of communication and consider them as terrain for cultural clash[32].

246

Molleindustria came into being in 2003, presenting brief games in Flash that accompany with irony and cynicism people who play in the contemporary worlds of atypical workers, simulated sex, flexibility and the precarious universe of our present. Yet a creativity that doesn't lead towards the self-referential resistance, it leads towards the theory and practice of the "soft, creeping, viral, guerrilla, subliminal [conflict] that produces our grey matter, which is also soft" (Molleindustria, 2003).

The first games found on the site are *Tuboflex*, the name of the job shop multinational that has the mission of deploying human resources in real time according to demand, therefore the worker is forced to survive in a universe of mobility; *Orgasm simulator*, which brings alive situations of simulated orgasm and precocious ejaculation; *TamAtipico*, the game of the virtual precarious worker who works, rests and has fun on command and who, when he doesn't want to play anymore, all you have to do is fire him without a justified reason. Then follow *Memory Reloaded*, the game of historic revisionism in which Italian politicians turn the tables and you have to press your memory to remember the associations of the past; *Papaparolibero*, holy words at large for composing the pontiff's messages for the Christian community, freely combining the Pope's words that shower from the sky; *Queer Power*, to each his own sex, which helps find the right companion, forgetting the stereotyped male/female categories; *Runaway embryos*, a critical-ironic videogame about the Italian referendum on Law 40 against experimentation on embryos; and *McDonald's Videogame*, which enables controlling each phase of the multinational's business process.

While waiting for the EuroMayDay Parade in 2004, Molleindustria started up the *MayDay NetParade* project. It is a parade of many virtual avatars, alter egos of the numerous temporary workers, co.co.co's (coordinated and continuing collaboration contracts), project collaborators, researchers and under-the-table or part-time workers. By the first of May 2004 it was possible to create one's own virtual avatar and insert it in the Parade, made up of many virtual multicoloured 2D characters who parade through musical floats and anti-precarious slogans. There are a great number of participants who parade with the real ones physically present in the streets of Milan and Barcelona. A cyber-procession that is a collective work. (www.euromayday.org/netparade).

Many of the practices described so far show that most of the Italian activists who grew up in the Social Centres, raves and fanzines, have a lot to teach regarding winning communication techniques and mass media strategies capable of making news. A background accumulated over the years that, as many emphasize, allows *maximum visibility with a minimum effort*. Luther Blissett teaches and many have learned the lesson. And they learned it so well that they decided to capitalise on it. In 2002 Guerrigliamarketing.it was established, a company that came about with the idea that it is possible to associate the politico-cultural experimentation of alternative and underground environments to the marketing activity of the business circuits (www.guerrigliamarketing.it). In Italy, the concept of guerrilla marketing assumed a political connotation alien to the rest of the world, just as many other experiences described earlier. Andrea Natella, one of the founders of Guerrigliamarketing.it, underlines that the concept of "guerrilla marketing" includes manifold practices that are outside the specification of "guerrigliamarketing.it", in spite of the fact that in Italy, above all in the marketing circles, the two terms overlap (Andrea Natella, 2006).

Some members of Guerrigliamarketing.it come from the Luther Blissett Project, the MenInRed (MIR) collective, a Radical Ufology experience (www.kyuzz.org/mir), from Indymedia and from the hacker movement. Moving for some time in the cultural jamming circuits are "a number of creative intervention practices on mainstream communication, by using detournement, fakes, the improbable and the absurd" (from the Guerrigliamarketing.it site). With their project, Guerrigliamarketing responds to the eternal gap between experimental underground environments and commercial companies. And they do it using techniques and strategies necessary to reach the mass media – learned over the course of their "opposing" activity.

As Andrea Natella tells,

what the underground teaches to the small cultural groups is that if you have an inconvenient or minority opinion, in order to succeed in publicising it without money to invest you have to find alternative routes. You have to invent something new or more often find a new way to say the same thing, prejudices have to be overcome and public opinion attention attracted to your topics. To do this, start moving like guerrilla. Set up an ambush, create a trap, build a hoax, action, news that the press can't avoid treating because of its nature of interest, curiosity, novelty. And whether they like it or not, they'll be forced to talk about you. It is the same type of attention that small companies very often need during start-up or relaunching phases. They need visibility, they need to be talked about, they need a dynamic image. (...) Our communication tactics foresee creating events that are improbable, paradoxical, science fiction, actions to be carried out during the night, at times at the limits of legality. (...) In this sense we have used the Internet above all as a parapet behind which to hide a product, or as a starting point to spread news. If only the horizontal mechanisms of communication are exploited and we wait for the networks of social relations to do the work for us, the resources to invest become huge, otherwise we need to resign ourselves to very long times for achieving minimally ambitious goals. This is why we have always aimed at broadcasting and often worked with hoaxes, false scoops specially constructed for the media, capable of echoing in the social networks along with our commercial communication (<www.percheinternet.it/autoformazione/guerriglia-mktg.html>).

Therefore the Guerrigliamarketing.it team offers itself directly to companies in search of notoriety with the idea of capitalising on their cultural background, which is very tempting to a lot of them. Why should they stay on the fringe when they are experts in the communications and social hack fields? Why leave the territory of action to just the large brands ready to swallow up any new experimentation attempt in the cultural industry? The Guerrigliamarketing.it team decided to become active in the new immaterial economy, offering «integrated and systematic reinvestment of our skills within a communications project serving anyone who still wants to risk and play, and above all has a beastly need for visibility» (from the <www.guerrigliamarketing.it> site).

Therefore profit-oriented communications strategies are put into action creating ad hoc pseudo-events for the companies accepting the invitation, working on their image and trying to obtain maximum visibility for them. Among the various successful campaigns, *La beffa di Riccione* (2001) was the first of the series. Conceived by Andrea Natella and Fabrizio Carli, again within the MenInRed experience, stages a fake UFO landing as a publicity campaign for the Emilia Romagna tourist promotion company. The city of Riccione accepted Guerriglia Marketing's proposal to simulate an invasion of aliens, leaving the incriminating "marks" in the parking lot of the Acquafan water amusement park and having it covered by the local and national press and the Radio Deejay commentators.

Naturally the news spread like wildfire up to the "revelation of the hoax", in the meanwhile everything "reinforced the image of a young, active city, inclined for experimentation" (from the <www.guerrigliamarketing.it> site).

Another initiative, the *Scrap the Brand* campaign "to relaunch employment and give back breathing space to Italian style communications creativity, we ask for a policy of incentives in favour of those companies that decide to scrap their obsolete marketing and communications strategies and replace them with mint campaigns!" (<www.guerrigliamarketing.it/campaign/rottamabrand.htm>). Or the *Illegal Art Show*, "bringing their own works to a public space with no need for asking permission. Objects, designs, bodies with which to make something happen in a space where nothing usually happens. Trying to interact with the people walking by as well as with the art enthusiasts, and trying to give a new meaning to the surrounding environment"[33].

Another innovative project, establishing a "Reality Trainer", a young escort (male or female) for a company manager who is tired of living from desks to hotel rooms and decides to go recharge his mind in the places where new cultures and trends are actually produced:

Young artist's studios and rehearsal rooms for musicians, squares and metropolitan meeting places, private parties and rave parties, social centres and association headquarters, dinners between hackers and poetry groups, spaces of urban and social degradation and more or less alternative consumption places, cult places and emerging micro-companies, situations of immigration or marginality and fashionable bars, headquarters of volunteer associations and semi-legal contexts. You will enter these places beside a young person who is absolutely at home with the people and the space he is guiding you through and who will highlight for you the more concrete and interesting aspects of each situation. (...) Thus you will be able to know and exchange ideas with people and personalities capable of giving a new impulse to your creativity and allow you to recuperate a concrete relationship with social reality (<www.guerrigliamarketing.it/solutions/realitytrain.htm>).

The Guerrigliamarketing.it project is actually a criticism of many of the situations of underground movement that *a priori* exclude contact with business reality, demonstrating that contamination can also be a winner and not always the mirror of identity loss. Or course, in doing so you have to be clever enough to avoid being swallowed up by what you want to swallow up: "Screw the market to enter it," is the Guerrigliamarketing philosophy. Naturally you have to have a good acting capability and a large dose of self-criticism, to the point that Guerrigliamarketing began being ironic about the movement of the precarious workers.

To respond to the various actions in supermarkets and commercial chains operated by some of the precarious workers who in 2004 seemed to lose the critical vision of the first battles a bit too much, making claims that were a little "slipshod" (and which put the more meditated ones in the shadows), Guerrigliamarketing created a hoax site for promoting the "proletarian expropriations". This is how the *Espropriproletari.com* project came about, "a unique opportunity for your company to become known throughout the national territory" <www.guerrigliamarketing.it/ep>.

The team was ironic about what seemed to become a fashion of people who signed themselves "the devout of Saint Precarious", and in 2004 expropriated books in the Feltrinelli book stores or ran out of restaurants without paying the bill (but left a tip for the waiter) after expensive fish dinners or baptism banquets for forty people. On the site called Espropriproletari.com the idea of expropriating goods to fight precarious employment and the high cost of living became a chance for recruiting young activists seeking new thrills or a business opportunity for companies looking for easy publicity. As is read on the site:

Espropriproletari.com is a revolutionary service capable of guaranteeing visibility to your brand or your emblem in all the national press; it is aimed at mass distribution chains, hypermarkets, catering companies, transport companies, small retailers. A group of specialised operators is sent to the shop to pilfer goods during a publicised sure-impact action. This is a unique action to give extreme desirability of your products through a national campaign in the main newspapers (<www.guerrigliamarketing.it/ep/it/index.html>).

A site that can even give cause for thought to the many precarious workers who, with their actions, often risk making indirect publicity for the brands they are fighting against. The Guerrigliamarketing.it project shows that they might as well be paid by the shopping malls, because it takes just a little knowledge of laws and market strategies to understand nowadays that sooner or later everything is capitalised by the cultural industry, or manipulated by power plays.

Otherwise critical strategies must be created, that play with the same "weapons" (as Serpica Naro has shown), because it isn't always true that the quantity of actions is proportional to the quality.

Yet not all companies seem to comprehend the irony of Espropriproletari.com and the benefits of indirect advertising, to the extent that in June 2006 the law firm representing Pam S.p.A and Panorama S.p.A., companies on the list of Espropriproletari.com "customers", sent a letter to the holder of the above mentioned site ordering the removal within three days of any reference and link to the Pam Group[34]. The two companies are on the list of "customers" along with others who were the object of previous proletarian expropriations and the law firm states that because of the incriminated page of the Espropriproletari.com site, suggesting an active role by the Pam Group in proletarian expropriations, there was damage to the image of the companies. This is also because several specialist publications considered the presumed partnership between Espropriproletari.com and the Pam Group to be a fact (once again, a Luther Blisset style ambush at the press officers who don't bother checking sources...). Consequently the references to Pam S.p.A and Panorama S.p.A were removed from the Espropriproletari.com site and the Pam Group image returned to normality. As many guerrilla marketing operations teach us, it's not sure that "returning to normality" nowadays is the right marketing strategy for these companies.

In this sense, the Guerrigliamarketing.it operations have undoubtedly turned out to be more astute compared to a normal marketing study, showing the ability of critical action in the sphere of advertising information techniques, as well as what concerns movement dynamics. Italy doesn't seem to have assimilated the concept of "indirect publicity" very much, and we should bear in mind that an international giant such as Nike, involved in the *Nike Ground* operation by 0100101110101101.ORG, after initial opposition to the artists, brought the lawsuit to nothing... Furthermore, today Nike Ground is considered a work of net.art by the majority of international critics.

Endnotes

1   As Maria Teresa Paoli mentions in her degree thesis titled "New media and independent political communication. Indymedia, between anti-global activism and hacktivism", defended at the University of Siena, Faculty of Letters and Philosophy, degree course in Sciences of Communications, academic year 2000-2001 (downloadable at: http://italy.peacelink.org/mediawatch/articles/art_14954.html). In particular, Maria Teresa Paoli writes: "The Reclaim the Streets activists have been connecting for some time through websites and e-mail whereas the street rallies are already equipped with video cameras. Some of the videos of their protests are already on the web, easily downloadable by the rest of the world. Thus we come to one month before the WTO summit, in October 1999, when five or six activists meet to set up an actual media center. Among them some have participated in the Countermedia project three years earlier. The group succeeds in finding a headquarters and the funds necessary by rallying the country's other independent media groups. Donations from individuals as well as local computer companies come in. When the protests start, the first media center in the world has an available budget of $75,000, two chairs, cell phones, dozens of computers and video editing systems. Approximately 500 people are actively involved in the media center during the November 1999 protests. Surprisingly enough the site is linked by the home pages of important portals such as Yahoo! and OneWorld. According to some of the American activists, the news agencies linked to Reuters, CNN and BBC, connect continually to IMC to have direct contact with the demonstrators." (pp. 93-94). On Countermedia, see: <www.cpsr.cs.uchica go.edu/countermedia> and on Reclaim the Streets: <http://rts.gn.apc.org/>.

2   In addition to the US and Canada, Europe, Latin America, Africa, Australia, the Middle East and India.

3   For information see the Contropiani site, among the organisers of the protests against the OECD summit, <www.contropiani2000.org>, today found at: <www.bologna.social-forum.org>.

4   A vast review on net.art and hacktivism with the subject "Art as actual practice: reflections on the use of technology in the artistic experimentation from avant-gardes to network art", organised by Tommaso Tozzi, Snafu and the undersigned, which involved numerous sector theorists and experts in a thick series of interventions on June 16th and 17th, 2000, at the Forte Prenestino cinema in Rome, Hackmeeting 2000. On the 17th of June, Franco Berardi "Bifo" and Matteo Pasquinelli tell about the protest experience of the OECD meeting and present the budding project called Indymedia Italia. Info about the meeting can be found at the Hackmeeting 2000 site: <www.ecn.org/hackit00/text/proposte/arte.htm>.

5   Message sent to the "Net_Institute" mailing list, subject: " quick netin-NOOCSE theoretic notes", 6th June 2000.

6   Franco Berardi and Matteo Pasquinelli, message sent on the "Net_Institute" mailing list with the subject line: "Rekombinant - September 2000, Bologna", 16th July 2000.

7   Simultaneously Indymedia texts and images and Radio GAP audio files were used in various underground contexts in other Italian cities. For example, in Florence, as the Strano Network collective, we organised the evening of counterinformation about the G8 days in the summer outdoor space called Parterre. The initiative was called "Voices and images from the G8" and for three days the Florentine passers-by were informed of the events in real time.

8   Among the more active counterinformation sites, in addition to Indymedia and Radio GAP, we mention the historical movement sites Isole nella Rete <www.ecn.org/g8>, Tactical Media Crew <www.tmcrew.org>, Carta <www.carta,org>, Decoder <www.decoder.it>, Genoa Social Forum <www.genoa-g8.org>.

9   The matter is described at length in Maria Teresa Paoli's degree thesis, pp. 142-144. The thesis reports the communication written by Indymedia in reaction to the accusation in the "Porta a Porta" broadcast, from which we derive the above mentioned phrase.

10   On the Radical Software site (www.radicalsoftware.org) are the issues of the magazine in pdf format, freely downloadable.

11   Simonetta Fadda's first CCTV installation is in Giuseppe Chiari's concert for *Il fido maestro giardiniere*, organised by Nanni Balestrini, Pratolino Park (Florence), Summer of 1987. The CCTV installations made by Simonetta Fadda at that time were a stimulus for reflecting on the forms of social control and surveillance, an opportunity to create *situations*, in the *situationist* meaning of the word, where the spectators end up participating actively, interacting with the work of art. In *Videogame* (1987), the spectator observes himself and his gestures within the exhibition space, in *Sistema* (1987) "the spectator was placed before his 'being there at the time', with the fact of having entered a situation that was asking him a question (who are you?), was asking him to do something (what do you want?)" (Fadda, 2006), whereas in *Sorveglianza totale* (1989), "the spectator confronts himself through the eye of the other person (the surveillance video camera observing the naked exhibition space), with no possibility for communication", as Simonetta Fadda explains in notes sent to me by e-mail (2006). The cross reference to the situationist concept of situation is not accidental, given that Simonetta Fadda is an enthusiastic scholar and critic of desecrating, ironic and provocative practices in art circuits and beyond. Among the texts translated by her, we mention the book by Stewart Home, 1995, *Neoism, Plagiarism and Praxis*, AK Press, Edinburgh-San Francisco *(Neoismo e altri scritti. Idee critiche sull'avanguardia contemporanea*, Genoa, Costa & Nolan, 1997).

12   Press release of the *Still Life* one man show at the Maria Cilena gallery in Milan, 1996.

13   Simonetta Fadda, *Bassa definizione*, intervention for the Hacker Art seminar organised by Tommaso Tozzi, held on the 5th of June 1998, during the 1998 Hackmeeting, Florence, CPA Social Centre.

14   Among the members of the Church of Electrosophy are Robert Chroscicki, Enzo Taglialatela, Giuseppe Serse, Manolo Luppichini, Cécile Glevarec, Stefano Aria, Myriam Laplante, Pierfrancesco Savona, Luca Nepi, Massimo Di Felice, initiator and first priest who in 2000 founded the independent production company Elettrosofia srl. A similar attitude, combining the broadcast world and underground scene, is found in the Link Project, starting up in Bologna in 1994 and author of a series of musical, performance and artistic events during experimental reviews and shows in Bologna's Link space. The *Netmage* project, an international audiovisual festival and a series of correlated events <www.netmage.it>, started from a "rib" of the Link Project and other subjectivities active in the audiovisual spheres.

15   One of the members of the Church of Electrosophy, Manolo Luppichini, was active in the first phase of the AvANa.net collective and is part of the Candida TV collective. Also members of Candida TV are Agnese Trocchi, Cristina Petrucci, Antonio Veneziano, Tora Krogh, Emanuele Bozzo and others.

16   I received this information from the Candida TV collective during an interview for the magazine "Neural". The article, *Candida, la televisione elettrodomestica*, was published in "Neural", 15, May-October 2000.

17   E-mail sent by Agnese Trocchi, on [AVANA-BBS] the subject being "Candida: una televisione elettrodomestica" (a household appliance television), dated 24th September 1999. As Agnese Trocchi writes in her e-mail, the layout proposed by Candida TV for the Teleambiente broadcasts, she proposed: "medical-surgical suburban hybrid columns, open spaces on detention-territories, information cut-ups with socio-economic studies, impossible poetry readings, underground musical cuts, alternative and anti-prohibitionist chronic cuisine (...), the hyperfiction of role-playing immersive videogames, forays in the global and Roman network with associations that deal with telematic law and subversive telematics,

women's rooms, insane quizzes, organic and inorganic sexuality, nihilistic ecology, radical astronomy, intervals".

18 Emanuele Bozzo, as Supervideo, continues making speeches under the name ManuelBo. Among these, "an attempt to reanimate information, which sees the means of communication (television, radio, computers) carried on a stretcher, complete with doctors and nurses, around the Telecommunications Ministry; newspaper pages served as a means because, as the author writes, 'in the information society, the hunger for communication needs to be fed'; the exhibition – the same day as the beginning of the Tele Padre Pio broadcasts, in the presence of Minister Gasparri – of a TV set shedding tears of blood, in a sort of secular 'miracle'. These performances of ManualBo's, playing on making the now worn out metaphors literal ('sick' information, indigestion of news, etc.) to relaunch the possibility of grassroots communication, daring and free, within the reach of everyone". This description of ManuelBo's work is taken from the site of the underground magazine "Cut-Up" <www.cut-up.net>.

19 From *Reality Hacking*, video collection, Candida TV, 2003.

20 Fabrizio Manizza specifies: when the word telestreet (lower case first letter) appears in his quotes, it is just a synonym for street TV or neighbourhood TV, but when Telestreet (upper case first letter) appears, reference is to the whole movement or network that groups and connects the individual telestreets.

21 Notes sent to me by Fabrizio Manizza, written on June 6, 2006, after I had requested to tell about the present status of the Telestreet phenomenon according to his personal viewpoint. Fabrizio Manizza answered this invitation with a long stimulating essay.

22 Remember that one of the Radio Alice members, Franco Berardi "Bifo", is also propeller and supporter of the Telestreet phenomenon.

23 Fabrizio Manizza, Senigallia, June 2006, *Ibidem*.

24 The event was organised by me along with the German filmmaker Alexandra Weltz from 14-16 July 2004, at the Muffathalle Cultural Centre in Munich, Germany. The event-meeting presented projects and reflections on the "guerrilla media" and independent information in Italy. It took place in an international convention and video show with Candida TV, Disco Volante TV, Minimal TV, New Global Vision, Rekombinant, P2P-FightSharing, infoAccessibile and video contributions on the circuit of Italian Telestreets. The following year the Telestreet project, and in particular Telestreet Disco Volante TV, were present at the show-event "Hack.it.art, Hacktivism in the Context of Art and Media in Italy", again organised by the Bazzichelli-Weltz pair at the Kunstraum Kreuzberg/Bethanien in Berlin, Germany. "Hack.it.art" is an exhibition on Italian Hacktivism and on the independent forms of artistic and media production, taking the experience of a country like Italy to an international context. There were debates, workshops and various events on Hacktivism from the 14th of January to the 15th of February 2005, presenting many old and recent experiences of the Italian hacker scene. The show-events enter in turn in the *AHA: Activism-Hacking-Artivism* <www.ecn.org/aha> project.

25 In the essay *Dalle Telestreet agli Hackmeeting: il network del fare informazione*, I amply wrote about the New Global Vision project, in the text edited by Marcello Pecchioli, *Neo televisione. Elementi di un linguaggio catodico-glocalle*, Milan, Costa & Nolan, 2005, pp. 93-109.

26 The article written by Giancarlo "Ambrogio" Vitali, which comes from the project document created by the T.CAP (Public Access Community Televisions), was published on the Telestreet site on the 8th of March 2004, at the URL: <www.telestreet.it/modules.php?%20op=modload&name=News&file=articl e&sid=41>.

27 For more information about the new broadband Internet TVs, see the article *La nuova tv che cambierà il mercato*, by Giuseppe Turani, published in "Affari & Finanza" ("La Repubblica") on May 9, 2005, and on the web at the Telestreet site forum <www.telestreet.it>.

28 MayDay Parade 2001 organisation appeal, in Chaincrew, *Chain Workers, lavorare nelle cattedrali del consumo*, Rome, Derive Approdi, 2001, pp. 111-112. The Milan MayDay was promoted in 2001 by ChainWorkers.org, Deposito Bulk and Cub. MayDay exists in a European version in various cities in Europe; information can be found at <www.euromayday.org>.

29 Text from: <www.chainworkers.org/imbattibili>.

30 The experience of the Sexyshock collective will be dealt with extensively in the next chapter.

31 An interesting DVD-video in which hacker ethics, Telestreet, activism and precarious battles meet is P2P-FightSharing (I + III), a collection of videos that show the state of Italian underground video culture in 2003-2005. Version I came about during the events external to the World Summit on Information Society (WSIS) in Geneva in 2003 and presents forms of networking and Trans-European cooperation among those who create political and media activism. The central themes are: city protest action, media activism, guerrilla information and media sabotage. Versions II and III are video compilations about precarious work and protest actions among ChainWorkers and MayDay. The DVDs, devised by Francesca Bria, Tora Krogh and Lize De Clercq, were presented by Candida TV <candida.thing.net> and Greenpepper Magazine in Amsterdam <www.greenpeppermagazine.org>.

32 Paolo Pedercini is interviewed by Claudia D'Alonso, "Molleindustria, quando il gioco si fa duro", published in *Digimag, periodico di informazione digitale*, April 2006, at: <www.digicult.it/digimag/article.asp?id=330>.

33 Guerriglia Marketing, "Illegal Art Show", at: <www.guerrigliamarketing.it/campaign/ias.htm>.

34 As Andrea Natella wrote me in a personal e-mail in July 2006.

Extra Gender

Cyberfeminism on the Net

Today, technology is still generally considered to be a male domain. But while this is true for many I.T. networks, the phenomenon becomes more ambivalent and complex if the subject of analysis is the network of experiences related to body and identity. Here sexuality becomes liberated and becomes an input to go beyond the categories of gender. In 1991, Donna Haraway published *Cyborg Manifesto* (1995), in which the feminist experience is considered from a new perspective, thinking about technology and the networks as a territory for the construction of new cultural and social processes.

Sexuality in this vision becomes a code of open and playfully radical communication. The identity of the woman is no longer based on the opposition of gender (feminine/masculine), but it becomes a fluid entity, capable of manifesting itself through a network of diffused and reticular ties which instead of stressing the differences, stress proximity, showing a chameleonic imitation of identities on a technology plane. It is no longer an "exclusively feminine" identity, but it becomes something more open and hybrid. The role of the woman, according to Haraway's approach, becomes active within the dynamics of production of culture and knowledge, acquiring importance in the construction of technological processes. At the same time, the cyber feminist techno-culture sees the body of a woman as a place of active experimentation, with particular attention to the radical and ludic aspect of the artistic practices which regard identity and sexuality, no longer stranded in the portrayal of pain and suffering as an answer to the forms of control.

Also in 1991, VNS Matrix, a group of Australian female artists and activists heavily inspired by the theories of Donna Haraway, wrote the *Cyberfeminist Manifesto for the 21st century*, a radical and ironic text in which overcoming rigid and patriarchal categories was at the centre of the group's reflections[1]. Through the proliferation of a fluid matrix of digital data, a mirror of a new "expanded" conception of sexuality, the seed of Cyberfeminism spread from Australia to Europe, all the way to America. Its key concepts were the radical use of the body, the enthusiasm for technological utopias and cyber-fantasies and the conviction that it is possible to subvert the patriarchy, through new hybrid identities, irony and political activism.

Equating feminism and technoculture on a critical plane and analyzing the consequences of the feminine use of technology in the workplace, in domestic life, in society and in the dimension of pleasure, Cyberfeminism has signalled the spirit of an era: the 1990s. But at the same time, Donna Haraway's *Cyborg Manifesto* and VNS Matrix's *Cyberfeminist Manifesto*, were fundamental in order to reflect on the cultural dualisms closely tied to the technological dominion, showing how the network and the cultural processes are still mainly dominated by men. Donna Haraway describes the technological development as *informatics of domination* through which surveillance and control become a constant of daily life and condition cultural development and social relationships.

From 1997 to 2001, these reflections were brought to an international level by the women's network Old Boys Network <www.obn.org>, organizing different meetings and events such as the *First Cyberfeminist International* (Kassel, Germany, September 1997 at *Documenta X*), *Next Cyberfeminist International* (Rotterdam, Holland, March 1999) and *Very Cyberfeminist International* (Hamburg, Germany, December 2001), constructing relationships between different female artists, activists and theorists working with net.art and media criticism[2].

The women working within this network demonstrate how the feminine approach to technology presents a very sophisticated critical capacity, aiming to deconstruct the social, cultural and gender categories. The feminine reflection on the use of technology aims at overcoming labels, subverting cultural prejudices

258

and common sense convictions through irony and parody. The power structures and the hierarchies, which are perpetuated even in the so-called "free networks" of *net culture,* are brought to light and overturned. Examples of this include the *Female Extension* project by German net.artist Cornelia Sollfrank, the disturbing and viral action in the *net culture* mailing list by Netochka Nezvanova and the poetry in programming code written by the Australian artist Mez with her unique poetic language called *mezangelle.*

For example, in *Female Extension,* Cornelia Sollfrank shows how it is possible to create cultural hacking with elegance and irony. In 1997 the Hamburg Museum of Contemporary Art promoted a net.art competition called "Internet as Material and Object", inviting registrants to create artistic works for the web, which were entered in a database-gallery accessible with a username and password. On the Internet it would appear that considering a net.art work as a finished product destined for a collection is limiting, when instead a collective process should be favoured. At the same time, it appears limiting to reduce a person (the artist) to a precise individuality made up of name, last name, telephone, address, e-mail, bringing the traditional categories of the artistic system into a context where they are usually overturned. Cornelia Sollfrank registered approximately two hundred fictitious women in the competition, aided by the web community to generate just as many working email addresses.

Using the *net.art generator* programme (the first version was created by Ryan Johnston), the artist succeeded in producing a work of web art for each of the two hundred female artists, combining different web pages in a sort of collage. In this way, not only was she able to register all the women for the competition in a short time, but she was also able to do it in such a way that each of these presented her work of art, amounting, in reality, to a collection of randomly assembled data. The organizers, although seemingly surprised by the high number of women who registered for the competition, did not uncover the "trick". After the publication of the names of the winners (three male artists, despite the high percentage of women registered in the contest), Cornelia Sollfrank went public with her experiment, which she named *Female Extension.* The vacuity of the contest, as well as the lack of knowledge on the part of the critics who promoted it, became clear. Furthermore, it showed that even when women on the web become active subjects, rarely do they achieve high positions or receive prestigious recognition, this is also true on an international level[3].

In 1999 these considerations pushed Cornelia Sollfrank to research women hackers, subsequently published in the reader of the event-meeting *Next Cyberfeminist International*. The research reveals that a scarce number of women were active in the field of hacking. Cornelia Sollfrank observed that not only are few women really involved in the commercial development of technology and only a few have an important role in the business world, but even fewer are present in underground culture and in the area of media criticism. Contrary to the utopias of the 1990s, in which technology via computer and the digital networks seemed to open and promise new communication horizons beyond the sexes, the boundaries between the sexes were still intact and, after fifteen years, this aspect seems to persist. Cornelia Sollfrank wrote that "the majority of women seem to prefer to dedicate themselves to politically subordinate tasks in a purely cultural environment, at a non-technological level. The women were not actively influencing the development of the hardware and software and therefore they were relinquishing the possibility of sharing the power that goes with it" (Sollfrank, 1999). Cornelia Sollfrank concluded her research with a fact: there are very few women in the production of new technologies and in the creation of new techno-paradigms. In reality, in those years, experiments such as the *Old Boys Network* (of which Cornelia Sollfrank is a member) and the international mailing list *Faces, Women in Media*, show that there are many active women in the field of technology. In any case, whether women are really influential in the creation of new techno-paradigms and the dynamics of power, which determine the production of hardware and software, is still debateable. Seven years after Cornelia Sollfrank's research, there is still no in-depth research which describes the current state of the situation (this is an invitation to do it). The situation seems to be decidedly better in terms of women's participation, even if the gap remains. For example, the *Faces, Women in Media* mailing list community, founded in the spring of 1997 by Kathy Rae Huffman, Diana McCarty and Valie Djordjevic (Ushi Reiter joined in 2003), is 400 members strong today <www.faces-l.net>.

Furthermore, in the last few years the numerous international networking events on the gender-tech theme demonstrate how the number of women working in the art and new technology sectors has increased. *Les HTMlles*, based in Montreal, Québec <www.htmlles.net>, is a Canadian new media art festival promoted by the Study XX community. Founded in 1995 in Montreal, Study XX is the most important centre for the study of new technologies by women <www.studyxx.org>. In Europe, the impact of technology on our daily lives and the increasing role that women play in it is analysed by *Digitales*, an international technology festival orientated towards the creation of a feminine network, held in Brussels in 2001, 2002 and 2004 <www.digitals-online.org>.

In 2002 in Pula, Croatia, the *Eclectic Tech Carnival* event was launched and was subsequently hosted in Athens, Greece in 2003, in Belgrade, Serbia in 2004, in Graz, Austria in 2005, in Timisoara, Romania in 2006 and in Linz, Austria, in 2007. A carnival organized by women for women who love computers and who experiment with technology. It is a sort of feminine hackmeeting offering basic computer courses on PC hardware, Linux (even for beginners), networking, privacy and PGP, scripting language, open publishing and hacker ethic ("get your hands into computers!") <http://etc.genderchangers.org>.

The *City of Women* festival <www.cityofwomen-a.si> (Ljubljana, Slovenia, since 1995) presents the work of many female artists and activists from all over the world, mostly from Eastern Europe[4], through panel meetings, workshops, performances and video projections.

Another mailing list bringing together women who are principally working in research, is NextGENDERation, a transactional European network of scholars, researchers, activists and individuals interested in feminist theory and politics and the relationships with antiracist themes, migration, anti-capitalism and lesbian and queer culture <www.nextgenderation.net>[5].

At the international level these experiences demonstrate the central role of the networking dynamics in connecting women artists, activists, theorists and hackers who work with art and new technologies. It is in these instances that technology is used with artistic, cultural and political goals, the joint action of different subjectivities which show how it is possible to create a first step in redefining powers and hierarchies, in terms of dismantling and opening social, cultural and sexual categories.

Pink Action and Queer Networks

In Italy, the critical reflection on sexuality and identity, like many of the free practices already described, could not but take on the shape of a network. In particular, this network shows that it knows how to concretely work on cultural codes in order to blow holes in the cultural basis of the codes. These holes reach beyond any form of sterile dualism that perpetuates the categories of existing power. It does this by bringing its own body into play and using sexuality as a critical territory to reach beyond the confines, the barriers and the rigid forms of thinking.

According to a theory created by anthropologist Victor Turner (1920-1983) to describe the phases of socio-cultural passage, performance is seen as a corporeal practice necessary for a critical redefinition of reality. The concept of the anthropology of the performance is used by Victor Turner to describe these *liminal* practices (potentially fertile areas of rewriting of the cultural codes) as well as to understand the transformation of the social itself. In the same way in which in theatrical practices it is possible to elaborate the lived starting from bodily experimentation, in daily life the fact of appealing to spontaneous creative improvisation can facilitate the understanding of the present and generate something new, recomposing the cultural symbols according to unedited modalities.

The body, placed within specific communicative and expressive contexts, in which the dynamics of interaction, dialogue and collective exchange acquire a particular relevance, allows for play with otherness and the other. At the same time, it makes the conflicts of dominion, which characterize a large part of our present, difficult. In this free, active, experimental space, new cultural elements and new combined rules can be introduced and above all it is possible to work on a critical reflection of corporate structure itself starting from putting one's own body on the performance stage.

As Victor Turner writes: "the essence of liminality consists in the decomposition of the culture in its constitutional factors and in the free or 'ludic' re-composition of these in every, and any, possible configuration, as bizarre as it may be" (1986, p. 61). Performance therefore has an experimental, and at the same time, critical character: through bodily action it is possible to live out an experience[6] and bring it to term and in the act of putting our body on the scene in free contexts, it is possible to reflect on the same experiences. On a more general level, performance constitutes a form of *social metacomment*, it therefore represents "a story that a group narrates to itself about itself" (*ivi*, p. 185).

Returning to the topic of networking, the importance of putting into play one's own body and sexuality in territories beyond the confines, lives inside the pink network and the free-actions and ludic-tactics strategies which commonly take on the names *pink block, macchia rosa* [pink spot] or *pink action*. Francesco "Warbear" Macarone Palmieri, cultural agitator active in the Roman queer sphere, describes the practices of the pink network as putting an accent on their playful and transforming character:

> Desiring something else from oneself, and doing it by transforming it into a theatrical event of maximum sociability, visibility and publicity – echoing with the romantic-surrealist idea of the Coney Island freak show in N.Y., is a typical pink action where the element of confusion, induced by the stirring up of pleasures/fears in a continuously overturning state, creates the dynamic of criticism. The theme of our monster cannot but pass for the theme of the body, which is the primary focus for the pink movement. To celebrate the body and to extend beyond the socially established confines of the culturally defined and of the morally accepted, means expanding it and altering it in a nomadic architecture of ecstatic wars, of moments of celebration swinging between the *grand guignol* circus and an orgiastic rush which provoked the mass use of MDMA[7]. From this equalizing point of view, we can mark time inside and outside of the concept of *pink block*, proposing a geography of individuality, entity, groups, organizations and structures. The *pink block* updates itself from time to time, in ever differing ways – organized and at the same time immediate – as a moment of aggregation on libertarian themes: therefore in primis deconstruction, criticism and the refusal of the practices of dominion based on total war and everything that is a consequence of it, such as neo-colonialism, sexism, neo-liberalism, misogyny, anti-environmentalism, homophobia, racism, prohibitionism, censure, religious movements, negation of the sharing of knowledge through freedom of information and much more. The *pink block* represents the pleasure of becoming through the freedom of being (2005, p. 57).

The pink block actively enters onto the scene at an international level in the demonstrations which involve a large part of the movement: in Prague (2000), Genoa (2001), Rome[8], Milan and Bologna (2004), and answers to the strategies of the clash and violence with the *détournement* of codes, the frivolity tactic, the playful action which is, at the same time, incisive because it is aimed at creatively overturning its symbols and the stronghold of power. Everything takes place characterized by blinding colours. Pink (or shocking pink), therefore substitutes the more "traditional" black of other antagonistic practices proposing a different vision from the nihilistic vision of *no future*.

"Think pink, for a rosy future. With a simple pink gesture it is possible to conquer the centre of the scene. *Empowerpink* diffused through the air like a perfume, it captures the optic nerve like a beam of light in twilight" (<www.ecn.org/sexyshock/xpink.htm>).

Even if inserted within the dynamics of the networking of movement, the "macchia pink" proposes a different political and strategic vision which creates a crisis for those used to opposition and clashes, composed of contrasts which do not legitimize the forms of traditional power, the subalternity which live in the dualistic hierarchies (for example culture and counter-culture, power and counter-power) and in the clashes between opposing and excluding ideals. At the same time, the pink block communicates a different vision of sexuality and of the identity which refuses every type of label and substitutes the more open *queer* vision for the g.l.b.t. (gay, lesbian, bisexual and transgender) vision. To describe the queer attitude, we quote Francesco "Warbear" Macarone Palmieri:

Pink is synonymous with queer and vice versa, they are both expressed in a bipolar arch which travels on semantic and pop/elitist focalizations. In this sense, pink is a space of hybridization of the battles, in which all the forgotten realities are taken into consideration; forgotten by the sweeping, so-called second class movements and the themes, such as the forms of sexual alienation and repression. Freedom from the oppression and control cannot but start from a semantic stripping and from a reconstruction of the meaning of the body and of its socio-sexual relationship practices. To rebel against one's own body, freeing sexuality and orientations and experimenting with new forms of socio-sexual relationships. (...) To incarnate the other, the monstrosity, perceiving the other one as one's own, multiplying the desiring self-transforming politics into desire, and deconstructing the concept of need as a demagogic, populist and generalizing narration: is both a pink and queer practice understood also and above all as a criticism of those processes of political g.l.b.t. (gay, lesbian, bisexual and transgender) claim which propose themselves as libertarian but in reality claim the norm and the similar more than the extremisation of the different. Queer culture proposes a radical vision, criticism and libertarianism of this type of process (2005, pp. 60-61).

Therefore pink practices live through a *processes of politically incorrect theatralization*, playful and libertarian jokes and pranks and group mud-fights in which the practice of the struggle becomes a form of ludic contact between the mud-stained bodies, together with colourful actions during a parade, electropunk music nights and videos of radical and hybrid bodies, pornography synonymous with rebellion, openness and cultural criticism. A bulletin of an action in Lausanne (Switzerland) against the Evian G8 in 2003, describes the pink (and silver) strategy (another network of freed bodies) of the tactical frivolity:

A form of direct action and creative, happy, fun, diversified, fluid and vital, civil disobedience. A splendid self-organized hybrid of parties and protests, based on values of autonomy, solidarity, diversity, personal initiative, indiscipline and mutual support. (...) Pink and Silver in our view are neither a "pacifist" group nor a "violent" group, because we think that these categories are useless and a dichotomy based on these is absurd. (...) We respect the fact that there are different ideas with respect to comparing themselves with us, and we welcome this diversity. Therefore together we want to think and create an open and fluid space of creative and vital protests/actions. A space where our gestures of freedom can coexist, where everyone has control over what happens, and where each one of us can choose what to do and how to do it, and make a different decision (<http://ch.indymedia.org/it/2003/05/9025.shtml>, 2003).

In Italy pink action and queer attitude live through a network of bodies and minds which travels, participating in local events or national demonstrations, but in reality it is the point of a pink triangle which plants its base in many collective projects that make the critical reflection on diversity and sexuality the principal field of action.

Among these is Sexyshock, the first independent sexshop in Italy created by women for women, a collective laboratory in which the members have all taken on the name Betty <www.ecn.org/sexyshock>. In 2001 a self-managed sex shop was created inside the Bologna TPO Social Centre. It is a space in which to reflect on the themes of sexuality, pornography, sex-toys and post-feminism, currently located in a shop-bookstore-space for meetings known as "Betty & Books" <www.betty-books.com>. Along with the physical space, there is a national mailing list on the following topics: women, technology, sexuality, prostitution, etc. <sexyshock@inventati.org>. But let's let Betty present Sexyshock directly:

265

Sexyshock is the first sex shop self-managed by 'women' in Italy. A hyper-space disseminated with links, an interactive circuit leading to other circuits. A space in which to remove sexuality from the mercantile culture and return it to a culture of relationships capable of positively exploiting the differences; far from judgements and simplifications, far from identifying roles and constraints. It is a meeting place, a space in which to archive material; a point for information gathering which can become a point of reference. It is a "mental space" in which to make the women's journeys visible and useable, open planning that interfaces with other plans. Then it reproduces like a stem cell creating new tissues: within gender, beyond gender. Betty is the collective name used by Sexyshock. Betty has many and no identities and for this reason s/he cannot be represented, s/he does not have a gender because s/he is completely loved: *s/he loves everybody*. Betty does not have colour because s/he loves the *melange* (even if s/he has an inclination for pink), Betty is a polyglot, Betty is a nomad, Betty does not need resident status documents because (until now) s/he has had the good fortune of being a citizen (<www.ecn.org/sexyshock/menu2.php, 2001).

Since 2001 the Bettys have brought forward numerous actions and campaigns, taking on the themes of sexuality, of freed pleasure, of pornography, but they have also touched on topics such as prostitution, sex trade workers and precarious employment <www.ecn.org/sexyshock/xprostitu.htm>, assisted reproduction technology and biotechnology and the cultural, political and social implications of technology on gender and identity <www.ecn.org/sexyshock/xbiotech.htm>.

In particular, with respect to the relationship between women and technology, the Sexyshock Bettys have developed an original position with regards to hacking and to the use of machines, whatever they might be. For the Bettys, computers are not the only machines which need to be taken into consideration, but also household appliances, therefore it is equally possible to apply the hacker ethic and logic of "get your hands into machines". This comes in the *détournement* of the images of the blender, washers, irons and vacuum cleaners commonly associated with women, to make them something different: an instrument of pleasure and play, an occasion to break the relationships of power and the sexual hierarchies. Machines can be seen from another point of view, as sex-toys or vibrators.

As the Bettys write: "women and housewives are a terrain of stereotypes, cemented in time: in order to understand it, just flip through the *Grazia* magazine of the 1950s, which intermingles a dangerous relationship with an undeclared, ambiguous eroticism, geared towards a male public, belonging to that time" (Betty, March 2006). This approach, designed to carry out a deconstruction and reconstruction involving the stereotypes and new fantasies, trying to rewrite, expand and de-structure the same images, was the point of view of different initiatives by Sexyshock within the Italian hacker movement <www.ecn.org/sexyshock/xbiohack.htm>.

For example, at the 2002 Hackmeeting in Bologna, the Bettys created a conference on the theme of "Betty and her/his technology", focusing on biotechnology and identity on the Web, divided in three sessions: the first, with a focus on research on the experiences of prostitution and pornography on the Web; the second, focused on the technical possibility of assisted reproduction possible today; the third, was on line, seen as a space of action to redefine the parameters of gender and identity at an individual and collective level. Also, at the 2003 Hackmeeting in Turin, the Bettys proposed a "dildo" performance with a coloured vibrator, and a group game-challenge between identitaries and post-identitaries, involving all the hackers who, for the occasion, finally "disconnected" from their own computers. The process of reflection on relationships between women and new technology was summarized with the term "Bettytech":

Tech stands for technology (clear, isn't it?) and Betty for identity (less obvious, but just as important): a name which indicates a journey of freedom through and by means of technology. Betty becomes a technologue and does not leave it up to the experts and the systems analysts to find the directions to the way of desire and revolution. Betty knows her/his own business. Bettytech is one and an infinite cyborg and invokes the death of the effeminate goddess in the name of an anti/romantic and fantastical freedom. Betty is against biopolitical abuses. We must not leave the construction of new sexual configurations and new organisms in the hands of the biopowers (multinationals, medical specialists, media magnates). Today we have Bettytech and tomorrow, who knows... (<www.ecn.org/sexyshock/xbio5.htm>).

At the same Hackmeeting in Turin, the Bettys organized an acrobatic ironing competition with winners and prizes (among which a feather duster and an apron for domestic chores): suspended in the air by a rope, many hackers attempted to iron a shirt from above, while the rope was made to oscillate at a "critical" velocity... The winners were two male hackers, who won both the feather duster and the apron!

During the 2004 Genoa Hackmeeting, it was the turn of web pornography, in particular amateur feminine pornography, as a possible vehicle of transformation of images tied to sexuality. Several porn sites on the Web were analyzed and pornography became a territory of open comparison among all the participants. We cite the comment of one of the female hackers present at the workshop, Maya[9], who describes the atmosphere which is usually experienced during a Hackmeeting on the most successful occasions:

It had been years since I had found myself in a situation of public discussion that gratified me so much. Years since I found myself talking about or listening to subjects such as pornography and women and networks and every time it happened there were only a few women, they were silent, they did not have the courage to speak their mind, or they would go on and on about the same old things: "this filth is not made for women, it is exploitation and nothing else". Burn them, burn them!! In Genoa for the first time, all the women present spoke their mind, they expressed their own opinion freely on pornography, and all were in favour. They even had the courage, seeing their young age and seeing the precise and very explicit questions they asked regarding their relationship with pornography and how they lived it, if they used it and in what way it excited them. The debate where everyone got involved went well beyond the time frame that we had established, and was interrupted only by hunger, but it continued along the hallways and staircases at least until midnight, when I left go to the station. I would like to thank all of the women who were present who have shown once again the capacity that we have to progress and to surpass our limits, in particular cultural and induced ones. A woman is beautiful and a woman Hacker is better!

This comment reminds us of the spirit of sharing and exchange felt in such meetings, which increasingly involve not only the male *smanettoni* [users who have discovered all there is to know about the software and hardware of a computer system and can manipulate it as they wish], but also women, active in the technology and computer sectors. The Sexyshock activity has been very important over the course of the years, and it is important even now, for it highlights, in these contexts, with their predominantly masculine participation, the fact of interpreting the use of technology as situated, showing that the derived relational relationships are the mirror of the dynamics of strength and of power at a corporate level.

268

Within the queer network, Phag Off is another Italian experience, which answers the taboos, the morals and the ethics (and labels) defined by freed radicalness, situational actionism, confusion/loss and nomadism, and musical and video experimentation in a critical manner. Phag Off, created in Rome by Francesco "Warbear" Macarone Palmieri and Bernardo "Noisy Pig" Santarelli, changes the derogatory and alienating concept of Phag (fag), with the Off universe, beyond hybridized and fluctuating queer parameters. It proposes a surpassing of the hetero-homosexual dualism, acting within the nerves of the unpredictable, of the grotesque, of sexual radicality, of the game and of the joke. For this reason, it is directly connected to the pink experiences and brings the irreverent tactic of the frivolous to punk, claiming to be the spokesperson of all those entities that don't want to belong to a socially defined universe, opposed and rigid, whether one is hetero or gay. Even in Phag Off, the traditional dynamics of power and belonging are upset because they are ridiculed, putting into play one's own body, pulling pranks and playing eccentric, surreal, dirty and carnally unforeseeable games.

Phag Off comes to life in a radical party thrown at the Metaverso club located in the Testaccio neighbourhood of Rome. In addition, many other events are included within its contaminating libidinous flux, from the presentation of books and movies (such as the Tekfestival <www.tekfestival.it>), to the self production of fanzines, magazines and editorial products (among which the pop counter-culture historical magazine "Torazine" and the recent magazine "Catastrophe" <www.catastrophe.it>), to the promotion of queer and homochorus musical groups together with performances on themes such as the body and other sexualities. During the evenings at the Metaverso, the musical electro-punk experimentation is mixed with video, as in Nikky's vjing, *activist-lady* of many of the Phag Off prank-performances[10].

As Francesco "Warbear" Macarone Palmieri narrates describing the Phag Off experience:

...if the debate arising from gender studies and the proliferation of continuous sexual subcultures based on micro-social re-aggregation has opened large fractures in the ideology of the unique colour, today the moment of using them like openings for the new wave has arrived. (...) The Phag Off queer project in this sense represents an erogenous zone of convergence pro/posing itself as a space of experience of the new wave understood as something *otherwhen* sexual, using its strength in research and discoveries of unknown constellations of diversity which are composed of hybrid and vague visions, continuous individualizations, cultural frankensteins, polyhedric identities, sexual war machines (2005, pp. 61-62).

Phag Off is inserted within a larger network of projects which equally present a critical view on sexuality, many with a distinct queer attitude[11]. Among these the Vida Loca Records, an independent music label and national booking agency with a distinct punk and queer attitude, dedicated to lesbian/fem themes and area of reflection on the sex trade, <www.vidalocarecords.com>. Part of the Vida Loca Records, is the *Porca Ma Donna Distro* project, an independent distribution house of self-produced material, from fanzines to records, magazines and pins, who are also active in mail art.

Hup Withcerti who organizes queer musical evenings should also be mentioned <www.hupconcerti.net>. "Speed Demon" is a national historical homocore fanzine close to the queer and punk universe in Milan <www.speeddemon.it>. Hot Skin is a group of gay Swiss skinheads who create radical bodily performances <www.hotskin.it>. Pornflakes is the Milanese queer collective that organizes electronic musical evenings and performances pertaining to the theme of liberated sexual identity <www.pornflakes.it>. Queering Sapienza, is a group of students from the Faculty of Literature of "La Sapienza" University in Rome who act with the motto "another sexuality is possible" promoting initiatives, parades and debates. Sex & Genders is the section of Indymedia Italy relating to the debate on gender and sexuality <http://italy.indymedia.org/features/sex>. Global Groove are queer graphic artists who create publications and host art and advertising events contaminating and appropriating iconographic, textual and mediatic sound sources and who work on plagiarism and graphic collages <www.globalgroove.it>. She Strikes is a group of post-feminists active in the self-governed Roman space Strike <http://strike-spa.net/shestrike.html>. Antagonismo Gay is a Bolognese collective composed of gay, lesbian and transgender individuals, working since 1999 on themes of sexuality collaborating with women, migrants and prostitutes, and fighting for those oppressed in the expression of one's own otherness <www.ecn.org/agaybologna>.

To these links, we add a series of current events, queer parties who work on sexuality and creative experimentation: in Bologna there is Gender Bender, a

270

festival created by the Cassero space <www.genderbender.it>; HomoBeat is tied to the relationship of bodies, sexuality and electronic music <www.cassero.it/homobeat> and Carni Scelte is a new queer radical party <www.carniscelte.info>. In Florence a new queer party experience called Milking was recently created. In Rome we note the Coq Madame, the queer dance evening in which many DJs of the city participate <www.coqmadame.com>. SHErocco is a new feminine Roman party, which applies femininity through the free use of the body, created by Nikky from Phag Off together with Maria Francesca Bianchi of Coq Madame <http://sherocco.superfluo.biz>.

On the theme of sex trading and prostitution, we note the committee for the rights of the prostitute <www.lucciole.org>, who recently invented a Monopoly style board game based on this subject, called Puttanopoly, which represents a trip between the different risks and accidents in the journey of a prostitute <www.puttanopoly.com>. In the trans area, an active reality in Italy, we have MIT, the Movimento di Identità Transessuale, a volunteer association which deals with defending the rights of transsexuals, transvestites and transgenders <www.mit-Italy.it>.

At an international level, there are many groups that work on queer issues and it would not be possible to list them all in this work, but in particular we choose to list a few because of their direct connection with the Italian experiences. In particular, the queer evening Poopsy Club in Berlin was created by Noisy Pig, Double Agent and A.Ona; the first two also worked on the Gogogozip party, in collaboration with Ria Stern until July 2006.

Poopsy Club, together with Gogogozip, were created out of the idea of developing a Berlin non-scene, *not* mainstream, *not* underground, *not* hetero, *not* gay, but queer. The parties live through live-acts, DJ-sets, art shows and diffusion through independent publications, animating the Berlin nights in several of the city's clubs with the idea of creating an open-platform suitable for every type of musical scene, even if the preferred one is garage-punk and electro <www.poopsyclub.com>. Poopsy Club was inaugurated on August 10, 2006 in Berlin[12], during Ladyfest, a week-long art, music, creative and workshop event created by a network of European women <www.ladyfesteurope.org>.

From Punk to Netporn

In the preceding chapters we used the concept of hacktivism, a term derived from *hacking* plus *activism*, to describe many of the artistic and activist practices which took place in Italy in the last twenty years. According to this vision, the use of technology should be seen as an attitude that allows one to reach common interest goals, in which exchange, sharing, freedom of information and experimentation are central elements. We saw that hacking is a created practice; an irreverent and playful way of using computers which indicates an ethical and cooperative modality of relating to knowledge, in all its forms; activism indicates the forms of the individual or collective direct action not bound by the logic of profit or by a rigid copyright and it is beyond every censure.

In this sense, the hacktivist technology is an instrument of social change and a critically cultural and politically active terrain. To these priorities a particular "method" of interacting with technology is added, for which self-management, DIY, becomes a mirror of a way of thinking that is autonomous, decentralized and anti-hierarchical. In Italy, this type of attitude is connected to the punk phenomena, seen as an optimal diffuser of the DIY logic and of the production of creative projects and actions realized according to an autonomous spirit.

But the punk and hacker attitude are not exclusive to the creative use of computers and technology. Because they are signals of a specific train of thought, they can be applied even to one's own corporeity, to the intimate relationship that everyone has with sexuality. In this sense, even sex becomes a territory of hacker experimentation and a context in which to express the *do it yourself* punk attitude. And while hacktivism is the direct political and social action online, pornography becomes the direct political and social action on one's own body (outside and inside the network).

Pornography is the obvious demonstration of how different dynamics of power are written and perpetuated through the body. At the same time, it can even become a territory of both radical and ludic conflict.

Contrary to the "traditional" approach of a type of feminism that considers itself *politically correct*, but that does not perpetuate and consolidate the conservative hierarchies pointing out porn as a form of exploitation, it is necessary to start to consider pornography no longer as an enemy, but as something which should be appropriated from below. As long as we continue to label pornography as sexist, chauvinist and macho, we will be leaving it in the hands of those who really want it as such, making it a mirror for relationships of hierarchical power between men and women, and a territory of repetitive banalities.

Instead, making porn punk, or rather making Punk Porn, pornography becomes a territory of knowledgeable experimentation for everyone, and another occasion for breaking the dynamics of crystallized power, self-governing one's own sexuality. The conscious role of women (and men) in this vision is to personally enter inside the mechanisms of bodily expression and the production of desire, to subvert them from within, in favour of a fluid dimension; a mirror of a fanciful expressive everyday life.

Pornography, eroticism and sexual pleasure become territories in which to play, into which to bring a form of open desire, expression of the pleasure of the different men and women, in which diversity and otherness can cohabitate. To interact with pornography together with many other open identities, which go beyond the sterile definitions and cataloguing of gender, means to hack porn from within to make it a new form of free artistic experimentation. It is an expressive occasion in which people can consciously choose their own role.

On the one hand, 80% of online spam has links offering up bodies and objects of desire, new possibilities for augmenting sexual performance, a container of reassuring sterile certainties as an antidote for a progressive virtualization of the flesh and erotic pleasure. On the other hand, individuals and collective groups act increasing more pervasively to drive a different vision of sexuality, creating projects, products and creative actions for which pornography becomes an artistic platform, an autonomous and experimental network.

While at an international level there are milestones such as Lydia Lunch <www.lydia-lunch.org> who was a champion for a punk attitude open to sexuality in the 1980s, mostly due to her involvement in the Richard Kern film <www.richardkern.com>, in Italy Helena Velena's journey as a nihilist, situationist, transgender, fetishist, hardcore punk must be retold. Her biography, thoroughly described on her website <www.helenavelena.com>, follows the various experiences described in this book and looks at the connections between her activities at the end of the 1970s and those of today, mirroring many networking dynamics present here.

In the late 1970s, Helena Velena was still a punk. She was called Jumpy Velena, and participated in Radio Alice's Bolognese experience, learning the art of *détournement* and situationist subversion of communicative codes in the editorial office. "With a name and a sexual identity which was already 'transgender', but without having already acquired any consciousness of it" (Helena Velena, 2006), she was, in 1979, among the initiators of the Bolognese and Italian punk scene, with an anarchical-libertarian tendency. She founded the RAF Punk band which then became Trans XXX. She spread Crass music and founded Multimedia Attak, an independent record company specialized in musical experimentation and hardcore, which lists among its projects the first four CCCP records (*Fedeli alla linea*) and the promotion of different underground groups who worked critically on sexuality, among which the Yugoslav *Borghesia* group.

The band Trans XXX to which Helena belongs, "is the first Italian group to base not only its own sexual images, but also its own poetic expression on the centrality of their own journey of gender identity and on extreme sex practices as a moment of vindication of their own antagonistic being" (*ibidem*). The same libertarian punk attitude is subsequently found in the New Justine cabaret group, an entirely female theatre of excess in which Helena Velena performs.

As we saw in the 1990s in Italy, the computer represented a red line, linking the opposing punk instances with the cyberpunk practices. Helena Velena actively participated in the Italian cyberpunk context giving life to *Cybercore*, an editorial services company which she managed together with Maya for eight years. It is within this company that a videotel platform for hot-chats and a BBS were created and geared towards "*sex minorities*", such as Lady Domina, Trans X, Lesbian Love, etc. <www.cybercore.com>. In this period, Helena Velena is seen as an icon for cybersex[13] theory, "which uses communicative technology to reawaken, develop and create its own negated sexual image, which will subsequently be created in reality" (*ibidem*). In the 1990s, in fact, Helena affirmed herself as one of the few women in Italy who brought forth a critical reflection on new technology and its relationship to themes of freed sexuality and corporeity and that, above all, put these themes into practice proposing a conscious use of technology and of the computer. However, the putting into practice of punk and cyberpunk attitudes, was not exclusive to the technological field, the experimentation also occurred directly on Helena Velena's own body, transforming it forever in 1993.

Helena worked on technology as a vehicle for otherness, but also on pure telematics, creating conferences on networks and their impact on the social and the everyday life: in the panorama of Cyberpunk, her public performances together with porn star Milly D'Abbraccio as part of the promotion of the *Tuta Cybersex* (1994), which allows direct bodily contact through technology, through sensors applied in the Cybersex suit, are now historical events.

Returning to reflect on the possibility of going beyond social restrictions through the knowledgeable and critical reflection on one's own body, Helena worked a long time on the *Transgender International* project (<www.helenavelena.com/page11/page11.htm>), "dedicated to the diffusion of the transgender, a vision of reality and identity of gender which negates the traditional dualism of 'male/female', 'hetero/gay', 'white/black' etc., to propose instead a vision of continuity and 'transit' of the experiences, of the desires and of the concept of identity seen as an unequivocal experience and not as a need of belonging" (*ibidem*).

Currently Helena Velena is active both at an artistic level with the travelling theatrical shows *TRANSizione di Sex/Mutaction di GENDER and Not Politically Correct*, based on going beyond the limits of corporeity. She is also active on a video and radiophonic level (for four years Helena Velena produced a segment on Rome's *Radio Città Futura*, based on themes of sexuality and underground music); and, in the musical arena in both the punk group Helenavelena and in the free jazz group Lendormin. Moreover she is active on a political level safeguarding civil, sexual and computer rights.

In the Italian panorama, the reflection on sexuality applied to new technology is a field of research and experimentation with a tight network of projects and journeys (as described in the preceding chapter), but in the 1980s and 1990s it lists only a few individuals as its diffusers[14]. Because of this, Helena Velena's experience appears to be at once, both singular and fundamental, and provides the vehicle for a break-away from many political and cultural experiences of the era, for which reason the fight for sexual rights excluded the practice pornography *a priori*.

Helena Velena's experience teaches us instead how the thread woven through punk, sexuality and technology can become a critical journey of research and an instrument of artistic, musical and cultural experimentation in step with the times.

At an international level, the connection between punk, computer and pornography is found in the text by the Neoists Florian Cramer and Stewart Home, *Pornographic Coding* (2005). It is a sort of *porno-prank* in which the two authors called far and wide for a *shamanic pornography* that would be created through an interaction with the computer and "computer coding".

The programmer at the computer becomes a psychedelic elevator, which allows one to reach the seventh heaven (level) of sexual pleasure, in which the pornography becomes a copulation made up of zeros and ones. This is the last stage to be reached after having passed first stage five, which requires both chemical support as well as long hours of arduous interaction with the computer, and that does not necessarily presuppose coitus, and then stage six, in which one is directly telepathically and sexually connected with the network hacker.

The text, which should be interpreted as a Neoist happening, combines irony and linguistic *détournements* and contains an original and quite current point of view with regards to the reflection on independent pornography or *indie porn*, seen as resulting from the connection between punk attitude and the amateur use of technology. In this approach the traditional view of pornography is seen as an arena of such repetitive banality that achieving an erection would be a triumph of the imagination, to transform into a source of sexual pleasure the same codes found equally throughout all porn films.

Instead, indie porn seems to finally suggest something different, in which anyone can become porn stars; men and women who decide to do things on their own and who self manage their own pornography through the use of amateur video cameras, digital cameras, computers and independent web sites created practically at no cost. A territory which becomes an active testing ground for everyone who wants to challenge the world of porn, experiment with one's own body and even make some money thanks to Internet users who pay (affordable amounts) to see photos and video.

On this subject, Florian Cramer and Stewart Home add:

There is no doubt that indie porn is the pornography of this decade, if not of the whole century. Furthermore, it appears to be the first significant new movement of the millennium. Indie porn has substituted net.art in the Internet avant-garde aesthetic. Web sites like <www.suicidegirls.com>, <www.cleansheets.com>, <www.thatstrangegirls.com> and <www.fatalbeauty.com>, combine the punk style of their models with the visual aesthetic of punk, and with the *do-it-yourself* punk attitude[15]. The website <www.indienudes.com> presents a list of all the sources and linked[16] sites which seem to finally show the presence of non-commercial pornography able to stimulate erotic fantasies for hetero- and bisexuals, after the avant-garde of lesbian and gay pornography already reached the same level in the first part of the 1990s with magazines such as "On Our Backs", and the porn videos created by the "Cazzo Productions" label. In reality, indie porn is just like indie pop. It demands to be different from the industry, but it works along the same business models. Just like punk and indie pop saved the musical industry in the 1980s and 1990s, indie porn will save the pornographic industry of today. It has become the research and development branch of the pornographic industry. It is an industry which would otherwise go bankrupt because of the free sharing of its products on the Internet (Cramer, Home, 2005).

Currently in fact, the exchange of clip porn in peer-to-peer channels is starting to create a financial crisis in the porn industry since everyone can freely distribute and obtain videos by simply going on line. Indie porn, therefore, could even become a new source of income and a new territory for business if it were to become a part of the cultural industry sector (something which is already occurring). Furthermore, Home and Cramer draw our attention to the normal men and women who make underground porn and are now putting themselves on line, as at <www.ishotmyself.com> in which one films oneself and then downloads one's video for public consumption on the Internet. They use this example to illustrate how these individuals can bring a growth of artistic experimentation and make porn materials less banal and stereotyped, but at the same time give the user a pre-packaged product, where the imaginative work is reduced to the bare minimum because the impulses of desire have already been encoded.

Through indie porn, the idea of authenticity and accessibility is communicated, perhaps it is because blogs, websites and chats are independently created, or it is because in order to communicate with the "models" one must only write an email and a prompt reply will arrive. Furthermore, on the websites there are authentic models, in the sense that their bodies are not altered with graphics programmes or through plastic surgery, but they are as they are, uniquely distinguishable by their tattoos, piercings and dyed hair (as in the photographic Suicide Girls website).

But as it happens with commercial porn, the sensation of reality is only a chimera and as Cramer and Home write, it is not possible to find any form of "authentic" sexuality in these products. They therefore add that commercial pornography is perhaps preferable, because at least it offers a less sophisticated content to train one's own imagination and in which to find pleasure, starting from the repetitive banal images. Therefore, "pornography which truly and honestly proves to deal with reality and imagination, should reduce and not augment the visual variation. In other words, it should not present itself differently than as a simple programming code, teaching us how to elaborate simple zeros and ones, in a way to surpass the false dichotomy between the artificial and the authentic" (*ibidem*).

Therefore, Cramer and Home conclude:

In contrast to commercial indie porn, we ask for a real, independent, open-source pornography. Pornography should be created by everyone, a populist and radical pornography collectively produced, made up of pure and formal codes. This pornography will reconcile rationality and instinct and will overcome alienation, because the code will be recreated in the sexual imagination produced by the right side of the brain. Software, converted into *dirty code* cleaned by formalism and subjectivity, will be the paradigm of this pornography, a code for putting the processes in motion[17] (*ibidem*).

Recently, without necessarily arriving at the conclusion that Florian Cramer and Stewart Home (ironically) auspicate, different on- and off-line projects using the theme of pornography as a source of independent artistic, musical and visual experimentation have been created. Beyond Sexyshock in Bologna, Phag Off in Rome and Pornflakes in Milan and many other collective projects which stud the queer network and Italian pink, the CUM2CUT festival was created in Berlin. It is an Indie-Porn-Short-Movies Festival (October 2006-2007, <www.cum2cut.net>) - a short film competition centred on independent pornography, created by Gaia Novati and me in collaboration with the Berlin PornFilmFestival <www.pornfilmfestivalberlin.de>.

Also at the international level, the experience of the collective of women Girlswholikeporno <www.girlswholikeporno.com>, based in Barcelona, Spain is worthy of mention. The website shows the activity of the group which was created in 2005 and took part in the 2006 occupation of the Mambo; a building in the city in which different workshops were organized. These "girls who love porn" work on the themes of freed sexuality, pornography, identity, the surpassing of sexual hierarchies, desire and ludic pleasure, and they do it by creating performances, workshops, videos (downloadable from the website), events and by informing the Internet populous through the website which acts as a blog on their activity.

Girlswholikeporno, even if they place prime importance on their being women (girls), act for the criticism on the division of gender, thinking that:

it no longer makes sense to talk about the differences between men and women, because perhaps there are neither women nor men. Furthermore, the theory of gender is a construction destined to disappear. Just like the concept of race. Who thinks in terms of Black, White or Asian today? They are only people with different colour of eyes or skin, people with tits, with a penis, with a penis and a pair of tits, with a beard and a vagina, with a vagina and a penis: people who like to mate with people - bodies with bodies. Their hair or eye colour does not matter. It does not matter where body hair or protuberances are found on the body. And perhaps sooner or later it will no longer make sense to say "girlswholikeporno". Because perhaps there will no longer be girls and guys. And the way of making porn will be different as the people will be different. Girlswholikeporno may not be for girls, or for guys, but for people who like to have sex with people (<www.girlswholikeporno.com/?page_id=66>).

On the website we find information on the activity of the collective beginning with the summer 2005. It is a useful networking platform for getting an idea of what it means to create independent porn, as an artistic and politically-activistic activity. Among the various events, the Girlswholikeporno were present at the first international festival of pornography on the Web, called The Art and Politics of Netporn, held in Amsterdam, Holland, from September 30 to October 1, 2005. It was a conference on *netporn criticsm* and on pornography created through the media and the web <www.networkcultures.org/netporn>.

The event, organized by the Institute of Network Cultures of Amsterdam and managed by Geert Lovink, Katrien Jacobs[18] and Matteo Pasquinelli, with the support of Interactive media, Hogeschool van Amsterdam, Amsterdam

School for Cultural Analysis, Cut-Up magazine <www.cut-up.com>, and de Condomerie in Amsterdam <www.condomerie.com>, presented different points of view on the debate on pornography on the Web, discussing the emergence of a Netporn Society and exploring the ties between porn and the themes of censure, surveillance and aesthetics of the digital media. The event, which involved those who really create porn and those who use it as a form of artistic and political freedom, proposed to reflect on the theme of porn as an everyday ingredient of *network culture*[19].

The Art and Politics of Netporn started off commenting upon on-line pornography and on the fact that, from blogs to amateur video, the current mass media panorama is always more pervasive and "pornographic". In this sense, pornography becomes a channel for direct and highly experimental expression. But the question is naturally more complex. Even the images of violence that television and the rest of the mass media present to us on a daily basis and which directly touch our physicality are pornographic. Porn is also the communication traffic between big multinationals and fringe cultures, between ISP and clients, pop stars and public. In particular, speaking of the politics of Netporn and drawing on his text *Warporn! Warpunk! Videopoiesis in the West at War* (2004), Matteo Pasquinelli, underlines:

> More and more frequently we find ourselves labelling any mass media events that represent an improvised and violent connection between our animal instincts and the sphere of collective fantasy as "pornographic". The images do not necessarily have to have a sexual overtone; but just think of the pornography of death, of violence, of war. On the other hand, in the Western territories not directly affected by conflicts, advertising images find themselves imitating underground porn attitudes and images in order to renew their own *appeal*. (...) The performance and Internet community increasingly involves more hypertrophic representations of desire and "animal" instincts of the human being. It is a molecular and intimate development of the media biosphere. It does not necessarily have to be a negative process: it is simply about social evolution. The *Politics of Netporn* means: how do we live with this process?[20].

In the text *Warporn! Warpunk!*, Pasquinelli presents an interesting analysis of the relationships between war, media, technology, body and desire, in a political society that is, in its entirety, becoming increasingly more pornographic. The focus is on the use of mass media images as an instrument of collective enchantment (*warporn*) in contrast with the use of radical images as a new territory of action for subversive political strategies (*warpunk*). Therefore we return to the theme of punk, this time seen as "a challenge for the movement to not equal horror, but to produce images that wake up the drowsy body" (Pasquinelli, 2004). It is a challenge therefore to not respond as a victim in front of images of violence which we are subjected to today, but to construct new images of movement that don't negate physicality, but become radically "flesh", to use a term from David Cronenberg.

As Matteo Pasquinelli writes,

While utopically searching for the perfect image, the one image that will be able to stop the war, make the empire fall and move the revolution, the global movement has theorized and practiced videoactivism (from Indymedia to Telestreet) and mythopoiesis (from Luther Blissett to Wu Ming), but still has not tried to fuse the two strategies together, producing a videopoiesis with a mythical impact; icons that know how to steal the mediascape scene from Bin Laden and Bush; seductive and disturbing formats like the video fragments diffused on the Web in *Pattern recognition* by William Gibson. Videopoiesis does not mean the banal proliferation of videocameras in the hands of videoactivists, but the creation of video narrations that have the strength of the body and that of the myth; it means to work on the genre and on the format more than on the informative content. The challenge is the image-body (*ibidem*).

With regards to reflecting on the body and sexuality, and at the same time the mechanisms of fascination with video, the Italian artist Franca Formenti has been working on the concept of the Bio Doll for a few years. It is a virtual creature that she invented, capable of snaring in her erotic web everyone who is fascinated by her. The Bio Doll, protagonist of several performances and videos beginning in 2002, is "a real, cloned doll, for public consumption" (Formenti, 2003), who is born out of the incarnation of pure desire, of an image that sees the women reduced to clones, losing all capacity for child bearing and whose belly button, symbol of the uterine and maternal relationship, disappears. The only remaining way out for the Bio Doll is to directly communicate with the digital world and to obtain nourishment and information through it. This occurs by putting one's own body into play on the Web, giving life to contexts of sexually freed interaction through which the Bio Doll can receive the vital lymph.

As Franca Formenti explains:

The object of my interests is geared towards the family nucleus, the period of gestation, the birth and therefore life. We are inundated with images of naked bodies that provoke us in every which way, from television to advertisements, etc., and we think this is a lack of creativity. I believe instead that it is a sort of swan song of humanity which is slowly losing the most direct contact with what it means to create life. Perhaps the feminine uterus will become an organ that will atrophy over time, and conception along with sexual relationships will take place in a different way. In this vision, the figure of the mother, father, children andthat of the prostitute too, will disappear. I therefore imagine a future where human beings will no longer be conceived by a man and a woman, but by a machine and therefore they will not be birthed: this is why I created the Bio Doll, to communicate new images in which the corporeity is redefined through technology as a channel of sexual freedom and a new form of conception (personal notes, 2003).

For this reason the *Biodoll's mouse* project was created at the end of 2005. It is an open on-line space, where one can examine the current themes, of the feminine use of the technology, from eroticization of the mass media, to new expressive prospects offered by the internet, to artistic creativity on the Web <www.biodollsmouse.org>. The new creature "conceived" by the Bio Doll is a *Bloki*, a blog which becomes *wiki* (a platform that allows any user to edit web pages on-line), which is reached after having passed a rain of virtual spermatozoa. As we read in the bulletin, everyone can enter the *Bloki* and ask direct questions to an ever-rotating interviewee. The interviewee might be an important person, a theorist, an artist, a performer or an entrepreneur who decides to be part of the project from time to time. The first person interviewed was Derrick de Kerckhove, who accepted to be "hacked" by Bio Doll, with questions which range from social hacking to the digital divide to online art.

In this sense, thanks to the action of the sensual and buxom Bio Doll who weaves a web in which to attract the interviewee, the same figure of the intellectual or artist is "de-structured" and thanks to the fascination of the seductive and erotic mechanisms, it becomes accessible and available to everyone who wants to interact through their own questions. The project, constantly in progress, is a form of disturbance in the concept of static art by being open to interactions and participation from the public. As Franca Formenti ironically points out:

The world revolves around the uterus: this is my concept of eroticism. Derrick de Kerckhove had never participated in a blog before and yet he fed himself to the Bio Doll. However, since she does not have a uterus, other than a virtual one, makes the world revolve around her neurons, tying her maternity and her fertility to the concept of being a mother, which can be expressed in many ways. (...) The relationship between her and Derrick de Kerckhove, in fact, becomes the legitimization of the *bloki*. Through the information that he gives her, the Bio Doll rearranges the contents that, once pushed out, are "birthed", they bring a "creation" or more precisely the *bloki*, to life[21].

In her voyage of searching for the necessary digital information for the development of her own *bloki*, the Bio Doll allies herself with Serpica Naro, the activist-designer already mentioned in the previous chapter, using the Serpica Naro meta-brand.

In June 2006 the Bio Doll created a small purse, which represented a sex-toy pouch instead of the usual cell pouch. It was signed by Serpica Naro and designed by the Bio Doll, two virtual female figures that don't exist, but who make a real object available for public consumption. The small purse is presented in a video created by Franca Formenti, called *Use Condoms* (2006), which involves several famous fashion, political and show business personalities who are fascinated by the figure of the Bio Doll (a *provocateuse* standing at the very edge of hardcore boundaries) and are, subconsciously accepting to participate in a project which in reality is intended to publicise a product, the small purse, created by a professional artisan bearing the Serpica Naro meta-brand, the designer who is the protector of the temporary workers[22]. The various characters answer five questions on current events, how women use technology, open-source, Internet TV, sex toys, social hacking and mass media activism, even if we question the extent to which they really know these subjects.

New victims (or executioners?) of a world that raps to the beat of mass media images and in which the dynamics of networking become fascinating instruments where numerous so-called communication, fashion and political "experts" can be made to fall into the web. It is another invitation to the creation of a sensual and palpitating videopoiesis which we hope becomes ever more radical and incisive in the years to come.

(Open) Conclusion

To conclude the journey between the dynamics of networking, we cite the text of the pink block bulletin written for MayDay 2004 in Milan, which has, even in this context, a playful, creative and irreverent approach. It is a point of view that sees beyond the genres and rigid categories and is capable of making the most of the networking dynamics, which have made the underground Italian movement an important experience over the course of the years.

Articolo XY: Italy is a Republic founded on relationships [not based on labour, as we read in the first Article of the Italian Constitution]. Labour is no longer the social glue that guarantees a dignified survival, we are more than harnessed between families, friendships, affinities and others forms of more or less conventional ties that are the last (and only) network of security that is given to us. At MayDay in Milan, starting with the Pink Block, we will invade the parade trying to make this network visible and tangible through inclusive and interactive performating actions. Many pink threads will construct improbable architectures, they will lacerate bridges, intersect connections. Fragile and precarious threads like our existences, are ready to break and freely reconnect to represent ties as we want them, based on consensus and play (loose weaves, not knots, from which it is possible to slip out without having to break them). If we have lost the thread of the discourse, let's knot up the threads of communication. Ensuring that they are pink threads) (...) Wear your pink thread and intertwine yourself: the network moves and it expands. Let's follow each other like discretely invasive lovers[23].

And from this pink block bulletin we extend an invitation to all those who have read with us this far, to continue to weave new threads of relations between activism, hacking and art. This is also the reason why we decided to leave this book "open", without including a concluding chapter to end our reflections. With regards to the rest it could not be otherwise, for a topic in development such as networking, which for each and every one of us became the incentive to experiment with many possibilities, to be free through relationship networks on the Internet or in the spaces of daily life.

Endnotes

1 The VNS Matrix collective was formed by Josephine Starrs, Francesca da Rimini, Julianne Pierce and Virginia Barratt. The text of the *Cyberfeminist Manifesto for 21st Century* can be found at: <http://lx.sysx.org/vnsmatrix.html>.

2 Old Boys Network was founded in Berlin by Susanne Ackers, Julianne Pierce, Valentina Djordjevic, Ellen Nonnenmacher and Cornelia Sollfrank. In addition to the website <www.obn.org>, there is also a mailing list found at: <www.nettime.org/oldboys>.

3 This and others of Cornelia Sollfrank's activities are published in *net.art generator*, a volume that retraces the artist's activities and her struggles to demonstrate that a single identity does not exist, what exists rather is an extensive multiplicity of identities that are widespread and have found vital energy on the Internet. The text helps to reflect upon the activities of hacker culture, on the concept of identity, originality and copyright.

4 City of Women is an international contemporary art festival created by women focusing on art and culture, from performance to art and video. The 2004 City of Women Festival took place in the wake of a unique political event in Slovenia (its admission to the European Union), during which many of the country's socio-cultural norms were redefined and it seemed important to write new codes and alternative artistic visions. Among those in attendance were important historic (and otherwise) figures in cyberfeminism, such as Mara Verna, Barbara Albert, Shilpa Gupta, Olga Kisseleva, Suzanne Treister, Tamara Vukov, Lizzie Borden, Cornelia Sollfrank, Nadia El Fani, Hans Scheirl, Peggy Ahwesh, Nina Mesko, Tanja Lazetic, Dara Birnbaum, CocoRosie, Pamela Z, Hiroko Tanahashi, Alicja Zebrowska, Misoura and the feminist *electropunk* musical group Le Tigre from New York.

5 At the academic level, the ATHENA network has been active for years in the fields of feminism and Gender Studies. This network connected more than 100 European institutions that specialized in Women's Studies and in research on gender. The University of Utrecht in Holland stands out among the various universities taking part, where the Department of Women's Studies, managed by Rosi Braidotti, has been active for 15 years in the area of research and post-graduate training <www.let.uu.nl/womens_studies>.

6 To clarify: the term "experience" is intended here to mean a lived experience, bearing in mind the concept of *Erlebnis* proposed by Wilhelm Dilthey (1833-1911). As an exponent of "contemporary historicism" Dilthey proposed a method of social analysis based on *Verstehen* - Comprehension; theorizing a divide between spiritual and natural science. One cannot study the spiritual sciences using physical and natural scientific methodologies (thereby distancing herself from a sociology with a positivistic matrix), however, in order to understand the spiritual world, and the world of historic-social and human reality, the analyses must have has their starting point man's interior world, seeing the self common to all experiences (that is, the *Verstehen*). In Dilthey's writings one can find the "cultural relativism" foundations, the fundamental concept for subsequent anthropological studies. According to Dilthey there are social entities and cultural configurations, created by humans that condition their vision and perception of the world and that are at the root of specific cultural models and modes of social interaction. One can, therefore, understand otherness only by being intimately involved with oneself.

7 An amphetamine with stimulant and empathogenic properties, it was very popular in the U.S. during the 1980s and, later, widely used throughout Europe in the 1990s at *raves* and at night clubs. For this reason, it came to be known as the *club drug* (N.d.A.).

8   Specifically, the demonstration in Rome took place on June 4, 2004 in conjunction with the arrival of George W. Bush in Italy. The blocco pink (pink block) organized a PPP-Pink Paint Party in the city's streets, to protest against the political and economic 'made in USA' vision. Various videos of the blocco pink's actions can be found on NGV, under the heading "identità, genere, sessualità": <http://www.ngvision.org/mediabase/category/14>. A representational and ironic short-film about the event was made by Cotoletta, a pink activist. The short-film, entitled, "PinkCorps" was submitted to Tekfestival 2005: <www.tekfestival.it/filmdb/scheda_film.php?id=357>.

9   Maya has been active in the new technology arena for several years. She has recently written *Hackers. La storia, le storie (Hackers. The History, the Stories)*, Rome, Malatempora, 2004. It is a brief but interesting retrospective on hacking in Italy, historic hacker figures and women hackers.

10 Nikky started off in the experimentational graphic and video sector of the Delirio Universale project <www.deliriouniversale.com>. She is closely aligned with Rome's queer-party *Coq Madame* experience, and collaborates with ShockArt, the web and digital art factory launched in 1999 as part of an initiative of the Vernice association under the direction of Gianluca Del Gobbo <www.shockart.net>. In her video performances, Nikky uses the Flxer platform, conceived by Shockart for use by anyone for VJ-ing and audio-video mixing. Flxer was creted in 2001 as a tool to combine audio, video and multimedia during live performances and it is circulated in free software. Even the <www.flxer.net> website is a community of individuals who exchange videos and other multimedia products that are uploaded and downloaded by all members.

11 The majority of the projects of this list were pointed out to me by Francesco "Warbear" Macarone Palmieri, whom I thank for this valuable information.

12 Sexyshock and AHA: Activism-Hacking-Artivism also took part in the event where they curated a video projection on pink action, hacktivism, and women and technology: <www.ecn.org/aha/English/netporn.htm>.

13 Cybersex theory was disseminated on an editorial level by Helena Velena in 1995, with the publication of the first edition of the book *Dal Cybersex al Transgender, tecnologie, identità e politiche di liberazione* [*From Cybersex to Transgender: Liberating Technologies, Identities and Politics*), published by Helena by Castelvecchi in Rome. The book explores the relationship between technology and sexuality and the expressive possibilities that this relationship provides through networking. The book is the product of collective discussion groups, through networks and sensory applications in the guise of cybersex. The book is a critical exaltation of technology and virtual sex, rather it analyses their implications on daily life, always having as its point of reference "real sex" involving physical bodies and between individuals in real encounters. In this sense, technology is seen as enhancing sexual prosthesis, not as an alternative to "real" sex, which continues to be a practice that is central to sharing.

14 To this end, within an artistic scope we have already spoken of the work of Pigreca, Flavia Alman and Sabine Reiff. In the scope of Italian cyberfeminist publications of the 1990s, directly connected to the Italian cyberpunk universe, we highlight the magazine "Fikafutura, secrezioni acide cyberfemministe e queer" ("Fikafutura, cyberfeminist and queer acidic secretions"), edited by Shake Edizioni Underground, 1997-1998, Milano and reviewed by DeadRed, Rosie Pianeta and Wonder Women.

15 A note by the authors: "<www.nerve.com> is the top-ranking leader of these sites that creates 'sophisticated' porn for an intellectual audience" (Florian Cramer and Stewart Home, 2005).

16 A note by the authors: "The sites <www.ishotmyself.com> and <www.beautifulagony.com> directly substitute Avant-garde art concepts into commercial porn styles; the first involves female models who create their own images of themselves, the second plagiarizes the Andy Warhol film, "Blow Job", showing the faces of individuals at the moment of orgasm" (Florian Cramer and Stewart Home, 2005).

17 A note by the authors: "A rare example of this dirty-porn-code is the writing of the Australian artist and programmer Mez ".

18 Katrien Jacobs recently wrote the book *LIBI_DOC. Journey in the performance of SEX ART*, Maska, 2005, in which the author describes her own journey into the world of artists who explore porn and sexuality with the point of view of a participant and with a direct, incisive, first-hand experience approach <www.libidot.org>.

19 Among the various collectives and individuals present, were the Phag Off group, mentioned in the preceding paragraph, and the director and media artist Shu Lea Cheang who directed, among other projects, a SF-porno-movie *I.K.U.* (2000). Filmed in 2000 and produced by Uplink Co. of Tokyo. The film won an award at the 2000 Sundance Film Festival, generating considerable success. Following immediately along *I.K.U.*'s vision, a Japanese-erotic-visionary reality was projected that was reminiscent of the worlds of Blade Runner and Ridley Scott, while transporting them into a liquid psychedelic universe in which the protagonists are a group of seven avatar-heroines. In the film women, men, fluid and hybrid beings take the stage, for an overdose of pleasure that is often barely realistic but does have a strong emotional impact that does not intend to victimize any of the characters <www.i-k-u.com>.

20 A personal interview with Matteo Pasquinelli, entitled *Netporn: nuovi territori 'tattici' (Netporn: new 'tactical' territories)*, published in "Digimag, periodico d'informazione digitale" [Digimag, the digital information periodical], December 2005-January 2006. On line at: <www.digicult.it/digimag/article.asp?id=284>.

21 From Francesca Tarissi's article, *Hackeriamo gli intellettuali [Let's hack the intellectuals]*, published on "Linus", June 2006, and available on line at: <www.portalinus.it/redazione/penne.asp?idpenne=186&st artposition=6>.

22 Along with the Bio Doll idea there was a legal probe aimed at either at subsequent preventive protection or a better understanding of the legal aspects of hacking and media art. To this end, in the Bio Doll video, an introduction to these issues was presented by the lawyer Giovanni Ziccardi, an expert in computer programming law.

23 From the message "[MayDay] la lega del filo rosa" ("[MayDay] the pink thread league"), sent by Sexyshock, April 28, 2004. On line at: <http://italy.indymedia.org/news/2004/04/536393.php>.

Afterword
The Threads of the Web
and the Tools of the Trade
by Simonetta Fadda

> At a certain point I felt that a work of art
> was an invitation to participate, sent by the
> artists, directly to each and every one of us.
> Carla Lonzi, *Autoritratto*, 1969

Hacktivism, Mail art, Netstrike, Punk, Netporn, Fluxus, Neoism, Net art, Hacker art: these and many other phenomena are at the heart of Tatiana Bazzichelli's analysis in *Networking: The Web as Art*. Some of these phenomena are usually counted among the practices or the "political" expressions, within, and by way of the Internet, while others are relegated, in general, to the art sphere. In addition, they are typically analyzed individually and separately, as artistic or political phenomena, as practices or movements, either in the sphere of political and sociological reflection, or in the sphere of the criticism of the history of art, and interpreted using different keys of interpretation.

Herein lies instead the originality of Bazzichelli's work: she analyses them together, including many other phenomena in her list, in order to highlight a very important common trait which until now has remained at the threshold of critical attention: being created and being developed on the basis of networking. In other words, thanks to and through the creation of connections (that is: the network), on whose stage heterogeneous subjects came together and examined each other, they united in the exchange to produce works, and to also create relationships and cultural communities. Bazzichelli talks about artists and fellow organizers, who, at different times and independently of the material or virtual vehicles or supports used, formed networks. They created discussion and comparison platforms, worked together on the formation of ideas and works, shared information, knowledge and techniques, and spawned organizations, or more simply, friendships. Networking for these artists has meant significant exchange and collective production, interaction and research, activism and experimentation; it meant making connections and exploring common performances and actions.

It's well known that the work of art, given its nature, needs a response from the world (from the public). It's also well known that this is one of its fundamental prerequisites because art can be created and shown off only when starting from a debate; from a dialogue with a live community. From Albrecht Dürer to the net artists, Bazzichelli's analysis underlines the fact that artists, will communicate/ collaborate as soon as they can (as soon as the media that they have at their disposal allows them[1]), trying to simultaneously create multimedia works, and works in progress which transcend the categorizations of genre and style, surpassing them. A bit like what must have happened in the case of primitive graffiti, whose actual ideological genesis can not be reconstructed due to a historical void. Similarly, in the case of the construction of the Gothic cathedrals blossoming all over Europe between the thirteenth and fifteenth centuries (examples of great collective artistic creation), which remain mysteries in some ways. When they are able to, artists exchange things: be they works, ideas or techniques, the result (and the origin) is the creation of networks.

Until now, the network of artists depicted in the somewhat gossipy anecdotal nature of the biographies, has not been analyzed as the real creative axis on which the production and diffusion of ideas and works of art, spin. The object analysed within the realm of the criticism of history and art, has been the work: the piece, or rather, the result of the process. Bazzichelli shuffles the cards and brings our attention to the genesis of this process; to the preconditions which render the production of the work possible; to the solicitations that accompany the realization, to the reactions that receive it, modifying it at the same time. From Albrecht Dürer's lithographs to George Maciunas' diagrams, from the Neoist *prank* to media jokes and plots, from Netstrike to guerrilla marketing (and the list should be much longer), the analysis reunites a series of heterogeneous artistic practices, distant both in time and in method. Bazzichelli frames the artistic practices in the context of networking considered here a form of art in itself. A form of art whose plurality lies in its expressions, in its modalities and its objectives, as both the matrix and the terrain of its creative cultivation, and in whose sphere such practices have been able to produce themselves.

Just as Carla Lonzi foreshadowed in 1969, experimenting with her "relational method"[2] in an attempt to open the field up to a new figure of the critic, able to accompany the artist in the production of the work. Taking for granted that the work of art is always and in any case an invitation to participation, Bazzichelli's *sui generis* approach jumps from one place to the other; it connects distant sectors and practices; it connects tangential discussions on disciplines and different interpretative codes. It multiplies the points of view in order to reveal how indispensable it is to the analysis of the worlds of art, that one start from the context. It also reveals how the context can surpass the work itself, the (unique) piece which is very dear to the market. In this way it also shows that the work intended as a unique piece, as "original", is a hologram borne of mercantile reasoning: an ideological construction that in any case, in the era of the internet and the digital age decidedly proves a historical fake.

The type of networking that Bazzichelli talks about, in fact alludes to an idea of art as a process in progress: an idea of art that is beyond, but also present before, during and after the crystallization of this process in the artwork.

In any case, underlining the importance of networking means, above all, paying attention to that which is at the origin of artistic practices in general: the fabric of relationships. This entails revealing the relationships of exchange which make it possible, it means bringing to light the pre-eminence of the relational context with respect to the results produced. In addition, by highlighting the plural, contradictory, ever progressing context in which art grows, the idea of otherness is implicit as a value in itself, since it is from the fruitful meeting of the "other" reciprocal heterogeneities that the network can develop. Choosing to describe the practices of networking that emerged as conspicuous phenomena, especially in the last twenty years, thanks to the birth of the web, Bazzichelli decides to accentuate the work of weaving the web, more than focusing on the individual nodes. She brings to the forefront the fact that the heterogeneous and "complex reasons", from which the practice of art moves and is unravelled are "true motors, capable of determining choices and orientations"[3], despite the fact that they are almost invisible within the traditional historical-critical reconstruction. Bringing networking to the centre of the critical discourse therefore means radically changing the point of view. It means not only considering art starting from the context of the production of the work, more than a finished product, but also re-examining the roles and the contributions that define themselves in the artistic creation. It means expanding the field of investigation to new elements capable of correcting the asymmetrical positions peculiar to languages, or rather, in other terms, it means adopting a feminist reading in the study of art.

It is that feminine knowledge that searches for and adds value to relationships: otherness, transits, "networking". It is, as Bazzichelli recounts, participation, the pooling of knowledge, the creation of networks of relationships between heterogeneous subjects and between different disciplinary circles, whose specificity and individuality result in being developed and enriched in virtue of these crossing-overs and meetings. The same idea of networking, in the positive sense of being open to sharing and exchange, and to interaction and reciprocity, seems for the most part, a common trait in the cultural practices of women over time. Upon closer examination, what is that "domestic" world, that *private* sphere of the affects where the feminine presence in art and in culture in general (with women artists mentioned by historiography as being simply students, friends or lovers of male artists) is traditionally classified and therefore effaced, if not a constant work of weaving of relationships, a practice of construction of relational webs inside which it is possible to weave meetings and comparisons between people/ideas/works? That is the "networking" that Bazzichelli talks about, describing today's practices and expressions developed, above all, on the web.

According to Bazzichelli's suggestion (and also beyond the single phenomenon taken into examination in her work), observing the practice of art in general through the lens of networking, implies the repositioning of the terms of discourse on the basis of the method of the "geographies and generations of visual arts" examined by Griselda Pollock. This obliges one to keep in mind, the "genealogical time and the semiotic space"[4] that are shaped on a social plane, consequently crossing and defining the artistic practices in order to introduce new variables capable of registering the plurality of the dynamics and journeys without levelling it in an ideological way. The "other" is by definition (traditionally) removed from observation, in as much as it is *invisible* to the monocular view of the logos, founded on the principle of identity. Analysing the ideas and practices of art, in light of networking, brings us to a revision of the same criteria of evaluation adopted in critical discourse: to recognize the importance of (new) phenomena and (ancient) subjects which emerge today, due also to the technology available which allows one to free oneself from rigid and pre-constituted identities, roles, methods and categories. Therefore, the idea of networking can modify the point of view of art in a

291

fruitful way. It can frame the practice of art and the subjects at play differently, even suggesting unusual perspectives, if transferred into the sphere of study of cultural practices and productions in general[5]. When Pollock in fact hopes for "a feminist analysis" capable of "putting the existence of a general and universal meaning up for discussion" (*ivi*, p. 21), therefore capable of breaking free from the imperative reasoning of the *reductio ad unum* at the foundation of the Western thought, she opens up the possibility of opening and re-reading even those practices, phenomena and subjects that are *not exclusively* feminine, from a *situated* point of view. Just as Bazzichelli does, in her study of the dynamics of networking, by encompassing multiple and transforming identities and practices, not necessarily characterized/ identified on the basis of the sex or sexual orientation, even when heavily connoted by these factors.

At the same time, the inaugurated method by the *feminist reading* proposed by Pollock gives some conditions, so that the possibility of a situated re-reading can reverberate also on whoever constructs the critical discourses. Today it is just as necessary to "keep a record of the stories, of the geographies and of the generations, not only for the person who creates art, but also for those who tell it, curate it, popularize it (…) including the places in which the actions, the works, the art processes take shape" (Trasforini, 2006, p. 19) and Bazzichelli does not shirk away from this. In presenting networking as a form of choral, plural, complex art, Bazzichelli, the networker, reunites voices without homologizing them, gathers the contradictions together without dissolving them, confronts the problems without manipulating them, and does so explicitly declaring her position: as a scholar, but also as a direct and sympathetic participant. The narration proceeds as in a "subjective shot" among the arguments addressed, always with Bazzichelli's "voice in", within the shot. For study and analysis are first of all subjective experiences: fruits of interior dialogue between those who study and the objects of study. They are expressions of orientations, propensities and alliances, even if they are rarely shown and presented as such when they are made public. With feminine responsibility, the moment in which Bazzichelli writes, she clearly indicates her own partiality, for "declaring 'where one narrates from', expands the points of view and the richness of vision" (*ivi*, p. 35). Underlining one's own power to narrate/construct a history means not forgetting that what is being narrated is only one of the possible stories. Remembering that the subjects treated are evolving contemporaneously as the telling of their stories and even in different and unsuspected directions by the teller. It means looking for a constructive comparison with their own interlocutors, stimulating them towards the expression of different ideas. As a consequence, it means eventually modifying one's own point of view; it means to really communicate. Therefore, it is a completely different thing, with respect to the arrogance of the Western *reductio ad unum* thought...

Probably, however, it might be necessary to dwell on the fact that in some way it is the network itself, the Web, to allow, perhaps to demand, the multiple approaches rooted in the feminist viewpoint. The Web, in fact, in a certain sense does not only represent a "materialization" of the networking awareness, demonstrated by women over the centuries as the practices described in Bazzichelli's work highlight, but it also lends itself as a powerful metaphor of a new symbolic order capable of offering new *mediations*[6] and proposing a "meaningful interaction between feminine experience and codified culture" (Muraro, 1991, p. 103). If feminism developed by looking for an authenticity in relationships, in order to cancel out the inauthenticity of the discrimination against women, thanks to the web, this research of authentic relations can today become a concrete practice, an attitude encouraged by the same functioning of the medium used (internet), through its circular and reciprocal nature. "The ability to articulate depends on the mediations that a certain culture ensures" (*ivi*, p. 98). Only what emerges in the language, that which can be said, and therefore *seen*, has a place in reality. The means (internet) is also a medium (the Web) and as such is capable of giving visibility to the phenomena (desires) that can take shape especially because they are finally *mediated* or rather legitimized to exist.

Endnotes

1   It is not a coincidence that the first example quoted by Bazzichelli is that of Albrecht Dürer, because during that time, what allowed the creating of a network of artists who would exchange lithographs was the invention of printing, with its possibility of reproducing in series, as it is possible today, through the web, the creation of multiple and heterogonous networks. The unique piece has always been a great problem for cultural transmission, while the "technical reproducibility of the work of art" has always represented an advantage for the artists; another possibility for playing with the culture.

2   Expression used by Maria Antonietta Trasforini regarding the *Autoritratto* in her *Introduction* to *Donne d'arte. Storie e generazioni* (AA.VV., edited by Maria Antonietta Trasforini, Rome, Meltemi, 2006, p. 16). Reading this book offered me great cues and suggestions for the draft of my brief text and I thank the authors.

3 Emanuela De Cecco, *Artiste nel contesto*, in AA.VV., quotation., p. 201. In the article, De Cecco dialogues with different female artists proposing to go "from the study of work of art as a product that is consummated *to a reflection on art as practice*" for "*tracing the components of a practice*, where different elements interact among themselves as dictated limits of reality, but more precisely of external conditions (and internal conditions which are inevitably traced) which *contribute to the development of an artistic language*" (*ibidem*; the italics are mine).

4 Griselda Pollock, *Visions and Difference*, London, Routledge, 1988, p. XXIX.

5 For example, I am thinking of the scientific world, where single "inventions" or "discoveries", often take place within very close exchanges, "networks", among scientists and between these and their subordinates (students, partners, colleagues in life/work). I think of teamwork in the realization of experiments and research: networking! For it to be successful not only are the "physical" (space and technical possibilities) and relational (the structure and organization of the work) contexts fundamental and determinant, (including the dynamics that are created within them), but also the creative interaction and collaboration with the assistants, who are always thanked in the footnotes, are essential. And above all, I wish for a review of the same sexist, scientific presuppositions from which the concepts of scientific thought originate. I further wish that the work taken on by Evelyn Fox Keller in *Sul genere e la scienza* (1987) is brought forward.

6 In particular, I am referring to the idea of mediation suggested in the context of reflection on the women in the Italian circle. To this end, cfr. the works of Diotima in general (la Tartaruga, Milan) or *L'ordine simbolico della madre* by Luisa Muraro (Rome, Editori Riuniti, 1991).

Bibliography

This bibliography lists the editions used by the author, hence some titles are Italian translations of sources in English and other languages. The original year of publication is reported at the beginning of each listing.

AA.VV.
1998   *Falso è vero. Plagi, cloni, campionamenti e simili*, Bertiolo, AAA Editions.

AA.VV.
1999   *New Media Culture in Europe*, Amsterdam, Uitgeverij De Balie and The Virtual Platform.

AA.VV.
2000   *Piermario Ciani. Dal Great Complotto a Luther Blissett*, Bertiolo, AAA Editions.

AA.VV.
2003   *CODE. The Language of Our Time, Ars Electronica 2003*, Linz, Hatje Cantz Verlag.

AA.VV.
2003   *Next Five Minutes 5 Reader*, International Festival of Tactical Media, Amsterdam, De Balie.

Abruzzese A.
1979   *La grande scimmia – Mostri, vampiri, automi mutanti*, Rome, Napoleone.

1994   *Nemici a se stessi*, in *La scena immateriale. Linguaggi elettronici e mondi virtuali*, edited by A. Ferraro e G. Montagano, Genoa, Costa & Nolan.
1995   *Lo splendore della TV – Origini e destino del linguaggio audiovisivo*, Genoa, Costa & Nolan.

Albertini R. and Lischi S. (edited by)
1988   *Metamorfosi della visione – Saggi di pensiero elettronico*, Pisa, ETS Edition.

Anderson L.
1984   *Mister Heartbreak*, Warner Bros Record (music CD).

Arnheim R.
1954   *Arte e percezione visiva*, Milan, Feltrinelli, 1996.

Arns I.
2002   *Netzkulturen*, Hamburg, EuropaeischeVerlagsanstalt.
2004   *Interaction, Participation, Networking. Art and Telecommunication*, in Daniels D., Frieling R., *Medien Kunst Netz 1: Medienkunst im Überblick*, Vienna/New York 2004, <www.medienkunst.de>.

A/traverso collective
1976-1977   *Alice è il diavolo. Storia di una radio sovversiva*, Milan, Shake, (edited by Bifo and Gomma), 2002.

Ballard J.G.
1973   *Crash*, Milan, Fabbri Editions, 1994.

Balderi I. and Senigalliesi L. (edited by)
1990   *Graffiti Metropolitani – Arte sui muri delle città*, with texts of A. Abruzzese, G. Dorfles, D. Origlia, Genoa, Costa & Nolan.

Balzola A., Monteverdi A.M. (edited by)
2004   *Le arti multimediali digitali*, Milan, Garzanti.

Bandera P.
1998   *Re/Search. Manuale di cultura industriale*, Milan, Shake.

Barba E.
1985   *Aldilà delle isole galleggianti*, Milan, Ubulibri.

Baroni V.
1997   *Arte postale. Guida al network della corrispondenza creativa*, Bertiolo, AAA Editions.
2005   *Postcarts. Cartoline d'artista*, Roma, Coniglio Editions.

Barratt V., Da Rimini F., Pierce J., Starrs J.
1991   *Cyberfeminist Manifesto for 21st Century*, Adelaide, Australia, on-line at <http: //lx.sysx.org/vnsmatrix.html>.

Barthes R.
1980   *La camera chiara*, Torino, Einaudi.

Bassi B., Bassi D., Biagini G., D'Antongiovanni S.
2005   *Arte telematica negli anni Ottanta*, video-interview with Maria Grazia Mattei, Fine Art Academy of Carrara, Course: Theory and Methods of Mass Media.

Baumgärtel T.
1999   *net.art – Materialien zur Netzkunst*, Verlag für moderne Kunst, Nürnberg.
2001   *net.art 2.0 – Neue Materialien zur Netzkunst*, Verlag für moderne Kunst, Nürnberg.

Bazzichelli T.
1998   Interviews with F. Alman, F. Bucalossi, M. Cittadini, A. Glessi, C. Parrini, S. Reiff, T. Tozzi, G. Verde, published at: <www.strano.net/bazzichelli/tesi.htm>.
1999   *Pratiche reali per corpi virtuali. Per una riformulazione del concetto di opera d'arte nell'arte digitale interattiva italiana / Dissertation on Italian interactive digital art*, Laurea in Sociology of Mass Media, Faculty of Sociology, University "La Sapienza", Rome.
       On-line at <www.strano.net/bazzichelli/tesi.htm>
2000   *Candida, la televisione elettrodomestica*, article published in "Neural", 15, May-October 2000.
2001   *Intervista con la PublixTheatreCaravan. Dopo il G8 a Genova*, in Ponte di Pino O., Monteverdi A.M. (edited by), *Il meglio di ateatro 2001-2003*, Pozzuolo del Friuli (Ud), Principe Costante Editions, 2004.
2003   *Artivism, quando l'arte diventa consapevole*, interview with *0100101110101101.org*, *Jaromil and Giacomo Verde*, published in "CyberZone",, 18, Year VIII, 2003.
2005   *Dalle Telestreet agli Hackmeeting: il network del fare informazione*, in Pecchioli M. (edited by), Neo televisione. Elementi di un linguaggio catodico-glocal/e, Milan, Costa & Nolan.

Belile L.
2000   *Gynomite: Fearless, Feminist Porn*, New Orleans, New Mouth from the Dirty Soul.

Benjamin W.
1955   *L'opera d'arte nell'epoca della sua riproducibilità tecnica*, Turin, Einaudi, 1991.

Berardi F. (Bifo) (edited by)
1996   *Cibernauti, Tecnologia, comunicazione, democrazia*, Rome, Castelvecchi.

Berardi F. (Bifo), Pasquinelli M.
2000   *Rekombinant-Settembre 2000*, Bologna, email sent to the "Net_Institute" mailing list, 16 July 2000.

Bettetini G., Colombo F.
1993   *Le nuove tecnologie della comunicazione*, Milan, Bompiani, 1996.

Bianchi F.
1995   *Antropologia della Performance: il corpo limen attraverso la videoarte*, Thesis of Laurea in Sociology, University "La Sapienza," Rome.

Bieber A., Caras J.
2004   *Rebel Art: connecting art & activism*, Frankfurt, Rebel Art Media Foundation.

Blank J.
1997   *What is net.art? :-)*, in *ZKP4, The Nettime Sping Conf*, Lubiana 23-25 maggio 1997, Beauty and The East <www.ljudmila.org/nettime/zkp4/toc.htm>.

Block F.W., Heibach C., Wenz K.
2004   *Poes1s, Digitale Poesie: The Aesthetics of Digital Poetry*, Berlin, literaturWERKstatt.

Bonito Oliva A., De Mila G., Cerritelli C.
1990   *Ubi fluxus ibi motus 1962-1990*, Mazzotta, Milan.

Bosma J.
1997   *Vuk Cosic interview: net.art per se*, 27 September 1997, *at net.art.per.se conference in Trieste (1997)* <www.nettime.org/Lists-Archives/nettime-l-9709/msg00053.html>.
1997-2006   *Josephine Bosma's Database*, on-line at <http://laudanum.net/cgi-bin/media.cg i?action=frontpage>.

Braidotti Rosi
1994   *Soggetto nomade, femminismo e crisi della modernità*, Rome, Donzelli Edition, 1995.
2002   *In metamorfosi. Verso una teoria materialista del divenire*, Milan, Feltrinelli, 2003.

Brener A., Schurz B.
2000   *Demolish Serious Culture!!!*, Wien, Selene Edition.

Bria F., Krogh T. e De Clercq L.
2003-2005   *P2P-FightSharing (I + III)*, DVD collection, Rome, Candida TV/
Amsterdam, Greenpepper Magazine.

Broeckmann A., Jaschko S.
2001   *Do it yourself: Art and Digital Media: Software, Participation, Distribution*, Berlin,
Transmediale 2001, Printfactory Berlin.
2004   *Runtime Art: Software, Art, Aesthetics*, Berlin, published at <http://
runtimeart.mi2.hr/TextAndreasBroeckmann>.

Bucalossi F.
1996   *Tribù astratte*, in Strano Network, *Net strike-No Copyright*, Bertiolo, AAA Editions,
1996.
1998   *Brain Machine, come costruirla e utilizzarla*, Strano Network Bioenciclopedia, self-
production of the author.

Burroughs W.
1959   *Il pasto nudo*, Carnago (VA), SugarCo Editions, 1994.

Butler J.
1990   *Gender Trouble, Feminism and the Subversion of Identity*, New York, Routledge.

Calvesi M.
1966   *Le due avanguardie – Dal Futurismo alla Pop Art*, Rome-Bari, La Terza, 1998.

Candalino N.
1996   *Palestra Elettronica* (conferences), Rome, University "La Sapienza", Faculty of
Sociology.

Candalino N., Gasparini B., Pasquali F., Vittadini N.
1996   *La trasformazione dei linguaggi espressivi: un cammino verso la performatività*,
Catalogo *Summit della comunicazione 1996 – Quattro anni dal 2000*, Naples,
Castel dell'Ovo.

Candida TV (edited by)
2001   *Supervideo>>> G8*, video, Roma, self-made production.
2003   *Reality Hacking*, video collection, Rome, self-made production.

Canevacci M.
1993   *La città polifonica – Saggio sull'antropologia della comunicazione urbana*, Rome,
SEAM.
1995   *Antropologia della comunicazione visuale*, Genoa, Costa & Nolan.

1995   *Sincretismi – Un'esplorazione sulle ibridazioni culturali*, Genoa, Costa & Nolan.

Capucci P.L.
1993   *Realtà del virtuale – Rappresentazioni tecnologiche, comunicazione, arte*, Bologna, Clueb Editions.
1994   *Il corpo tecnologico – L'influenza delle tecnologie sul corpo e sulle sue facoltà*, Bologna, Baskerville.

1994   *La Natura Virtuale II – Telepresenze e telecomunità*, Netmagazine, Baskerville.
1996   *Arte e Tecnologie – Comunicazione estetica e tecnoscienze*, Bologna, Edizioni dell'Ortica.

Capucci P.L., Terrosi C.
1993   *Cybernauti. Un mondo rovesciato / Cybernauts: a reversed World*, Bologna, "Lo specchio di Dioniso".

Carlotti G. (edited by)
1992   *William S. Burroughs, Brion Gysin*, Milan, Shake.

Caronia A.
1985   *Il Cyborg. Saggio sull'uomo artificiale*, Milan, Shake, 2001.
1996   *Il corpo virtuale. Dal corpo robotizzato al corpo disseminato nelle reti*, Padova, Muzzio Editions.

Castells M.
2001   *Galassia Internet*, Milan, Feltrinelli.

Celant G.
1977   *OFF MEDIA. Nuove tecnologie artistiche: video disco libro*, Bari, Dedalo Libri.

Chaincrew
2001   *ChainWorkers, lavorare nelle cattedrali del consumo*, Rome, Derive Approdi.

Chandler A., Neumark N.
2005   *At a Distance. Precursors to Art and Activism on the Internet*, Cambridge, Massachusetts Institute of Technology.

Chiccarelli S., Monti A.
1997   Spaghetti Hacker, Storie, tecniche e aspetti giuridici dell'hacking in Italia, Milano, Apogeo Editions <www.spaghettihacker.it>.

Cimino T., Ester F. (edited by)
1997   *Meduse Cyborg*, Milan, Shake.

300

Cirifino F., Rosa P., Roveda S., Sangiorgi L.
1999   *Studio Azzurro, Ambienti Sensibili, Esperienze tra interattività e narrazione*, Milan, Electa.

Cittadini, M. (Contrasto)
1993   *Uomo Macchina – Texts*, Genova, Galleria Leonardi, no-copyright self-production.

Clifford J.
1988   *I frutti puri impazziscon – Etnografia, Letteratura ed Arte nel secolo XX*, Turin, Bollati Boringhieri, 1993.

City of Gallarate, National Prize Visual Art
1997   *Segnali d'Opera, Arte e Digitale in Italia, per l'aggiornamento di un museo*, Civic Gallery of Modern Art, Gallarate.

Cosic V.
1996   *The net.artists*, email by Pit Schultz, "Nettime" mailing list, 31 May 1996, online at <www.nettime.org/Lists-Archives/nettime-l9606/msg00011.html>.

Costa M.
1990   *Il sublime tecnologico*, Salerno, Edisud.
1994   *Nuovi media e sperimentazione d'artista*, Naples, Edizioni Scientifiche Italiane.

Cramer F.
2002   *Language, a virus?*, catalogue of *I love you – Computer_viren_hacker-Kultur* (edited by Franziska Nori), Frankfurt, MAK, 2002.

2003   *Social Hacking, Revisited*, in Sollfrank C., *net.art generator*, Nuernberg, Verlag fuer moderne Kunst Nuernberg, 2004.
2003   *Ten Theses about Software Art*, 10/2003, in Gohlke G., *Software Art – Eine Reportage über den Code*, Berlin, (Künstlerhaus Bethanien), 2003.
2005   *Words Made Flesh. Code, Culture, Imagination*, Rotterdam, Media Design Research, Piet Zwart Institute, online at <http://pzwart.wdka.hro.nl>.

Cramer F., Home S.
2005   *Pornographic Coding*, Crash Conference, London, Tate Gallery, February 2005.

Cremaschi M.
1997   *L'arte che non c'è 1987-1996. Indagine sull'arte tecnologica*, Bologna, Edizioni dell'Ortica.

Dall'Ongaro M.
1998   *Elettroshock, 50 anni di musica elettroacustica. 35° Festival di Nuova Consonanza*, American Accademy, Acquario Romano, Goethe Institut, Rome.

D'Alonso C.
2006   *Molleindustria, quando il gioco si fa duro*, published in "Digimag, periodico di informazione digitale", April 2006, online at <www.digicult.it/digimag/article.asp?id=330>.

D'Avossa A.
2001   Joseph Beuys, *Difesa della natura*, Milan, Skira Editore.

Decoder (edited by)
1987-1998   *Decoder. Rivista Internazionale Underground*, issues nr. 1-13, Milan, Shake Edizioni, <www.decoder.it>.

Debord G.
1956   *La théorie de la dérive*, in "Les Lèvres Nues", 9, Bruxelles, 1956, later published in "Internazionale Situationniste", 2, Paris, 1958.
1967/1988   *La società dello spettacolo – Commentari sulla società dello spettacolo*, Milan, Baldini & Castoldi, 1997.
1989   *Panegirico*, Rome, Fanucci Editore, 1998.

Deleuze G., Guattari F.
1980   *Rizoma, Millepiani, Capitalismo e schizofrenia, Sez. I*, Rome, Castelvecchi, 1997.

De Micheli M.
1986   *Le avanguardie artistiche del novecento*, Milan, Feltrinelli, 1997.

De Paz A.
1980   *Sociologia e critica delle arti*, Bologna, Clueb.

Deseriis M., Marano G.
2003   *Net.Art. L'arte della connessione*, Milan, Shake Edizioni.

Dick P.K .

1953/1959 *I racconti di Philip K. Dick – Souvenir – James P. Crow*, Rome, Fanucci Edition, 1995.
1968   *Blade Runner*, Rome, Fanucci Edition, 1996.
1969   *Ubik*, Rome, Fanucci Edition, 1998

Di Corinto A., Tozzi T.
2002   *Hacktivism. La libertà nelle maglie della rete*, Rome, Manifestolibri.

Di Marino B., Nicoli L.
2001   *Elettroshock. 30 anni di video in Italia 1971-2001*, Rome, Castelvecchi Arte.

Dorfles G.
1961   *Ultime tendenze nell'arte d'oggi – Dall'Informale al Postmoderno*, Milan, Feltrinelli, 1998.

Eco U.
1962   *Opera aperta*, Milan, Bompiani, 1997.
1990   *I limiti dell'interpretazione*, Milan, Bompiani, 1995.

Equizzi M.
2006   *Dal Cyberpunk all'Industrial. Una involuzione crudele di Mariano Equizzi (considerando la sua simbiosi techno-creativa con Luca Liggio e Paolo Bigazzi)*, inedito, New York-Tokyo.

Fadda S.
1998   *Bassa definizione*, written for Hacker Art conference by Tommaso Tozzi, 5 June 1998, Hackmeeting 1998, Florence, CPA Social Center.
1999   *Definizione zero. Origini della videoarte fra politica e comunicazione*, Milan, Costa & Nolan.

Fagone V.
1990   *L'immagine video. Arti visuali e nuovi media elettronici*, Milan, Feltrinelli.

Featherstone M.
1990   *Cultura del consumo e postmodernismo*, Rome, SEAM, 1994.

Felsenstein L.
1985   *The Hacker's League, from Real Hackers Don't Rob Banks initial published in"Byte Magazine", online at <www.welcomehome.org/hl.html>.*
2005   *The Arming of Desire, Counterculture and Computer Revolution, Conference at the Waag Institute, Amsterdam.*

Ferraro A. e Montagano G. (edited by)
1994   *La scena Immateriale. Linguaggi elettronici e mondi virtuali*, Genoa, Costa & Nolan.

Ferry Byte, Parrini C.
2001   *I motori di ricerca nel caos della rete*, Milan, Shake, online at <www.strano.net/chaos>.

Fikafutura
1997   *Frutta interattiva*, interview with Flavia Alman and Sabine Reiff, "Fikafutura, secrezioni acide cyberfemministe e queer", 1, Milan, Shake.

Finelli A., Galluzzi F., Righetti S.
2005   *La Stanza Rossa. Trasversalità artistiche e realtà virtuale negli anni Novanta*, San Lazzaro di Savena (Bo), Fabula O.

Formenti C.
2000   *Incantati dalla rete. Immagini, utopie e conflitti nell'epoca di Internet*, Milan, Raffaello Cortina Editions.
2002   *Mercanti di futuro. Utopia e crisi della Net Economy*, Turin, Einaudi.

Francalanci E.L.
1994   *Artriti*, Civic Museum of Albano Terme Editions.

Freschi A.C., Leonardi L. (edited by)
1998   *Una ragnatela sulla trasformazione*, Firenze, City Lights Italia.

Fusco A.
1995   *La dimensione ludica nella Realtà Virtuale*, Thesis of Laurea in Sociology, "La Sapienza" University, Rome.

Galluzzi F., Parrini C.
2002   *Dieci anni (e forse più). Appunti per una storia possibile della net art*, in "Making Art On the Web", conference curated by Undo.net, at the Pistoletto Foundation of Biella, 9 November 2002 <www.undo.net>.

Galluzzi F., Righetti S.
1996   *La Stanza Rossa. Immaginario collettivo e linguaggi della comunicazione*, Bologna, Edizioni dell'Ortica.

Gibson W.
1984   *Neuromante*, Milan, Nord Edition, 1993.
1986   *Giù nel ciberspazio*, Milan, Arnoldo Mondadori Edition, 1995.
1988   *Monna Lisa cyberpunk*, Milan, Arnoldo Mondadori Edition, 1995.

Glass P.
1986   *Songs from liquid days*, CBS inc. (music CD).

Goriunova O., Shulgin A.
2003   *Read_me 2.3 Reader, about software art*, Helsinki, Nifca Publication.

Greene R.
2004   *Internet Art*, London, Thames & Hudson.

Gubitosa C.
1999   *Italian Crackdown. BBS amatoriali, volontari telematici, censure e sequestri nell'Italia degli anni '90*, Milan, Apogeo.

Hakim Bey
1985   *T.A.Z. Zone Temporaneamente Autonome*, Milan, Shake, 1997.
1995   *Utopie pirata*, Milan, Shake, 1996.
1996   *Millennium*, Milan, Shake, 1997.

Haraway Donna J.
1991   *Manifesto Cyborg*, Milan, Feltrinelli Interzone, 1995.

Hawthorne S., Klein R.
1999   *Cyberfeminism: Connectivity, Critique and Creativity*, North Melbourne Victoria, Australia, Spinifex Press.

Held Jr. J.
1999   *L'arte del timbro – Rubber Stamp Art*, Bertiolo, AAA Editions.

Himanen P.
2001   *L'etica hacker e lo spirito dell'età dell'informazione*, Milan, Feltrinelli.

Hodges N. (a cura di)
1993   *Word Wide Video*, London, Art & Design.

Home S.

1995   *Neoismo e altri scritti. Idee critiche sull'avanguardia contemporanea*, Genoa, Costa & Nolan, 1997.
1988   *Assalto alla cultura. Correnti utopistiche dal Lettrismo a Class War*, Bertiolo, AAA Editions, 1996.

Infusino G.
1998   *Oltre il villaggio globale. Storia e futuro della comunicazione dai primi esperimenti al dopo Internet*, Naples, CUEN.

Ippolita
2005   *Open non è free, Comunità digitali tra etica hacker e mercato globale*, Milan, Elèuthera, online at <http://www.ippolita.net/~ippolita/>.
2005   *Laser, il sapere libertario*, Milan, Feltrinelli.

Iusco I., Ludovico A.
1991   *Virtual Reality Handbook*, Bari, Minus Habens Records.
1995   *Internet Underground Guide*, Bari, Minus Habens Records.

Jacobs K. (Libidot and Dr. Jacobs)
2005   *LIBI_DOC. Journey in the performance of SEX ART*, Ljubljana, Maska.

de Kerckhove D.
1991   *Brainframes – Mente, tecnologia, mercato*, Bologna, Baskerville, 1993.
1995   *La pelle della cultura – Un'indagine sulla nuova realtà elettronica*, Genoa, Costa & Nolan, 1996.
2001   *L'architettura dell'intelligenza. La rivoluzione informatica*, Testo&Immagine, Turin, 2001.

Kerouac J.
1959   *Sulla Strada (On the Road)*, Milan, Mondadori, 1995.

Krueger M.W.
1991   *Artificial Reality II*, Addison-Wesley Publishing Company

Lampo L. (edited by)
2005   *Connessioni Leggendarie, Net.Art 1995-2005*, catalogue of exhibition, Mediateca di Santa Teresa, Milan, 20 October-10 November 2005, Ready-made Editions, Milan.

Leary T.
1994   *Caos e cibercultura*, Milan, Apogeo-Urra.

Levy S.
1984   *Hackers. Gli eroi della rivoluzione informatica*, Milan, Shake, 1996.

Liang L.
2004   *Guide to Open Content Licenses*, Rotterdam, Piet Zwart Institute.

Link Project (edited by)
2000   *Netmage. Piccola Enciclopedia dell'immaginario tecnologico. Media, arte,*
        comunicazione, Milan, Arnoldo Mondadori Editions.

Livraghi E. (edited by)
1999   *La carne e il metallo. Visioni storie pensiero del cybermondo*, Milan, Il Castoro
        Edition.

Lotti G. (edited by)
1997-2003   *Simultaneità. New Media Arts Magazine*, Rome, <www.simultaneita.net>.

Luc Pac, Marta McKenzie
1998   *Kriptonite, Fuga dal controllo globale. Crittografia, anonimato e privacy nelle reti*
        telematiche, Bologna, Nautilus Editions. Online at <www.ecn.org/crypto>.

Ludovico A.

2000   *Suoni Futuri Digitali*, Milan, Apogeo Editions.
1993-2006 (a cura di) "Neural, hacktivism, e-music and new media art", magazine, issues
        nr. 1-24, Bari, <www.neural.it>.

Luther Blissett
1996   *Totò Peppino e la guerra psichica*, Bertiolo, AAA Editions.
1996   *netgener@tion*, Milan, Mondadori.
1999   *Q*, Turin, Einaudi.
2000   *Mind Invaders. Come fottere i media: manuale di guerriglia e sabotaggio culturale*,
        Rome, Castelvecchi.

Macarone Palmieri F. "Warbear"
2005   *Pink-Punk-Queer. Frivolezza tattica ed estetica del disastro*, "Avatar", 5, Theme:
        "Corpo: bodyscape: corpographie", Rome, Meltemi Edition.

Macrì T.
1996   *Il corpo postorganico. Sconfinamenti della performance*, Genoa, Costa & Nolan.

Majer L.
1994 *Cybervideo. Il video vecchia frontiera dell'arte?*, Santa Maria di Sala, Blended.

Manizza F.
2006   *Memoriale Telestreet*, inedito, Senigallia.

Manovich L.
2001   *Il linguaggio dei nuovi media*, Milan, Edizioni Olivares, 2002.

Mattei M. G., Giromini F.

1998   *Computer Animation Stories – Nuovi linguaggi e tecniche del cinema d'animazione*, Rome, Mare Nero.

Mattei M.G.

1996   *Correnti Magnetiche. Immagini Virtuali e Installazioni Interattive*, Perugia, Umbria Entertainment Foundation, Ed. Arnaud-Gramma.

1999   *Interattività. Studio Azzurro opere tra partecipazione e osservazione*, Tecnoarte Project 1998, Perugia, Umbria Entertainment Foundation.

Maya

2004   *Hackers. La storia, le storie*, Rome, Malatempora.

McCarty D.

1997   *Nettime: the legend and the myth*, Berlin, published at <www.medialounge.net/lounge/workspace/nettime/DOCS/1/info3.html>.

McKenzie Wark

2004   *Un Manifesto Hacker*, Milan, Feltrinelli, 2005.

McLuhan M.

1964   *Gli strumenti del Comunicare*, Milan, Il Saggiatore, 1995.

Medosch A.

2005   *Roots Culture. Free Software Vibrations 'inna Babylon'*, in *How Open is the Future? Economic, Social & Cultural Scenarios inspired by Free & Open-Source Software*, Brussels, Crosstalks and VUB Press, <http://crosstalks.vub.ac.be>.

Milner M.

1982   *La fantasmagoria. Saggio sull'ottica fantastica*, Bologna, Il Mulino, 1989.

Monty Cantsin

1987   *Neoism Now. The first Neoist Anthology and Sourcebook*, Berlin, Artcore Editions.

Morris M., Sava S.

1999   *Ray Johnson*, University of British Columbia, Morris and Helen Belkin Art Gallery.

Nori F.

2002   (edited by) *I love you – Computer_viren_hacker-Kultur*, catalogue of exhibition, 23 May-13 June, Frankfurt, MAK, 2002.

Old Boys Network

1997   *First Cyberfeminist International*, reader, Kassel, Documenta X, Hybrid Workspace.
1999   *Next Cyberfeminist International*, reader, Rotterdam.
2001   *Very Cyberfeminist International*, reader, Hamburg.

Ortoleva P.
1995   *Mass Media: nascita ed industrializzazione*, Florence, Giunti.
1995   *Mediastoria. Comunicazione e cambiamento sociale nel mondo contemporaneo*, Parma, Nuova Pratiche Edition.

Paoli M.T.
2001   *Nuovi Media e Comunicazione Politica Indipendente. Indymedia tra Hacktivismo e Attivismo No Global*, Thesis of Laurea in Science of Communication, Faculty of Humanities, University of Siena.

Parrini C.
1993   *Interrogativi allo specchio – Autointerview of Claudio Parrini*, "La Stanza Rossa", 9, Year II, 1993.
1998   *Dispotismo dell'Autore*, Hacker Art Seminar, Hack-IT '98, CPA Social Center, Florence, 1998.

Pasquinelli M. (edited by)
2002   *Media Activism. Strategie e pratiche della comunicazione indipendente*, Rome, Derive Approdi.
2004   *Warporn! Warpunk! Videopoiesi nell'Occidente in guerra*, online at <http://multitudes.samizdat.net/article.php3?id_article=1495>.

Pecchioli M. (edited by)
2005   *Neo televisione. Elementi di un linguaggio catodico glocal/e*, Milan, Costa & Nolan.

Perciballi R. (edited by)

1998   *Come se nulla fosse*, Rome, Castelvecchi.
2001   *Bloody Riot. Ardecore de Roma, 1983-2001*, Rome, Radio Onda Rossa.

Perneczky G.
1993   *The Magazine Network. The trends of alternative art in the light of their periodicals 1968-1988*, Koeln, Soft Geometry.

Perniola M.
1994   *Il sex appeal dell'inorganico*, Turin, Einaudi.

Perretta G.

1994   *Nodale*, Brescia, Allegrini Gallery Editions.
1996   *Laboratorio politico di fine secolo*, Macerata, Per Mari e Monti Gallery.
1997   *Laboratorio politico di fine secolo 2*, Bologna, Edizioni dell'Ortica.
2002   *art.comm, collettivi, reti, gruppi diffusi, comunità acefale nella pratica dell'arte: oltre la soggettività singolare*, Rome, Cooper Edizioni.

Perretta G., Marino A., Marino P., Canciotta Mendizza A
1996   *Virtual Light*, Bari, Palazzo Fizzarotti.

Philopat M.
1997   *Costretti a sanguinare. Romanzo sul punk 1977-84*, Milan, Shake.

Plant S.
1997   *Zeros+Ones: Digital Women+The New Technoculture*, New York, Doubleday.

Popper F.
1993   *Art of the Electronic Age*, London, Thames and Hudson.

Quaranta D.
2004   *NET ART 1994-1998, La vicenda di Ada'web*, Milan, Vita e Pensiero.

Raymond E.S.
1998 *The Cathedral and the Bazaar*, in *The Cathedral and the Bazaar*, online at <www.catb.org/~esr/writings/cathedral-bazaar/>.

Reggiori A.
1997   *Arte e Tecnologia in Italia – Un museo da cliccare* in *Virtual, il mensile dell'era digitale*, 47, Year V, November 1997.

Reiche C., Kuni V.
2004   *Cyberfeminism, next protocols*, New York, Autonomedia.

Rheingold H.
1992   *Virtual Reality*, New York, Touchstone Books.

Rossi E.G.
2003   *Archeonet. Viaggio nella storia della net/web art*, Siena, Lalli Edition.

Salaris C.
1997   *Il movimento del settantasette. Linguaggi e scritture dell'ala creativa*, Bertiolo, AAA Editions.

Saper C.J.
2001   *Networked Art*, Minneapolis/London, University of Minnesota Press.

Scelsi R. (Raf "Valvola")
1990   *Cyberpunk. Antologia di testi politici*, Milan, Shake.
1994   *No Copyright. Nuovi diritti nel 2000*, Milan, Shake.

Schechner R.
1983   *Notizie, sesso e teoria della performance*, in *Il teatro nella società dello spettacolo*, edited by Claudio Vicentini, Bologna, Il Mulino, 1983.
1984   *La teoria della Performance 1970-1983*, Rome, Bulzoni.

Schmidt-Burkhardt A.
2005   *Maciunas' Learning Machines, From Art History to a Chronology of Fluxus*, The Gilbert and Lila Silverman Fluxus Collection/Vive Versa Verlag, Berlin.

Scuola RAI/Multibox
1998   *DOCUMEDIA, percorsi multimediali, "Video-Performance, Riflessione sulle psicologie delle percezioni"*, Rome, RAI, Multimedia Productions.

Sega Serra Zanetti P., Tolomeo M.G.
1998   *La coscienza luccicante. Dalla videoarte all'arte interattiva*, Rome, Gangemi Edition.

Shulgin A.
1997   Net.Art. The origin, "Nettime" mailing list, 18 March 1997, <www.nettime.org/Lists-Archives/nettime-l-9703/msg00094.html>.

Sollfrank C.
1999   *Women Hackers, a report from the mission to locate subversive women on the net*, reader of *Next Cyberfeminist International*, Rotterdam.
2004   *net.art generator*, Nuernberg, Verlag fuer moderne Kunst Nuernberg.

Speroni F.
1995   *Sotto il nostro sguardo. Per una lettura mediale dell'opera d'arte*, Genoa, Costa & Nolan.

Stallman R.
2002   *Software libero, pensiero libero. Vol. I*, Viterbo, Nuovi Equilibri, 2003 (Italian translation edited by Parrella B. and Free Software Foundation).
2002   *Software libero, pensiero libero. Vol. II*, Viterbo, Nuovi Equilibri, 2004 (Italian translation edited by Parrella B. and Free Software Foundation).

311

Sterling B.

1986   *Prefazione a Mirrorshades* in Raf "Valvola" Scelsi (edited by) *Cyberpunk, Antologia di testi politici*, Milan, Shake, 1990.

1992   *Giro di vite contro gli Hackers / Hacker Crackdown*, Milan, Shake, 1993.

Strano Network

1996a   *Net Strike – No Copyright – Et (-:*, Bertiolo, AAA Editions.

1996b   *Nubi all'orizzonte. Diritto alla comunicazione nello scenario di fine millennio. Iniziativa nazionale in difesa della telematica amatoriale*, Rome, Castelvecchi.

2001   (edited by), *Le giornate di Genova. Cronache dal G8*, Florence, CD-Rom self-production.

subRosa (Fernandez M., Wilding F., M.Wright M.)

2002   *Domain Errors! Cyberfeminist Practices*, New York, Autonomedia.

Taiuti L.

1996   *Arte e Media. Avanguardie e comunicazione di massa*, Genoa, Costa & Nolan.

Tanni V.

2004   *Net Art. Genesi e generi*, in Balzola A., Monteverdi A.M. (edited by), *Le arti multimediali digitali*, Milan, Garzanti, 2004.

Tarissi F.

2006   *Hackeriamo gli intellettuali*, "Linus", June 2006, online at <www.portalinus.it>.

Terrosi R.

1997   *La filosofia del postumano*, Genoa, Costa & Nolan.

The Yes Men

2004   *The True Story of the End of the WTO*, New York, The Disinformation Company.

Tozzi T. (edited by)

1991a   *Opposizioni '80. Alcune delle realtà che hanno scosso il villaggio globale,* Milan, AMEN.

1991b   "HACKER ART" (1989) in *Gmm Hacker Test – Tecnomaya in Infotown* catalogue of exhibition, June-July 1991, Luigi Pecci Contemporary Art Museum in Prato.

1992a   *Conferenze Telematiche Interattive*, Rome, Paolo Vitolo Gallery.

1992b   *Happening Digitali Interattivi – Musica, testi, immagini realizzate e rimanipolabili in modo interattivo*, Florence, no-copyright self-production.

1992c   *Comunità virtuali/opposizioni reali*, "Flash Art", 167, April-May 1992.

1997   *Arte, Media e Comunicazione*, "La Stanza Rossa", 25, Edizioni dell'Ortica, Bologna.

1998   *Cotropia: Lifeware e Coevoluzione Mutuale*, in *Una ragnatela sulla trasformazione*, Freschi A. C., Leonardi L. (edited by), Florence, City Lights Italy.

Tozzi T., Sansavini S., Ferry Byte e Di Corinto A. (edited by)

2000   *La nuova comunicazione interattiva e l'antagonismo in Italia*, online at <www.hackerart.org/storia/cybstory.htm>.

Trocchi A.

1999   *Candida: una televisione elettrodomestica*, email sent to [AVANA-BBS] mailing-list, 24 September 1999.

Turkle S.

1996   *La vita sullo schermo. Nuove identità e relazioni sociali nell'epoca di Internet*, Milan, Apogeo, 1997.

Turner V.

1982   *Dal rito al teatro*, Bologna, Il Mulino, 1986.

1986   *The Anthropology of Performance*, New York, Paj Publication.

Vale V., Juno A.

1987   *Pranks!*, San Francisco, Re/Search Publications.

Valeriani L.

1999   *Dentro la Trasfigurazione. Il dispositivo dell'arte tra cibercultura e Vangelo*, Milan, Costa & Nolan.

Velena H.

1995   *Dal Cybersex al Transgender, tecnologie, identità e politiche di liberazione*, Rome, Castelvecchi.

Verde G.

1997   *Dalla strada al virtuale*, "Teatro da quattro soldi" street-theatre magazine, 4 October 1997.

1998   *Documenta Percorsi Multimediali*, conference, Rome, RAI, May 1998.

2005   *Pensieri dietro la Minimal TV*, in Pecchioli M. (edited by), *Neo televisione. Elementi di un linguaggio catodico glocal/e*, Milan, Costa & Nolan.

Verde G., Voce L. (edited by)
2001   *Solo Limoni. Videotestimonianza sui fatti di Genova (Genoa G8)*, Milan Shake. More info online at <www.verdegiac.org/sololimoni>.

Welch C. (edited by)
1995   *Eternal Network. A Mail Art Anthology*, University of Calgary Press.

Vicentini C. (edited by)
1983   *Il teatro nella società dello spettacolo*, Bologna, Il Mulino.

Zingoni A.
1999   *Gino the chicken – Le mirabolanti avventure del primo pollo perso nella rete*, Rome, Castelvecchi.

.Zip!
1997   *Hot web. Guida ai siti alternativi e radicali su Internet*, Rome, Castelvecchi.

Webliography

There are many more internet sites than are mentioned in this book, and even more are those which are part of the Italian and international networks. In order to better limit the subject, we wanted to apply an inevitable selection process and listed only those which contributed in the weaving of the Hacktivism, political activism and artistic experimentation networks in Italy. Conscious of the partiality of this list, we refer the reader to the variegated world of the Web in order to discover new connections for other Internet sites not listed in this webliography, which were equally important in the writing of this book.

0100101110101101.org
avana.forteprenestino.net
candida.thing.net
copydown.inventati.org
epidemic.ws
indivia.net
it.wikipedia.org
italy.indymedia.org
kyuzz.org
ordanomade.kyuzz.org
ordanomade.kyuzz.org/tora.htm
oziosi.net
papuasia.org/radiocybernet
poetry.freaknet.org/
punto-informatico.it
reload.realityhacking.org

strano.net/mutante
zonegemma.cjb.net
www.28blog.splinder.com
www.aaa-edizioni.it
www.adolgiso.it
www.arcnaut.it
www.ateatro.it
www.autistici.org
www.bfsf.it
www.biodollsmouse.org
www.carniscelte.info
www.catastrophe.it
www.chainworkers.org
www.connessionileggendarie.it
www.creativecommons.it
www.criticalmass.it

www.cryptokitchen.net
www.cut-tv.com
www.cut-up.net
www.cybercore.com
www.cyberzone.it
www.d-i-n-a.net
www.decoder.it
www.deliriouniversale.com
www.deliriouniversale.com
www.digicult.it
www.dvara.net/HK/
www.dyne.org
www.ecn.org
www.ecn.org/aha
www.ecn.org/crypto
www.ecn.org/cybr
www.ecn.org/nautilus
www.ecn.org/sciattoproduzie
www.ecn.org/sexyshock
www.ecn.org/xs2web
www.elasticgroup.com
www.euromayday.org/index_it.php
www.flxer.net
www.freaknet.org
www.giardini.sm
www.globalgroove.it
www.gmm.fi.it
www.gnu.org/home.it.html
www.guerrigliamarketing.it
www.hackerart.org
www.hacklabs.org
www.hackmeeting.org
www.helenavelena.com
www.idrunners.net
www.imbattibili.org
www.infoxoa.org
www.inventati.org
www.ippolita.net
www.kyuzz.org/mir

www.lacritica.net
www.linux.it
www.lutherblissett.net
www.marianoequizzi.com
www.minimaltv.cjb.net
www.mit-italia.it
www.molleindustria.it
www.mutoto.org
www.netmage.it
www.netstrike.it
www.networkingart.eu
www.neural.it
www.ngvision.org
www.noemalab.org
www.nothuman.net
www.olografix.org
www.parrini.net
www.phagoff.org
www.pigreca.com
www.pornflakes.it
www.puttanopoly.com
www.quintostato.it
www.qwertyu.net
www.radioalice.org
www.radiogap.net
www.rekombinant.org
www.sanprecario.info
www.serpicanaro.com
www.shake.it
www.shockart.net
www.simultaneita.net
www.strano.net
www.strano.net/chaos
www.strano.net/contrasto
www.strano.net/stragi
www.tekfestival.it
www.telestreet.it
www.thanitart.com
www.thething.it

www.tmcrew.org
www.topolin.it
www.transhackmeeting.org
www.verdegiac.org
www.vidalocarecords.com
www.wikiartpedia.org
www.wumingfoundation.com
www.x-8x8-x.net
www.zeusnews.it
www.ziobudda.net

1   2

1) Drawing by Pete Horobin, "Neoist Altar". Eighth Apartment Festival of the Neoist Network, London, May 1984.
2) One of the covers from the Neoist magazine "Smile", published by Vittore Baroni in 1985.
3) Vittore Baroni, "Organic Tree", 1992.

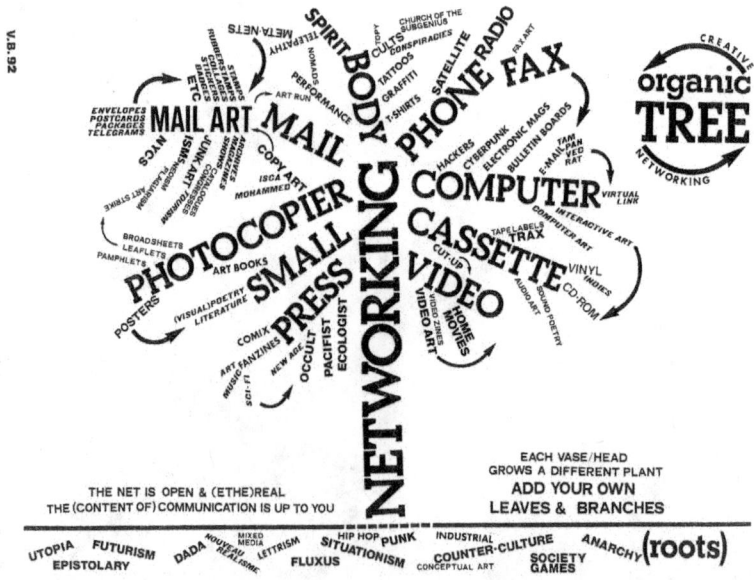

3

4a

4b

5

6

7

8a

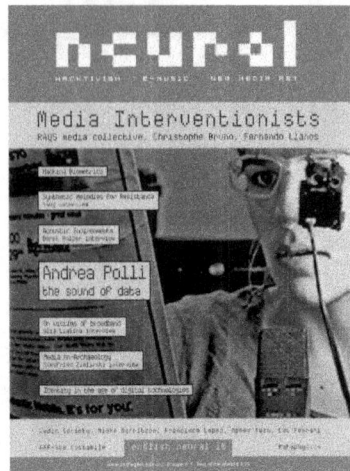

8b

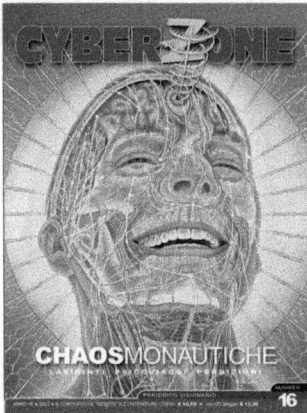

9

10

4A) Piermario Ciani, "Art in Europe" postcard, 1990.

4B) Piermario Ciani, "Art is the Beginning of Something Else", 1991.

5) Andrea Alberti and Edi Bianco, "official" Luther Blissett portrait, achieved in 1994 by combining photos from the 1930s and 1940s of three of his great uncles and one of his great aunts; by Wu Ming 1.

6) Cover of "Decoder", number 8, Underground International Magazine, Shake Edizioni, 1993.

7) Wu Ming Foundation, "This revolution is faceless", 2000.

8A) Cover of the first issue of "Neural" magazine, Bari, 1993.

8B) Cover of the 25th issue of "Neural" magazine, English version, Bari, 2006.

9) Cyberzone, "The greatest philosophers of the imaginary and the most visionary artists of the planet interrogate themselves on the future of humanity", 1996-2006.

10) Strano Network, "Against all Kinds of Social Barriers, Cyber-Rights Now!", 1991. Logo of the Cyber-Rights BBS (today a mailing list) managed by Ferry Byte.

11

12

13

11) Strano Network logo, 1993.

12) Strano Network, "Virtual Town Television (V.T.T.V)", 1994.

13) "Right to Communication in the End of the Millennium Scenario" poster. Amateur BBS Networks Conference promoted by Strano Network, Museo L. Pecci in Prato, 1995.

14) COMA, the computer virus, from the movie Syrena by Mariano Equizzi, 1996-98 <www.lucaliggio.com>.

14

15

15) Agent Plotkin in action, by <www.28blog.splinder.com>, the narrative-participative-paranoid blog by Mariano Equizzi, 2006.

16) The three GMM in flesh and blood in 1985: Roberto Nistri, Rolando Mugnai and Paola Pacifico.

17) The original Giovanotti Mondani Meccanici (GMM) nucleus in a series di re-touched photos with an Apple II computer: Antonio Glessi, Marco Paoli, Andrea Zingoni, Maurizio Dami, Loretta Mugnai. The colour image appeared on the back of the GMM LP (1985).

16

17

19

20

18

18) Tommaso Tozzi, "419695, Fanzine d'arte per segreteria telefonica", [419695, Art Fanzine for the Answering Machine] Florence, 1986. The 419695 project, conceived in 1984, continued up until 1989.
19) Tommaso Tozzi, "Hacker Art", 1989.
20) Tommaso Tozzi, "Happening Digitali Interattivi" [Interactive Digital Happenings]. Book, CD-ROM and floppy disc contained in a self-made case, 1992.
21) Simonetta Fadda, "Genova Pissing", 1993 (Still image from the video)

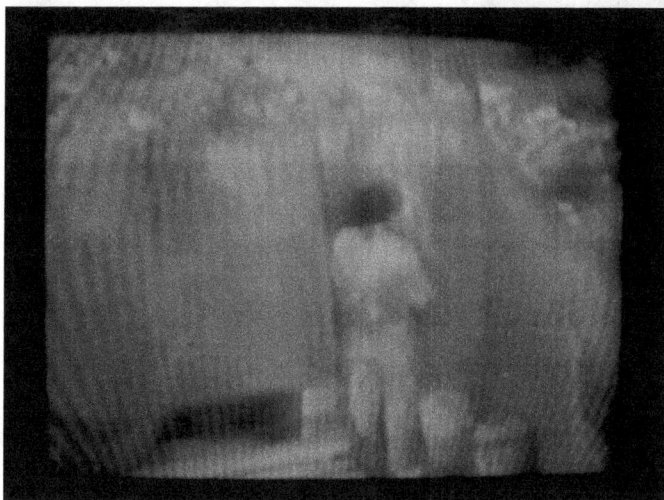

21

22a

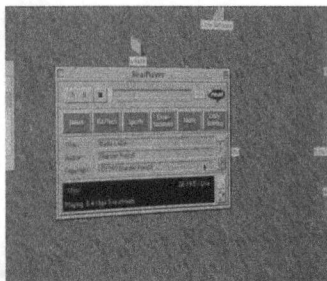

22b

22c

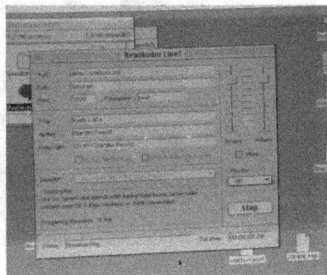

22d

22) Festival L'Arte dell'Ascolto LADA 97 [Festival of the Art of Listening], Recycling the Future (third session). Live Rimini-Vienna streaming, live on ORF Kunstradio, November 6 1997. Participants: Roberto Lucanero, Jaromil, Enrico Marchesin, Isabella Bordoni, Roberto Paci Dalò.

23) Frank Nemola, Flavio Bertozzi and Giacomo Verde, "BandaMagnetica" [MagneticBand], street action; postcard from a photo by Andrea Fabbri Cossarini, 1986-87.

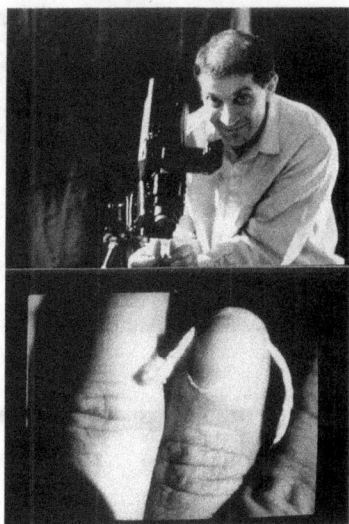
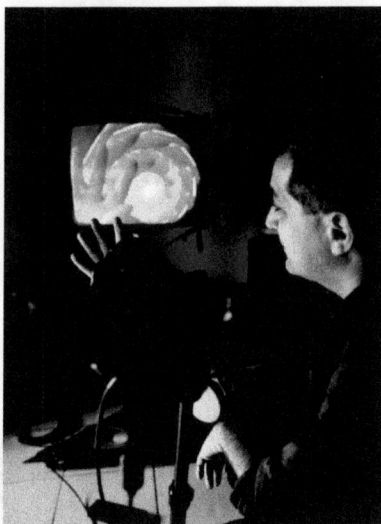

24a   24b

24A) Giacomo Verde, "H&G TV" *Teleracconto* [Television story], inspired by the *Hansel and Gretel* fable, 1990.

24B) Giacomo Verde, "Video Loop Interattivo" [Interactive Video Loop], photo by Jacopo Benassi, 2000.

25) Giacomo Verde, "Qwertyu", a work of net.art, 1999.

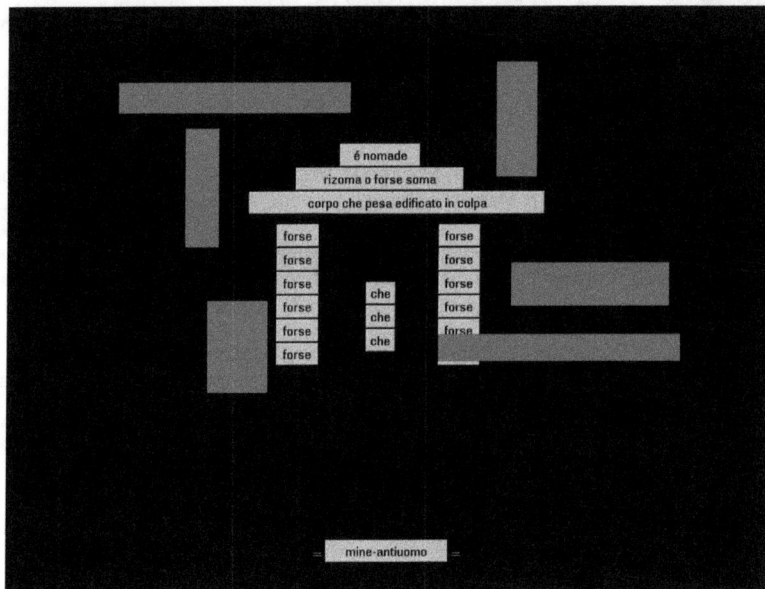

26a

26b

27

28

26A) Massimo Contrasto (Cittadini), "Uomo-Macchina" [Man-Machine], interactive installation with Mandala System, 1993. Inspired by Marcel Duchamp's artwork, "Fountain", 1917.

26B) Massimo Contrasto (Cittadini), "Uomo-Macchina" [Man-Machine], interactive installation with Mandala System, 1993. Inspired by Kasimir Malevich's artwork: "Black Square and Red Square", 1915.

27) Massimo Contrasto (Cittadini), "Mr Regular", interactive installation with Mandala System, within the "La Coscienza Luccicante" [The Shiny Conscience] show, Rome, Palazzo delle Esposizioni, 1998.

28) Quinta Parete Network, Minimal TV logo, Vinci (Fi), 1996.

29

29) Flavia Alman and Sabine Reiff (Pigreca), anamorphic images from the "Bacchatio" video, third in the "Hierophante" series, filmed in video and processed with Conic Anamorphosis computer software, 1997.

30) Federico Bucalossi, "SensualZone – Sappiamo più di quanto possiamo dire" [We know more than we are allowed to say], interactive installation, 1996.

31) Federico Bucalossi, "nothuman.net" video and website, 2001-2006. Sequence of audio-visual de-humanizing frequencies: "Sei ancora umano? - Dichiarati NonUmano" [Are you still human? – Declare yourself non-human].

Sensual*Zone*
Interactive installation and CdRom [mac/pc]
We know more than we can say
Select your preferite mood ... and enjoy your experience

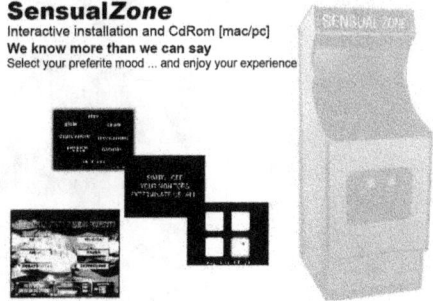

30

31

32

32) Claudio Parrini, "Etere-Arte-Rete" [Ether-Art-Web] project, inter-medial artistic operation, Museo L. Pecci, Prato, 1995.
33) A group of activists attacks the Venice Biennale. 0100101110101101.ORG disseminates Darko Maver stickers with the Biennale space, September 1999.
34) Eva and Franco Mattes (0100101110101101.ORG) "Vaticano.org", Website, 1998-1999.

33

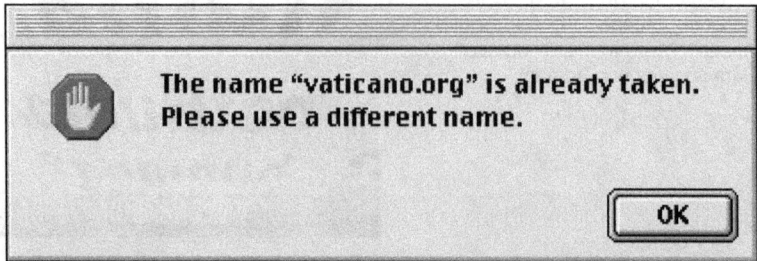

The name "vaticano.org" is already taken. Please use a different name.

OK

34

35   36

35) Print on paper with annotations from the "biennale.py" virus designed and diffused by [epidemiC] and 0100101110101101.ORG at the 49th Venice Biennale, 2001.

36) Eva and Franco Mattes (0100101110101101.ORG), "Life Sharing", screenshot, 2000-2003. Networking Flux triggered by the 0100101110101101.ORG duo, seen in this image through the *Web Stalker* spatial representation browser developed by the London collective I/O/D (1997).

37) [epidemiC], "You Are Not Alone", AntiMafia The Action Sharing (2002). Advertising poster of the peer-to-peer AntiMafia programme presented at the " I love you – computer_viruses_ hacker_culture" show, Digitalcraft, Museum of Applied Arts in Frankfurt, May 2002.

37

38

38) Jaromil, "HasciiCam", 2000.
39) View of the Bulk Deposit (now demolished), 1999 Hackmeeting place, Milan, June 18-20, 1999.
40) The tents of some of the Hackmeeting 2000 participants, Forte Prenestino, Rome, June 16-18, 2000.
41) Open computer at the 2001 Hackmeeting, Centro Sociale Auro, Catania, June 22-24, 2001.

39

40

41

42

43

44

45

42) Candida TV logo and Supervideo image, 2001.
43) Entrance of the Teatro Polivalente Occupato, Hackmeeting 2002 location, Bologna, June 21-23, 2002.
44) Table of [female] hackers' underpants with the Linux penguin, self produced by the FreakNet Medialab, Hackmeeting 2003, El Barrio, Turin, June 20-22 2003.
45) Molleindustria, "Tuboflex – La flessibilità attraverso un tubo" [Flexibility through a tube], sequence strip taken from the Flash videogame which summarize the ungrateful destiny of many temporary workers "rented out" by the multinationals, 2003.
46) The Serpica Naro meta-brand, anagram of "San Precario". With a media hoax by temporary workers in Milan, they overthrew the Settimana della moda milanese, [Milanese Fashion Week] 2005.
47) Molleindustria, "MayDay Netparade". April 2004, while waiting for the EuRomeyDay more than 17,000 people added their own avatar to this virtual procession.
48) Banner pink-silver block, MayDay, May 1, 2005.
49A and 49B) Stickers of the unbeatables, WonderBra and SpiderMom, May 1, 2005.

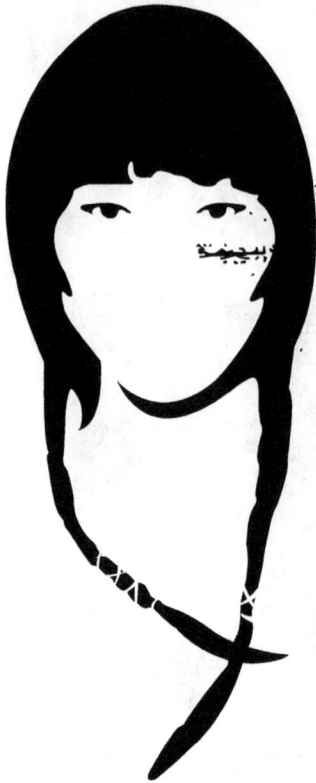

46

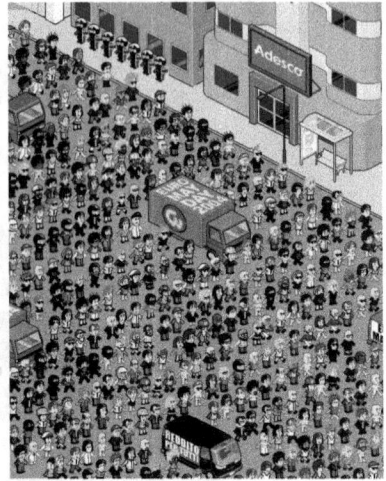

47

sexworkers
e
precariato

pink silver block

48

SPIDER MOM

49a

WONDER BRA

49b

50

51

52

50) Phag Off @ Metaverso during the "Fuck Me Like You Hate Me" evening, Rome, March 2005, photo by Slavina.

51) Photo in the sex toys room by Betty&Books. A shop in downtown Bologna where the Sexyshock collective meets, March 2006.

52) "Use Condoms", video by Franca Formenti, photo by Hajime Morita, Photoshop by Massimiliano Mazzotta, 2006.

53

53) Francesco "Warbear" Macarone Palmieri during a Phag Off performance-evening, at Metaverso, Rome, 2005. Photo by Slavina.